Creating
ACTIVE X
Controls
with
VISUAL BASIC 5

Creating
ACTIVE X
Controls
with
VISUAL BASIC 5

Al Williams

CORIOLIS GROUP BOOKS

an International Thomson Publishing company I(T)P®

Albany, NY • Belmont, CA • Bonn • Boston • Cincinnati • Detroit • Johannesburg • London • Madrid
Melbourne • Mexico City • New York • Paris • Singapore • Tokyo • Toronto • Washington

PUBLISHER	KEITH WEISKAMP
PROJECT EDITOR	SCOTT PALMER
COVER ARTIST	GARY SMITH
COVER DESIGN	ANTHONY STOCK
INTERIOR DESIGN	BRADLEY O. GRANNIS
LAYOUT PRODUCTION	SHADY LANE GRAPHICS AND EDITORIAL
PROOFREADER	MARISA PEÑA
INDEXER	LAURA LAWRIE

Visual Developer Creating ActiveX Controls with Visual Basic 5
Copyright © 1997 by The Coriolis Group, Inc.

Limits of Liability and Disclaimer of Warranty

The author and publisher of this book have used their best efforts in preparing the book and the programs contained in it. These efforts include the development, research, and testing of the theories and programs to determine their effectiveness. The author and publisher make no warranty of any kind, expressed or implied, with regard to these programs or the documentation contained in this book.

The author and publisher shall not be liable in the event of incidental or consequential damages in connection with, or arising out of, the furnishing, performance, or use of the programs, associated instructions, and/or claims of productivity gains.

Trademarks

Trademarked names appear throughout this book. Rather than list the names and entities that own the trademarks or insert a trademark symbol with each mention of the trademarked name, the publisher states that it is using the names for editorial purposes only and to the benefit of the trademark owner, with no intention of infringing upon that trademark.

The Coriolis Group, Inc.
An International Thomson Publishing Company
14455 N. Hayden Road, Suite 220
Scottsdale, Arizona 85260

602/483-0192
FAX 602/483-0193
http://www.coriolis.com

Printed in the United States of America
10 9 8 7 6 5 4 3 2 1

*For my daughter Amy and her new husband Bryan. May they find
as much joy and happiness in their marriage as
her Mother and I have found.*

Acknowledgements

One of the best things about working on a book is all the great people you get to impose upon. For all the impositions, they get a crummy mention at the front of the book. Kind of like one of those shirts that says, "Someone went to Hawaii, and all I got was this lousy shirt." Except, someone probably reads the shirt. Nevertheless, to me, this is the most important page in this book. I hope you'll take a moment to find out why. I'm sure I can't remember everyone who deserves a pat on the back, but here goes, anyway.

My thanks to the Coriolis folks including: Jeff Duntemann for all of his encouragement over the years and for saving me from driving perpetually through the Arizona desert; Keith Weiskamp for turning me on to what a big deal ActiveX really is; and—not least—Scott Palmer for having to put up with my schedule and running interference for me.

Thanks, too, to Jon Erickson of *Dr. Dobb's Journal* for many things, the least of which was allowing me to reuse several examples which appeared in a different form in that magazine.

Normand and Yvette Damien—our local movie experts—cross-checked my cinema references, which helped keep me honest. Next time we are at the movies, I guess I'll have to buy the popcorn.

Thanks to William Shakespeare for the quotes. Or thanks to Sir Francis Bacon. It depends on your opinion (sorry, Rebecca).

As always, I am greatly indebted to my lovely wife, Pat, and our kids (Jerid, Amy, and Patrick) for putting up with my lunacy when the deadlines draw near. Especially since this book was wrapping up right when Amy was getting married! Nothing I do would be possible without Pat's help and support. Thanks for some great years!

No thanks, I'm afraid, can go to Madison, our spoiled Dachshund, whose contribution to this book was limited to forcing me to get up every few minutes to let her in or out of the house. We gotta get a doggie door!

—Al Williams

http://www.al-williams.com/awc

CONTENTS

CHAPTER 3   ONE MILE UP   29

CHAPTER 5   VB ACTIVEX IN DETAIL   87

Chapter 10   ActiveX Documents   307

Chapter 11   The End?   325

APPENDIX D   JUST A LITTLE C++   359

APPENDIX E   CALLING THE WINDOWS API   369

BONUS CHAPTER   377

INDEX   407

The Future Of Windows, The Web, And Everything

The undiscovered country from whose bourn
No traveler returns, puzzles the will,
And makes us rather bear those ills we have
Than fly to others that we know not of.

—Hamlet

What does WWW stand for? Okay, it is supposed to stand for *World Wide Web*. But sometimes when I'm in one of my more cynical moods, I think it stands for *Wow! What a Waste*. On the other hand, when I'm being more charitable, I think it means *Whatever, Whenever, Wherever*. If Microsoft gets its way, however, it will stand for the *Wonderful Windows Workplace*, or something like that.

1

Microsoft's vision of the future (apparently) is to integrate Windows with the Internet as seamlessly as possible. This vision—today known as *AIP* or Active Internet Platform—is really two pieces. The piece the users see looks suspiciously like a Web browser that can browse everything (not just Web pages). The part programmers see is a bit more complicated, but it supports several things you need to successfully integrate Windows, the Internet, and networks in general. It also helps programs browse things (on or off the Net) with a minimum of fuss. ActiveX is an integral part of AIP. AIP uses ActiveX, and you must use ActiveX to fully utilize AIP.

A Peek Over The Shoulder

Suppose in the near future, you are browsing the Web and you wind up on my home page. My latest white paper expounds that the key to programmer productivity is to have an office with a door and one programmer per office. You think this is rubbish (perhaps you sell Herman Miller cubicles) and decide to set me straight. First, you click on the telephone icon at the bottom-right corner of the Web page—you'd like to talk to me directly.

The telephone obligingly rings (complete with an animation of a phone shaking). After a minute, my answering machine page comes on the screen. An AVI file plays a video of me telling you that I'm not in but you can leave a message. You click on the back button to go back to the original page and disconnect the call. You then click on the mailbox icon (next to the telephone) to send me a flaming note.

You are still working in the "Web browser" but now it looks slightly different. The menus and toolbars look suspiciously like Microsoft Word (or whatever your favorite word processor is). A dialog box pops up, prompting you to select one of my "in-boxes." Annoyed that you can't start composing your mail, you pick *Complaints* and dismiss the dialog. After the automatically generated mail header, you begin typing your point of view about cubicle workspace synergy.

As you compose your message, you remember that you have a nice chart showing that the ideal number of programmers per cube is three. You click on the *Favorite Places* menu item and open the Charts folder. Nothing changes—you are still in the browser, but it shows you a list of chart documents. You click on one to open it (just a single click) and you copy it to the clipboard. Two clicks on the back button bring you back to your email in progress. You paste the chart in and smugly press *Send* on the toolbar.

Satisfied that you have made your point, you decide to pay some bills. Another click on *Favorite Places* brings you to a page that looks very much like Quicken. It isn't Quicken, however. You are still working in the browser. The only differences are that the "page" you are browsing looks like Quicken and the browser's menus and toolbars merge with Quicken's toolbar. The Quicken/browser automatically and securely logs you into your bank over the Internet.

This is AIP's *Page View* (see Figure 1.1). You don't have to use page view. If you prefer, you can still do things the way you do now: open a program or a document and manage multiple windows. However, the page view is quite simple and mimics a Web page in every way. In the above scenario, you can't tell when you are working on a local application, a Web page, or something else. For example, the answering machine application runs on my machine, not yours. The ringing telephone control also belongs to me. The dialog box where you select my mail in-box belongs to me, too. My computer made your copy of Word display it.

What About Us?

That's the user's view. But what does this mean to programmers? Does this mean we just write plug-in modules for Microsoft's Web browser? No. Although the programming part of AIP supports the page view, that's just the tip of the iceberg.

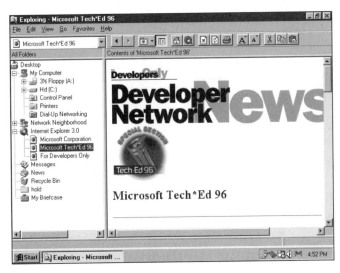

Figure 1.1 Page View in action.

Here's a list of the major components integral to AIP. They're illustrated in Figure 1.2.

1. WinInet, an API that presents a high-level interface that allows you to easily fetch files (and perform other common operations) from the Internet without bothering with details.

2. Local caching of resources over a network.

3. A generalized browsing mechanism that keeps track of the navigation portion of a browsing application.

4. An ActiveX-enabled browser that allows any ActiveX (OLE) server to reside on a browser page.

5. ActiveX controls that know how to display common data types (GIF, JPEG, AVI, and so on).

6. Support for ActiveX controls that reside on remote machines or store data on remote machines; Web pages can automatically download ActiveX controls and install them.

7. More efficient ways of communicating information about ActiveX controls in the system registry without creating them (Categories).

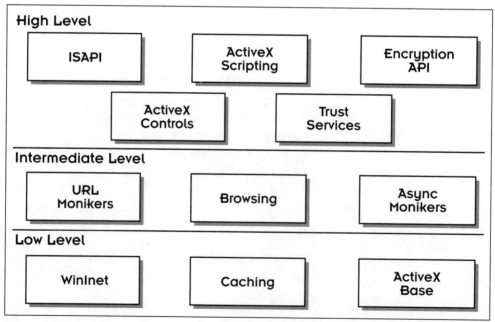

Figure 1.2 AIP components.

8. A method to represent a URL (for example, *http://www.coriolis.com*) at the operating system level (URL Monikers).

9. A mechanism (Asynchronous Monikers) that allows ActiveX to load large blocks of data over a potentially slow network connection (and using the cache mentioned above in item 2).

10. A programming API (the Internet Server API or ISAPI) to customize Web server functionality.

11. A generalized scripting service that you can use to control Web pages (or any other compatible program, for that matter).

12. Methods to verify that downloaded code is safe, encrypt data, and rate content (similar to rating movies).

Nearly all of the AIP uses ActiveX controls—that's why you need to know how to use ActiveX and how to create your own ActiveX components. This has several advantages. First, ActiveX does a great deal of work to make certain that you don't care much if a component and its user are on the same machine. Also, ActiveX is extensible. Suppose a new graphics format becomes popular on the Web next week (not hard to imagine, eh?). With ActiveX, you only need to install a new component to take advantage of it.

In the following sections, I'll show you what each of the above pieces means to you. Don't worry about the details; I'll get into those in the next few chapters. For now, try to see how each piece is important. The same goes for terms. In this chapter, I'll throw around some terms without rigorously defining them. That, too, will come in later chapters.

WinInet

Since the goal of AIP is to integrate seamlessly with the Internet, it isn't surprising that one of the core AIP technologies is a simple way to work with networks. If you've been frustrated trying to write WinSock programs in the past, then WinInet is for you. As an example of how easy this is, consider the case where you want to read a file from a Web server. You can use simple calls like *InternetOpen*, *InternetOpenUrl*, and *InternetReadFile* to retrieve the file. Similar services make it easy to work with the FTP and Gopher protocols, too.

Before you use the WinInet calls, you always call *InternetOpen*. Like many other API calls, this one returns a handle to you. However, this handle refers to the Internet (it is a hINTERNET). Imagine what you can do with that. WinInet takes care of all the messy details of establishing the connection, negotiating protocols, and those other things that you don't care about.

Local Caching

The Internet isn't necessarily speedy. True, connections are getting faster, but the connection speed usually pales compared to the raw speed of the machine. Even if the network connection is fast, there are many, many users on the Internet (make that many, many, *many*). This makes data caching very important. Instead of loading a file over and over again, why not load it once, keep a copy of it, and satisfy future requests from the same file?

That is the purpose of the Cache API. It allows programs to associate a file on disk with a URL. You can specify if the cache system will automatically free these associations and files when the cache begins to fill. WinInet calls can also specify that they wish to bypass the cache. You might want to directly reread a file from the Internet if its contents are volatile or you suspect it has changed.

Browsing

Because browsing is so integral to AIP, Microsoft provides two ways you can easily create browsing applications. The first is an ActiveX component that manages browsing. What you browse—URLs, files, database records—isn't important. The browsing component helps you maintain a context where you can move backwards, forwards, and maintain a history regardless of the actual content.

Since some programs don't use ActiveX, there is a simplified API you can use to support browsing. This API is not as powerful as the ActiveX version because it is a simple wrapper around the base ActiveX objects.

ActiveX Controls And Containers

ActiveX is more than just the technology that Microsoft uses to build AIP—it is an integral part of how programmers use and extend AIP. The page view I described above is little more than a Web browser that can contain ActiveX controls and some special ActiveX controls to provide views on a variety of objects.

More importantly, the browser can automatically download ActiveX controls on demand. In the above example, my Web page specified a ringing telephone icon. If your machine didn't already have it, the browser would automatically download it from my computer.

Any ActiveX program can use any ActiveX control. If you want an ActiveX container to display your data or special control, you can write your own ActiveX controls. That's what this book is all about.

ActiveX Categories

OLE controls (the precursor to ActiveX) relied on the registry to alert containers to their presence. However, this didn't tell the container what the control does. Categories allow ActiveX components to notify clients that they are present, and also what they can do. In this way, you can be reasonably certain that it is worthwhile for a container like the browser to create a component (which may take a while).

Consider this example: In an old-style container, you need to create a control that can load a BMP file. First you create a control and ask it if it can load BMPs. If the answer is no, you destroy the control and move on to the next one. This is very inefficient, particularly when the controls may reside on the Internet.

ActiveX components can place entries in the registry (using unique Category IDs or CATIDs) that signify that they can handle certain operations (for example, loading BMP files). A container need only scan the registry to determine which component can load BMP files. Then, if the container creates the component, it is reasonably sure it will do the right things. The user can also associate a default component with a particular CATID. Then containers that want to display BMP files, for example, can use the default component even if several components have that capability.

Categories also allow components to request certain functions from a container. This allows containers to not waste time creating components they can't use.

Some containers may want to display categories graphically (for instance, in a tool box). To this end, the registry can also contain icons for each category type.

Monikers: URL And Asynchronous

Writing simple ActiveX controls isn't the entire picture, however. You need to take special care when writing controls that may stretch over a slow data link (like the Internet). AIP deals with this in several ways. For many years, traditional OLE programs have had the notion of a moniker. A moniker is a special ActiveX component that contains the name of some other object. In a simple case, suppose you want to link to a file on your hard disk. The moniker might simply contain the file's name. As a more complex example, what if you were linking just three paragraphs from a document on disk? Then the moniker contains the file name and some way to indicate which three paragraphs you

want. You don't need to know what that indication is—you ask the moniker to get the data and it does it. You can think of a moniker as an object-oriented file name—it knows where the data is and how to get it.

Now that AIP encapsulates the Internet, Windows provides a standard moniker for URLs. You know URLs; they are those odd strings you use to identify resources on the Internet. For example: *http://www.coriolis.com* or *ftp:// coriolis.com.* Using the moniker, you can get an object or a storage that corresponds to a URL.

There is one other special twist to monikers you'll use with AIP. Suppose you have a URL moniker that points to a 25-megabyte video clip on the Internet. If it were a traditional moniker, your program–when asked to give you an object for the video clip–would grind to a halt while the 25 megabytes crawled through cyberspace. This isn't a good idea. Instead, you'll use an asynchronous moniker, which allows things to continue while the download proceeds. This is how Web browsers work today. When a large graphic or sound bite loads, you can view text, move on to another page, and generally continue to work as usual.

ISAPI

Web pages that supply simple text and graphics are easy to create. But what about interactive Web pages like search forms or games? These special Web pages require some code to run on the server to handle requests. That's where ISAPI (Internet Server API) comes into play. This special API allows you to write custom code that executes in response to input from a Web page and to create new Web content on the fly.

You can also create ISAPI filters to monitor or alter data in conjunction with a server. You might use a filter to encrypt stock market data, for example. Another use for a filter might be to log transactions.

Although ISAPI is part of AIP, it isn't of much use to the casual Web page creator. You don't use ISAPI to create Web pages; you use it to customize an HTTP server.

Scripting

Scripting isn't really new. It's what Microsoft used to call OLE Automation (see the *ActiveX Thesaurus* in Appendix A). Any script-capable program (including the page view browser) can accept commands from generic script languages. The best example of such a script language today is Visual Basic Scripting

Edition (similar to the older Visual Basic for Applications). However, any program that can control ActiveX objects (C++ or Visual Basic, for example) can participate. There are already a few third-party scripting languages that work the same way, and you can look for more in the near future. Remember: The language doesn't have to be Basic—as long as it can drive ActiveX objects, it can be a scripting language.

Why should you care about scripting? Scripting is an easy way to control other applications, especially the page view browser. For many Web programmers, scripting can take the place of more complicated techniques like ISAPI or CGI (Common Gateway Interface) programming.

Security

With the increased connectivity afforded by AIP, security is even more of an issue than usual. How do you transmit data securely? If a Web page wants to run an ActiveX component, how can you be sure it isn't a virus? There are several parts of AIP that deal with this problem. In particular, PCT (Private Communication Technology) and the new cryptography API can ensure privacy. The Windows Trust Verification Services system, combined with digital signatures, allows network administrators to allow (or disallow) certain ActiveX components to run on their network.

Another security issue arises when you set up an *Intranet*. An Intranet is a private network you can set up to work like the Internet (and possibly connect to the Internet as well). For example, suppose your company maintains a Web site for your customers. However, if someone accesses this Web site from the local network (the Intranet), you want some links to appear that go to special pages that are not accessible to the general public. You might have inventory data, private messages, or a time and expense entry form protected this way. AIP allows you to authenticate users—only certain users may have access to specific information on your Intranet.

Summary

Wow! If that seems like a lot of information, that's because it is. AIP is a major architecture change for Windows. There is even more, but these 12 items are the high points. Luckily, if you want to develop Web pages, most of this technology hides in the background. Some of it is mainly used by other parts of AIP. For example, URL monikers use the cache and WinInet to actually do the work. You only need to worry about URL monikers.

This book focuses on ActiveX because it is the core of AIP and it is the part that most programmers will deal with. The ability to run controls over the Internet allows unprecedented control and flexibility for Web programming.

Two issues immediately come to mind, however: Java and portability. Of course, Java targets the same applications as ActiveX. Both attempt to run programs over the Internet. However, Java isn't as robust as ActiveX. Besides, it is a new programming language and not a very powerful one at that. Why not stick with Visual Basic (or whatever language you choose to use to develop ActiveX controls)?

Portability is a bit trickier. Obviously, Microsoft is aiming AIP at Windows platforms. However, they have agreements with other companies to bring ActiveX to multiple platforms. As we examine the architecture of ActiveX, you'll see this isn't as far-fetched as it may sound. Not only can ActiveX components operate easily over a network, but with the automated downloading of ActiveX, you can run your controls on the user's machine. A mechanism exists that allows you to specify different versions of an ActiveX control depending on the user's operating system and CPU type.

No one knows the future. But with Microsoft betting the Windows farm on AIP, you can bet it's going places. And if you want to go those places too, you're going to need to learn ActiveX.

2
No Pain...
No Siree Bob!

Why, all delights are vain; but that most vain
Which, with pain purchased doth inherit pain.

—Love's Labour's Lost

Most people think component software is a good idea. It is easy to use components to obtain impressive results. However, only a few people are creating components. It is just too hard. The fitness gurus on television say, "No pain...no gain." My creed is, "No pain...No siree Bob!" Although I have written ActiveX controls using C++, it isn't much fun.

Luckily, Visual Basic 5 allows you to create ActiveX controls almost painlessly. Truthfully, it allows you to create controls as easily as you currently create form-based applications. In this chapter, you'll jump right in and create a control. It's easy! In later chapters, you'll see more details about what you did and why it worked. For now, you can just jump right in and get started.

VB5 creates ordinary ActiveX controls. In theory, you can use these ActiveX controls in VB, Web pages, C++, Delphi, Power-Builder,or any other environment that understands ActiveX controls. If you are already a VB programmer, you'll have little or no trouble creating controls. If you haven't tried VB, it isn't difficult to get started. If you are accustomed to using an older version of VB, you'll notice that Microsoft has introduced a new user interface that is more comfortable for programmers accustomed to their Microsoft Developer's Studio program. Don't worry. If you prefer the traditional VB interface, you can still approximate it.

User Interface Options

VB5 departs from the usual look and feel of previous versions. Sort of. By default, the environment looks more like the Microsoft Developer's Studio (the C++, J++, and Fortran environment). If you are already familiar with VB5's user interface, you might want to skip ahead to the section titled *ActiveX Fundamentals.*

The interface centers around one mainframe window that contains all the other windows you'll use. The subordinate windows can float around, or you can dock them to an edge of the frame window. The code editor shows you the entire module (it draws lines between the various subroutines and functions).

I find the new interface pleasant to use. However, you might like the old style of interface better. That's no problem. Microsoft will let you turn off practically all the new enhancements. Just go to the Tools menu and select Options. Then pick the Advanced tab. Check the SDI Development Environment check box. The change won't take effect until you restart the program. Before you shut down, you might want to pick the Editor tab and uncheck the Default to Full Module View check box. This makes the code editor behave the way it did in older versions of VB. Shut VB5 down and restart it. Things will look more familiar.

Even with those changes, some windows will not behave the way you remember. For example, the project window and the object inspector are stuck together. To fix that, right click on each window and uncheck the dockable box. This will allow the windows to float about the desktop.

So, you can make the environment look almost exactly like previous versions of VB. However, try the new interface for a while and see if you like it. You can always change back and forth until you decide.

ActiveX Fundamentals

If you've ever used any kind of component software, you won't be surprised to hear that the fundamental pieces of an ActiveX control are: properties, methods, and events. VB-created ActiveX controls are no different.

Properties are similar to variables. These are values that the program using the component (the container) can set or read. In VB, you may place these values in actual variables, or you can connect them to components that you use to create your component. You'll see how that works shortly.

Methods are just functions and subroutines that the container can call. Again, you can define your own, or expose methods from components that you use internally.

Events notify the container when something interesting happens. Guess what? You can define custom events or you can pass events from other components.

Fail To Plan...Plan To Fail

To get the most from an ActiveX control you should carefully plan what properties, methods, and events it will handle. You can tweak things later, but it helps if you have a good idea from the start what you want to use. The example control I'll show you in this chapter is a simple scanning bar of lights (see Figure 2.1). You know, the sort of thing you see under the view screen on the Enterprise (the original Enterprise). It exposes four properties:

1. **Delay**—The number of milliseconds to delay between each lamp turning on.
2. **Direction**—**TRUE** to scan from left to right or **FALSE** to scan from right to left.
3. **ForeColor**—The color of lights when they are on.
4. **Hold**—Stops the lights from scanning when **TRUE**.

The control also supports a single event: **TICK**. This event fires each time the lights change state (that is, once for each period set by **Delay**). The control doesn't have any methods.

Figure 2.1 The example control.

Laying Out The Control

Once you have a plan, you can fire up VB5. From the start up dialog, select ActiveX Control under the New tab. The program will create an empty project. VB certainly looks different by default (see Figure 2.2). The toolbox on the left-hand side is familiar enough. At the top right is the project window. This window shows a hierarchical list of projects you have open. VB5 allows you to open multiple projects at once. This is especially useful if you have a control in one project and a test program that uses the control in another.

Looking at Figure 2.2, you'll notice that the familiar property browser window appears. Beneath that is a description window that describes the selected property. When you create a component, you'll want to control what appears in this window when programmers use your component. Even farther down is a layout window. This shows where your form will appear when it runs. If you right click on this window you can create grid lines to show the common screen resolutions and select options for where your forms will show up when your program runs.

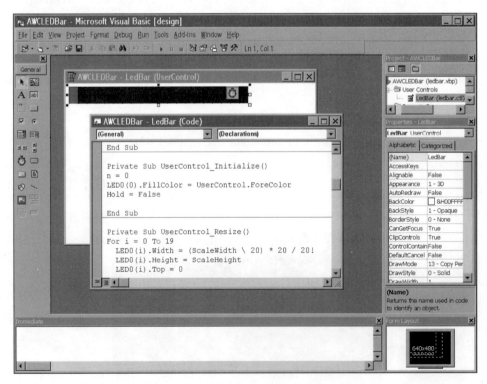

Figure 2.2 The Property browser window.

In the center of the screen, you'll see windows that hold forms and Basic code. By default, the code window shows you all the code at once and draws lines between sections. If you prefer the old style, you can click the small button at the bottom left corner of the code window. In fact, you can change just about any aspect of the interface. You can easily move, resize, or hide any of the windows or toolbars. You can customize everything. Right clicking anywhere brings up interesting menus.

Defining The Interface

To create the LEDBAR control (the scanning lights), I used the normal Basic shape component. Each of the 20 lights is a rectangle shape. I created the first one, copied it to the clipboard, and then pasted it to form a control array. Then I pasted it 18 more times to complete the array. By using a control array, I can refer to each light as an element in an array (or collection, if you prefer). The array's name is **LED0** and the elements range from 0 to 19.

Obviously, the control also needs a timer. Each time the timer expires, the control should turn off the current light and then turn on the light to the right or left of the current light (depending on the setting of the **Direction** flag).

At this point you could start writing code to take care of the logic. However, you'll need some of the properties (for example **Direction**), and they don't exist yet. To define properties, methods, and events, you'll use the Interface Wizard (from the Add-Ins menu). This Wizard (see Figures 2.3-2.6) allows you to select members (that is, properties, methods, and events) that many controls support (see Figure 2.3). You can also create custom members (Figure 2.4). On the next screen (see Figure 2.5) you attach the members to corresponding members in the components the control contains. I attached the **Delay** property directly to the timer component and the **ForeColor** property to the **UserControl** component (**UserControl** corresponds to a form in a regular VB program).

At this point, it would be tempting to attach the **Tick** event to the timer's **Timer** event. You can do this as long as you haven't already put a **Timer** handler in the code. If you have an existing handler, the Wizard will write an extra event handler that causes a compile error.

On the final Wizard screen (Figure 2.6) you can define any unattached members. The description text will appear in the design environment (below the property browser in Figure 2.2). You can also specify types, properties, etc. The wizard creates variables for your unattached properties. For example, the **Direction** property causes the Wizard to create a variable named **m_Direction**.

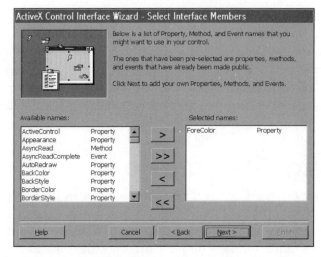

Figure 2.3   Selecting common members.

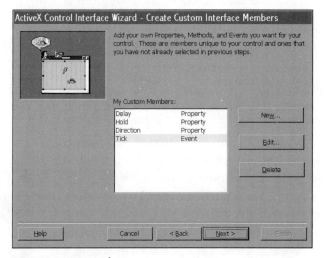

Figure 2.4   Creating custom members.

Methods get skeletal function definitions that you must complete. The Wizard also handles events. Of course, any members that you connect to other components don't show up on this screen.

After you finish this Wizard, all of your external members are complete. Of course, you'll need to write code that handles any custom methods, and fire any custom events at the appropriate time. You also have to write all the other code that makes your control work.

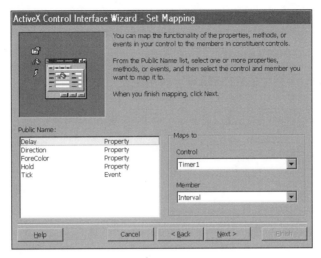

Figure 2.5 Connecting component members.

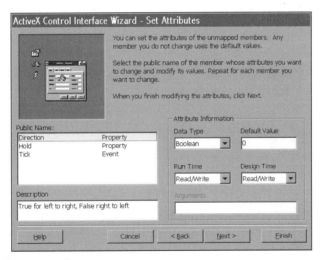

Figure 2.6 Defining members.

Writing The Code

The code to handle the light bar is fairly simple. A **Timer** event handler cycles the lights based on the **m_Direction** flag (see Listing 2.1). Also, the **UserControl_Initialize** event takes care of some setup issues. If you attached the **Tick** event to the **Timer** control, you already have a **Timer** handler. It will contain the line:

```
RaiseEvent Tick
```

You can simply add your code in the same handler. If you didn't hook up the **Tick** event, you can now create a **Timer** handler and add the **RaiseEvent** line to raise your custom event.

LISTING 2.1 THE LEDBAR CONTROL.

```
VERSION 5.00
Begin VB.UserControl LedBar
    BackColor       =   &H00FFFFFF&
    ClientHeight    =   432
    ClientLeft      =   0
    ClientTop       =   0
    ClientWidth     =   4788
    FillColor       =   &H00FFFFFF&
    PropertyPages   =   "ledbar.ctx":0000
    ScaleHeight     =   432
    ScaleWidth      =   4788
    ToolboxBitmap   =   "ledbar.ctx":001A
    Begin VB.Timer Timer1
        Interval        =   125
        Left            =   4212
        Top             =   0
    End
    Begin VB.Shape LED0
        FillStyle       =   0   'Solid
        Height          =   492
        Index           =   19
        Left            =   4560
        Top             =   0
        Width           =   252
    End
    Begin VB.Shape LED0
        FillStyle       =   0   'Solid
        Height          =   492
        Index           =   18
        Left            =   4320
        Top             =   0
        Width           =   252
    End
    Begin VB.Shape LED0
        FillStyle       =   0   'Solid
        Height          =   492
        Index           =   17
        Left            =   4080
        Top             =   0
        Width           =   252
    End
```

```
Begin VB.Shape LED0
   FillStyle      =    0   'Solid
   Height         =    492
   Index          =    16
   Left           =    3840
   Top            =    0
   Width          =    252
End
Begin VB.Shape LED0
   FillStyle      =    0   'Solid
   Height         =    492
   Index          =    15
   Left           =    3600
   Top            =    0
   Width          =    252
End
Begin VB.Shape LED0
   FillStyle      =    0   'Solid
   Height         =    492
   Index          =    14
   Left           =    3360
   Top            =    0
   Width          =    252
End
Begin VB.Shape LED0
   FillStyle      =    0   'Solid
   Height         =    492
   Index          =    13
   Left           =    3120
   Top            =    0
   Width          =    252
End
Begin VB.Shape LED0
   BackColor      =    &H00000000&
   FillStyle      =    0   'Solid
   Height         =    492
   Index          =    12
   Left           =    2880
   Top            =    0
   Width          =    252
End
Begin VB.Shape LED0
   BackColor      =    &H00000000&
   FillStyle      =    0   'Solid
   Height         =    492
   Index          =    11
   Left           =    2640
```

```
       Top             =   0
       Width           =   252
    End
    Begin VB.Shape LED0
       BackColor       =   &H00000000&
       FillStyle       =   0   'Solid
       Height          =   492
       Index           =   10
       Left            =   2400
       Top             =   0
       Width           =   252
    End
    Begin VB.Shape LED0
       FillStyle       =   0   'Solid
       Height          =   492
       Index           =   9
       Left            =   2160
       Top             =   0
       Width           =   252
    End
    Begin VB.Shape LED0
       FillStyle       =   0   'Solid
       Height          =   492
       Index           =   8
       Left            =   1920
       Top             =   0
       Width           =   252
    End
    Begin VB.Shape LED0
       FillStyle       =   0   'Solid
       Height          =   492
       Index           =   7
       Left            =   1680
       Top             =   0
       Width           =   252
    End
    Begin VB.Shape LED0
       FillStyle       =   0   'Solid
       Height          =   492
       Index           =   6
       Left            =   1440
       Top             =   0
       Width           =   252
    End
    Begin VB.Shape LED0
       FillStyle       =   0   'Solid
       Height          =   492
```

```
            Index         =    5
            Left          =    1200
            Top           =    0
            Width         =    252
         End
         Begin VB.Shape LED0
            FillStyle     =    0    'Solid
            Height        =    492
            Index         =    4
            Left          =    960
            Top           =    0
            Width         =    252
         End
         Begin VB.Shape LED0
            FillStyle     =    0    'Solid
            Height        =    492
            Index         =    3
            Left          =    720
            Top           =    0
            Width         =    252
         End
         Begin VB.Shape LED0
            FillStyle     =    0    'Solid
            Height        =    492
            Index         =    2
            Left          =    480
            Top           =    0
            Width         =    252
         End
         Begin VB.Shape LED0
            BackColor     =    &H00000000&
            FillStyle     =    0    'Solid
            Height        =    492
            Index         =    1
            Left          =    240
            Top           =    0
            Width         =    252
         End
         Begin VB.Shape LED0
            BackColor     =    &H000000FF&
            FillColor     =    &H000000FF&
            FillStyle     =    0    'Solid
            Height        =    492
            Index         =    0
            Left          =    0
            Top           =    0
            Width         =    252
```

```
    End
End
Attribute VB_Name = "LedBar"
Attribute VB_GlobalNameSpace = False
Attribute VB_Creatable = True
Attribute VB_PredeclaredId = False
Attribute VB_Exposed = True
Attribute VB_Ext_KEY = "PropPageWizardRun" ,"Yes"



Dim n As Integer
'Default Property Values:
Const m_def_Direction = True
Const m_def_Hold = False
'Const m_def_ForeColor = 255
'Property Variables:
Dim m_Direction As Boolean
Dim m_Hold As Boolean
'Dim m_ForeColor As OLE_COLOR
'Event Declarations:
Event Tick()
'Event Timer() 'MappingInfo=Timer1,Timer1,-1,Timer



Private Sub Timer1_Timer()
If m_Hold = True Then Exit Sub
LEDO(n).FillColor = vbBlack
If m_Direction Then
   If n = 19 Then n = 0 Else n = n + 1
Else
   If n = 0 Then n = 19 Else n = n - 1
End If
LEDO(n).FillColor = UserControl.ForeColor
RaiseEvent Tick
End Sub

Private Sub UserControl_Initialize()
n = 0
LEDO(0).FillColor = UserControl.ForeColor
Hold = False

End Sub

Private Sub UserControl_Resize()
For i = 0 To 19
```

```
  LED0(i).Width = (ScaleWidth \ 20) * 20 / 20!
  LED0(i).Height = ScaleHeight
  LED0(i).Top = 0
  LED0(i).Left = i * (ScaleWidth \ 20) * 20 / 20!
Next i
End Sub
'WARNING! DO NOT REMOVE OR MODIFY THE FOLLOWING COMMENTED LINES!
'MappingInfo=UserControl,UserControl,-1,BackColor
'Public Property Get BackColor() As OLE_COLOR
'    BackColor = UserControl.BackColor
'End Property
'
'Public Property Let BackColor(ByVal New_BackColor As OLE_COLOR)
'    UserControl.BackColor() = New_BackColor
'    PropertyChanged "BackColor"
'End Property
'
'Public Property Get ForeColor() As OLE_COLOR
'    ForeColor = m_ForeColor
'End Property
'
'Public Property Let ForeColor(ByVal New_ForeColor As OLE_COLOR)
'    m_ForeColor = New_ForeColor
'    PropertyChanged "ForeColor"
'End Property


'WARNING! DO NOT REMOVE OR MODIFY THE FOLLOWING COMMENTED LINES!
'MappingInfo=Timer1,Timer1,-1,Interval
Public Property Get Delay() As Long
Attribute Delay.VB_Description = "Returns/sets the " & _
    "number of milliseconds between calls to a Timer " & _
    "control's Timer event."
    Delay = Timer1.Interval
End Property

Public Property Let Delay(ByVal New_Delay As Long)
    Timer1.Interval() = New_Delay
    PropertyChanged "Delay"
End Property

'Initialize Properties for User Control
Private Sub UserControl_InitProperties()
'    m_ForeColor = m_def_ForeColor
    m_Hold = m_def_Hold
    m_Direction = m_def_Direction
End Sub
```

```
'Load property values from storage
Private Sub UserControl_ReadProperties(PropBag As PropertyBag)

'    UserControl.BackColor = PropBag.ReadProperty("BackColor", &HFFFFFF)
'    m_ForeColor = PropBag.ReadProperty("ForeColor",
'    m_def_ForeColor)
    Timer1.Interval = PropBag.ReadProperty("Delay", 125)
    UserControl.ForeColor = PropBag.ReadProperty("ForeColor", &H80000012)
    m_Hold = PropBag.ReadProperty("Hold", m_def_Hold)
    m_Direction = PropBag.ReadProperty("Direction", m_def_Direction)
End Sub


'Write property values to storage
Private Sub UserControl_WriteProperties(PropBag As PropertyBag)

'    Call PropBag.WriteProperty("BackColor", UserControl.BackColor,
&HFFFFFF)
'    Call PropBag.WriteProperty("ForeColor", m_ForeColor, m_def_ForeColor)
    Call PropBag.WriteProperty("Delay", Timer1.Interval, 125)
    Call PropBag.WriteProperty("ForeColor", UserControl.ForeColor,
&H80000012)
    Call PropBag.WriteProperty("Hold", m_Hold, m_def_Hold)
    Call PropBag.WriteProperty("Direction", m_Direction, m_def_Direction)
End Sub


'WARNING! DO NOT REMOVE OR MODIFY THE FOLLOWING COMMENTED LINES!
'MappingInfo=UserControl,UserControl,-1,ForeColor
Public Property Get ForeColor() As OLE_COLOR
Attribute ForeColor.VB_Description =
"Returns/sets the foreground color " &_
    "used to display text and graphics in an object."
    ForeColor = UserControl.ForeColor
End Property


Public Property Let ForeColor(ByVal New_ForeColor As OLE_COLOR)
    UserControl.ForeColor() = New_ForeColor
    PropertyChanged "ForeColor"
End Property


Public Property Get Hold() As Boolean
Attribute Hold.VB_Description = "Set to TRUE to freeze LEDs"
    Hold = m_Hold
End Property


Public Property Let Hold(ByVal New_Hold As Boolean)
    m_Hold = New_Hold
    PropertyChanged "Hold"
```

```
End Property

Public Property Get Direction() As Boolean
Attribute Direction.VB_Description = "True for left to right, False right
to left"
    Direction = m_Direction
End Property

Public Property Let Direction(ByVal New_Direction As Boolean)
    m_Direction = New_Direction
    PropertyChanged "Direction"
End Property
```

With those two handlers in place, the control will work as advertised. However, you have to make the control the exact size of the 20 shape controls. Not very programmer-friendly. To improve the behavior, you can add a **UserControl_Resize** event handler to resize the shape controls dynamically.

To calculate the new size and position for each shape control, you take the **ScaleWidth** of the **UserControl** object and round it so that it is divisible by 20 (the number of shape controls). Then you divide it by twenty. Given the width of each control, it is a simple matter to decide where the left edge of each control should be. You can set the shape controls' height to the **UserControl**'s **ScaleHeight** property.

Finishing Touches

Now you are about finished. You can set the **ToolboxIcon** property to a bitmap so that your control shows up with your choice of pictures in toolboxes. You can also edit the project properties and change the name of the control.

If you want a property sheet for the control, just run the property sheet Wizard. It will allow you to select a standard page to select colors (the foreground color in this case). You can also define custom pages and place properties (like **Direction** and **Hold**) on them. The Wizard automatically creates appropriate pages (see Figures 2.7 and 2.8).

Using The Control

Once you have finished, you can easily test the control. Simply select Add Project from the File menu. When prompted, tell the environment that you want an EXE file project. You'll see your control appears in the toolbox. Simply grab it and place it on the form as you would any other component. Use

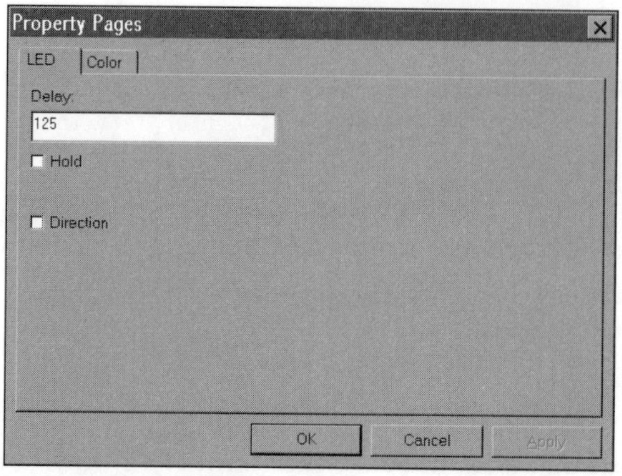

Figure 2.7 Defining property sheets.

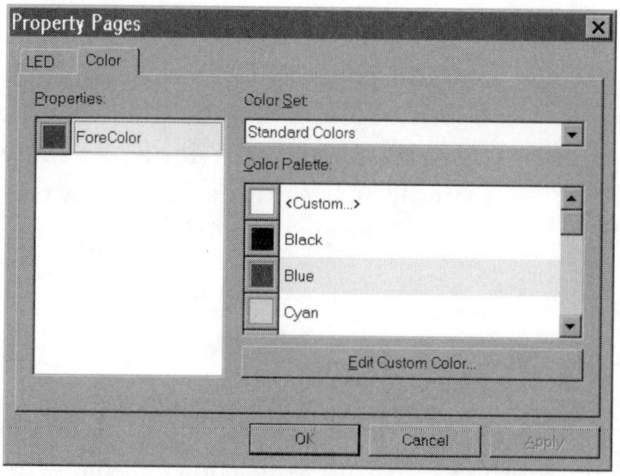

Figure 2.8 Property sheets.

the object browser to set the properties and double click the control to write event handlers. It's easy.

If you want to use the control in a regular project, generate an OCX file (you'll find the choice on the File menu). Then, you'll have to add the component to your toolbox using the Components command on the Project menu. Once you add it to the toolbox, you are ready to go. Some other environments may require you to register your control. That's no problem since VB5 automatically generates self-registration code. You only need to run REGSRVR32.EXE and specify the OCX file that contains your control.

Packaging Your Control

What happens if you want to distribute your control to other users? VB5 provides a special tool to create distributions (see Figure 2.9). You run this tool directly from the Start menu (or Program Manager if you are using NT 3.51). It allows you to create setup files for your project, or files appropriate to download over the Internet. You simply tell it what project you want to distribute and it does the rest.

Summary

All this sounds too good to be true, right? Well, there is one catch. Your control requires a special runtime DLL before it can run. If you are using your control with conventional programs, that isn't a big problem. However, if you want users to download your control over the Internet, it could be annoying. The good news is that once users download the DLL once, they don't have to do it again. Then, they only need to download your control.

Speaking of the Internet, you can even set up asynchronous properties using VB5. This advanced technique allows you to load a large property (perhaps a picture) asynchronously over the network. You'll find out more about these things in later chapters.

OLE controls are usable almost everywhere. Now they are easy to create too. Don't worry if you don't fully understand the process. In the next few chapters, I'll tell you more about ActiveX theory, then—armed with that information—you'll see how to build some more controls.

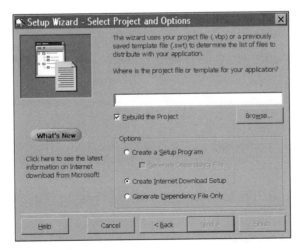

Figure 2.9 Creating a distribution.

ONE MILE UP 3

Like one that stands upon a promontory,
And spies a far-off shore where he would tread,
Wishing his foot were equal with his eye.

—King Henry VI

ctiveX might be the Next Big Thing, but how do you get started? Do you have to write OLE programs? Before you can write ActiveX servers and clients, you need to know about a few other things (like the system registry). In most cases, you don't have to write what most people think of as an OLE program. Traditional OLE programming allows you to embed or link one document inside another. This is a complex process involving many different ActiveX objects. However, writing ordinary ActiveX components isn't hard at all. Writing ActiveX controls is only a bit more difficult. This is especially true with Visual Basic. Thanks to VB's support, you don't need to know a lot to just get started. After all, we wrote a nice control in Chapter 2 and didn't care much about why it worked.

I don't remember who said it, but someone once told me, "You don't have to know how engines work to drive a car. But, the best drivers do." The same is true in this case. VB conceals many of the details that other programmers have to grapple with to make ActiveX controls. However, if you have any troubles, or just want to do something out of the ordinary, you'll need to understand more.

This chapter will introduce a few terms and some basic ideas you should know about. Much of the material will talk about pointers, and other things that sound like C programming. That's

natural, since the underlying Windows API and ActiveX specifications use C as a base. If you want to brush up on some of these concepts, you might want to stop and read Appendix D now. Be aware, however, that there isn't any C code in this chapter. Everything here covers abstract concepts you should know, not implementation details. Those will appear in later chapters.

Definitions

In the last two chapters, I used several terms without defining them rigorously. Let's define a few of them a little better now:

- **ActiveX Component.** An ActiveX object that other programs can use

- **ActiveX Control.** A special component that works like a control window

- **ActiveX Client.** Any program that uses any ActiveX component

- **ActiveXContainer.** A program that can accept ActiveX document objects or controls

- **ActiveX Server.** A DLL or executable program that provides one or more ActiveX objects

- **ActiveX Document Object.** A document that you can embed or link into a container (this is the traditional OLE functionality)

Currently, Microsoft calls any ActiveX object a control. Personally, I don't think that's a good idea. I prefer to call any ActiveX object a component. Some components know how to act like traditional windows and those are controls. For example, an ActiveX object that converts names to Internet addresses is just a component. You can't drag it onto a Visual Basic form, for instance. On the other hand, the ringing telephone control from Chapter 1 is both a component and a control. Controls are similar to the older-style OCX (OLE Control Extensions) or VBX (Visual Basic Extension) controls.

The Structure Of An ActiveX Object

Here is the most startling and important sentence in this book: *To a client program, an ActiveX object is nothing more than a table of function pointers.* That's it. Read it again. When a client accesses an object, it simply calls functions using the pointers in the table (see Figure 3.1). Objects can supply any number of tables for different purposes, but the client works with one at a time. These tables are called *interfaces.* Of course, the client and server must completely

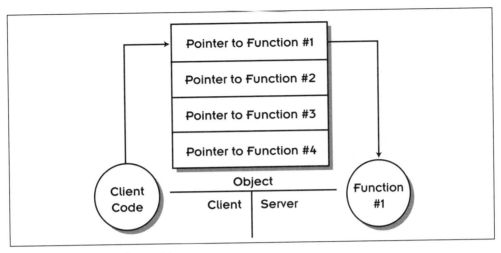

Figure 3.1 An interface table.

agree on the order and form of these functions. The calling convention, parameters, and return value must match both sides' expectations.

Consider this example: You are writing a system that allows users to retrieve stock market data. You create an ActiveX object with functions to validate the user's ID, make an entry in the user's account (so you can charge him for the transaction), and get the data. The object then has three methods, **LogIn**, **AccountLog**, and **GetStockData**. You might use two interface tables; one for the logging and accounting (the **ILog** interface); another for the data retrieval (**IGetStockInfo**; see Figure 3.2). Could you use one single table? Yes, you could. However, consider another example.

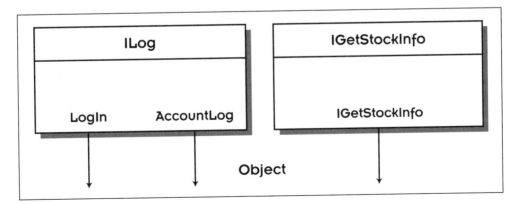

Figure 3.2 The stock market object.

Your stock market data program is so successful, you branch into providing data for mutual funds, too. You might then create the object in Figure 3.3. Notice that two of the functions are the same and they appear in the same interface. Only the **GetStockData** function changes. Keep this example in mind. We'll look at it more closely in just a minute. By the way, it is customary (although not mandatory) to specify interface names that begin with **I**, like **IGetStockInfo** and **ILog**.

It doesn't matter what language you use to create your object. You can use C, C++, Delphi, or Visual Basic. The only thing that is important is that your language can create the magic table of function pointers. ActiveX servers can reside in DLLs or EXE files and supply objects to other programs. It doesn't matter what language you use to write the client or the server.

That's An Object?

That seems too simple, doesn't it? (In truth, there is a bit more to it than this, but not much more.) If you are familiar with objects from C++, this doesn't seem like the same thing. Well, it isn't exactly the same thing, but if you look closely, it allows you to do the same fundamental operations as C++ objects. Visual Basic has class modules, of course. These classes are more similar to ActiveX interfaces and less similar to traditional C++ objects.

Objects, in general, are important for several reasons:

1. Objects hide their implementation of functions. You ask the object to perform, and it does, but you shouldn't have to know how it performs. This is encapsulation and allows you to make major changes in the way an object operates without affecting any other code.

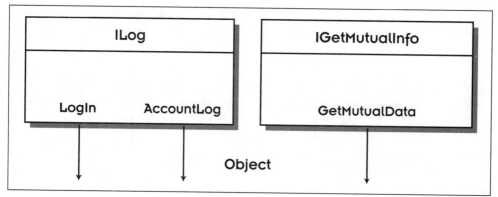

Figure 3.3 The mutual fund object.

2. Objects allow you to reuse their code to build other objects. In C++, you do this via *derivation*. When you derive one class from another, the derived class inherits all of the code from the base class.

3. Objects are *polymorphic*. If you have a base object for vehicles, for example, you can create more specific classes for cars, trucks, and vans. Polymorphism allows you to treat cars, trucks, and vans as vehicles. In other words, you can define a list of vehicles that may contain cars, trucks, and vans without knowing which is which. C++ handles this via derivation, also. If all three classes derive from the vehicle class, you can store pointers to them in a vehicle pointer.

How does ActiveX accomplish these goals? Encapsulation is easy. Since each ActiveX object exposes interfaces (and nothing else), client programs must call using the pointers in those interfaces. You are free to change the object in any way as long as the interface table contains pointers that work the way they originally did. If you agree that Slot 6 in the interface table prints its five-integer arguments, then that's what it has to do. However, exactly how you do that is up to you. You could write the object in C++ or Visual Basic, or you could connect over the Internet to a mainframe and print it there using Fortran. The client doesn't know or care.

That still leaves the question of derivation, right? Not exactly. C++ uses derivation to support code reuse and polymorphism. Derivation is not especially important to object orientation. It is simply one way to meet the goals of code reuse and polymorphism. ActiveX uses different mechanisms to provide these features.

Code Reuse

There are two ways ActiveX components can reuse other ActiveX components: aggregation and containment. Aggregation requires a good deal of work and design (which we'll talk about later). Containment, on the other hand, is quite simple. There is no reason why an ActiveX object can't use another ActiveX object in its implementation. The new object can provide the same interfaces as the base object as well as additional interfaces. When the object receives a call to one of the contained interfaces, it can do any of the following:

1. Handle the call itself (this is similar to a C++ override).

2. Call the contained object (this is similar to doing nothing in C++).

3. Execute some code, call the contained object, and—perhaps—execute some more code (this is similar to C++ overrides that call their base class).

This allows you to reuse any number of other ActiveX components the same way a C++ derived class reuses its base classes. Look at the advantages to this method:

- You don't need the source code for the base class

- The base class doesn't even have to use the same language

- If the base class changes, the containing class will automatically use the new version without recompiling

- You don't have to expose all the interfaces an object supplies, which allows you to selectively expose interfaces from a base class

Since ActiveX components only expose interface functions (and never variables), you don't have the problems you see in C++, where the derived class depends on some internal state of the base class. The only communication permitted is via the interfaces.

Figure 3.4 shows an example of a contained object. Notice that the outside client has no idea what the contained class is. If the object later decides to use a different object to provide an interface, or provide the entire interface internally, it is free to do so. If the object needs to inherit from multiple base classes, it can simply contain multiple objects.

Polymorphism

Because objects can support multiple interfaces, they can be polymorphic. Returning to the vehicle/car/truck/van example, look at Figure 3.5. These three

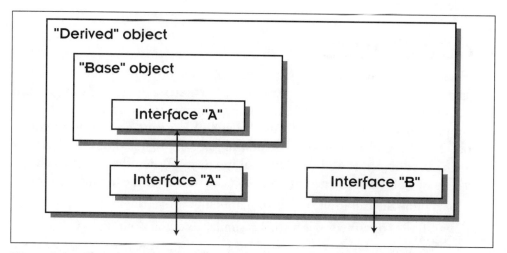

Figure 3.4   Object containment.

| Car Object | IVehicle |
| | ICar |

| Truck Object | IVehicle |
| | ITruck |

| Van Object | IVehicle |
| | IVan |

Figure 3.5 Polymorphic objects.

objects are polymorphic because they all support the **IVehicle** interface. A client can treat all of these objects the same by requesting their **IVehicle** interface table. If the client requires more detail, it can get the more specific interface table, too. Notice that if there is an object for vehicles, the other objects can reuse it through containment.

The only problem here is when you want the vehicle class to be abstract. In C++, an abstract base class is one that you can't create. You can only derive from it. If you plan to reuse an ActiveX object via containment, then the "derived" classes must create it. Therefore, anyone else can create it too.

There are some *ad hoc* solutions to this problem. For example, if you don't tell clients about the vehicle class, they can't create it. That isn't a very good answer, however. Usually, the idea of an abstract base class in ActiveX is just that: an idea.

Polymorphism has many advantages (some of which are similar to the advantages of containment):

- You can create unrelated objects that are polymorphic with respect to each other

- The objects don't need to be in the same language, nor do you require the other object's source code

- Any program can work with your polymorphic objects, regardless of the language or origin of the program

Another example of polymorphism occurs in the stock market/mutual fund example (see Figures 3.2 and 3.3). Here the parts of your code that deal with

logging in the user and computing his charges need not change. Regardless of the object in use, the interface remains the same. Only the data interface is special. If you want another object later that has a more complicated data interface, so what? The login interface remains constant.

A Few Miscellaneous ActiveX Oddities

There are a few other oddities that you ought to know about before you start exploring ActiveX. These aren't fundamentally important, but they are peculiar to ActiveX.

HRESULT And SCODE

By convention, many ActiveX functions return a type known as an **HRESULT**. This is simply a 32-bit value that indicates success or failure along with an explanation in either case (see Figure 3.6). The top bit indicates the error status. The next 15 bits identify what system causes the success or failure (the facility code defined by Microsoft). Finally a 16-bit code tells you more information. On 32-bit platforms, an **HRESULT** is the same thing as an **SCODE**.

An **HRESULT** is almost never zero—even when it succeeds—so you can't just test it for being zero or non-zero. While you can break the fields apart manually and test them, it is usually easiest to use the **SUCCEEDED** and **FAILED** macros to test for success or failure.

The ActiveX headers define many codes that you can return as **HRESULT**s. For example, you might return **S_OK** to indicate success or **E_FAIL** to indicate a failure. Other codes are more specific. For example, **E_OUTOFMEMORY**, **E_NOTIMPL**, or **S_FALSE** indicate specific failures. This last code means that

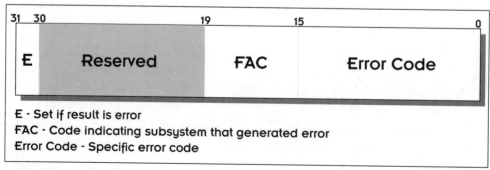

Figure 3.6 An HRESULT.

the function succeeded, but the answer is **FALSE** (whatever that means for a particular function).

Notice that not all ActiveX functions return **HRESULT**s—they can return any type you want. However, if your functions are to work across process boundaries (or over a network), they must return **HRESULT**s. When an **HRESULT** indicates failure, you can't assume anything about the state of any output parameters. A function that wants to succeed partially must return some sort of successful **HRESULT**.

GUID/UUID/IID

One of the daunting problems with ActiveX is identifying particular components uniquely—even across the Internet. This problem crops up whenever you have networking considerations. The Open Software Foundation's Distributed Computing Environment defines a Universally Unique Identifier (UUID) that addresses this problem. Microsoft calls UUIDs, GUIDs (for Globally Unique Identifier), and often calls them CLSIDs (Class IDs) or IIDs (Interface IDs) depending on their use. All of these terms refer to the same thing. Which name you use depends on how you are using the UUID.

What does a UUID look like? It is a 128-bit number formed in such a way as to be unique (or at least reasonably so). When you create a UUID, the system builds it using the current date and time and unique information about your machine (for example, a network card's hardware address).

So how do you create a magic UUID? You can call **CoCreateGuid** if you need one at run-time. More often, you'll run a program named UUIDGEN (this comes with most development tools). UUIDGEN will create as many IDs as you need at random, or in a sequence. For example, consider the following:

```
C:\>UUIDGEN
f6d0f800-992a-11cf-a7b2-444553540000

C:\>UUIDGEN -n3
0c10ba20-992b-11cf-a7b2-444553540000
0c10ba21-992b-11cf-a7b2-444553540000
0c10ba22-992b-11cf-a7b2-444553540000
```

By the way, I ran these two invocations of UUIDGEN about 10 seconds apart. You can also ask UUIDGEN to create C structures (-S) and in a few other formats. Enter UUIDGEN -H to see a list.

VB will usually create UUIDs for you automatically. However, you may still need to know UUIDs to cooperate with other ActiveX systems. Also, you'll need them when you want to embed controls in Web pages, as you'll see later.

UUIDs usually go in your code, the system registry, and type information files. You'll learn more about the registry and type information in later chapters. When you see text representations of a UUID in places like the registry, they will look like this:

```
{f6d0f800-992a-11cf-a7b2-444553540000}
```

The braces and dashes are not optional, although they serve no good purpose. You also have to be careful not to get extra spaces anywhere in the UUID. This is especially bothersome at the beginning and end of the string where the blank isn't apparent.

Not all objects require a UUID. Only objects you need to identify uniquely to the system require one. It turns out most interesting objects will have a UUID, but you could have private objects that don't have a UUID.

When you use VB, the system automatically assigns a new UUID each time you build your component. This is no problem until you ship programs that know about that UUID. Then you'll want future components to use the same UUID. VB allows you to do this by setting the **Binary Compatibility** option on the **Component** tab of the **Project Properties** dialog box. You can specify an existing DLL or ActiveX control and VB will use the same UUID for your project and the existing component.

About IUnknown

Does all this sound too easy? How does this simple protocol work so much magic? Well, there is one little thing I forgot to mention. There is one pseudo-interface called **IUnknown**. It isn't a true interface because it is really a part of every interface.

Remember earlier when I said that an interface is a table of function pointers? That's true, but ActiveX reserves the first three slots in the table for the **IUnknown** interface functions. This allows you to treat any interface as an **IUnknown** interface. You never know or care exactly how many functions are in any interface—as long as there are at least as many as you plan on calling. If you think an interface is **IUnknown**, then it is because every interface has the same three functions appearing first in its table.

In C++ jargon, **IUnknown** is the base interface from which all other interfaces derive. What could be so important about three functions that every interface needs them? The **IUnknown** functions are vital. Two of them manage the object's reference count. When you create an object, it has a reference count of one. Each time you acquire a different interface for the same object, or copy an existing interface pointer, the count should go up by one. That's what **AddRef** does. When you no longer need an interface, you call **Release**, which decreases the count. If the count falls to zero, the object can destroy itself. Notice that the reference count is usually per object, not per interface. Interfaces may implement their own **AddRef** and **Release** logic, or they may call a common routine to do the work. Either way, they usually manage a single reference count per object.

Creating Objects And Finding Interfaces

The third function that **IUnknown** specifies is **QueryInterface**. You call **QueryInterface** with an IID (remember, that's a UUID that identifies an interface). If the object supports that interface, **QueryInterface** returns a pointer to the appropriate interface table. Let's go back to the stock market and mutual fund data objects in Figures 3.2 and 3.3. Suppose you are in some part of your code that doesn't know which of the two objects it is working with. It only knows it has an **IUnknown** interface. (Note: Figures 3.2 and 3.3 don't explicitly show **IUnknown**, but assume it is there.)

The first thing your code will do is call **QueryInterface** on the pointer it has, specifying the IID for **ILog**. Of course, the pointer might have been an **ILog** interface already. That's okay. **QueryInterface** will just return the same pointer. The difference is that now your code knows it is an **ILog** interface. In any case, **QueryInterface** will search the object, looking for an interface that matches the IID. If it finds it, it returns a pointer to the interface. Otherwise it returns **E_NOINTERFACE** (a standard **HRESULT**).

All this assumes you know how to create an object. There are many ways you might get an initial interface pointer to an object. Here are the four most common ways:

1. Call some function that specifically returns a particular interface pointer to you. This function might be part of ActiveX, or it might be code in a private library.

2. You might call an interface function that belongs to one object to create another object.

3. Someone else might pass you an interface pointer via a function or interface function in your code.

4. Call a function that can create any ActiveX component. Usually, this is **CoCreateInstance**. You can think of this like the VB **CreateObject** call. You supply an object ID (a CLSID) and an interface ID (IID). The function creates the object and returns a pointer to the interface you requested (or returns an error if, for any reason, that didn't work).

More About Reference Counts

It seems like a lot of trouble to call **AddRef** each time you make a copy of an interface pointer, doesn't it? Luckily, you don't have to do it in every case. A little common-sense reasoning will show you that it doesn't always make sense. Consider this pseudo-code:

```
AnInterface p, p1
p=GetTheObject   'ref count == 1
p1=p             'make "copy" of object for function
p1.AddRef   'ref count == 2
DoSomething p
p1.Release 'ref count == 1
p.Release  'ref count == 0; object destroyed
```

Assuming that **DoSomething** doesn't start a new thread, it is pointless to call **AddRef** and **Release** a second time. The original **AddRef** won't **Release** until the function returns. We really don't care what the value of the reference counter is as long as it won't go to zero until the object is not in use. While the above code would work, it is wasteful.

Consider what could happen if **DoSomething** started a new thread to work with the interface pointer passed into it. Then you wouldn't code the first **Release** statement above. Instead, the **DoSomething** code would call **Release** at the end of the thread (or when it finished with the interface). You'd need the first **AddRef** since the final release in the code might occur while the second thread is still using the object. It is very impolite to destroy an object while some other part of your code is using it.

Here are the two most common rules on when you must call **AddRef**:

1. Any function that returns an interface pointer (like **QueryInterface** or **CoCreateInstance** must call **AddRef** so the object has an initial count of one.

2. Anytime you pass an interface pointer to another thread, you'll need to call **AddRef** first (as in the above example).

If you think about it, it is usually apparent where you'll need to call **AddRef**. Just make sure the reference count stays above zero until the object is no longer in use.

About Aggregation

Earlier, I told you about two methods you can use to support code reuse: containment and aggregation. Containment is very simple, but aggregation requires you to know about **IUnknown** and reference counting. So armed with that information, we are ready to tackle the idea of aggregation.

The only thing wrong with containment is that you usually have to write little stub functions for the entry points that you want to pass directly to the contained object. This is an advantage for the functions you want to override or alter, but it seems stupid if you just want to directly expose the contained object's interface (contrast Figure 3.7 and Figure 3.4).

You might try this simple solution. What if the main object creates another copy of the subordinate object? Using **QueryInterface**, the main object learns the address of the exposed interface. Then, when the main object receives the correct **QueryInterface** call from a client, it simply returns that address. That sounds good, but there is a slight problem.

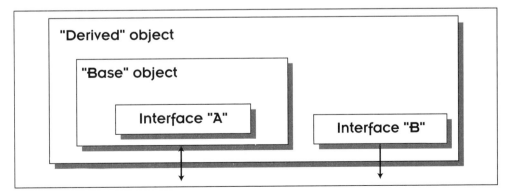

Figure 3.7 First attempt at aggregation.

What happens if a client gets the exposed interface and calls **QueryInterface** on it to learn another interface that belongs to the main object? It won't work. The subordinate object doesn't know about the main object. The **AddRef** and **Release** calls won't work correctly either because the main object's reference count won't reflect calls made against the subordinate.

The answer is to use special features that ActiveX supplies to support aggregation. Both the main object and the subordinate object must do special things, so you may not be able to aggregate just any object. When the main class creates the subordinate one, it passes an address to an **IUnknown** interface (the controlling **IUnknown**). If the subordinate object supports aggregation, it will pass any calls directed at its **IUnknown** to the controlling interface (see Figure 3.8).

The subordinate object still has a private set of **IUnknown** functions, and the main object requests a pointer to them when it creates the object. This allows the main object to call **IUnknown** in cases where that is necessary. If this seems a bit complicated, don't worry. You'll usually use containment to reuse any ActiveX component.

More Oddities

There are a few other things you should be aware of regarding ActiveX, which we'll explore more fully later. For now, you should just know they exist.

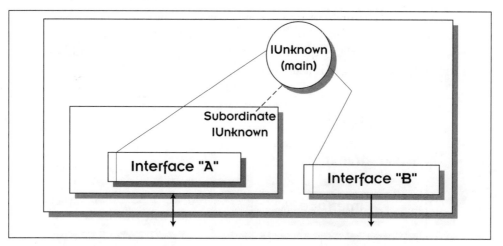

Figure 3.8 Correct aggregation.

Predefined Interfaces

Part of ActiveX is the definitions of many standard interfaces. You'll use some of these (like **IMalloc** to allocate memory), and you'll create others (**IDispatch**). In certain cases, you'll have to supply certain interfaces to work with some other part of the AIP or Windows (for example, the browser).

However, there is nothing to stop you from adding your own interfaces. If you are writing an object that requires three interfaces, there is no reason why you can't supply other custom interfaces, too. That's polymorphism again. If certain clients never ask for particular interfaces, who's the wiser?

Of course, you can also design your own objects with whatever interfaces you desire (predefined, custom, or both). The only thing you must support is **IUnknown**, and you need that in every interface. Other than that, you are free to do what you want. The only restrictions come when you want to interact with other ActiveX programs that you don't control (like the browser or Word). Then you have to follow their specific protocols, at least.

Here's a specific example: Suppose you want clients to create your component by calling **CoCreateInstance**. Then you must provide a specific object (a class factory) that has an **IClassFactory** interface. This component knows how to create your component, and **CoCreateInstance** uses it. However, if you have another method for creating your component and don't care about **CoCreateInstance**, you don't need a class factory object or the **IClassFactory** interface. Don't worry about the specifics of **IClassFactory** just yet. Just realize that to work with certain parts of ActiveX, you need to provide certain interfaces.

Type Libraries

Because you are free to design your own objects and interfaces, how can any program know what to expect? That's where type information comes into play. In brief, a type library contains information about objects and their interfaces in machine-readable format. You can use special function calls to read this information from a database that each component contains. You can also use functions to create the type library (often a TLB file or resource). However, you usually let VB automatically generate your type library which is a great convenience.

Proxies, Stubs, And Marshalling

One key aspect of the ActiveX object structure is that clients don't know or care where the interface table's function pointers go. If an ActiveX server is in a DLL, then the pointers probably go directly to the proper functions. The DLL loads into the client's address space and the functions run fast and efficiently.

What if the server is in an EXE file? You can't pass pointers across process boundaries. In this case, ActiveX creates a proxy. The proxy is just a simple function that resides in the client's address space and forwards calls to a stub function in the server's address space. Then the stub calls the actual server function. Of course, the functions have to move any data back and forth between the address spaces (see Figure 3.9). ActiveX calls the process of translating data across process boundaries *marshalling*.

Here's an interesting twist on proxies: Why not have a proxy that forwards calls across network boundaries, not just process boundaries? Figure 3.10 shows a typical situation. The proxy receives a call, marshalls the data, and passes the call to a stub on the remote machine. The stub receives the data and makes the call to the server. Neither the server nor the client need ever know they are not on the same machine. The exact mechanism used to pass the data (named pipes, remote procedure calls, and so on) is unimportant and subject to change. ActiveX hides these details from both the client and the server.

The nice part about proxies and marshalling is that they usually happen automatically—at least for predefined interfaces. There are a few exceptions, but mostly they all happen with no effort on your part. The only problem is when

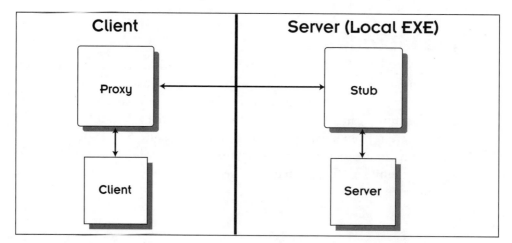

Figure 3.9 Proxy to an EXE.

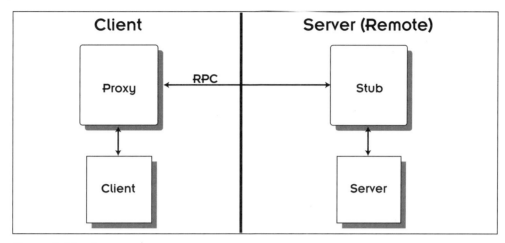

Figure 3.10   A network proxy.

a certain data type can't pass between process boundaries. For example, consider a device context (an **HDC**). What good would it do to send an HDC to another machine? You can't draw on it or even find out much about it. In cases like this, you'll often have a two-part server. One part (either a DLL or an EXE) can run on the remote machine. The other part (always a DLL) handles functions that must occur on the local machine and passes the other requests to the main server. If the main server is an EXE, this technique also can improve local performance since code in the DLL runs in the client's address space. An EXE server always runs in a different process space and requires marshalling.

It is possible, too, for your custom interfaces to have marshalling support over networks. The easiest way to do this is to describe your interface using Microsoft Interface Description Language (MIDL). If you've ever done Remote Procedure Calls (RPC), this will look familiar. You pass an MIDL script through the MIDL compiler and it generates all the marshalling code you need. You'll use that code to build a DLL. Then you'll need to inform ActiveX that it needs to use the DLL for your interface. This requires you to compile some C code. However, there is no reason why you can't support network marshalling with your own personal interfaces.

About Multiple Threads

If all this seems simple, it's because it is. There is one small complication, however. An ActiveX server can contain multiple threads of execution, but clients can also call servers from multiple threads. This can lead to problems. ActiveX supports a threading model known as the Apartment Model. This is just an odd way to say that ActiveX treats each thread in a process as a separate process (or apartment, if you prefer).

This has several ramifications. First, each thread that will make ActiveX calls must initialize the ActiveX library separately. Also, each object belongs to a particular thread. Other threads that access the object must use a form of marshalling—just as if they were in separate processes. This special marshalling isn't to share data—it is to ensure that only one thread modifies the object at any time. If the object uses any shared data (like a reference count), it must take steps to protect that data using a critical section, a mutex, or some other synchronization method. Supporting multiple threads using the apartment model is fairly complex. However, when you use VB to create servers—and you will in later chapters—it will handle these details automatically.

ActiveX under NT 4.0 supports a different threading standard called the Free Threading model, which uses a pool of worker threads that handle each call to an object and requires more synchronization on the part of the object. You can also write servers that are not thread-safe. ActiveX will attempt to load these servers into the main apartment. However, most multithreading clients (for example the Windows 95 shell) will fail if a server is not thread-safe.

The ActiveX/C++ Connection

If you've worked with C++ in detail, you might notice that an interface table looks suspiciously like a C++ VTBL (the table that stores virtual function pointers). Conveniently, most C++ compilers do generate VTBLs in the exact format required by an interface table.

This is a tremendous aid to C++ programmers, as you can express objects easily using C++. However, this in no way ties ActiveX to C++. You can write objects in any language. You may have to "manually" create the interface table, but you can do it. Of course, VB5 is well-suited to creating interfaces (using class modules) and controls (using the **UserControl** component). You'll see examples of building both types of ActiveX components in later chapters.

The ActiveX SDK is usually C++ biased, although sometimes it has a slight C flavor to it. For example, the online help often uses the :: notation to indicate an interface function, as in:

```
IUnknown::Addref();
```

This means that the **IUnknown** interface has a function named **AddRef**. On the other hand, some versions of Help show function calls with an extra first parameter that you don't need with C++. The parameter, of course, is the C++ **this** pointer that points to the object. In C, you'd need to specify that parameter directly. This makes Help a little difficult to read because you have to switch gears depending on what you are doing. If you are writing in C, you have to remember to insert the **this** pointer manually (regardless of what Help says to do). If you are writing in C++, you have to ignore any **this** pointer argument that Help specifies. The Help is completely confusing if you are using VB or some other language. You'll find some advice on mentally shifting gears in Appendix D.

Why Not Use C++ Directly?

For all this trouble, you might wonder why Microsoft didn't elect to use C++ directly. The key is that Microsoft wanted ActiveX to be a binary standard. You should be able to work with objects without having their source and without recompiling. You should be able to distribute objects without having to give away your source code.

ActiveX meets these goals. Although it may be easier to create ActiveX objects in C++, you can create them in practically any language. You can reuse code at the binary level via containment and aggregation, regardless of the language you use. You can design objects that are polymorphic with other objects, even if you don't have access to the source code for all the objects.

Why Not Use Java?

The biggest competitor to ActiveX is Java (from Sun Microsystems). This is an advanced interpreter that allows you to write code that runs over the Internet. However, Java is a relatively simple C++-like language (though it isn't *exactly* like C++). Switching to Java means losing support for many advanced C++ features. It also means embracing new development tools. With ActiveX, you can continue to write code in whatever language you like. If you like the simplicity of Visual Basic, use it. If you need the power of C++, go ahead and use that.

Of course, Java is much simpler than ActiveX, but class libraries and other tools (like VB) can make ActiveX relatively easy, too. And as Java is an interpreter, you can often expect it to run more slowly than fast, compiled ActiveX code.

The other advantage to ActiveX is that it isn't just for the Internet. There's no such thing as an "ActiveX Internet Control." Any ActiveX control is usable on the Internet, in Microsoft Word, or in Visual Basic. If you design a control with the Internet in mind, you can make it more efficient, but there is nothing about ActiveX that forces it to work with the Internet.

Although Java can make the same claim—you can run Java programs locally—its limited scope prevents you from writing general, large projects with it (at least for now). Also, Java won't easily integrate with other programs like Word and other ActiveX applications from Microsoft and other vendors.

Summary

In their basic form, ActiveX objects are a simple table of function pointers, with three predefined functions and any number of custom ones. More complex objects provide multiple tables (interfaces). That's it. It can't be much simpler than that.

You won't often deal with many of these constructs directly. Instead, you'll use VB5 to do most of the dirty work for you. For example, VB5 can automatically creates a class factory and provides all of the **IUnknown** functions for you. You'll see how soon. But for now, just concentrate on the fact that none of these things is very difficult. The hard part is knowing what objects and interfaces you must supply to integrate with the rest of ActiveX.

INFORMATION, PLEASE 4

For many men that stumble at the threshold
Are well foretold that danger lurks within.

— King Henry VI

What do you think of when someone says database? Oracle, Jet, Access, Sybase, DB2, and dBase? Sure, those are the traditional database products, but you usually don't use these in ordinary programs. In Windows 3.1, the most common database you might use in a regular application is an INI file. INI files are easy to use—you just need to know a few easy-to-learn API calls.

However, another system-level database exists: the system registry. In the past, only a few types of programs used the registry. With the advent of Windows NT and Windows 95, though, Microsoft recommends using the registry instead of INI files. So, what's that got to do with ActiveX?

In Chapter 3, you saw that servers can reside in DLLs or EXE files. Each object a server can create often has a CLSID (those long 128-bit numbers) that identifies it. How does the system know that a particular CLSID goes with a given server? The registry. There are many other ActiveX-related items found in the registry—not just CLSIDs. To program ActiveX, you'll need to know all about the registry. Luckily, the registry isn't very hard (although it isn't as easy as INI files). The registry database resembles a file system with directories (keys) and files (values). You use special APIs to create, manipulate, and destroy these items. In short, if you can navigate the hard disk on your computer, you can learn to use the registry.

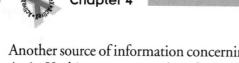
Another source of information concerning ActiveX objects is *type libraries.* These ActiveX objects can provide information about the objects a server provides and their interfaces. After you find out more about the registry, you can tackle type libraries.

This chapter will show you how to use the registry to control ActiveX. You'll also learn more about type libraries at a conceptual level. When you start writing components in the next chapter, you'll see how easy it is to make type libraries.

Give Up INI Files?

Giving up INI files causes most programmers to experience a slight panic. INI files are friendly, easy to use, easy to modify, and well-understood. However, INI files have a few limitations:

- INI files can't exceed 64K on some platforms

- Adding entries to WIN.INI and SYSTEM.INI quickly clutters those files up and may push them past 64K

- Accessing a large INI file can be slow since Windows performs a linear search for the item

- INI files are not easily protected or remotely administered over a network

- Data in INI files is untyped—you must store the data as a string and convert it in your program

The registry addresses all of these problems. In essence, it is a hierarchical database. You access a key and obtain its values. Keys may have subkeys as well as values. This is very similar to the file system. Think of a key as a directory and values as files. The registry has been around for a while, but most programs didn't use it until recently. Traditionally, only OLE programs and the old program manager used the registry. Now, however, most new Windows features (the advanced shell, ActiveX, and so on) rely on the registry.

Have INI files gone away? No, not at all. You can still use the INI file calls if you like. However, to interact with the shell, get Windows logo compliance, or be a good Win32 citizen, you'll want to use the registry. Since you must use the registry for ActiveX, you might as well store your private profile data there as well. Once you use the registry a few times, you'll find that it is an improvement over INI files.

To use the registry with VB, you'll need to call the Windows API. If you've never called the API from VB before, you'll find the details in Appendix E.

The built-in procedures **GetSetting** and **SaveSetting** manipulate the registry, but they refer to fixed locations in the registry that are not suitable for most ActiveX work.

The Registry: Up Close And Personal

Figure 4.1 shows REGEDIT, the standard Windows 95 registry editor (the equivalent NT 3.5 program is REGEDT32; you may use either name under NT 4.0). As you can see, the registry resembles a file system with folders and files. The root of this pseudo file system contains six items:**HKEY_CLASSES _ROOT, HKEY_CURRENT_USER, HKEY_LOCAL_MACHINE, HKEY_USERS, HKEY_CURRENT_CONFIG,** and**HKEY_DYN_DATA.** These items loosely segregate the various entries in broad categories.

Suppose you want to work with a value called **PATH** in the **HKEY_ CURRENT_USER\SOFTWARE\AWC\REALFAST\1.0** key. You have several choices. The best plan is to open the **HKEY_CURRENT_USER\SOFT-WARE\AWC\REALFAST\1.0** key and then modify the **PATH** subkey. However, you could simply open the **HKEY_CURRENT_USER** key and work with the **SOFTWARE\AWC\REALFAST\1.0** subkey. On Windows NT, you may have security issues with the latter method, so it is best to open the most specific key possible.

You'll use an **HKEY** variable (a key handle) to refer to an open registry key. You can obtain an **HKEY** with **RegOpenKeyEx** or **RegCreateKeyEx** (see Table 4.1 for a list of registry-related calls). These calls present a chicken-and-egg problem: The first argument required is an **HKEY**. However, you can use a

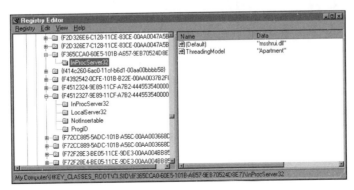

Figure 4.1   The Windows REGEDIT program.

Table 4.1 Selected registry calls.

Function	Description
RegCloseKey	Close an open registry key
RegConnectRegistry	Connect to a remote registry
RegCreateKeyEx	Create a new subkey
RegDeleteKey	Delete a key
RegDeleteValue	Delete a value
RegEnumKeyEx	Enumerate subkeys (returns a different key on each call)
RegEnumValue	Enumerate values (returns a different value on each call)
RegFlushKey	Flush (write) key values (only required if you demand immediate update)
RegLoadKey	Load a key from a special file (see RegSaveKey)
RegOpenKeyEx	Open a key
RegQueryInfoKey	Query key information
RegQueryValueEx	Read value
RegReplaceKey	Replace a key after system restart
RegSaveKey	Save a key to a file
RegSetKeySecurity	Set key security
RegSetValueEx	Set a value
RegUnloadKey	Unload a set of entries

constant to refer to any of the root entries (as mentioned above). For example, you might write:

```
Dim Key as LongInt
errv=RegCreateKeyEx(HKEY_CURRENT_USER,
  "SOFTWARE\AWC\REALFAST\1.0",0,
  NULL,REG_OPTION_NON_VOLATILE,
  KEY_ALL_ACCESS,NULL,key,NULL)
```

Once you have a key, you can do any of the following (see Table 4.1):

1. Read the key's default value (**RegQueryValue, RegQueryValueEx**).
2. Read a specific value that belongs to the key (**RegQueryValueEx**).
3. Open a subkey of the specified key (**RegOpenKey**).
4. Delete the key (**RegDeleteKey**).

5. Change or add any value that belongs to the key (**RegSetValue**, **RegSetValueEx**).

6. Create a new subkey (**RegCreateKey**, **RegCreateKeyEx**).

7. Enumerate the key's subkeys (**RegEnumKey**, **RegEnumKeyEx**).

8. Enumerate the key's values (**RegEnumValue**).

The functions that end in *Ex* have new parameters for Win32 programs. The Win32 registry supports many features not found in the old Windows 3.1 registry. Most of the old-style calls are still around for compatibility, however. Registry calls return **ERROR_SUCCESS** when they succeed or an error code when they fail.

The registry has additional features I won't cover in this book. For example, Windows NT includes advanced security features to protect portions of the registry. A particular program may not have access rights to work with every registry key on the system. Also, with Windows NT or Windows 95, you can connect to a remote registry and manipulate it over the network. But these features don't have anything to do with ActiveX. Besides, once you understand the concepts, the remaining features are not difficult.

Since these are Windows API functions, you need to declare them in Visual Basic before you can call them (see Appendix E). The API expects fixed-length strings (which VB supports). Since these are inconvenient to process, I wrapped all of the functions that want fixed-length strings into a function with a similar name. These wrapper functions convert temporary fixed-length strings to variable-length strings (see, for example, VBRegEnumKey in Listing 4.1). This makes it easier to manipulate the strings in other parts of the program.

In addition to reading and writing the registry, you'll often want to enumerate a key's subkeys or values. This is useful when you have a key and you'd like to know what other entries are available. The enumerators accept an integer value as an argument. The first time you call the enumerator, set the integer to zero. On subsequent calls, increment the integer by one. Eventually, the enumerator will not return **ERROR_SUCCESS** and you can assume you've completed the entire list.

Registry Oddities

There are a few things about the registry that don't work the way you'd expect. Here, in no particular order, are some of the more unusual things I've noticed.

RegEnumValue

RegEnumValue() has a peculiar property. The documentation says that this function walks through the values for a particular key. If the key only has a default value, the function returns it. However, if the key has non-default values, this function will return them but not the default value. That means if you want to be sure to get all the values, you'll need to get the default value explicitly (**RegQueryValue**()) and then enumerate. If you retrieve the default value during enumeration (it will have an empty string as its name), just discard it.

RegDeleteKey

If you attempt to delete a key that has subkeys under Windows NT, the **RegDeleteKey**() call will fail. Under Windows 95, the call succeeds but wipes out the key and all subkeys! Not surprisingly, this can be very dangerous. In particular, you can get into lots of trouble under Windows 95 with code like the following:

```
Dim subkey as String
GetSubKeyName subkey // this fails—subkey is empty
RegDeleteKey HKEY_CLASSES_ROOT,subkey
// if subkey is empty, the entire HKEY_CLASSES_ROOT
// branch is now gone!
```

Error Returns

Don't depend on **GetLastError** to check for error values from the registry functions. These functions all return the error code directly. Calling **GetLastError** will simply return whatever error some other API call generated earlier in your program.

Typed Data

If you browse the Help files, you'll see that the registry can contain many exotic data types (see Table 4.2). The system doesn't pay attention to these types in any real way. For example, the **REG_EXPAND_SZ** type is for strings that should have environment variables expanded in-line. Don't think that the registry will do this expansion for you. The flag implies that you should do the expansion yourself (use the Win32 function **ExpandEnvironmentStrings**()).

There are a few exceptions. For example, Windows 95 will add a terminating zero to a **REG_SZ** string if you forget to do it. Windows NT, however, will not add the zero. Neither system adds the extra **NULL** to **REG_MULTI_SZ** or **REG_EXPAND_SZ** types.

Table 4.2 Registry data types.

Type	Description
REG_BINARY	Binary data in any form
REG_DWORD	A 32-bit number
REG_DWORD_LITTLE_ENDIAN	A 32-bit number in Intel-style format
REG_DWORD_BIG_ENDIAN	A 32-bit number in Motorola-style format
REG_EXPAND_SZ	A null-terminated string that contains unexpanded references to environment variables (for example, "%PATH%")
REG_LINK	A Unicode symbolic link
REG_MULTI_SZ	An array of null-terminated strings, terminated by two null characters
REG_NONE	No defined value type
REG_RESOURCE_LIST	A device-driver resource list
REG_SZ	A null-terminated string

An Example

To demonstrate how the registry works, I decided to write a specialized registry viewer that only shows file types (see Figure 4.2). This program, FILEINFO, shows all the file extensions, their symbolic names, and any OLE extensions they use. If you click on the CLSID of an OLE extension, you'll learn the symbolic name of the OLE server. While you are viewing a file type, you can export it to an ASCII file (using the same format REGEDIT uses) or you can delete it. Deleting or exporting the entry processes all the keys associated with the file type: the extension, the symbolic name, and (optionally) the OLE servers.

The code in Listing 4.1 implements this simple VB program. Notice that calling the API requires some declare statements (see Appendix E and Listing 4.2). Otherwise, this is a perfectly normal VB program. You may be able to use many of the access routines directly in your code (**WriteKeys**, and **GetFileType** are especially useful).

Many things you want to do with the registry are recursive. For example, to write a key to a file, you first write its values to the file, and then write each subkey. This leads naturally to recursive functions. If you find yourself writing lots of looping code to handle the registry, step back and see if recursion will simplify your program.

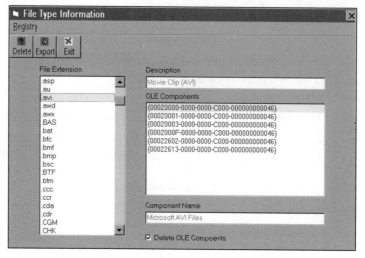

Figure 4.2 FILEINFO.

LISTING 4.1 MANIPULATING THE REGISTRY.

```
VERSION 4.00
Begin VB.Form Form1
    BorderStyle       =   1  'Fixed Single
    Caption           =   "File Type Information"
    ClientHeight      =   4935
    ClientLeft        =   435
    ClientTop         =   1785
    ClientWidth       =   8220
    Height            =   5535
    Left              =   375
    LinkTopic         =   "Form1"
    MaxButton         =   0   'False
    MinButton         =   0   'False
    ScaleHeight       =   4935
    ScaleWidth        =   8220
    Top               =   1245
    Width             =   8340
    Begin VB.TextBox Component
        Enabled       =   0   'False
        Height        =   285
        Left          =   3240
        TabIndex      =   9
        Text          =   "Text1"
        Top           =   4080
        Width         =   4215
    End
```

```
Begin VB.CheckBox OLEDelete
    Caption          =    "Delete OLE Components"
    Height           =    255
    Left             =    3240
    TabIndex         =    6
    Top              =    4560
    Value            =    1  'Checked
    Width            =    2055
End
Begin VB.ListBox OLEServers
    Height           =    2205
    Left             =    3240
    Sorted           =    -1  'True
    TabIndex         =    2
    Top              =    1560
    Width            =    4215
End
Begin VB.TextBox FileType
    Enabled          =    0  'False
    Height           =    285
    Left             =    3240
    TabIndex         =    1
    Text             =    "Text1"
    Top              =    960
    Width            =    4215
End
Begin VB.ListBox List1
    Height           =    3765
    Left             =    720
    Sorted           =    -1  'True
    TabIndex         =    0
    Top              =    960
    Width            =    2055
End
Begin VB.Label Label4
    Caption          =    "Component Name"
    Height           =    255
    Left             =    3240
    TabIndex         =    8
    Top              =    3840
    Width            =    2175
End
Begin MSComDlg.CommonDialog SaveDlg
    Left             =    6720
    Top              =    0
    _Version         =    65536
    _ExtentX         =    847
```

```
    _ExtentY         =    847
    _StockProps      =    0
    DefaultExt       =    "REG"
    DialogTitle      =    "Select file"
    Filter           =    "*.REG"
    Flags            =    2129926
End
Begin ComctlLib.ImageList ImageList1
    Left             =    7440
    Top              =    0
    _Version         =    65536
    _ExtentX         =    1005
    _ExtentY         =    1005
    _StockProps      =    1
    BackColor        =    -2147483643
    ImageWidth       =    16
    ImageHeight      =    16
    NumImages        =    3
    i1               =    "InfoForm.frx":0000
    i2               =    "InfoForm.frx":03BF
    i3               =    "InfoForm.frx":077E
End
Begin ComctlLib.Toolbar Toolbar1
    Align            =    1    'Align Top
    Height           =    600
    Left             =    0
    TabIndex         =    7
    Top              =    0
    Width            =    8220
    _Version         =    65536
    _ExtentX         =    14499
    _ExtentY         =    1058
    _StockProps      =    96
    ImageList        =    "ImageList1"
    ButtonWidth      =    1005
    ButtonHeight     =    953
    NumButtons       =    3
    i1               =    "InfoForm.frx":0D35
    i2               =    "InfoForm.frx":0EEC
    i3               =    "InfoForm.frx":10A7
    AlignSet         =    -1   'True
End
Begin VB.Label Label3
    Caption          =    "OLE Components"
    Height           =    255
    Left             =    3240
    TabIndex         =    5
```

```
          Top            =    1320
          Width          =    2055
      End
      Begin VB.Label Label2
          Caption        =    "Description"
          Height         =    255
          Left           =    3240
          TabIndex       =    4
          Top            =    720
          Width          =    2055
      End
      Begin VB.Label Label1
          Caption        =    "File Extension"
          Height         =    255
          Left           =    720
          TabIndex       =    3
          Top            =    720
          Width          =    2055
      End
      Begin VB.Menu MainMenu
          Caption        =    "&Registry"
          Begin VB.Menu Delete
              Caption    =    "&Delete"
          End
          Begin VB.Menu Export
              Caption    =    "&Export"
          End
          Begin VB.Menu Sep1
              Caption    =    "-"
          End
          Begin VB.Menu About
              Caption    =    "&About"
          End
          Begin VB.Menu Sep2
              Caption    =    "-"
          End
          Begin VB.Menu Exit
              Caption    =    "&Exit"
          End
      End
  End
End
Attribute VB_Name = "Form1"
Attribute VB_Creatable = False
Attribute VB_Exposed = False

Sub AddUniqueServer(s As String)
' Search OLE list before adding item
```

```
For i = 0 To OLEServers.ListCount
  If OLEServers.List(i) = s Then Exit Sub
Next i
OLEServers.AddItem s
End Sub


Function DblSlash(s As String) As String
'Double backslashes in string
i = 1
Do
  i - InStr(i, s, "\")
  If i <> 0 Then s = Left$(s, i) _
      + Right$(s, Len(s) - (i - 1)): i = i + 2
Loop While i <> 0
DblSlash = s
End Function


Function GetFileType(s As String) As String
' Get file type from registry
Dim key As Long
Dim kname As String
Dim l As Long
l = 255
FValue = Chr$(0)
' Open key and read value
Aerr = RegOpenKeyEx(HKEY_CLASSES_ROOT, s, 0, KEY_ALL_ACCESS, key)
If Aerr = ERROR_SUCCESS Then
  Aerr = VBRegQueryValue(key, "", kname, l)
  If Aerr = ERROR_SUCCESS And kname <> "" Then
    GetFileType = kname
  Else
    GetFileType = ""
  End If
  RegCloseKey (key)
End If
End Function


Function VBRegEnumKey(key As Long, i As Long, _
      value As String, ByRef l As Long)
Dim tmpstring As String * 256
l = 255
VBRegEnumKey = RegEnumKey(key, i, tmpstring, l)
value = ZRTrim(tmpstring)
```

```
End Function

Function VBRegEnumValue(key As Long, i As Long, VName As String, _
    ByRef l As Long, rsvd As Long, ByRef typ As Long, StrData As String, _
    ByRef ct As Long)
    Dim tmpname As String * 256
    Dim tmpdata As String * 256
    l = 255
    ct = 255
    VBRegEnumValue = RegEnumValue(key, i, tmpname, _
        l, rsvd, typ, tmpdata, ct)
    VName = ZRTrim(tmpname)
' Don't trim data! It could contain zero bytes
    StrData = Left$(tmpdata, ct)
End Function

Function VBRegQueryValue(key As Long, subk As String, _
    ByRef kname As String, ByRef l As Long)
Dim tmpstr As String * 256
l = 255
VBRegQueryValue = RegQueryValue(key, subk, tmpstr, l)
kname = ZRTrim(tmpstr)
End Function


Private Sub Write_Keys(ByVal s As String)
' Write keys out to file #1
Dim i As Long
Dim key As Long
Dim kname As String
Dim SkName As String
Dim VName As String
Dim StrData As String
Dim s1 As String
Dim l As Long
Dim rsvd As Long
Dim typ As Long
Dim dat As Long
Dim ct As Long

Aerr = RegOpenKeyEx(HKEY_CLASSES_ROOT, s, 0, KEY_ALL_ACCESS, key)
' Write key name
Print #1, "[HKEY_CLASSES_ROOT\"; s; "]"
i = 0
' Write all values
Do
    Aerr1 = VBRegEnumValue(key, i, VName, l, rsvd, typ, StrData, ct)
```

```
     If Aerr1 = ERROR_SUCCESS Then
       If VName = "" Then
         Print #1, "@=";
       Else
         Print #1, Chr$(34) + VName + Chr$(34); "=";
       End If
       If typ = REG_SZ Then
           Print #1, Chr$(34) + DblSlash(StrData) + Chr$(34)
       End If
       If typ = REG_BINARY Then
           Print #1, "hex:";
           For jj = 1 To ct
             Print #1, Hex$(Asc(Mid$(StrData, jj, 1)));
             If jj <> ct Then Print #1, ",";
           Next jj
           Print #1, ""
       End If
       If typ = REG_DWORD Then
           v = Asc(Mid$(StrData, 1, 1)) * 256 * 256 * 256
           v = v + Asc(Mid$(StrData, 2, 1)) * 256 * 256
           v = v + Asc(Mid$(StrData, 3, 1)) * 256
           v = v + Asc(Mid$(StrData, 4, 1))
           Print #1, "dword:"; Hex$(v)
       End If
     End If
     i = i + 1
   Loop While Aerr1 = ERROR_SUCCESS

   ' Recurse for all subkeys
   i = 0
   Do While Aerr = ERROR_SUCCESS
     SkName = ""
     Aerr = VBRegEnumKey(key, i, SkName, 255)
     If Aerr = ERROR_SUCCESS And SkName <> "" Then
       s1 = s + "\" + SkName
       Write_Keys s1
     End If
     i = i + 1
   Loop
     RegCloseKey (key)
   End Sub




   Function ZRTrim(ByRef s As String) As String
   ' Right trim + remove trailing zero byte
     If Len(s) = 0 Then Exit Function
```

```
  If Len(RTrim(s)) = 0 Then
    s = RTrim(s)
    ZRTrim = s
  Else
    If Right$(RTrim(s), 1) = Chr$(0) Then
      ZRTrim = Left$(s, Len(RTrim(s)) - 1)
      s = Left$(s, Len(RTrim(s)) - 1)
    Else
      ZRTrim = RTrim(s)
      s = RTrim(s)
    End If
  End If
End Function


Private Sub About_Click()
MsgBox "File Type Information by Al Williams"
End Sub


Private Sub Delete_Click()
' Confirm
If (MsgBox("Warning! Deleting a file type may affect other file " & _
    "types. Be sure you delete all references to this file type. " & _
    "OK to proceed?", vbOKCancel + vbExclamation) = vbCancel) Then
  Exit Sub
End If
RegDeleteKey HKEY_CLASSES_ROOT, GetFileType(List1.Text)
If OLEDelete.value Then
  For i = 0 To OLEServers.ListCount - 1
    RegDeleteKey HKEY_CLASSES_ROOT, "CLSID\" + OLEServers.List(i)
  Next i
End If
RegDeleteKey HKEY_CLASSES_ROOT, List1.Text
Form_Load
End Sub



Private Sub Exit_Click()
End
End Sub

Private Sub Export_Click()
On Error Resume Next
SaveDlg.ShowSave
On Error GoTo 0
' Pressed cancel?
If Err.Number <> 0 Then Exit Sub
Open SaveDlg.filename For Output As 1
```

```
  Print #1, "REGEDIT4"
  Write_Keys List1.Text
  Write_Keys GetFileType(List1.Text)
  ' Write OLE server keys
  For i = 0 To OLEServers.ListCount - 1
    Write_Keys "CLSID\" + OLEServers.List(i)
  Next i
  Close (1)
End Sub


Private Sub Form_Load()
Dim key As Long
Dim i As Long
Dim kname As String
' Set up everything
List1.Clear
Aerr = RegOpenKeyEx(HKEY_CLASSES_ROOT, "", 0, KEY_ALL_ACCESS, key)
i = 1
Do While Aerr = ERROR_SUCCESS
  Aerr = VBRegEnumKey(key, i, kname, 255)
  If (Aerr = ERROR_SUCCESS And Left$(kname, 1) = ".") Then _
      List1.AddItem kname
  i = i + 1
Loop
RegCloseKey (key)
List1.Selected(0) = True
End Sub


Private Sub List1_Click()
' Read Description
Dim key As Long
Dim key1 As Long
Dim kname As String
Dim FValue As String
Dim l As Long
' New selection in main list, so update file type, and OLE list
FValue = Chr$(0)
Aerr = RegOpenKeyEx(HKEY_CLASSES_ROOT, List1.Text, 0, _
    KEY_ALL_ACCESS, key)
If Aerr = ERROR_SUCCESS Then
  OLEServers.Clear
  OLEFill key, List1.Text
  Aerr = VBRegQueryValue(key, "", kname, 1)
  If Aerr = ERROR_SUCCESS And kname <> "" Then
    Aerr = RegOpenKeyEx(HKEY_CLASSES_ROOT, kname, 0, _
        KEY_ALL_ACCESS, key1)
    If (Aerr = ERROR_SUCCESS) Then
```

```
      OLEFill key1, kname
      Aerr = VBRegQueryValue(key1, "", FValue, 1)
      RegCloseKey (key1)
    End If
  End If
RegCloseKey (key)
End If
If Aerr = ERROR_SUCCESS And FValue <> "" Then FileType.Text = _
    Fvalue Else FileType.Text = "????"
End Sub


Private Sub OLEFill(key As Long, Keyname As String)
Dim subkey As Long
Dim value As String
Dim l As Long
Dim i As Long
' Fill up OLE list box
' I assume anything that starts with { is a CLSID
Component.Text = ""
If Left$(Keyname, 1) = "{" Then AddUniqueServer Keyname
' Get key value
VBRegQueryValue key, "", value, 1
' If starts with { add to list
If Left$(value, 1) = "{" Then AddUniqueServer value
' Enum subkeys
i = 0
Do
Aerr = VBRegEnumKey(key, i, value, 1)
If Aerr = ERROR_NOERROR Then
  RegOpenKeyEx key, value, 0, KEY_ALL_ACCESS, subkey
' Call OLEFill on each enum
  OLEFill subkey, value
  RegCloseKey subkey
  i = i + 1
End If
Loop While Aerr = ERROR_NOERROR
If OLEServers.ListCount <> 0 Then
  OLEServers.Selected(0) = True
  OLEServers_Click
End If
End Sub


Private Sub OLEServers_Click()
' Current OLE Server changed, so update server name box
Dim key As Long
Dim VName As String
```

```
Dim 1 As Long
VBRegQueryValue HKEY_CLASSES_ROOT, "CLSID\" + OLEServers.Text, VName, 1
Component.Text = VName
End Sub


Private Sub Toolbar1_ButtonClick(ByVal Button As Button)
' Vector toolbar to menu
Select Case Button.key
    Case "Delete"
        Delete_Click
    Case "Export"
        Export_Click
    Case "Exit"
        Exit_Click
    End Select

End Sub
```

LISTING 4.2   DECLARATIONS FOR LISTING 4.1.

```
Attribute VB_Name = "Module1"
' Autogenerated by API Viewer


Public Const STANDARD_RIGHTS_ALL = &H1F0000
Public Const REG_BINARY = 3
' Free form binary
Public Const REG_CREATED_NEW_KEY = &H1
' New Registry Key created
Public Const REG_DWORD = 4
' 32-bit number
Public Const REG_DWORD_BIG_ENDIAN = 5
' 32-bit number
Public Const REG_DWORD_LITTLE_ENDIAN = 4
' 32-bit number (same as REG_DWORD)
Public Const REG_EXPAND_SZ = 2
' Unicode nul terminated string
Public Const REG_NOTIFY_CHANGE_ATTRIBUTES = &H2
Public Const REG_NOTIFY_CHANGE_LAST_SET = &H4
' Time stamp
Public Const REG_NOTIFY_CHANGE_NAME = &H1
' Create or delete (child)
Public Const REG_NOTIFY_CHANGE_SECURITY = &H8
Public Const REG_OPTION_RESERVED = 0
' Parameter is reserved
Public Const REG_OPTION_VOLATILE = 1
' Key is not preserved when system is rebooted
Public Const REG_OPTION_BACKUP_RESTORE = 4
```

```
' open for backup or restore
Public Const REG_OPTION_CREATE_LINK = 2
' Created key is a symbolic link
Public Const REG_OPTION_NON_VOLATILE = 0
' Key is preserved when system is rebooted
Public Const REG_FULL_RESOURCE_DESCRIPTOR = 9
' Resource list in the hardware description
Public Const REG_LEGAL_CHANGE_FILTER = (REG_NOTIFY_CHANGE_NAME Or
REG_NOTIFY_CHANGE_ATTRIBUTES Or REG_NOTIFY_CHANGE_LAST_SET Or
REG_NOTIFY_CHANGE_SECURITY)
Public Const REG_LEGAL_OPTION = (REG_OPTION_RESERVED Or
REG_OPTION_NON_VOLATILE Or REG_OPTION_VOLATILE Or REG_OPTION_CREATE_LINK
Or REG_OPTION_BACKUP_RESTORE)
Public Const REG_LINK = 6
' Symbolic Link (unicode)
Public Const REG_NONE = 0
' No value type
Public Const REG_OPENED_EXISTING_KEY = &H2
' Existing Key opened
Public Const REG_REFRESH_HIVE = &H2
' Unwind changes to last flush
Public Const REG_RESOURCE_LIST = 8
' Resource list in the resource map
Public Const REG_RESOURCE_REQUIREMENTS_LIST = 10
Public Const REG_SZ = 1
' Unicode nul terminated string
Public Const REG_WHOLE_HIVE_VOLATILE = &H1
' Restore whole hive volatile
Public Const REGDB_E_CLASSNOTREG = &H80040154
Public Const REGDB_E_FIRST = &H80040150
Public Const REGDB_E_IIDNOTREG = &H80040155
Public Const REGDB_E_INVALIDVALUE = &H80040153
Public Const REGDB_E_KEYMISSING = &H80040152
Public Const REGDB_E_LAST = &H8004015F
Public Const REGDB_E_READREGDB = &H80040150
Public Const REGDB_E_WRITEREGDB = &H80040151
Public Const REGDB_S_FIRST = &H40150
Public Const REGDB_S_LAST = &H4015F

Public Const HKEY_CLASSES_ROOT = &H80000000
Public Const HKEY_CURRENT_CONFIG = &H80000005
Public Const HKEY_CURRENT_USER = &H80000001
Public Const HKEY_DYN_DATA = &H80000006
Public Const HKEY_LOCAL_MACHINE = &H80000002
Public Const HKEY_PERFORMANCE_DATA = &H80000004
Public Const HKEY_USERS = &H80000003
```

```vb
Public Const READ_CONTROL = &H20000
Public Const STANDARD_RIGHTS_EXECUTE = (READ_CONTROL)
Public Const STANDARD_RIGHTS_READ = (READ_CONTROL)
Public Const STANDARD_RIGHTS_REQUIRED = &HF0000
Public Const STANDARD_RIGHTS_WRITE = (READ_CONTROL)


Public Const KEY_NOTIFY = &H10
Public Const SYNCHRONIZE = &H100000
Public Const KEY_CREATE_LINK = &H20
Public Const KEY_CREATE_SUB_KEY = &H4
Public Const KEY_ENUMERATE_SUB_KEYS = &H8
Public Const KEY_EVENT = &H1
Public Const KEY_QUERY_VALUE = &H1
Public Const KEY_SET_VALUE = &H2
Public Const KEY_ALL_ACCESS = ((STANDARD_RIGHTS_ALL Or _
KEY_QUERY_VALUE Or KEY_SET_VALUE Or KEY_CREATE_SUB_KEY Or _
KEY_ENUMERATE_SUB_KEYS Or KEY_NOTIFY Or KEY_CREATE_LINK) And _
(Not SYNCHRONIZE))
Public Const KEY_READ = ((STANDARD_RIGHTS_READ Or _
KEY_QUERY_VALUE Or KEY_ENUMERATE_SUB_KEYS Or KEY_NOTIFY) And _
(Not SYNCHRONIZE))
Public Const KEY_EXECUTE = (KEY_READ)
Public Const KEY_WRITE = ((STANDARD_RIGHTS_WRITE Or KEY_SET_VALUE _
Or KEY_CREATE_SUB_KEY) And (Not SYNCHRONIZE))




Type SECURITY_ATTRIBUTES
        nLength As Long
        lpSecurityDescriptor As Long
        bInheritHandle As Boolean
End Type

Type ACL
        AclRevision As Byte
        Sbz1 As Byte
        AclSize As Integer
        AceCount As Integer
        Sbz2 As Integer
End Type


Type SECURITY_DESCRIPTOR
        Revision As Byte
        Sbz1 As Byte
```

```
        Control As Long
        Owner As Long
        Group As Long
        Sacl As ACL
        Dacl As ACL
End Type


Type FILETIME
        dwLowDateTime As Long
        dwHighDateTime As Long
End Type


Declare Function RegCloseKey Lib "advapi32.dll" (ByVal hKey As _
    Long) As Long Declare Function RegConnectRegistry Lib _
    "advapi32.dll" Alias "RegConnectRegistryA" _
    (ByVal lpMachineName As String, ByVal hKey As Long, _
    phkResult As Long) As Long
Declare Function RegCreateKey Lib "advapi32.dll" Alias _
    "RegCreateKeyA" (ByVal hKey As Long, ByVal lpSubKey As String, _
    phkResult As Long) As Long
    Declare Function RegCreateKeyEx Lib "advapi32.dll" Alias _
    "RegCreateKeyExA" (ByVal hKey As Long, ByVal lpSubKey As String, _
    ByVal Reserved As Long, ByVal _
    lpClass As String, ByVal dwOptions As Long, ByVal samDesired _
    As Long, lpSecurityAttributes As SECURITY_ATTRIBUTES, _
    phkResult As Long, lpdwDisposition As Long) As Long
Declare Function RegDeleteKey Lib "advapi32.dll" Alias _
    "RegDeleteKeyA" (ByVal hKey As Long, ByVal lpSubKey As String) _
    As Long
Declare Function RegDeleteValue Lib "advapi32.dll" Alias _
    "RegDeleteValueA" (ByVal hKey As Long, ByVal lpValueName _
    As String) As Long
Declare Function RegEnumKey Lib "advapi32.dll" Alias _
    "RegEnumKeyA" (ByVal hKey As Long, ByVal dwIndex _
    As Long, ByVal lpName As String, ByVal cbName As Long) As Long
Declare Function RegEnumKeyEx Lib "advapi32.dll" Alias _
    "RegEnumKeyExA" (ByVal hKey As Long, ByVal dwIndex _
    As Long, ByVal lpName As String, lpcbName As Long, lpReserved _
    As Long, ByVal lpClass As String, lpcbClass _
    As Long, lpftLastWriteTime As FILETIME) As Long
' Modified so that data parameter is "any"
Declare Function RegEnumValue Lib "advapi32.dll" Alias _
    "RegEnumValueA" (ByVal hKey As Long, ByVal dwIndex _
    As Long, ByVal lpValueName As String, lpcbValueName _
    As Long, lpReserved As Long, lpType As Long, ByVal lpData _
```

```
    As Any, lpcbData As Long) As Long
Declare Function RegFlushKey Lib "advapi32.dll" (ByVal hKey _
    As Long) As Long
Declare Function RegGetKeySecurity Lib "advapi32.dll" (ByVal hKey _
    As Long, ByVal SecurityInformation As Long, pSecurityDescriptor As _
    SECURITY_DESCRIPTOR, lpcbSecurityDescriptor As Long) As Long
Declare Function RegLoadKey Lib "advapi32.dll" Alias "RegLoadKeyA" _
    (ByVal hKey As Long, ByVal lpSubKey As String, ByVal lpFile _
    As String) As Long
Declare Function RegNotifyChangeKeyValue Lib "advapi32.dll" _
    (ByVal hKey As Long, ByVal bWatchSubtree As Long, ByVal _
    dwNotifyFilter As Long, ByVal hEvent As Long, ByVal fAsynchronous _
    As Long) As Long
Declare Function RegOpenKey Lib "advapi32.dll" Alias _
    "RegOpenKeyA" (ByVal hKey As Long, ByVal lpSubKey _
    As String, phkResult As Long) As Long
Declare Function RegOpenKeyEx Lib "advapi32.dll" Alias _
    "RegOpenKeyExA" (ByVal hKey As Long, ByVal lpSubKey As String, _
    ByVal ulOptions As Long, ByVal samDesired As Long, phkResult _
    As Long) As Long
Declare Function RegQueryInfoKey Lib "advapi32.dll" Alias _
    "RegQueryInfoKeyA" (ByVal hKey As Long, ByVal lpClass _
    As String, lpcbClass As Long, lpReserved As Long, lpcSubKeys _
    As Long, lpcbMaxSubKeyLen As Long, lpcbMaxClassLen As Long, _
    lpcValues As Long, lpcbMaxValueNameLen As Long, lpcbMaxValueLen _
    As Long, lpcbSecurityDescriptor As Long, lpftLastWriteTime _
    As FILETIME) As Long
Declare Function RegQueryValue Lib "advapi32.dll" Alias _
    "RegQueryValueA" (ByVal hKey As Long, ByVal lpSubKey _
    As String, ByVal lpValue As String, lpcbValue As Long) As Long
Declare Function RegQueryValueEx Lib "advapi32.dll" Alias _
    "RegQueryValueExA" (ByVal hKey As Long, ByVal lpValueName _
    As String, ByVal lpReserved As Long, lpType As Long, ByVal lpData _
    As Any, lpcbData As Long) As Long
' Note that if you declare the lpData parameter as String,
' you must pass it By Value.
Declare Function RegReplaceKey Lib "advapi32.dll" Alias _
    "RegReplaceKeyA" (ByVal hKey As Long, ByVal lpSubKey _
    As String, ByVal lpNewFile As String, ByVal lpOldFile As String) _
    As Long
Declare Function RegRestoreKey Lib "advapi32.dll" Alias _
    "RegRestoreKeyA" (ByVal hKey As Long, ByVal lpFile As String, _
    ByVal dwFlags As Long) As Long
Declare Function RegSaveKey Lib "advapi32.dll" Alias _
    "RegSaveKeyA" (ByVal hKey As Long, ByVal lpFile As String, _
    lpSecurityAttributes As SECURITY_ATTRIBUTES) As Long
Declare Function RegSetKeySecurity Lib "advapi32.dll" _
```

```
      (ByVal hKey As Long, ByVal SecurityInformation As Long, _
      pSecurityDescriptor As SECURITY_DESCRIPTOR) As Long
Declare Function RegSetValue Lib "advapi32.dll" Alias _
    "RegSetValueA" (ByVal hKey As Long, ByVal lpSubKey As String, ByVal _
    dwType As Long, ByVal lpData As String, ByVal cbData As Long) As Long
Declare Function RegSetValueEx Lib "advapi32.dll" Alias _
    "RegSetValueExA" (ByVal hKey As Long, ByVal lpValueName _
    As String, ByVal Reserved As Long, ByVal dwType As Long, lpData _
    As Any, ByVal cbData As Long) As Long
' Note that if you declare the lpData parameter as String,
' you must pass it By Value.
Declare Function RegUnLoadKey Lib "advapi32.dll" Alias _
"RegUnLoadKeyA" (ByVal hKey As Long, ByVal lpSubKey _
    As String) As Long
```

That's It?

Is that all there is to manipulating the registry? Hmm, yes and no. Physically working with the registry *is* this easy. However, you also need to know what goes where so that other programs (and Windows) can work with the information you provide. The registry API is like an alphabet. Even if you know all the letters, you can't communicate without words.

There are many standard places in the registry that you should use to store data. For example, you can register a file type so that the shell can display custom icons, context menus, and so forth for your files. Another example is profile information (what you used to store in INI files). You should put your profile information in **HKEY_CURRENT_USER\SOFTWARE** *company_name\product_name\version_number* if it applies to the current user, or under the **HKEY_LOCAL_MACHINE\SOFTWARE***company_name* *product_name\version_number* key if it applies to the machine.

This book doesn't cover the myriad places you can put registry information, only the places that apply to ActiveX. If you want to find more information about the registry's format, you'll find it scattered throughout the Microsoft documentation.

Registering Objects

For the ActiveX programmer, the burning question is: Where do I enter servers (or classes, if you prefer) in the registry? There are several answers to that, depending on what you need to do.

Nearly all of the ActiveX registry entries appear under the **HKEY_CLASSES_ROOT** root key. The first thing you'll need is something to identify the server. You place a key equal to the CLSID (with all the curly braces and dashes) under the **\HKEY_CLASSES_ROOT\CLSID** key. The value of this key is a human readable name that identifies the server. The name can contain any characters you like—it is just for display. Further subkeys identify the location of the server. Consider the following example:

```
HKEY_CLASSES_ROOT
    CLSID
        {73FDDC80-AEA9-101A-98A7-00AA00374959} = Word Pad Document
            LocalServer32=C:\PROGRA~1\ACCESS~1\WORDPAD.EXE
            InprocHandler32=OLE32.DLL
            PROGID=WordPad.Document.1
            Insertable=""
```

This entry, which is part of the one Windows 95 uses for Word Pad, identifies WORDPAD.EXE as the server for this object. It is an EXE server because it uses the **LocalServer32** keyword. If the server were in a DLL (an inproc server), the key would read **InprocServer32** instead. Don't confuse this with the **InprocHandler32** key. This key specifies a DLL that stands in for the local server. The client communicates with the handler, and the handler communicates with the local server. This allows the client to avoid making calls across process boundaries. It also allows the local server to perform operations in the client's address space. You almost always use the default system-supplied handler, OLE32.DLL.

It is permissible to have both types of servers for a single CLSID. Clients can request a particular type of server when they create an object. Inproc DLLs are very efficient because all operations occur in the client's address space. However, users can't start a DLL. What if you were writing a word processor program? You certainly need an EXE file that users can run. However, for better ActiveX performance, you might make a DLL that also serves the word processor objects.

Naturally, if you were dealing with old-style 16-bit OLE objects, you'd omit the "32" suffix from all of the above items. Technically, 16-bit components are not part of the ActiveX standard, but you'll probably run into some older OLE objects if you deal with Win32S or Windows 95.

The **ProgID** key serves as a short (hopefully unique) ID for the object. Some languages that don't support GUIDs will use the ProgID when creating objects. You can use any character in a ProgID, except for spaces. In theory, it doesn't matter what you use for a ProgID because end users should never see it. However, in practice, the ProgID needs to be unique. The convention is to use your company name and a component name together. For example:

```
Coriolis.AutoMail
```

You can also support multiple versions of a component by tacking the version number at the end, as shown in the following code line:

```
Coriolis.AutoMail.2
```

The ProgID has its own entry under **HKEY_CLASSES_ROOT**.

```
HKEY_CLASSES_ROOT
    Coriolis.AutoMail.2=Coriolis Group Auto Mailer Version 2.0
        CLSID = {c353e4a0-9ce6-11cf-a7b2-444553540000}

    Coriolis.AutoMail=Coriolis Group Auto Mailer
        CurVer = Coriolis.AutoMail.2

    CLSID
        {c353e4a0-9ce6-11cf-a7b2-444553540000} =
                        Coriolis Auto Mailer
            ProgID=Coriolis.AutoMail.2
            VersionIndependentProgID=Coriolis.AutoMail
            .
            .
            .
```

The version-independent ID is for clients that want the current version, regardless of what that is. You can use **ProgIDFromCLSID**() and **CLSIDFromProgID**() to convert back and forth between CLSIDs and ProgIDs. In C++ programs, you won't often use the ProgID, but it is important for many other types of clients.

Notice the single **Insertable** key in the previous Word Pad example. This indicates that the client can display this class in a list of objects to insert. For example, many programs have an Insert Object menu item. When you select this item, a dialog appears that allows you to create a new object (see Figure 4.3). The items on this list all have an **Insertable** key. If you have objects that are not for users to see, simply omit the **Insertable** key.

Many of the other keys you'll notice in registry entries pertain to specific types of objects. For example, embedded documents may support a **DefaultIcon** key

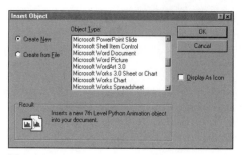

Figure 4.3 The Insert Object dialog.

and a **Verb** key. However, for simple ActiveX components, this is all you need. Remember, you don't always need a CLSID and registration for simple objects. Components that require registration include:

- Any object that clients will create with **CoCreateInstance**() (including most objects that other parts of ActiveX will create)

- Objects that want to expose information about themselves to clients before they are created

- Objects that marshal their interfaces

One of the best ways to learn about the registry is to open yours up and browse through it. Many of the entries make sense right away. Others you'll read about later (or, if you can't wait, look them up in a Windows reference). You'll also find a brief summary for many entries in Table 4.3.

Table 4.3 Registry entries.

Key	Description
LocalServer32	Name of EXE file that contains the server
InprocServer32	Name of DLL file that contains the server
InprocHandler32	Inprocess handler DLL (usually OLE2.DLL)
Insertable	Indicates that server is an insertable object
ProgID	Short name for class (may include version information)
VersionIndependentProgId	Short name for class (independent of version)
TreatAs	Replacement class for this class (see text)
AutoTreatAs	Replacement class for this class (see text)
Interfaces	List of all IIDs that this object may support (optional)

Class Installation

Now that you know where to register classes, do you have to write a lot of code to do it? Not necessarily. There are three ways you can inform a machine about your registry entries:

- Write code to manipulate the registry in an installation program

- Write a REG file and call REGEDIT (or REGEDT32) to insert it for you

- Make your servers self-registering by adding code to them

Each of these methods has advantages and disadvantages. The first case is tedious, but not difficult to figure out. Just use the calls outlined in Table 4.1 to put whatever you like in the registry.

Using REGEDIT or REGEDT32 is the easiest way to add entries to the registry. You simply construct an ASCII file (see below) and use **WinExec()** (or any other method) to launch the appropriate program. You pass the file name as a command line argument to the editor, and it provides a dialog box that reports its success or failure. If you don't want the user to see anything, pass a /S argument to REGEDIT and it will remain silent.

Self-registration is a convenient feature that allows servers to automatically register themselves. Of course, servers can reside in DLLs or EXE files, too. As you might expect, the mechanism you use to self-register is different for these two types of servers. Self-registration isn't really a technique in itself. It is just a protocol for the system to ask your server to register itself. When you respond to the request, you'll use one of the other two methods (direct API calls or REGEDIT) to complete the task.

Using REGEDIT

By far, the easiest way to make entries in the registry is by using REGEDIT (or REGEDT32 in Windows NT). You simply create an ASCII text file, which you can install in several different ways:

- You can import the file using the commands on REGEDIT's menu

- You can run REGEDIT with the file name to import the file and receive feedback

- You can run REGEDIT /S with the file name to import the file silently

- If your system associates REG files with REGEDIT (the default association), you can simply use the shell (or **ShellExec()**) to register the file if it has a REG extension

Listing 4.3 shows a simple REG file. Notice that it has three main sections. The top line, REGEDIT4, denotes that this is a REG file and what version of REGEDIT it supports.

The next part of the file is a key name surrounded by square brackets. REGEDIT will create as many keys as necessary to generate the full key. For example, if you specify [HKEY_CLASSES_ROOT\X\Y\Z] when there is no X subkey, REGEDIT will create all three subkeys. However, if any (or all) of the keys already exists, REGEDIT will not complain.

After the key name, you specify any values for the key. The default value's name is "@." Other values may have any name you like and may appear up to the next key name. Then the whole process repeats until you have specified all the keys you want.

LISTING 4.3 AN EXAMPLE REG FILE.

```
REGEDIT4
[HKEY_CLASSES_ROOT\CLSID\{F4512327-9E89-11CF-A7B2-444553540000}]

[HKEY_CLASSES_ROOT\CLSID\{F4512327-9E89-11CF-A7B2-
444553540000}\LocalServer32]
@="c:\\activex\\aawsound\\debug\\aawsound.exe"
"ExampleValue"="Some string value"

[HKEY_CLASSES_ROOT\CLSID\{F4512327-9E89-11CF-A7B2-444553540000}\ProgID]
@="AAW.Sound"
```

The easiest way to see how to generate a particular REG file is to find a similar entry in the registry and export it using REGEDIT. Then you can modify the file to suit your needs instead of building it from scratch. Some programming tools automatically generate REG files, too.

Self-Registration

To simplify registration, ActiveX supports an optional means for component servers to register themselves. This self-registration protocol also allows the system to ask a server to remove itself. In most cases, self-registration is optional, but it is handy and not difficult to implement.

There are three basic strategies you might use to implement self-registration:

- Use the API calls to directly modify the registry
- Spawn a copy of REGEDIT to load a REG file
- Create a temporary file (perhaps from a resource) and run REGEDIT

Of course to remove entries, you'll always need to use the API calls. The second method, loading an existing REG file, isn't as useful as the other two methods because it requires a separate REG file. If a user forgets to copy the REG file with the component, the registration will fail. The other two methods allow a naive user to copy your server to another machine and still operate it.

It is optional, but you can indicate your server's ability to self-register by including a special version information string in your resources:

```
VS_VERSION_INFO VERSIONINFO
    .
    .
    .
BEGIN
BLOCK "StringFileInfo"
    BEGIN
    BLOCK "040904B0" // Unicode US English
      BEGIN
         .
         .
         .
      VALUE "OLESelfRegister","\0"
      END
    .
    .
    .
```

When your server self-registers, you'll need to make entries for every single object your server supports. You also need to register type libraries, if you have any. Unregistration should remove all the entries that registration makes.

Self-Registering EXEs

If your server resides in an EXE, you need to look for command line arguments to decide when self-registration should occur. For registration, the command line will contain **/RegServer**. Don't assume anything about the case of the string. Also, the option character may be a dash instead of a forward slash.

Not surprisingly, **/UnregServer** signals that you should remove everything. The same rules apply: The string may be in any case and may use a "-" character instead of the "/."

Self-Registering DLLs

DLLs don't typically process command line arguments. Instead, the system looks for two functions exported by name: **DllRegisterServer**() and **DllUnregisterServer**() (not too imaginative, eh?). These functions take no arguments, and must return an **HRESULT**.

If the routines succeed, they return **S_OK**. If they fail, you can return **SELFREG_E_CLASS**, indicating that class information failed to load, or **SELFREG_E_TYPELIB**, if the type information failed.

Impersonating Objects

There is a different way you can register a class in the registry that allows it to masquerade as a different class. This is handy, for example, if you upgrade to a new server with a different CLSID, but you don't want to break existing code. Another possibility is replacing a competitor's server with your own (which, of course, will be better in every way).

When you replace one server with another, you have to be sure you provide all the same interfaces with semantics identical to those that the existing server provided. You are free to implement them any way you wish, but the semantics must remain the same. You can also add additional objects and interfaces, as long as the server doesn't require clients to use them. Newer programs will use your "new" CLSID and can request the new objects or new interfaces. The old programs will use the "old" CLSID and will only request objects and interfaces they know about.

The entries required for this emulation might seem odd at first. Suppose we want to replace component **ALPHA** (in ALPHA.DLL) with the **BETA** component (in—surprise—BETA.DLL). The registry might look like this:

```
HKEY_CLASSES_ROOT
    {..Alpha CLSID here..}=The Alpha Component
        TreatAs={..Beta CLSID here}
        AutoTreatAs={Beta CLSID here}
        InprocServer32=ALPHA.DLL
            .
            .
            .
```

```
{..BETA CLSID here..}=The Beta Component
    InprocServer32=BETA.DLL
    .
    .
    .
```

So what's the difference between **TreatAs** and **AutoTreatAs**? When a new server completely replaces an old server, you make entries in both keys. This indicates a permanent replacement. If you are not replacing the existing server, you only make an entry in the **TreatAs** key. That way, when your server unregisters, the old server (either from **InprocServer32** or from **AutoTreatAs**) gains control.

To put it another way, you might use both keys if you were upgrading your existing server with a new version. However, if you install a software package and want to emulate your competitor's server, you only make an entry in **TreatAs**. After all, the user might remove your software and resume using your competitor's (surely not).

ActiveX will automatically manage this process if you call **CoTreatAsClass()** in your registration routines. This function requires two CLSIDs. If the IDs are different, the function creates a **TreatAs** entry in the registry. If the IDs are the same, it indicates that the replacement server is unregistering. Then, the function looks for **AutoTreatAs**. If it finds an entry there, it replaces any existing **TreatAs** key with the value from **AutoTreatAs**. If there is no **AutoTreatAs** key when both arguments are the same, then the **CoTreatAsClass()** function removes the **TreatAs** key.

Type Libraries

ActiveX is very extensible. You can add your own objects and your own interfaces. Your objects can mix predefined interfaces and custom ones. But how can you communicate information about your objects to clients you didn't write?

The answer is type libraries. A type library is a database associated with a server. The library contains type entries. There are five types of elements (see Table 4.4). The library and each of its elements can have attributes (see Table 4.5).

At run-time, the library appears as a set of ActiveX objects you work with using interfaces. You can query for elements or enumerate them, you can set up type libraries to work with different languages, and you can supply different libraries for particular languages.

Table 4.4 Type library elements.

Element	Description
importlib	Imports another type library
typedef	Defines a new elementary type
interface	Defines an interface
dispinterface	Defines an IDispatch interface
coclass	Describes a component class
module	Describes exported items from a DLL

Table 4.5 Selected type attributes.

Attribute	Description
odl	Required on all interface elements
in	Marks argument as an in-parameter
out	Marks argument as an out-parameter
vararg	Indicates that the function takes a variable number of arguments
optional	Marks argument as optional
lcid	Identifies a language for the element
public	Allows external visibility of typedef elements
uuid	Specifies the UUID associated with the element
version	Marks element's version number
appobject	Used with coclass to mark the class as an EXE application
control	Used with coclass to mark the class as an ActiveX control
dllname	Identifies the name of a DLL
entry	Specifies an exported item in a module
helpcontext	Context ID for help
helpfile	Specifies name of help file (no path; see text)
helpstring	Brief help
hidden	Indicates that the object should never appear to the user

Where Is The Type Library?

You can distribute a TLB file that contains the type information directly, or you can store it in the DLL or EXE server as a resource. If your application uses ActiveX compound files (as we'll discuss in Chapter 5), you can store it in a special stream.

To identify the type library for an object, you need more entries in the registry. First, you need a **TypeLib** key under the CLSID entry. Each type library has a GUID (which you create like any other). For example:

```
HKEY_CLASSES_ROOT
    {..object CLSID..} = Some Class With TypeInfo
    TypeLib={..TypeLib UUID}
```

Then you also need to define the type library:

```
HKEY_CLASSES_ROOT
   TypeLib
      {..TypeLib UUID..}=TypeInfo for Some Class
         DIR=c:\some_class\bin
         HELPDIR=c:\some_class\help
         1.0
            9
               Win32=English.TLB
            0
               Win32=Any.TLB
```

Some of these entries deserve some explanation. The **DIR** and **HELPDIR** entries specify the directories that contain the library and the help files, respectively. This is important, because it varies depending on the installation. Help files named in the library must not have an absolute path. Instead, their paths are relative to the directory named in **HELPDIR**.

The next entry is the library version number (1.0 in this case). You can have multiple versions registered, if you like. The numbers below the version are language IDs (a locale). This identifies the library's language. The 9 is generic English, and the 0 is for any language. It is always a good idea to specify at least an entry for language 0. You'll use locales anytime you write programs that support multiple languages. If you want to learn more about locales, see the sidebar *About Locales*.

The **Win32** key, of course, specifies the file that contains the library. This can be a TLB file, an EXE or DLL server, or a compound file.

About Locales

A locale is a 32-bit number that identifies a specific language. Although locales (or LCIDs) are 32 bits wide, only the bottom 16 bits are significant. Windows reserves the top 16 bits, which are always zero.

Of the significant 16 bits, bits 0 through 9 specify the major language. For example, 9 is English and 0x13 is Dutch. The top six bits specify divisions of the major language. Consider English, for instance. What is spoken in London is quite different from what you'll hear in New York. In addition, many words are spelled differently, too (honour vs. honor). Sometimes meanings are even different. For instance, in the U.S., the word "hood" is the part of a car that covers the engine. In the United Kingdom, it is a convertible's top (the engine cover is a bonnet). Also, time and money formats are different. So while 0x0009 is simply English, 0x0409 is U.S. English and 0x0609 is U.K. English.

You can find all the various language bits in WINNT.H. There are language IDs, ranging from Afrikaans to Ukrainian, defined symbolically there. You'll also find macros you can use in your code, like **MAKELANGID**, **PRIMARYLANGID**, and **SUBLANGID**. The first macro builds an LCID from the two IDs. The other two macros extract the parts from an LCID. You can also find definitions for the *neutral* language—that is, the language to use when you just don't care.

Creating Type Libraries

This all begs the question: How do I create a type library? VB takes care of this for you. The easiest way to manually create one is to write an Object Description Language (ODL) script that describes your objects. You compile this file with MKTYPLIB to generate a TLB file. You can then use that file or include it in your server as a resource.

There are three basic things you can describe in an ODL script:

- A module
- Custom data types
- An interface

You can also describe scripting (or automation) classes and interfaces, but that is a special case of interface.

Listing 4.4 shows a typical ODL file. There is a single line at the top that describes the library as a whole. This line contains the library's GUID, its help file, and any attributes (see Table 4.5). It also names the library. Then after the first curly brace, you can use several special keywords, discussed as follows:

IMPORTLIB

The **importlib** statement is similar to a C++ **#include** statement. It reads in another type library. You often use this to read standard types from a common library (such as STDOLE.TLB, which contains the predefined types).

TYPEDEF

Use **typedef** to define structures, enumerated types, and unions.

COCLASS

To define an ActiveX component, use the **coclass** keyword. You'll precede this with a **uuid** line to identify the object, its help file, and its attributes. This is the same modifier used in the first line of the script to identify the library as a whole.

Inside the **coclass** braces, you can name interfaces that the object supports. These interface lines consist of an optional attribute (see Table 4.5), the word **interface**, and the name of the interface. To describe the individual functions in the interface, see the **interface** keyword below.

INTERFACE

Not surprisingly, the **interface** keyword describes an interface. You'll precede this with a **uuid** line to identify the interface, its help file, and its attributes. This is the same modifier used in the first line of the script to identify the library as a whole.

MODULE

The **module** keyword describes any exported functions or constants from a DLL. You may precede it with any appropriate attributes (see Table 4.5).

LISTING 4.4   AN EXAMPLE ODL FILE.

```
/*
*EXAMPLE.ODL
```

```
* Neutral Language Type Library
*
* "Neutral" language is usually English.
*
*/


[
uuid (5889EE60-AE68-11CF-A7B2-444553540000)
    , helpstring("AAWSound Type Library")
    , lcid(0x0000)
    , version(1.0)
]
    library AAWSoundLibrary
      {
      #ifdef WIN32
      importlib("STDOLE32.TLB");
      #else
      importlib("STDOLE.TLB");
      #endif

/*
 * IID_IAAWSound
 * 'interface' entries must have 'odl' attribute
 */
[
uuid(F4512324-9E89-11CF-A7B2-444553540000)
  , helpstring("Definition of interface IAAWSound")
  , odl
]
interface IAAWSound : IUnknown
  {
  //Methods
  [helpstring("Play the specified sound")]
  HRESULT Play([in] char *file);
  HRESULT GetOptions([out] long *val);
  HRESULT SetOptions([in] long val);
  }


//CLSID
  [
  uuid (F4512327-9E89-11CF-A7B2-444553540000)
  , helpstring("Type information for AAWSound")
  ]
coclass AAWSound
  {
```

```
interface          IAAWSound;
  }
};
```

Type Library Wrap-Up

Some specifics of type libraries will have to wait until we look at other ActiveX details. For now, recognizing that they exist and understanding their basic form is enough. Soon, you'll see how MFC will create starter type libraries for you. You'll only need to maintain those libraries, not create them from scratch.

Summary

If this chapter seems unrelated to ActiveX and VB, don't worry. You really will need to know about the registry when you start writing real ActiveX code. Although VB handles many common cases, you really need to understand the registry to do anything out of the ordinary. When you do manipulate the registry by hand, don't be surprised if it doesn't work and the reason is incorrect formatting. This sort of problem is maddening because your code looks fine (and it probably is). Sometimes it is the dreaded extra-blank-in-the-registry problem. Maybe you forgot the curly brace in the CLSID. Whatever it is, the registry is one of the first places to look when you can't get an ActiveX program running.

Understanding the registry is key to ActiveX programming. It is also useful for programming shell extensions, file types, and many other common chores. Time you spend now learning how the registry operates will pay off down the road.

VB ActiveX In Detail

I see you stand like greyhounds in the slips,
Straining upon the start. The game's afoot...

— King Henry V

As an electrical engineer, you quickly find out that you can't just fiddle around with hardware. If you start poking around with a probe, you can start sparks, or even a fire. You've got to think things through carefully before you start trying things. Luckily, software is usually much more forgiving. You can try things out, and at best, the consequences are minor. Sure, if you are doing low-level programming, you could wipe out your hard drive, but that doesn't have to be a disaster if you back up, right? Poking around with VB is pretty safe. The worst you might do is lock up your machine. So? Just reboot and go on with your experiments.

In Chapter 2, you jumped right in and wrote an actual ActiveX control. Since VB takes care of many of the details for you, it worked even if you weren't 100% sure why. With any luck, no sparks appeared. In this chapter, you'll learn more about VB's ActiveX support. You'll also learn some details that we glossed over in earlier chapters.

If you recall the project from Chapter 2, it is exceedingly easy to write an ActiveX control using VB. However, what price does this simplicity exact? The actual code VB generates for your control is fairly efficient. The example control in Chapter 2 is only 17 Kbytes long. However, the code requires a special VB DLL that is about 1,300 Kbytes in size. (Note: these sizes are correct

for the beta version of VB I used to create the examples in this book; so your mileage may differ.)

If you only intend to use your control as part of a product you distribute (say, on disk or CD-ROM), then this isn't a big issue. Where it becomes a problem is when you want to use the control on Web pages. If the user loading the page already has the VB DLL, fine—the user only needs to download your specific control. If not, the user has to wait for the DLL to download (almost eight minutes with a 28.8 kbps modem).

What's the alternative? If you can't stand the possibility of downloading a large file, you'll have to abandon VB. You can write ActiveX controls using Visual C++. However that is fairly difficult. If you disbelieve, go out and buy my book *Developing ActiveX Web Controls* for the full story on developing ActiveX controls with Visual C++. Truthfully, it doesn't have to be very difficult if you use the Microsoft Foundation Class (MFC) library. Then you need the MFC run-time DLL. If you have to use a large DLL, you might as well stick with VB.

ActiveX Containers

There are two very exciting places you can use ActiveX controls in VB applications and in Web pages. Using controls in a VB program opens up new possibilities for code reuse. Experienced programmers can create controls and distribute them to other programmers. Controls can also promote consistency in large projects.

Web pages are a hot area right now. Allowing VB programmers to create Web-based controls opens up a vast new market. However, many other programming environments support ActiveX controls, too. The beauty of ActiveX is that it is perfectly acceptable to create controls in one language and use them in another. You can use ActiveX controls in programs written with Visual C++, Delphi, PowerBuilder, Optima, and many other programming languages.

ActiveX Without Controls

Although ActiveX controls are glamorous, they aren't the entire picture. As you saw in earlier chapters, you can create and use specific ActiveX interfaces without incurring the overhead of a control. Remember, a control is just a DLL that exposes a set of predefined interfaces.

VB has some limited support for what is known as OLE automation interfaces. You can place these interfaces in a DLL (inproc server) or an EXE (local server). What exactly is an automation interface? It is one that implements **IDispatch**.

About IDispatch

The **IDispatch** interface is arguably one of the most powerful ActiveX interfaces around. Yet it only contains four unique functions (see Table 5.1). These functions allow objects to expose variables and functions to other objects—even those from different programs. A good understanding of **IDispatch** is crucial if you want a detailed understanding of ActiveX. On the other hand, if you just want to use VB to quickly turn out ActiveX controls, you might want to skip the following material at first (skip ahead to the section titled *Is Your Head Spinning?*).

Like all other ActiveX technologies, the **IDispatch** interface has to have obscure names. Instead of exposing variables, **IDispatch**-aware objects expose properties. This may be actual variables, or the object may execute code to store and retrieve the property value. Either way, the object's user accesses properties as if they were simple variables.

IDispatch-aware objects also don't have functions or subroutines; they have methods. These are simple function calls.

The key to the **IDispatch** interface is the **Invoke** function. This function allows ActiveX objects to select, at run time, what variable (property) you want to access or what function (method) you want to call. Each property and method has a unique ID (a **DISPID**). This ID is just an integer that serves to distinguish the various methods and properties from each other. Microsoft predefines **DISPID**s of zero or less (see Table 5.2). You won't always use any of these predefined **DISPID**s.

When you want to call a method or access a property, you call **IDispatch::Invoke** passing it a **DISPID**, some control flags, an array of arguments, a locale ID, a place to store any return result, and places to store error information. Before you look at these arguments in detail, you need to learn about some special types ActiveX defines.

Table 5.1 The IDispatch interface.

Function	Description
Invoke	Provides access to properties and methods exposed by the object
GetIDsOfNames	Converts a single member name and an optional set of argument names to a set of integer DISPIDs
GetTypeInfo	Retrieves the type information for an object
GetTypeInfoCount	Returns 0 if GetTypeInfo is not supported; 1 if the object can provide type information

Table 5.2 Predefined DISPIDs.

DISPID	Value	Description
DISPID_VALUE	0	The default member
DISPID_NEWENUM	-4	Returns an enumerator object that supports IEnumVariant and should have the restricted attribute specified in the ODL script
DISPID_EVALUATE	-5	The Evaluate method
DISPID_PROPERTYPUT	-3	The parameter that receives the value of an assignment in a property put
DISPID_CONSTRUCTOR	-6	The C++ constructor function for the object
DISPID_DESTRUCTOR	-7	The C++ destructor function for the object
DISPID_UNKNOWN	-1	Value returned by IDispatch::GetIDsOfNames to indicate that it could not resolve a name

BSTR, SAFEARRAY, And VARIANT

ActiveX defines three unique data types that you can use in a variety of situations. The simplest of these is the **BSTR**. As the name suggests, this data type is for character strings. A **BSTR** pointer is just like a C string pointer since it points to an array of characters that end with a **NULL** byte. The only difference is that the four bytes *preceding* the **BSTR** pointer contain the count of characters in the string (not counting the **NULL** byte). You can see the string "ActiveX" in a **BSTR** in Figure 5.1. If you are using any C++ (MFC) code, you can convert a C++ **CString** into a **BSTR** by calling **CString::AllocSysString**.

A **SAFEARRAY** is a simple structure (see Figure 5.2) that contains information about the size and shape of an array, along with a memory handle (and possibly a pointer) that contains the data in the array. A **SAFEARRAY** can contain **BSTRs**, **IDispatch** pointers, **IUnknown** pointers, or **VARIANTs** (see below).

The **VARIANT** (or **VARIANTARG**) data type—called a data type in Visual Basic, but usually referred to as a "data structure" in C++—can hold almost anything. In essence, it is just a few bytes and a variable that indicates what kind of data is in the **VARIANT** at any given time (see Tables 5.3a and 5.3b). When a client passes a **VARIANT** to a server, you might expect it to be a simple matter to just read the value from the proper field in the union. But, what if the client didn't pass the type of data you expected? ActiveX has two C-language functions that can convert (or coerce) a **VARIANT** that contains one data type into a **VARIANT** that contains a different type (if the conversion is

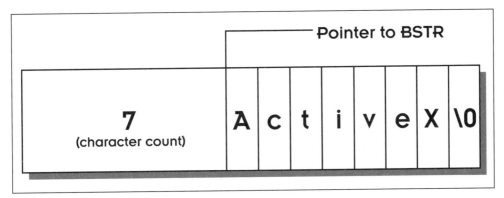

Figure 5.1 A BSTR.

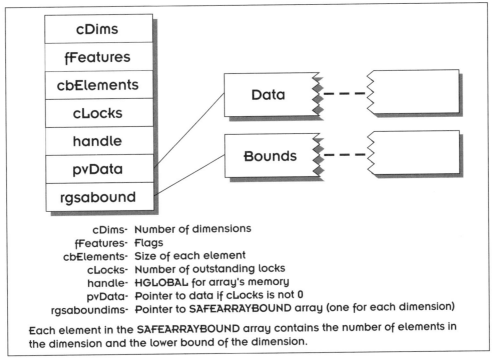

cDims- Number of dimensions
fFeatures- Flags
cbElements- Size of each element
cLocks- Number of outstanding locks
handle- HGLOBAL for array's memory
pvData- Pointer to data if cLocks is not 0
rgsaboundims- Pointer to SAFEARRAYBOUND array (one for each dimension)

Each element in the SAFEARRAYBOUND array contains the number of elements in the dimension and the lower bound of the dimension.

Figure 5.2 A SAFEARRAY.

possible). The functions are **VariantChangeType** and **VariantChangeTypeEx**. These functions are very similar in form, but the **Ex**-flavor function understands the current locale (important for date and currency formats). Don't attempt to convert a **VARIANT** in place with these functions; provide a separate output **VARIANT**.

Table 5.3a   The VARIANT data type.

Field	Type	Comments
vt	VARENUM	Type of data in VARIANT (see Table 5.3b)
iVal	short	Short integer
lVal	long	Long integer
fltVal	float	4-byte real
dblVal	double	8-byte real
bool	VARIANT_BOOL	Boolean
scode	SCODE	Error code
cyVal	CY	Currency
date	DATE	Date
bstrVal	BSTR	A BSTR
punkVal	IUnknown *	Note that this means IUnknown pointer, not an unknown data type
pdispVal	IDispatch *	Pointer to a dispatch interface
parray	SAFEARRAY *	An array
piVal	short *	Pointer to short
plVal	long *	Pointer to long
pfltVal	float *	Pointer to float
pdblVal	double *	Pointer to double
pbool	VARIANT_BOOL *	Pointer to Boolean
pscode	SCODE *	Pointer to error code
pcyVal	CY *	Pointer to currency
pdate	DATE *	Pointer to date
pbstrVal	BSTR *	Pointer to BSTR
ppunkVal	IUnknown **	Pointer to an IUnknown pointer
ppdispVal	IDispatch **	Pointer to a dispatch interface pointer
pvarVal	VARIANT *	Pointer to a VARIANT
byref	void *	Any pointer

Back To Invoke

Armed with information about **BSTRs**, **SAFEARRAYs**, and **VARIANTs**, we can return to examining **IDispatch::Invoke**. The **Invoke** method requires 8 parameters:

1. A **DISPID** that identifies the method or property the client wants to use.

2. A **GUID** that has no meaning; always use **IID_NULL**.

Table 5.3b   VARIANT types.

Type	Meaning	Ordinary Field	ByRef Field
VT_EMPTY	No data present	N/A	N/A
VT_NULL	NULL value	N/A	N/A
VT_I2	2-byte integer (signed)	iVal	piVal
VT_I4	4-byte integer (signed)	lVal	plVal
VT_R4	4-byte real value	fltVal	pfltVal
VT_R8	8-byte real value	dblVal	pdblVal
VT_CY	Currency	cyVal	pcyVal
VT_DATE	Date	date	pdate
VT_BSTR	BSTR	bstrVal	pbstrVal
VT_DISPATCH	IDispatch	pdispVal	ppdispVal
VT_ERROR	Error code	scode	pscode
VT_BOOL	Boolean	bool	pbool
VT_VARIANT	VARIANT	N/A	pvarVal
VT_UNKNOWN	IUnknown	punkVal	ppunkVal
VT_UI1	Unsigned character	iVal	iVal
VT_ARRAY	SAFEARRAY	parray	pparray
VT_BYREF	Adds with other VT_ types to indicate passing by reference	N/A	N/A

3. A locale ID to specify the current language in use.

4. A flag that specifies the operation (see Table 5.4).

5. A pointer to a **DISPPARAMS** structure (Table 5.5 identifies the arguments for this call).

6. A pointer to a **VARIANT** that will receive the result, if any (may be **NULL**).

7. A pointer to a structure that receives error information in the event that a **DISP_E_EXCEPTION** error occurs.

8. A pointer to an unsigned integer that receives the index of the parameter that caused a **DISP_E_TYPEMISMATCH** or **DISP_E_ PARAM NOTFOUND** error.

The **DISPPARAMS** structure requires a little explanation. This structure identifies all of the arguments for the call. Of course, to read a simple property, you don't need any arguments. However, to set a simple property requires one argument. An indexed property access may need many arguments. A method call may not require any arguments, or it may need several.

Table 5.4   Operation flags.

Flag	Meaning
DISPATCH_METHOD	Perform a function call
DISPATCH_PROPERTYGET	Read a property
DISPATCH_PROPERTYPUT	Set a property
DISPATCH_PROPERTYPUTREF	Set a property by reference

Table 5.5   The DISPPARAMS structure.

Field	Meaning
rgvarg	Pointer to array of VARIANTs
rgdispidNamedArgs	Named argument DISPIDs (see text)
cArgs	Number of total arguments
cNamedArgs	Number of named arguments

The first field in the **DISPPARAMS** structure points to an array of **VARI-ANTS** (the **rgvarg** field). This is the argument list. There are three kinds of arguments you may encounter: positional arguments, named arguments, and optional arguments. Although some arguments are optional, the **Invoke** function always receives the entire set of arguments. If the client wishes to omit an optional parameter, the corresponding **VARIANT** will have a type of **VT_ERROR** or **VT_EMPTY**. If the client uses **VT_ERROR** (the preferred method) it also sets the **scode** field to **DISP_E_PARAMNOTFOUND**.

Named arguments each have a unique **DISPID** (from the type information). The client sets the **DISPPARAMS** structure's **rgdispidNamedArgs** field to point to an array that contains the named argument's **DISPIDs** (if any). The length of the array (and therefore, the number of named arguments) appears in the **cNamedArgs** field. If that value is zero, there are no named arguments.

If there are any named arguments, they appear first (in a random order) in the **rgvarg** array. The positional arguments follow in reverse order. Consider the following call (from a Visual Basic program):

```
rv=ActiveXObject.Go(p1=30, p2="RESET", 14, "Command")
```

This call has two named arguments (named **p1** and **p2**) and two positional arguments. Figure 5.3 shows how the **rgvarg** array will look for this call.

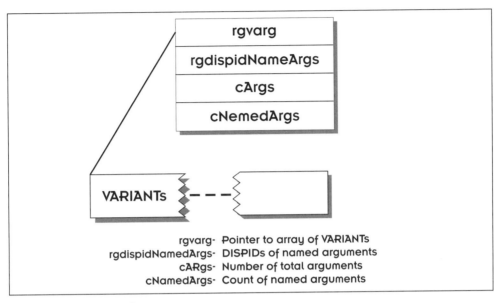

Figure 5.3 A dispatch argument array.

You can easily parse arguments out of the **DISPPARAMS** structure by calling the **DispGetParam** functions. This function accepts the **DISPPARAMS** structure, a proper index (that is, zero is the first argument, not the last), and a type you want that argument to be. The function automatically pulls the correct parameter from the **rgvarg** array and coerces it to the proper type. Since your type information knows about argument types, you can also call **ITypeInfo::Invoke** to magically coerce all of the **VARIANT**s in the argument list. You can also get a similar effect by calling the global function **DispInvoke**.

From the client's point of view, it is often more convenient to work with names instead of **DISPID**s for properties, methods, and named parameters. That's why the **IDispatch::GetIDsOfNames** function exists. Using this function, the client can convert the simple names of things into **DISPID**s.

Is Your Head Spinning?

Wow! **IDispatch** isn't easy, is it? However, did all the data types and members sound familiar? **VARIANT**s and properties? VB already uses these types and members in standard objects. In fact, to use an ActiveX object, you need only create it and treat it as though it were any other VB object. To provide objects to other programs, you can create a class and expose properties and methods for the class to the outside world.

If it is this easy, why learn the details? One of the most important uses of ActiveX objects is to achieve interoperability between languages. If you have to interface to other languages, these details can be important. Also, the ActiveX documentation assumes you know all of these things. Worse, it assumes you know them with the C++ flavor that the documentation tends to use.

To show you just how easy it is to create and use an ActiveX object with VB, let's try a simple project. First, you'll create an ActiveX inproc server. Then you'll use the server in a program. The program itself won't be anything special, but you'll be creating and using an ActiveX server. This isn't as capable as an ActiveX control, but for reusable processing code, it is quite efficient and simple to use.

A Simple Project

Before you start any ActiveX project, you should have a clear idea of four things:

1. What your object will do.
2. What properties you want to expose.
3. What methods you want to expose.
4. What events you want to expose (for controls only).

For this simple example, suppose you need a DLL that encrypts and decrypts a string. The ActiveX object has one property: **Key**. This is a string that controls the encryption or decryption. Next, you need a method for encoding (**Encrypt**) and decoding (**Decrypt**). Since this is not an ActiveX control (just an object), there are no events possible.

You can find the code for the DLL in Listing 5.1. Starting the project is simple. From the *New Project* dialog's *New* tab, select *ActiveX DLL*. Of course, if you wanted a local server, you'd select *ActiveX EXE* instead.

LISTING 5.1 THE MAGIC DECODER RING'S SOURCE.

```
' Magic Decoder Ring ActiveX DLL Source
' By Al Williams
VERSION 1.0 CLASS
BEGIN
  MultiUse = -1   'True
END
Attribute VB_Name = "MagicRing"
Attribute VB_GlobalNameSpace = False
Attribute VB_Creatable = True
```

```
Attribute VB_PredeclaredId = False
Attribute VB_Exposed = True
Option Explicit

' Property Named Key
Public Key As String


' Encrypt this string
' This version just XORs the string
' with the key
Public Function Encrypt(s As String) As String
Dim slen As Integer
Dim klen As Integer
Dim i, j As Integer
slen = Len(s)
klen = Len(Key)
For i = 0 To slen Step klen
  For j = 1 To klen
    If i + j <= slen Then
      Mid(s, i + j, 1) = _
        Chr(Asc(Mid(s, i + j, 1)) _
        Xor Asc(Mid(Key, j, 1)))
      If Mid(s, i + j, 1) = Chr(0) Then
        Mid(s, i + j, 1) = Mid(Key, j, 1)
      End If
    End If
  Next j
Next i
Encrypt = s
End Function


' Decrypt the string
' This version just XORs the string
' with the key
Public Function Decrypt(s As String) As String
Dim slen As Integer
Dim klen As Integer
Dim i, j As Integer
slen = Len(s)
klen = Len(Key)
For i = 0 To slen Step klen
  For j = 1 To klen
    If i + j <= slen Then
      Mid(s, i + j, 1) = _
        Chr(Asc(Mid(s, i + j, 1)) _
        Xor Asc(Mid(Key, j, 1)))
      If Mid(s, i + j, 1) = Chr(0) Then
```

```
        Mid(s, i + j, 1) = Mid(Key, j, 1)
      End If
    End If
  Next j
Next i
Decrypt = s
End Function
```

Your new project now contains a VB class module. This class module represents your ActiveX object. Any public variables you create in the module will become properties and any public Subs or Functions will show up as methods.

The **Key** property only requires a single line:

```
Public Dim Key as String
```

You can also create procedures that handle setting and reading properties (**Property Set**, **Property Let**, and **Property Get**) routines. These routines handle cases where you want to convert the data, validate properties, or otherwise act on the data. You'll see examples of using these when you create a true ActiveX object.

Two ordinary functions easily provide the logic for **Encrypt** and **Decrypt** (see Listing 5.1). In reality, the algorithm is exactly the same for both functions. However, you might alter the functions to use a different algorithm that isn't symmetrical.

That's really all there is to creating an ActiveX object using VB5. The system takes care of the class factory, self-registration, and all the other mundane details that aren't really all that interesting.

Notice that you can add more class modules to a project if you want multiple ActiveX classes. Just make sure the module's instancing property is set appropriately. What's the instancing property? It tells VB how to handle requests to create your object.

Table 5.6 shows the settings and their meanings. For a DLL project, usually setting 5 is what you want.

You can automate some of the tedium inherent in creating class modules by using the Class Builder add in (on the **Add-Ins** menu). This simple tool lets you add properties, methods, and events (covered soon) using a graphical interface. The tool writes all the declarations and procedures you need. Then you can alter them if you wish.

Table 5.6 Instancing settings.

Setting	Description
1	(Default) Private. Other applications aren't allowed access to type library information about the class, and cannot create instances of it. Private objects are only for use within your component.
2	PublicNotCreatable. Other applications can use objects of this class only if your component creates the objects first. Other applications cannot use the CreateObject function or the New operator to create objects from the class.
3	OnNewProcess. Allows other applications to create objects from the class, but every object of this class that a client creates starts a new instance of your component (applies to EXEs only).
4	GlobalOnNewProcess. Similar to OnNewProcess, except that properties and methods of the class can be invoked as if they were simply global functions (applies to EXEs only).
5	InSameProcess. Allows other applications to create objects from the class. One instance of your component can provide any number of objects created in this fashion, regardless of how many applications request them.
6	GlobalInSameProcess. Similar to InSameProcess, with one addition properties and methods of the class can be invoked as if they were simply global functions. It's not necessary to explicitly create an instance of the class first, because one will automatically be created.

Using The Object

Using the object is simple, too. The easiest way to test the program is to add a new project to your existing project. Select the *Add Project* item from the File menu. This brings up the *New Project* dialog. Select the *Standard EXE* choice to create an ordinary application. You'll see the layout of the sample program in Figure 5.4. Assuming the text fields are named **Data** and **Key**, you can write the button handlers simply:

```
Private Sub Encode_Click()
Dim ring As Object
Set ring = CreateObject("Crypt.MagicRing")
ring.Key = Key.Text
Data.Text = ring.Encrypt(Data.Text)
Set ring = Nothing
End Sub
```

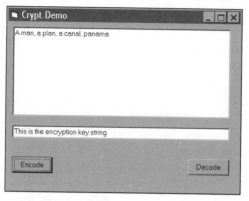

Figure 5.4 Testing the magic decoder ring.

The **Dim** statement defines a variable to hold the object reference. Next, a **CreateObject** call instantiates the object. The string you pass to **CreateObject** consists of the name of the ActiveX project (**Crypt**), a period, and the name of the class module within the project (**MagicRing**). Once you create the object, you can manipulate it by accessing the properties and methods the object exposes. Finally, assigning **nothing** to the object's variable allows VB to destroy the object. You can see the entire program in Listing 5.2.

LISTING 5.2   TESTING THE MAGIC DECODER RING.

```
' Crypt demo
' by Al Williams
VERSION 5.00
Begin VB.Form Demo
   Caption         =    "Crypt Demo"
   ClientHeight    =    3888
   ClientLeft      =    48
   ClientTop       =    360
   ClientWidth     =    5520
   LinkTopic       =    "Form1"
   ScaleHeight     =    3888
   ScaleWidth      =    5520
   StartUpPosition =    3   'Windows Default
   Begin VB.CommandButton Decode
      Caption         =    "Decode"
      Height          =    372
      Left            =    4320
      TabIndex        =    3
      Top             =    3120
      Width           =    972
   End
```

```
      Begin VB.CommandButton Encode
         Caption         =    "Encode"
         Height          =    372
         Left            =    120
         TabIndex        =    2
         Top             =    3120
         Width           =    972
      End
      Begin VB.TextBox Key
         Height          =    288
         Left            =    120
         TabIndex        =    1
         Top             =    2400
         Width           =    5172
      End
      Begin VB.TextBox Data
         Height          =    2052
         Left            =    120
         MultiLine       =    -1    'True
         TabIndex        =    0
         Top             =    120
         Width           =    5172
      End
   End
End
Attribute VB_Name = "Demo"
Attribute VB_GlobalNameSpace = False
Attribute VB_Creatable = False
Attribute VB_PredeclaredId = True
Attribute VB_Exposed = False
Option Explicit

Private Sub Encode_Click()
' Create an object reference
Dim ring As Object
' Create Magic Ring Object
Set ring = CreateObject("Crypt.MagicRing")
' Set key from form
ring.Key = Key.Text
' Encrypt form data and put back in field
Data.Text = ring.Encrypt(Data.Text)
' Get rid of magic ring
Set ring = Nothing
End Sub

Private Sub Decode_Click()
' See comments for Encode_Click
```

```
Dim ring As Object
Set ring = CreateObject("Crypt.MagicRing")
ring.Key = Key.Text
Data.Text = ring.Decrypt(Data.Text)
Set ring = Nothing
End Sub
```

Back To Controls

Writing controls is a straightforward affair thanks to the Wizards. Although you used the Wizards back in Chapter 2, you didn't get a chance to use all of the features.

The most important Wizard is the ActiveX Control Interface Wizard. This Wizard allows you to specify the properties, methods, and events for your control. The first screen allows you to specify common properties, methods, and events (see Figure 5.5). You are not limited to these, however. You can use the next screen (shown in Figure 5.6) to add any custom members you want.

Once you select all the members you want your control to expose, you can proceed to the next screen, shown in Figure 5.7. This dialog allows you to connect the members you specified on the first screen to members of internal objects. For example, if your component has a timer control. You can use this Wizard to connect the timer's **Timer** event to an external event. You could also expose the **Interval** property to external programs.

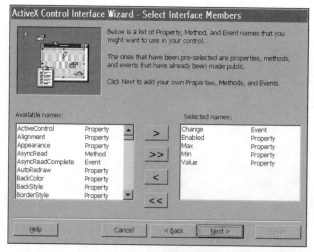

Figure 5.5 Using the Wizard to specify common members.

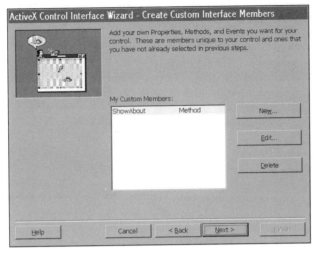

Figure 5.6 Using the Wizard to create custom members.

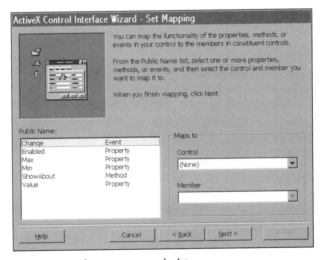

Figure 5.7 Connecting members to internal objects.

The final dialog, shown in Figure 5.8, shows all the otherwise unassigned members. You can set the member's attributes and the description text that appears in the design-time environment. For properties, you can specify the type, the default value, and specify if the property is readable and writable at design time and run time. You can also specify arguments to the properties. This allows you to create pseudo-array properties. However—at least in the beta version of VB5—the Wizard doesn't properly add the arguments to the **Property Let** and **Property Get** routines (see below). You'll have to do that by hand.

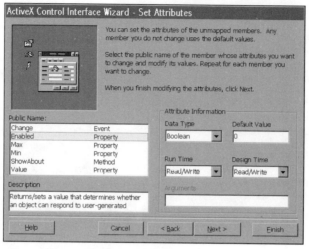

Figure 5.8 Specifying other members.

For methods, you specify the arguments the method requires, and the return type (if any). Events only require the arguments you want to pass with the event.

The UserControl Object

At the heart of each control is a UserControl object. This object serves a similar function to a form in an ordinary VB program. You place components on the UserControl to create your component. Table 5.7 shows the key properties and events you can access using UserControl.

Although UserControl is similar to a form, there are some differences. In particular, there are no **Activate**, **Deactivate**, **Load**, **Unload**, or **QueryUnload** events. However, other events serve similar purposes (see Table 5.7).

There are two ways to utilize the UserControl. The easy way is to drop one or more components from the standard VB toolbox onto the UserControl's display area. That's how the LEDBAR control in Chapter 2 works. The UserControl is simply a container for other components. You can use any of the standard VB components except for the OLE container (see Table 5.8).

The other alternative is to draw directly on the surface of the UserControl. To do that, you need to write a **Paint** handler. Inside the **Paint** handler, you use ordinary drawing commands (like **Line** and **Circle**) to define the look of your control. This is more difficult since you are responsible for every aspect of your control's appearance. Not only do you have to draw the usual appearance of the control, but you also have to fret over the proper display of focus rectangles and other mundane details. Of course, you can mix your own drawing code with components, too.

Table 5.7 Key properties and events of UserControl.

Name	Type	Description
Name	Property	Names the control—should be unique
AccessKeys	Property	Allows use of hot keys to shift focus to control
Alignable	Property	Allows control to align to edge of certain containers
Appearance	Property	Determines if control is flat or 3D
Ambient	Property	Allows access to container's ambient properties
AutoRedraw	Property	Set to True to let VB handle repainting of the control
BackColor	Property	Background color
BackStyle	Property	Set for opaque or transparent background
BorderStyle	Property	Determines type of border around control
CanGetFocus	Property	True if control can receive focus (see text)
ClipControls	Property	Determines if control can draw over child controls
ControlContainer	Property	True if control can act as a container that developers can place other controls inside (see Chapter 6)
Controls	Property	List of controls that make up the ActiveX control
DefaultCancel	Property	True if control simulates a standard command button
DrawMode	Property	Determines how drawings interact with existing window contents
DrawStyle	Property	Affects line style for graphics output calls
DrawWidth	Property	Sets line width for graphics output calls
EditAtDesignTime	Property	True if designers must use Edit menu
Enabled	Property	True if control is able to be active (see text)
Extender	Property	Allows access to container-managed (extended) properties
FillColor	Property	Color used to fill graphics interiors
FillStyle	Property	Determines how graphics use FillColor
Font	Property	Current font
FontTransparent	Property	True if text has transparent background
ForeColor	Property	Color used for foreground graphics
ForwardFocus	Property	True if control should forward focus events to next control
ScaleHeight	Property	Height of interior of control

continued

Table 5.7   Key properties and events of UserControl (continued).

Name	Type	Description
ScaleWidth	Property	Width of interior of control
InvisibleAtRuntime	Property	Determines if control is visible at run time (see Chapter 6)
KeyPreview	Property	True if control wants to process keys before child controls
MouseIcon	Property	Icon used for mouse pointer when MousePointer = 99
MousePointer	Property	Pointer used when mouse is over control
PropertyPages	Property	Name of ActiveX Property Page
Public	Property	True if other programs can create instances of this control
ScaleMode	Property	Sets units of measure used for ScaleHeight, ScaleWidth, etc.
ToolboxBitmap	Property	Picture used to represent the control
AccessKeyPress	Event	Signifies an access key was pressed
AmbientChanged	Event	Container's ambient property changed
EnterFocus	Event	Focus changed (see text)
ExitFocus	Event	Focus changed (see text)
Hide	Event	Control is hiding
Initialize	Event	Initialize control (properties not yet finalized)
InitProperties	Event	Initialize properties
LostFocus	Event	Focus changed (see text)
GotFocus	Event	Focus changed (see text)
Paint	Event	Must redraw control
ReadProperties	Event	Read properties from storage
Resize	Event	Control's size changed
Show	Event	Container is showing control
Terminate	Event	Control is terminating
WriteProperties	Event	Write properties to storage

Other UserControl Features

In addition to the ordinary properties that you define for your control, you can access ambient properties. These are properties that the control container provides for you to use. For example, your control might want to use the same background color that the container uses. To do this, the control can read the container's ambient background property and use it as the control's background color.

Table 5.8 Standard controls usable in an ActiveX control.

Name

PictureBox

Label

TextBox

Frame

CommandButton

CheckBox

OptionButton

ComboBox

ListBox

HScrollBar

VScrollBar

Timer

DriveListBox

DirListBox

FileListBox

Shape

Line

Image

Data

Of course, exactly what ambient properties are available depends on the particular container. However, there are many ambient properties that many
containers make available (see Table 5.9). VB always makes these properties
appear to your control even if the container doesn't really support them. Of
course, specific containers may provide other properties, too. To read these
properties, you use the **UserControl**'s **Ambient** property. Each ambient property is a property of the **Ambient** object. These properties are read-only and are
not available during the **Initialize** event.

When the container changes any ambient property, VB calls the **UserControl**'s
AmbientChanged event. You can use this event to change any properties that
should synchronize to an ambient property. Listing 5.3 shows the code changes
required to make the LEDBAR control use the container's background color.
The significant portions are in bold type. Note that the control reads the ambient color each time it darkens an LED. However, it also handles the
AmbientChanged event. When any ambient property changes, the control
sets all the LEDs to the (potentially new) background color and redraws itself.

Table 5.9 Common ambient properties.

Name	Description
UserMode	True if the control is in a run-time (as opposed to design-time) environment
LocaleID	The current locale (language ID)
DisplayName	The name the container uses to identify the control
ForeColor	The foreground color
BackColor	The background color
Font	The current text font
TextAlign	Default text alignment
DisplayAsDefault	Indicates if the control should appear as the default (for example, a button that is the default button appears slightly different than an ordinary button)

Try commenting out the code in this handler and see what happens. The new color takes effect one LED at a time as the control turns off particular LEDs.

LISTING 5.3 CHANGES TO LEDBAR FOR AMBIENT PROPERTIES.

```
Private Sub Timer1_Timer()
If m_Hold = True Then Exit Sub
LEDO(n).FillColor = UserControl.Ambient.BackColor
If m_Direction Then
  If n = 19 Then n = 0 Else n = n + 1
Else
  If n = 0 Then n = 19 Else n = n - 1
End If
LEDO(n).FillColor = UserControl.ForeColor
RaiseEvent Tick
End Sub


Private Sub UserControl_AmbientChanged(PropertyName As String)
For i = 0 To 19
  LEDO(i).FillColor = UserControl.Ambient.BackColor
Next i
Refresh
End Sub


Private Sub UserControl_Initialize()
n = 0
LEDO(0).FillColor = UserControl.Ambient.BackColor
Hold = False

End Sub
```

What's Inside?

What do the two ActiveX Wizards do? Of course, the first Wizard creates an empty **UserControl** object and initializes your project. The real action occurs in the interface Wizard. This Wizard handles the association of your properties, methods, and events with VB code.

Suppose your control contains a timer component. Further, suppose you want to expose the **Interval** property as your control's **Delay** property. The Wizard will generate two special pieces of code to handle this. Here's an example:

```
Public Property Get Delay() As Integer
Attribute Delay.VB_Description = "Component Delay"
    Delay = Timer1.Interval
End Property

Public Property Let Delay(ByVal New_Delay As Integer)
    Timer1.Interval = New_Delay
    PropertyChanged "Delay"
End Property
```

When the external program reads the **Delay** property, VB calls the corresponding **Property Get** routine. This simply transfers the timer's **Interval** property to the **Delay** property. The **Attribute** line describes the property. When the external program sets a property, VB calls the **Property Let** routine. This transfers data in the other direction and calls **PropertyChanged**. This important call informs VB that the object will require saving. It also serves to synchronize any multiple views of the control on the screen (e.g., the control and an open property sheet).

One function the Wizard doesn't write for you is a **Property Set** procedure. This is similar to **Property Let**, but it handles the case where the programmer assigns one object variable to another. For example, suppose you have an object reference named **anObj** and you execute the following statement:

```
Set objCopy=anObj
```

The **Property Set** procedure allows you to control the coping process in great detail. For most ActiveX controls, you don't really care about this unless you are trying to make a read-only property (discussed later in this chapter).

Properties that don't directly relate to an internal component's property are possible, too. The Wizard creates a variable for you that has the same name as the property but it begins with **m_**. In other words, a property named

SubInterval will have a variable named **m_SubInterval**. The Wizard then writes **Property Let** and **Property Put** routines that use the variable instead of another component property. Your code might look something like this:

```
Public Property Get SubInterval() As Integer
Attribute SubInterval.VB_Description = "Secondary time out period"
    SubInterval = m_SubInterval
End Property

Public Property Let SubInterval(ByVal New_SubInterval As Integer)
    m_SubInterval=New_SubInterval
    PropertyChanged "SubInterval"
End Property
```

If you want to validate property data, you can easily do it in these functions. You can also convert units. For example, what if you wanted a timer that took a delay in minutes instead of seconds? You might write:

```
Public Property Get Delay() As Integer
Attribute Delay.VB_Description = "Component Delay (minutes)"
    Delay = Timer1.Interval/60
End Property

Public Property Let Delay(ByVal New_Delay As Integer)
    Timer1.Interval = New_Delay*60
    PropertyChanged "Delay"
End Property
```

VB automatically creates three subroutines related to properties. The **UserControl_ReadProperties** and **UserControl_WriteProperties** arrange to read and write your control's properties using a file or other external storage (usually an ActiveX **IStream** or **IPropertyBag**). Remember, your control doesn't save a file like a regular application. Instead, the container program handles all saving and loading. Your control is only responsible for providing the container with a representation of the control's properties suitable for saving and loading.

Where does the container store your data? You don't care. The container might store the data in a file. Alternately, it might store the data in a database record. Your control shouldn't know or care.

If you have properties that don't map to another component's properties, VB will also create a **UserControl_InitProperties** subroutine. The purpose of this **Sub** is to set up each property using a default value. The default value resides in a variable starting with **m_def_**. In other words, **m_def_myprop** is the default value for **m_myprop**, which is the variable for the **myprop** property.

You might wonder why the **Write_Properties** routine has default values specified in it. VB uses this to reduce the amount of storage required to save a control. The VB routines only write a property out to storage if its value is different from the default value.

If you want to manually create properties, methods, and events, you can use the **Add Procedure** item from the **Tools** menu. You can also add ordinary **Sub**s and **Function**s with this menu command. Also on the **Tools** menu is the **Procedure Attributes** command. This command brings us a dialog (see Figure 5.9) where you can set the description text, the help ID to use for the procedure, and some other obscure details about the procedure. You'll find out more about the options on the Advanced button on this dialog later in this chapter.

When you create a property, you can specify additional arguments, if you like. These additional arguments pass directly to the appropriate **Property Get** and **Property Let** routines. What you do with them is up to you. For example, suppose you wanted a way to disable and enable specific LEDs in the LEDBAR control. You might create a property named **LEDEnable**. This property could take an extra integer parameter that you would use to index the **LED** control array. Keep in mind you can pass as many arguments as you like of practically any type.

Methods And Events

Methods are the easiest part of the control since they correspond to simple **Sub**s or **Function**s. Once again, you can use the Wizard to connect a method to a component you use internally, or to a stub **Sub** or **Function** that you then fill in with code. If you elect to connect (or delegate) the method to an internal component, the Wizard writes a simple routine that does nothing more sophisticated than calling the underlying routine.

Events are not much more difficult to manage. The Wizard declares each event you specify using a line like this:

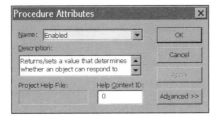

Figure 5.9 The Procedure Attributes dialog.

```
Event Timer()
```

If you connect an event to an event that originates with an internal component, the Wizard constructs code that handles the original event and calls **RaiseEvent** for your new event like this:

```
Private Sub Timer1_Timer()
    RaiseEvent Timer
End Sub
```

The event names need not match. That is, the internal **Timer** event might trigger a **Tick** event, and that's not a problem. Of course, you can add code to this event handler. For example, you might write:

```
If m_GenerateTicks = True Then RaiseEvent "Tick"
```

You can also write code that you want to execute for the event before or after passing it on to the container. The LEDBAR control does this. It updates the LEDs and then fires the **Tick** event.

If you don't connect the event to an existing internal event, then the Wizard doesn't write any code except the declaration. Then it is up to you to call **RaiseEvent** wherever it is appropriate for you to generate that event.

What Properties, Methods, And Events Should I Provide?

The flip answer to "What members should I provide?" is "Exactly as many as you need." However, Microsoft makes recommendations about the properties, methods, and events every control *should* supply. Keep in mind you are under no obligation to supply any of these, but they do make sense for most controls.

Microsoft suggests that you supply these properties: **Appearance, BackColor, BackStyle, BorderStyle, Enabled, Font,** and **ForeColor.** Of course, just adding them isn't sufficient. You also need to implement their behavior. Luckily, the **UserControl** object will handle most of these for you (see the section *Finishing Touches* for more about the **Enabled** property). You only need to expose them using the Wizard. You also have to respect them in any code you write where these properties are important.

The only one of these properties that is difficult to handle is the **Appearance** property. If your control consists of other controls, you'll quickly realize that your internal controls want you to set their **Appearance** property at design time. However, you need to handle the **Appearance** property at run time so that you can forward it to the internal components. There isn't a good answer for this, short of drawing your own control without using any components.

Many common properties are so important that they have a predefined **DISPID**. This allows any program to manipulate those properties even if they don't know the language used to define the control's strings. This leads to an interesting problem: If you create, for example, a **BackColor** property without using the predefined **DISPID**, it isn't really the **BackColor** property. That is, some containers may not recognize it as the background color property.

The answer is to use the special **Procedure Attributes** dialog (you can find this menu selection under the **Tools** menu). The dialog appears with a limited amount of information at first. When you click on the Advanced button, you'll see the dialog in Figure 5.10. This reveals (among other things) the **Procedure ID** selection. VB uses the term **Procedure ID** to mean the same thing as **DISPID**. You can select a predefined ID (see Table 5.10), or enter zero, or a negative number manually (all the predefined **DISPID**s are negative or zero). Selecting a particular ID doesn't automatically handle your property; it simply allows certain containers to recognize what the property is supposed to do. It is still up to you to write the code that makes the property behave appropriately.

The (**default**) selection is the same as using a **DISPID** of zero. Using (**default**) allows you to specify a default property (by convention, this property is named

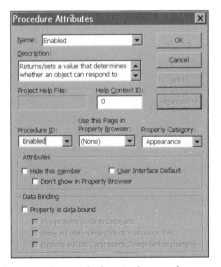

Figure 5.10 The Procedure Attributes dialog (advanced).

Value). Suppose your control has a **Value** property and you use the **Procedure Attributes** dialog to specify a **DISPID** of zero (or (**default**) if you prefer).

Table 5.10 Predefined procedure IDs.

Name	Type	Notes
(default)	Property	Sets the default property
Appearance	Property	
AutoSize	Property	
BackColor	Property	
BackStyle	Property	
BorderColor	Property	
BorderStyle	Property	
BorderWidth	Property	
Caption	Property	Window text for this control
DrawMode	Property	
DrawStyle	Property	
DrawWidth	Property	
Enabled	Property	
FillColor	Property	
FillStyle	Property	
Font	Property	
ForeColor	Property	
hWnd	Property	The control's window handle
TabStop	Property	
Text	Property	
RightToLeft	Property	
Click	Event	
DblClick	Event	
KeyDown	Event	
KeyPress	Event	
KeyUp	Event	
MouseDown	Event	
MouseMove	Event	
MouseUp	Event	
Error	Event	

Then you can write:

```
UserControl11 = "Howdy"
```

which is the same as:

```
UserControl11.Value = "Howdy"
```

What's the difference between using a (**default**) **DISPID** and selecting the **User Interface Default** check box? Using the **DISPID** controls what property is the default for programs that don't specify a particular property. The **User Interface Default** option determines what property, for example, shows up by default at design time. When you double click on a control, VB automatically supplies an event handler. This will be the handler for the event that has the **User Interface Default** option checked.

Another thing you can set using this dialog is the property's category. VB allows you to look at properties alphabetically or by category. You can specify a category in this dialog so that your custom properties appear in the correct place.

Methods

Microsoft's only recommendation for methods is the **Refresh** method. You only need this method if your control is visible (you'll learn about invisible controls in Chapter 6). Handling this method is very easy. Just call **UserControl.Refresh**. This will cause your **Paint** code to execute and will also cause any internal controls to redraw.

Events

The events that most controls should expose are **Click, DblClick, KeyDown, KeyPress, KeyUp, MouseDown, MouseMove**, and **MouseUp**. Implementing these can be as simple as writing the corresponding handlers for each control that makes up your component (including **UserControl**) and calling **RaiseEvent** for the appropriate event. Remember, the **Property Attribute** dialog applies to events. You can select a **DISPID** and also specify a user interface default by making the appropriate selections.

Finishing Touches

You now know enough to turn out almost any control you can design. However, there are a few pitfalls regarding some of the common properties. Also, you'd like your control to appear professional, with its own name, toolbar icon, and other flourishes.

Supporting Enable

One of the oddest properties you'll need to implement is the **Enabled** property. The problem is that the property is both a regular one and an *extended* property. An extended property is one that the container maintains on behalf of the control. For example, consider the property that determines the location of the control (usually **Top** and **Left**). These properties don't mean anything to the control. The container maintains these for the container's benefit. Usually extended properties show up in the control's **Extender** object. However, you ordinarily don't care about **Extender** since you can't predict what properties a container will provide.

If you want the container to see an **Enabled** property, you must also supply an ordinary **Enabled** property. This property isn't visible to the control's user: the user sees the container's extended property. However, your property must exist for the container's property to work properly.

Adding the property is no big deal. Just delegate it to the **UserControl** object using the Wizard. Also, you must use the **Procedure Attributes** dialog to set the ID to **Enabled**. Since this property is always an extended property, you can't change its property category. When you change it, it changes your copy of the property and the user never sees that. Instead, the user sees the extended property in the **Misc** category.

Focus

Another thing that robust controls need to consider is focus. Some controls can accept the focus: that is, they can receive keyboard input. Edit controls and buttons, for example, will accept focus. Labels don't. If you want your control to accept the focus and you are performing your own drawing, you can set the **CanGetFocus** property to **True**. Then, the control receives **GotFocus** and **LostFocus** events. You can use these to redraw your control as appropriate.

The situation is a little different when you compose your control from other components that may receive focus. Then, each constituent control that might get the focus can get the focus. For example, if your control contains an edit field and the user clicks on it, the edit field will get the focus regardless of the setting of the **CanGetFocus** property. If you have focus-accepting components in your control, VB won't let you set **CanGetFocus** to **False**. Conversely, if you set **CanGetFocus** to **False**, VB grays out many controls in the tool box. Your control now receives an **EnterFocus** event when the focus moves from outside your control to a component inside your control. When the focus leaves your control entirely, you'll get a **LeaveFocus** event.

Access Keys

Speaking of focus, one way users shift the focus is via accelerator or shortcut keys. For instance, in a dialog box, you might find a label with the caption **Name**. The user expects to be able to press Alt+N to jump to the corresponding edit field. Of course, the focus actually shifts to the label. Since the label can't accept the focus, it forwards it to the next control, which should be its edit control.

You can set up this type of behavior in your own controls. The trick is to use the **AccessKeys** property. This property allows you to set any number of keys that you want to use as access keys. When the user presses one of the access keys, your control gets an **AccessKeyPress** event. You can use the event's argument to determine which key caused the event.

You could hard code letters into the **AccessKeys** property at design time. However, that is bad form. You should probably examine your **Caption** (or comparable) property and search for an ampersand (&). If you find one, use the following letter as an access key.

A complex control that contains other controls can set access keys on the various internal controls and they will do all the work. Again, you may want to allow some way for the end designer to specify custom access keys.

Read-only And Run-time Properties

Sometimes you'd like to make a property that is read-only. Sometimes you want properties that are only available at run time (or design time). You might even want a property that you can write to at design time, but at run time it is read only. You can accomplish all of these effects. To make a property read-only, you just have to cause the **Property Let** and **Property Set** procedures to raise an error (usually error 31013). Of course, if the property isn't a variant, you won't need **Property Set**, since it is only for object types. For example:

```
Private m_iprop As Integer

Property Get iprop() As Integer
    iprop = m_iprop
End Property

Property Let iprop(newValue As Integer)
    Err.Raise Number:=31013, Description:= "Read-only"
End Property
```

If you want the behavior only during design (or run) time, just test the **Ambient.UserMode** property. If it is **True**, then the control is running. Otherwise, it is just in design mode. You can then either set the property or raise an error, as appropriate.

Toolbar Bitmaps And About Boxes

Although VB provides each control with a default picture to show in toolbars, it is a good idea to create your own. Just make an image that is 16 pixels wide by 15 pixels high. The image should be a bitmap, not a true icon. Then assign the picture to the **UserControl**'s **ToolboxBitmap** property. Another polite thing to do is to rename the **UserControl** object. Otherwise, everyone will try to create controls named **UserControl**.

Many controls have an **AboutBox** property that isn't a property at all. Instead, it brings up the control's About dialog box. This box can supply any information you want, but it usually displays your copyright notice and contact information.

It is very simple to add an About box. Just create a new, ordinary form. Arrange controls and write code to make the About box behave any way you wish. Then add a subroutine to display the box (assume it is named **dlgAbout**):

```
Public Sub ShowAboutBox()
    dlgAbout.Show vbModal
    Unload dlgAbout
    Set dlgAbout = Nothing
End Sub
```

This simply calls up the form as a modal dialog. Then when the user dismisses the dialog, it unloads the form and deletes the object reference to free up memory. If you use the standard About box that the **Add Form** dialog offers, it automatically unloads itself when the user clicks OK, so you don't need to explicitly write the **Unload** statement above.

All that is left is to tell VB that this is a special procedure that displays the About box. You can do this by using the **Procedure Attribute** dialog to set the subroutine's ID to **AboutBox**. You may use any subroutine and form name you wish. Just be sure that the subroutine's ID is **AboutBox**. In fact, you don't have to display an About box here (although, you'll usually want to do that). You might prefer to play a wave file that describes the control with an audio clip. Perhaps you'll start a Web browser and load your About box and documentation off the Internet. Use your imagination.

Exporting Constants

Often your controls will use constants to signal certain conditions. For example, the LEDBAR example can move lights from left to right or from right to left. Users have to remember if setting the direction to **True** moves from the left or from the right. Not very programmer-friendly.

Wouldn't it better if you could define two constants (**lbLeftToRight** and **lbRightToLeft**)? Not only is this easier to remember, but the VB design environment will automatically place a drop-down list box with the constants in them if we do things correctly.

The trick is to define a new type using a **Public Enum**. This type then becomes the type of the property. For example:

```
Public Enum LEDBARX
    lbLeftToRight
    lbRightToLeft
End Enum

Private m_direction As LEDBARX

Public Property Get Direction() As LEDBARX
    Direction = m_direction
End Property

Public Property Let Direction(ByVal NewDir    As LEDBARX)
    m_direction = NewDir
    PropertyChanged "Direction"
End Property
```

Of course, you have to modify your code to use the new flag instead of the old Boolean value. For example:

```
If m_Direction = lbLeftToRight Then
  If n = 19 Then n = 0 Else n = n + 1
Else
  If n = 0 Then n = 19 Else n = n - 1
End If
```

It is unfortunate that the beta version of VB's interface Wizard doesn't set this up for items such as **BackStyle** and **BorderStyle**. The Wizard creates these as integer properties, and so the browser doesn't offer you any special drop down list boxes for the properties. Of course, you can alter the definitions by hand, but at that point, you might as well write the entire property yourself. Hopefully, the release version of VB will fix this.

Adding Property Pages

Adding properties with the Property Page Wizard is simple. You can select standard property pages and create new pages on the first dialog (see Figure 5.11). Keep in mind that property pages need a unique name since they are actually ActiveX objects themselves.

The second page (Figure 5.12) allows you to associate properties with each page. The Wizard automatically places controls on the page for each property. That's all there is to it. Of course, you won't like where the Wizard places the controls. So, you just open up the form that the Wizard creates and move the controls around. You can also add labels or anything else you like. The property page is, for most purposes, a regular VB form.

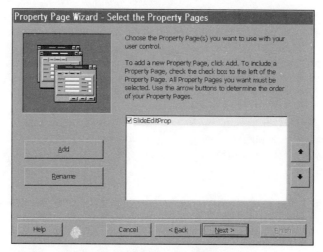

Figure 5.11 Selecting and creating property pages.

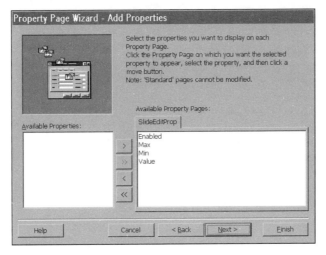

Figure 5.12 Assigning properties to pages.

You can examine the code the Wizard creates, but it is quite unremarkable. Once the Wizard creates the skeleton, you'll be able to easily modify the resulting custom property pages. The system pages that define things like colors and fonts are not something you can change. However, you don't have to use them. You can easily supply custom pages for all of your properties.

Putting It All Together

Figure 5.13 and Listing 5.4 show an example control that takes advantage of most of the refinements mentioned in this chapter. This control is a simple text editor and a scroll bar that affects the value in the text box. The control is straightforward for the most part. There are only a few oddities you should note.

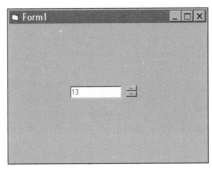

Figure 5.13 The SlideEdit control in action.

LISTING 5.4   THE SLIDEEDIT CONTROL.

```
' Slide Edit Control
' by Al Williams
VERSION 5.00
Begin VB.UserControl UserControl1
    BackStyle       =   0   'Transparent
    ClientHeight    =   576
    ClientLeft      =   0
    ClientTop       =   0
    ClientWidth     =   1980
    PropertyPages   =   "SlideEdit.ctx":0000
    ScaleHeight     =   576
    ScaleWidth      =   1980
    Begin VB.VScrollBar VScroll1
        Height      =   255
        Left        =   1440
        TabIndex    =   1
        Top         =   120
        Width       =   255
    End
    Begin VB.TextBox Text1
        Height      =   285
        Left        =   120
        TabIndex    =   0
        Text        =   "0"
        Top         =   120
        Width       =   1215
    End
End
Attribute VB_Name = "UserControl1"
Attribute VB_GlobalNameSpace = False
Attribute VB_Creatable = True
Attribute VB_PredeclaredId = False
Attribute VB_Exposed = True

'Event Declarations:
Event Change()

' Private variable to prevent recursion
Private ChgLock As Boolean

Private Sub Text1_Change()
' We need to prevent a change here from firing
' a scroll bar change which changes the text box,...
' so we resort to a lock variable
```

```
  If ChgLock = False Then
    ChgLock = True
    If Text1.Text < VScroll1.Min Or _
      Text1.Text > VScroll1.Max Then
      Text1.Text = VScroll1.Value
    End If
    VScroll1.Value = Text1.Text
    ChgLock = False
    RaiseEvent Change
  End If
End Sub

Public Property Get Enabled() As Boolean
Attribute Enabled.VB_Description = _
  "Returns/sets value indicating if object is user active"
    Enabled = UserControl.Enabled
End Property

Public Property Let Enabled(ByVal New_Enabled As Boolean)
    UserControl.Enabled = New_Enabled
    PropertyChanged "Enabled"
End Property

Public Property Get Min() As Integer
Attribute Min.VB_Description = _
  "Returns/sets minimum Value for scroll bar"
    Min = VScroll1.Min
End Property

Public Property Let Min(ByVal New_Min As Integer)
    VScroll1.Min = New_Min
    PropertyChanged "Min"
End Property

Public Property Get Max() As Integer
Attribute Max.VB_Description = _
  "Returns/sets maximum Value for scroll bar"
    Max = VScroll1.Max
End Property

Public Property Let Max(ByVal New_Max As Integer)
    VScroll1.Max = New_Max
    PropertyChanged "Max"
End Property

' Note that value is modified to reverse the
' sense of the scroll bar
```

```
Public Property Get Value() As Integer
Attribute Value.VB_Description = _
  "Returns/sets the value of an object."
    Value = VScroll1.Max - VScroll1.Value
End Property


Public Property Let Value(ByVal New_Value As Integer)
    VScroll1.Value = VScroll1.Max - New_Value
    PropertyChanged "Value"
End Property

' When scroll bar changes, we have to
' modify the value and change the edit box
Private Sub VScroll1_Change()
    If ChgLock = False Then
      ChgLock = True
      Text1.Text = VScroll1.Max - VScroll1.Value
      RaiseEvent Change
    End If
End Sub


'Load property values from storage
Private Sub UserControl_ReadProperties(PropBag As PropertyBag)
   UserControl.Enabled = PropBag.ReadProperty("Enabled", True)
   VScroll1.Min = PropBag.ReadProperty("Min", 0)
   VScroll1.Max = PropBag.ReadProperty("Max", 32767)
   VScroll1.Value = PropBag.ReadProperty("Value", 0)
' Compute text value from scroll bar value
   Text1.Text = VScroll1.Value
End Sub


'Write property values to storage
Private Sub UserControl_WriteProperties(PropBag As PropertyBag)
   Call PropBag.WriteProperty("Enabled", UserControl.Enabled,_
     True)
   Call PropBag.WriteProperty("Min", VScroll1.Min, 0)
   Call PropBag.WriteProperty("Max", VScroll1.Max, 32767)
   Call PropBag.WriteProperty("Value", VScroll1.Value, 0)
' No need to write text value since it is calculated
End Sub
```

First, for the purposes of this control, scroll bars work backwards. Clicking up makes the value of the scroll bar go down. This is the opposite of how it should work for this special edit control. To prevent this behavior, the component knows that the real value of the scroll bar **VScroll1** is **VScroll1.Max − VScroll1.Value**. This causes the scroll bar's value to operate correctly. Notice, however, that this requires manually touching up the Wizard-generated code that hooks the value to the outside world.

Another issue arises while handling the change events. It is imperative that the control keep the edit control and the scroll bar synchronized. The text control handles its change event and changes the scroll bar appropriately. The scroll bar also handles its change event and updates the text control. The problem is, when each change event procedure alters the other control, it fires the other control's change event. This in turn changes the original control, firing another change event. This continues until the stack overflows. To prevent this from happening, the code maintains a flag that locks out change events while it is processing a change event. A simple, yet effective, idea. Again, you'll have to modify the Wizard's code to handle this. By now, you can see why it is important to understand the Wizard's code. You'll often have to tweak it to do exactly what you want it to do.

Consider saving and loading properties. There is no need to save both the text value and the scroll bar value for this control since they depend on one another. Again, a manual tweak to the routines that save and load the properties takes care of things.

Only the **Enabled** and **ShowAbout** procedures require a special procedure ID. If you open the project and bring up the **Procedure Attribute** dialog, you'll see the IDs set. As a convenience to the programmer who uses this control, the **Value** property is set as the default property, too. The project marks the **Change** event as the user interface default. Again, this isn't strictly necessary, but it does make life easier for programmers using the control.

Look at Figure 5.14. This is another simple ActiveX control. However, if you examine the code in Listing 5.5, you'll notice that the control contains no visual components. It works by drawing directly in response to the **UserControl_Paint** event. It does use a timer component to generate events to control the drawing.

Figure 5.14 A Painted ActiveX control.

LISTING 5.5   PAINTING A CONTROL.

```
' Spin Wait Control
' by Al Williams
VERSION 5.00
Begin VB.UserControl SpinWait
    CanGetFocus     =   0   'False
    ClientHeight    =   1812
    ClientLeft      =   0
    ClientTop       =   0
    ClientWidth     =   1980
    BeginProperty Font
        Name            =   "MS Sans Serif"
        Size            =   18
        Charset         =   0
        Weight          =   400
        Underline       =   0   'False
        Italic          =   0   'False
        Strikethrough   =   0   'False
    EndProperty
    PropertyPages   =   "SpinWait.ctx":0000
    ScaleHeight     =   1812
    ScaleWidth      =   1980
    Begin VB.Timer Timer1
        Interval        =   250
        Left            =   240
        Top             =   1320
    End
End
Attribute VB_Name = "SpinWait"
Attribute VB_GlobalNameSpace = False
Attribute VB_Creatable = True
Attribute VB_PredeclaredId = False
Attribute VB_Exposed = True
Option Explicit

Private Tick As Integer


' When timer ticks, count it and
' redraw. Only 8 positions in the
' spin, so reset after 7 (positions
' are 0-7)
Private Sub Timer1_Timer()
Tick = Tick + 1
If Tick = 8 Then Tick = 0
Refresh
End Sub
```

```
' Here is the painting action
Private Sub UserControl_Paint()
Dim x2, y2, halfx, halfy
' We always draw from either coordinates 0, the
' full width, the full height, or half the height
' and width
x2 = ScaleWidth
y2 = ScaleHeight
halfx = x2 / 2
halfy = y2 / 2
' Just for fun, I wanted to use a print to
' put some text in the top left corner.
' Who'd have thought you'd use print in
' a Windows program?
CurrentX = 0
CurrentY = 0
Print "Wait!"
' True, half the cases are duplicates, but
' I figure, I might do different colors for each
' line or something someday.
Select Case Tick
  Case 0
    Line (halfx, 0)-(halfx, y2)
  Case 1
    Line (x2, 0)-(0, y2)
  Case 2
    Line (x2, halfy)-(0, halfy)
  Case 3
    Line (x2, y2)-(0, 0)
  Case 4
    Line (halfx, y2)-(halfx, 0)
  Case 5
    Line (0, y2)-(x2, 0)
  Case 6
    Line (0, halfy)-(x2, halfy)
  Case 7
    Line (0, 0)-(x2, y2)
  End Select
End Sub

'Load property values from storage
Private Sub UserControl_ReadProperties(PropBag As PropertyBag)
    UserControl.BackColor = _
      PropBag.ReadProperty("BackColor", &H8000000F)
    UserControl.ForeColor = _
      PropBag.ReadProperty("ForeColor", &H80000012)
    UserControl.Enabled = _
      PropBag.ReadProperty("Enabled", True)
```

```
    UserControl.BackStyle = _
      PropBag.ReadProperty("BackStyle", 1)
    UserControl.BorderStyle = _
      PropBag.ReadProperty("BorderStyle", 0)
    Timer1.Interval = PropBag.ReadProperty("Delay", 250)
    UserControl.DrawWidth = _
      PropBag.ReadProperty("LineWidth", 1)
End Sub


'Write property values to storage
Private Sub UserControl_WriteProperties(PropBag As PropertyBag)
    Call PropBag.WriteProperty("BackColor", _
      UserControl.BackColor, &H8000000F)
    Call PropBag.WriteProperty("ForeColor", _
      UserControl.ForeColor, &H80000012)
    Call PropBag.WriteProperty("Enabled", _
      UserControl.Enabled, True)
    Call PropBag.WriteProperty("BackStyle", _
      UserControl.BackStyle, 1)
    Call PropBag.WriteProperty("BorderStyle", _
      UserControl.BorderStyle, 0)
    Call PropBag.WriteProperty("Delay", _
      Timer1.Interval, 250)
    Call PropBag.WriteProperty("LineWidth", _
      UserControl.DrawWidth, 1)
End Sub


Public Property Get BackColor() As OLE_COLOR
Attribute BackColor.VB_Description = _
 "Returns/sets the background color for text and graphics"
Attribute BackColor.VB_ProcData.VB_Invoke_Property = _
   "StandardColor"
Attribute BackColor.VB_UserMemId = -501
    BackColor = UserControl.BackColor
End Property


Public Property Let BackColor(ByVal New_BackColor As OLE_COLOR)
    UserControl.BackColor = New_BackColor
    PropertyChanged "BackColor"
End Property


Public Property Get ForeColor() As OLE_COLOR
Attribute ForeColor.VB_Description = _
 "Returns/sets the foreground color for text and graphics"
Attribute ForeColor.VB_ProcData.VB_Invoke_Property = _
   "StandardColor"
```

```
   Attribute ForeColor.VB_UserMemId = -513
       ForeColor = UserControl.ForeColor
End Property

   Public Property Let ForeColor(ByVal New_ForeColor As OLE_COLOR)
       UserControl.ForeColor = New_ForeColor
       PropertyChanged "ForeColor"
End Property

   Public Property Get Enabled() As Boolean
Attribute Enabled.VB_Description = _
   "Returns/sets the enabled property."
Attribute Enabled.VB_UserMemId = -514
       Enabled = UserControl.Enabled
End Property

   Public Property Let Enabled(ByVal New_Enabled As Boolean)
       UserControl.Enabled = New_Enabled
       PropertyChanged "Enabled"
End Property

   Public Property Get BackStyle() As Integer
Attribute BackStyle.VB_Description = _
   "Indicates transparent or opaque"
Attribute BackStyle.VB_UserMemId = -502
       BackStyle = UserControl.BackStyle
End Property

   Public Property Let BackStyle(ByVal New_BackStyle As Integer)
       UserControl.BackStyle = New_BackStyle
       PropertyChanged "BackStyle"
End Property

   Public Property Get BorderStyle() As Integer
Attribute BorderStyle.VB_Description = _
   "Returns/sets the border style for an object."
Attribute BorderStyle.VB_UserMemId = -504
       BorderStyle = UserControl.BorderStyle
End Property

   Public Property Let BorderStyle(ByVal New_BorderStyle As Integer)
       UserControl.BorderStyle = New_BorderStyle
       PropertyChanged "BorderStyle"
End Property
```

```
Public Sub Refresh()
Attribute Refresh.VB_Description = _
  "Forces a complete repaint of a object."
Attribute Refresh.VB_UserMemId = -550
    UserControl.Refresh
End Sub


Public Property Get Delay() As Long
Attribute Delay.VB_Description = _
  "Returns/sets the number of milliseconds to delay"
    Delay = Timer1.Interval
End Property


Public Property Let Delay(ByVal New_Delay As Long)
    Timer1.Interval = New_Delay
    PropertyChanged "Delay"
End Property


Public Property Get LineWidth() As Integer
Attribute LineWidth.VB_Description = _
  "Returns/sets the line width"
Attribute LineWidth.VB_UserMemId = -509
    LineWidth = UserControl.DrawWidth
End Property


Public Property Let LineWidth(ByVal New_LineWidth As Integer)
    UserControl.DrawWidth = New_LineWidth
    PropertyChanged "LineWidth"
End Property
```

The paint event handler can use several calls to draw directly on the face of the **UserControl** object. **Circle**, **Line**, and **PSet** draw circles, lines, and individual pixels, respectively. **Line** can also draw boxes. You can coax **Circle** into drawing ellipses and arcs as well. If you want to write text, use the **Print** command. You may set the current printing coordinates using the **CurrentX** and **CurrentY** properties.

There are many properties that affect the drawing when you use the above calls. For example, the **DrawWidth** and **DrawStyle** properties set the width and style of the line. **DrawMode** lets you control how your drawing combines with the existing contents of the screen. This can be useful for selectively darkening areas or mixing colors, for example. When you want to make sure the control is up to date, call **Refresh**. The example code does this when it processes the timer event.

Debugging Notes

The biggest difference between debugging a control and an ordinary program is that controls run in one of two modes. Remember, your code runs at design time and while its host application is executing. To accommodate this, VB allows you to set breakpoints in a control that can fire when you place the control on a form at design time.

To make sure this works as you'd expect, VB disables everything having to do with a control while it is open for design. If you can see the control's layout in a form window, any program using the control is disabled. The toolbox entry for the control is grayed out as well. Before you can run a program that uses the control, or drag the control from the toolbox, you'll need to close the design window that contains the control.

What happens if you have a program in design mode that uses your control and you open the control for modification? The main program goes gray. When you make your changes to the control, VB destroys the old copies of the control in a special way so that the control doesn't receive any termination events (or any events, for that matter). Then VB creates a new instance of the control to replace the destroyed copy.

One side effect of this is that sometimes you'll leave a debugging session only to enter a new one. Suppose you are running a program that uses a control and you put a breakpoint in one of the control's procedures. While running the program, you decide to make a change. You press the Stop button on the VB tool bar. However, you still can't make any changes to the program. You notice on the VB title bar that you are in a breakpoint mode. Did the Stop button fail to work? No. The Stop button worked fine. However, the design time environment manipulated your control in the form designer and triggered an event that fired the breakpoint. The answer? Disable the break point, or click on the Run button to allow the design environment to continue processing.

Other than these caveats, debugging an ActiveX control is much the same as debugging a VB program. Just use the **Add Project** command to put a regular program in with the control project and debug the programs together. Most of the controls on the accompanying disk already have companion debugging programs in their project files.

A Few Things To Think About

One important thing to consider is the licensing of controls that you use to build your controls. If you are only using the standard Microsoft-supplied controls, you'll have no problems. Otherwise, be careful. Most companies that sell controls sell them for you to use in your programs, not to sell to other programmers.

Think about it. If you spent six months writing a great word processor control, you might like to sell it to other developers. But what if one of those developers buys your control for $99, and makes a new control out of it? The only change is that the new control has a built-in toolbar above the text area. This developer decides to sell his new control. His changes took about two hours, so he charges $14.99 for the new control. Who will buy your control for $99 now?

Each vendor of controls will have its own rules about distributing controls. You may need a license key to use the control on a Web page or in another program. Be sure to check first.

What does this mean if you want to create a new control for your own use but you want to use a component from a third party? If the third party allows you to do it, no problem. Also, if the third-party control uses a license key, you won't have any problems (see Chapter 6). If the control doesn't use a key, and you are not allowed to distribute it to developers, you might consider setting the **UserControl** object's **Public** property to **False**. Then, only your control can use the component and you can distribute it as though you were shipping an ordinary program.

When you compile a public ActiveX control, you generate an OCX file (which is just a fancy DLL). Private controls reside in source files with CTL and CTX extensions. Once you create the finished project, those files are mixed with all your other source files and are not independently accessible.

If you move controls from machine to machine, don't forget that the OCX needs to register itself on each machine. This registration process adds entries to the system registry. Just run REGSVR32 from a command line and specify the path to the OCX control as an argument. Then the control is ready to run on the machine.

Summary

The basic steps required to create an ActiveX control with VB are quite simple. The Wizards make things even easier. However, there are a few subtleties you need to keep in mind. Also, there are things you should do to make life easier for people who use your control.

If you want to have the maximum influence on a component's appearance, you can paint the entire control. However, it is easier to use other components to build your control. These constituent components can supply properties, methods, and events for your control with just a few clicks of the mouse. This is largely thanks to the Wizards that simplify nearly every aspect of creating ActiveX controls.

ADVANCED CONTROLS 6

O! for a Muse of fire, that would ascend
The brightest heaven of invention!

— King Henry V

I invented the World Wide Web. Well, not really. But I might have, and a lot of other people might have, too. It's just that we didn't. Tim Berners-Lee did. Let me explain. Years ago (when DOS was king) my company created two products in response to demands from our clients. One was E-book, a hypertext document system. It allowed text formatting and hyperlinks between documents. Another product we sold in those days was FORMZ, a form processor. You could define fields and choices and submit the form to a script for processing. Gee, kind of sounds like a web browser doesn't it?

There were at least two things that prevented AWC from taking the world by storm: first, I didn't merge the products into one. Besides that, I never saw the utility of making E-book and FORMZ network-aware to the point that the documents and scripts could reside on a remote host. Stupid me. Of course, many other companies had similar products. Microsoft had WinHelp that they tried to convert into a multimedia authoring language. Again, not really network-aware (besides, the file format isn't very good for a networked implementation). There are countless others.

If you think about it, what was revolutionary about Tim Berners-Lee's invention? The technology? No, many people had been writing hypertext and similar programs for a long time. A breakthrough in data representation? No, HTML is really a form of SGML. Tim

135

Berners-Lee's web revolution was because of an idea. An idea to juxtapose two well-understood technologies: hypertext and networking. Amazing.

Many great ideas are just that simple: putting things together in a way no one has ever thought of before. Look at the Weed Eater. If it had a blade on it, anyone could have thought of it (and many people did). No one would think of fishing line as a high-tech innovation. Someone put them together and changed the way you cut your lawn.

Isaac Newton once said, "If I have seen further...it is by standing upon the shoulders of Giants." Sir Isaac would appreciate component software. Imagine if my E-book and FORMZ programs had been components. Maybe I'd have put them together. Perhaps I'd have added a networking component too. Even better, maybe one of my clients would have made the connection that I failed to make.

In this chapter, I'll show you how you can reuse existing ActiveX components to make entirely new ActiveX components with Visual Basic 5. Since I've been talking about Web browsers, I'll make one that you can drag and drop into any ActiveX container. Of course, I don't want to write all the code to parse HTML, encode form data, and render pictures. Instead, I'll stand on Microsoft's shoulders and use Internet Explorer's (IE's) Web browser control.

In the last chapter, you saw the fundamentals of constructing ActiveX controls. In this chapter, you'll see more advanced techniques, including using resources, licensing controls, enumerated types, and handling errors.

Why A New Control?

If IE provides a browser control, why should you write another one? Primarily because the IE control doesn't provide a user interface. Sometimes this is what you want—just a blank window full of HTML. Many times, however, you'd like to have a complete browser with controls and the other accouterments you expect on a browser. Besides, perhaps you'll merge the browser with some other innocuous component and get rich and famous!

If you read the ActiveX SDK documentation, you might think Microsoft has a way for you to use a full-featured browser already. That's not really true. The SDK talks about the two browser objects: InternetExplorer and WebBrowser. The InternetExplorer object has a full interface. It is also a complete running instance of IE. InternetExplorer isn't a control; it is an OLE automation interface that you can use to control a copy of IE.

The WebBrowser control is a proper component, but it lacks any user interface. If you want to see the difference, open up VB5 and start a standard EXE project. From the *Project* menu, select *Components*. Then on the *Controls* tab, select *Microsoft Internet Controls* and press *OK*. Notice the new icon on the tool palette? That is the WebBrowser control. For now, open the **Form_Load** event handler and add this code:

```
Private Sub Form_Load()
Dim wb As New InternetExplorer
wb.Visible = True
wb.Navigate "http://www.al-williams.com/awc"
End Sub
```

Go ahead and run the program. Not exactly the results you'd like, right? Now try dragging a WebBrowser control on your main form. Then replace the **Form_Load** event code with this:

```
Private Sub Form_Load()
WebBrowser1.Navigate "http://www.al-williams.com/awc"
End Sub
```

That's better (assuming you have a connection to the Internet active; otherwise, you might want to specify a local URL). The only problem is that there are no controls to operate the browser. Sure, you can drag buttons onto the form and use them to trigger methods in the WebBrowser control. However, I want a true component that has all the necessary controls ready to go.

Getting Started

The first step to creating a new control that encapsulates the WebBrowser control is to plan it! Figure 6.1 shows the general appearance I wanted for the control. Notice the graphical buttons—the component should encapsulate these and not use external files that the final developer will have to carry around.

For this control, I decided to expose several members of the WebBrowser and UserControl objects (see Table 6.1). The only unique member is **ShowStatus**, a flag that determines if the browser shows its status bar or not.

Armed with a plan, it is trivial to start a new ActiveX Control project. This causes VB to create a blank UserControl object. This object is similar to a form, but it is really an ActiveX control.

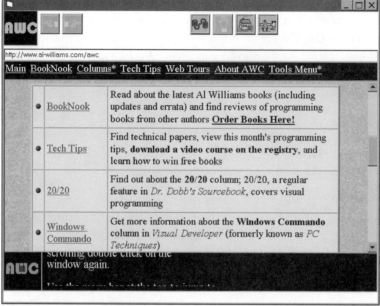

Figure 6.1   The finished control.

Table 6.1   Members of the browser control.

Member	Description	Handled By
BackColor	Background color	UserControl
ForeColor	Foreground color	UserControl
Enabled	Control responds?	UserControl
BackStyle	Background opaque?	UserControl
BorderStyle	Style of border	UserControl
Refresh	Redraw control	UserControl
GoSearch	Go to search page	WebBrowser
GoHome	Go to home page	WebBrowser
GoForward	Go to next history page	WebBrowser
GoBack	Go to previous history page	WebBrowser
LocationURL	Returns the current URL	WebBrowser
LocationName	Returns the current title	WebBrowser
Navigate	Move to a new URL	WebBrowser
ShowStatus	Show or hide status text	Internal
TitleChanged	Event fires when title changes	WebBrowser

You drag buttons, static text, and text boxes onto the UserControl just as you would any ordinary VB form. To get the WebBrowser control to appear, you'll have to add it using *Tools/Components* again (since this is a new project). The WebBrowser control may not draw correctly at design-time, but don't worry about it.

The browser needs to recalculate the layout of all the internal controls when the main control resizes. Therefore, you don't need to worry about the design-time layout (see Figure 6.2). After all the code is in place, the internal components will move to the correct places when the main control starts and every time it resizes, too.

Defining Members

Defining members in VB5 is simple. Simply use the ActiveX Interface Wizard to specify the members and connect them to the underlying components (see Figures 6.3, 6.4, and 6.5). In the case of the **ShowStatus** property, you'll need to manually define it, even though it corresponds closely to the **URL.Visible** property. You can do that on the final screen of the Wizard (see Figure 6.6).

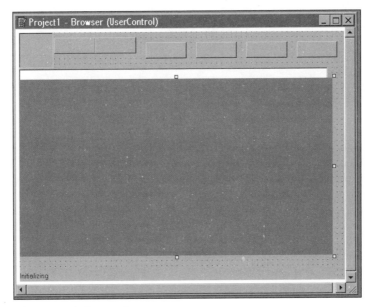

Figure 6.2 The control during design.

Figure 6.3 Assigning common members.

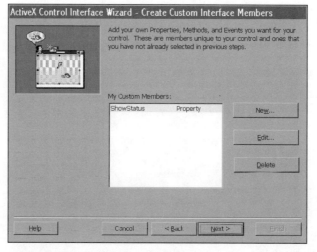

Figure 6.4 Creating custom members.

You would think that selecting default property names in the Wizard would cause the Wizard to assign the correct dispatch IDs for these properties. However, it doesn't. You'll need to go to the *Procedure Attributes* menu item (on the *Tools* menu), press the Advanced button, and change the *Procedure ID* field to match the names of the standard properties (see Figure 6.7). While you are at it, you can set the property categories, if you like.

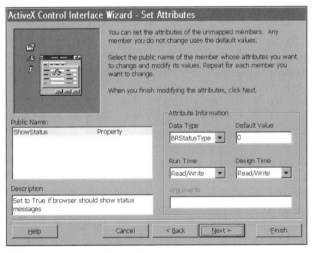

Figure 6.5 Connecting members.

Figure 6.6 Handling unconnected members.

Another annoyance is that the Wizard doesn't define certain members to be the correct type. Look at the properties for a form. Notice the **BorderStyle** property, in particular. It has six possible values (0-5). However, the property editor shows the values with descriptive tags (like **Sizable**, for example). It does this because VB defines an **Enum** for a special type used only with **BorderStyle**. However, the Wizard defines our **BorderStyle** property as an **Integer**. Therefore, the property editor doesn't show the descriptive tags for our **BorderStyle**.

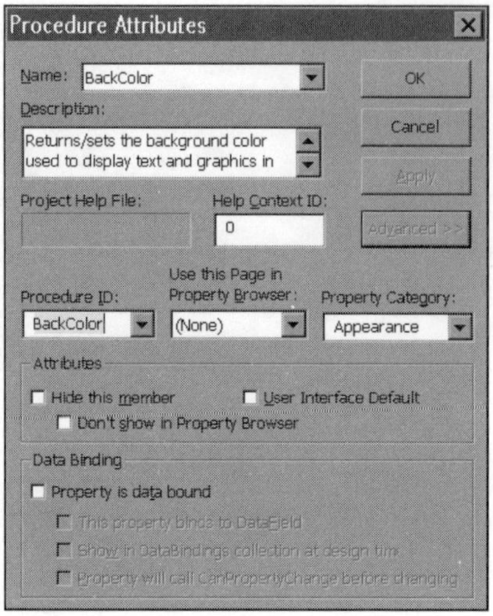

Figure 6.7   Setting procedure attributes.

I decided not to worry too much about this since I think the Wizard will work properly by the release of VB5. However, if you can find the name of the enumeration, just patch up the code to treat the property as the correct type. Most (but not all) of the types are visible in the object browser (look in the *View* menu). If you prefer, you can define your own enumeration. Look at the **ShowStatus** property in Listing 6.1 to see how that works. Here's the **Enum** for that property:

```
Enum BRStatusType
  brShowStatus = True
  brHideStatus = False
End Enum
```

Since the **ShowStatus** property uses the **BrStatusType**, the property browser works as you'd expect. For the ones that don't work right, the end programmer simply has to look up the numeric value in the help and plug it in directly. Remember, this is a beta copy of VB5, and I strongly suspect the release version won't have this problem.

LISTING 6.1   THE BROWSER COMPONENT.

```
VERSION 5.00
Object = "{EAB22AC0-30C1-11CF-A7EB-0000C05BAE0B}#1.0#0"; "SHDOCVW.DLL"
Begin VB.UserControl Browser
   ClientHeight   =   5748
   ClientLeft     =   0
```

```
ClientTop        =    0
ClientWidth      =    7740
PropertyPages    =    "browser.ctx":0000
ScaleHeight      =    101.388
ScaleMode        =    6   "Millimeter
ScaleWidth       =    136.525
Begin SHDocVwCtl.WebBrowser WebBrowser
   Height        =    4092
   Left          =    0
   TabIndex      =    1
   Top           =    1080
   Width         =    7452
   Object.Height        =    341
   Object.Width         =    621
   AutoSize      =    0
   ViewMode      =    1
   AutoSizePercentage=   0
   AutoArrange   =    -1   "True
   NoClientEdge  =    -1   "True
   AlignLeft     =    0    "False
End
Begin VB.CommandButton FwdCmd
   Height        =    372
   Left          =    1800
   Style         =    1   "Graphical
   TabIndex      =    9
   ToolTipText   =    "Go Forward"
   Top           =    120
   Width         =    972
End
Begin VB.CommandButton BackCmd
   Height        =    372
   Left          =    840
   Style         =    1   "Graphical
   TabIndex      =    8
   ToolTipText   =    "Go Back"
   Top           =    120
   Width         =    972
End
Begin VB.CommandButton SearchCmd
   Height        =    372
   Left          =    6600
   Style         =    1   "Graphical
   TabIndex      =    7
   ToolTipText   =    "Search"
   Top           =    240
   Width         =    972
End
```

```
Begin VB.CommandButton HomeCmd
    Height          =    372
    Left            =    5400
    Style           =    1    "Graphical
    TabIndex        =    6
    ToolTipText     =    "Return Home"
    Top             =    240
    Width           =    972
End
Begin VB.CommandButton StopCmd
    Enabled         =    0    "False
    Height          =    372
    Left            =    4200
    Style           =    1    "Graphical
    TabIndex        =    5
    ToolTipText     =    "Stop"
    Top             =    240
    Width           =    972
End
Begin VB.CommandButton RefreshCmd
    Height          =    372
    Left            =    3000
    Style           =    1    "Graphical
    TabIndex        =    4
    ToolTipText     =    "Refresh"
    Top             =    240
    Width           =    972
End
Begin VB.TextBox Url
    Height          =    288
    Left            =    0
    TabIndex        =    2
    Top             =    840
    Width           =    7332
End
Begin VB.PictureBox Logo
    AutoSize        =    -1    "True
    Height          =    816
    Left            =    0
    ScaleHeight     =    768
    ScaleWidth      =    768
    TabIndex        =    0
    Top             =    0
    Width           =    816
End
```

```
Begin VB.Label Status
      Caption         =    "Initializing"
      Height          =    252
      Left            =    0
      TabIndex        =    3
      Top             =    5520
      Width           =    7452
   End
End
Attribute VB_Name = "Browser"
Attribute VB_GlobalNameSpace = False
Attribute VB_Creatable = True
Attribute VB_PredeclaredId = False
Attribute VB_Exposed = True
Option Explicit
"Event Declarations:
Event TitleChange(ByVal Text As String)
"MappingInfo=WebBrowser,WebBrowser,-1,TitleChange
Enum BRStatusType
   brShowStatus = True
   brHideStatus = False
End Enum


Private Sub BackCmd_Click()
GoBack
End Sub

Private Sub FwdCmd_Click()
GoForward
End Sub

Private Sub HomeCmd_Click()
GoHome
End Sub

Private Sub RefreshCmd_Click()
On Error Resume Next
WebBrowser.Refresh
If Err.Number <> 0 Then Beep
End Sub

Private Sub SearchCmd_Click()
GoSearch
End Sub
```

```
Private Sub StopCmd_Click()
On Error Resume Next
WebBrowser.Stop
If Err.Number <> 0 Then Beep
End Sub


Private Sub Url_KeyPress(KeyAscii As Integer)
If KeyAscii = 13 Then
  On Error Resume Next
  WebBrowser.Navigate Url.Text
  If Err.Number <> 0 Then Beep
  KeyAscii = 0
End If
End Sub
Private Sub SetButton(b As CommandButton, n As Integer)
b.Picture = LoadResPicture(n, vbResBitmap)
b.Height = b.Picture.Height / 100
b.Width = b.Picture.Width / 100
End Sub


Private Sub UserControl_Initialize()
Logo.Picture = LoadResPicture(20, vbResBitmap)
SetButton HomeCmd, 10
SetButton StopCmd, 11
SetButton SearchCmd, 12
SetButton RefreshCmd, 13
SetButton BackCmd, 14
SetButton FwdCmd, 15


Url.Text = "http://www.al-williams.com/awc"
WebBrowser.Navigate Url.Text
End Sub
" When you resize, lots goes on
Private Sub UserControl_Resize()
Const offset = 1  " 1 mm margins
" Set Logo to top left corner
Logo.Top = 0
Logo.Left = 0
" Reposition everything relative to Logo
RefreshCmd.Top = offset
RefreshCmd.Left = ScaleWidth / 2
StopCmd.Top = offset
StopCmd.Left = RefreshCmd.Left + RefreshCmd.Width + offset
HomeCmd.Top = offset
HomeCmd.Left = StopCmd.Left + StopCmd.Width + offset
SearchCmd.Top = offset
SearchCmd.Left = HomeCmd.Left + HomeCmd.Width + offset
```

```
BackCmd.Top = offset
BackCmd.Left = Logo.Width + offset
FwdCmd.Top = offset
FwdCmd.Left = BackCmd.Left + BackCmd.Width + offset

Url.Top = Logo.Height + offset
Url.Left = 0
Url.Width = ScaleWidth
WebBrowser.Left = 0
WebBrowser.Top = Url.Height + Logo.Height + offset
WebBrowser.Width = ScaleWidth
WebBrowser.Height = ScaleHeight - WebBrowser.Top - Status.Height
Status.Left = 0
Status.Top = ScaleHeight - Status.Height
Status.Width = ScaleWidth
End Sub

Private Sub WebBrowser_CommandStateChange(ByVal Command _
  As Long, ByVal Enable As Boolean)
Select Case Command
  Case CSC_NAVIGATEFORWARD
    FwdCmd.Enabled = Enable

  Case CSC_NAVIGATEBACK
    BackCmd.Enabled = Enable
End Select
End Sub

Private Sub WebBrowser_DownloadBegin()
StopCmd.Enabled = True " Let user stop
End Sub

Private Sub WebBrowser_DownloadComplete()
" Reset logo and Disable stop button
Logo.Picture = LoadResPicture(20, vbResBitmap)
StopCmd.Enabled = False
End Sub

Private Sub WebBrowser_ProgressChange(ByVal Progress As _
  Long, ByVal ProgressMax As Long)
Static Logonum As Integer
" As progress is made, change logo image
Logonum = Logonum + 1
If Logonum = 3 Then Logonum = 0
Logo.Picture = LoadResPicture(20 + Logonum, vbResBitmap)
End Sub
```

```
Private Sub WebBrowser_StatusTextChange(ByVal Text As _
   String)
If Text <> "" Then Status.Caption = Text
End Sub
"WARNING! DO NOT REMOVE OR MODIFY THE FOLLOWING COMMENTED LINES!
"MappingInfo=UserControl,UserControl,-1,BackColor
Public Property Get BackColor() As OLE_COLOR
Attribute BackColor.VB_Description = "Returns/sets " & _
   "the background color used to display text and " & _
   "graphics in an object."
Attribute BackColor.VB_ProcData.VB_Invoke_Property = _
   ";Appearance"
Attribute BackColor.VB_UserMemId = -501
   BackColor = UserControl.BackColor
End Property


Public Property Let BackColor(ByVal New_BackColor As _
   OLE_COLOR)
   UserControl.BackColor() = New_BackColor
   PropertyChanged "BackColor"
End Property


"WARNING! DO NOT REMOVE OR MODIFY THE FOLLOWING COMMENTED LINES!
"MappingInfo=UserControl,UserControl,-1,ForeColor
Public Property Get ForeColor() As OLE_COLOR
Attribute ForeColor.VB_Description = "Returns/sets " & _
   "the foreground color used to display text and " & _
   "graphics in an object."
Attribute ForeColor.VB_ProcData.VB_Invoke_Property = _
   ";Appearance"
Attribute ForeColor.VB_UserMemId = -513
   ForeColor = UserControl.ForeColor
End Property


Public Property Let ForeColor(ByVal New_ForeColor As _
   OLE_COLOR)
   UserControl.ForeColor() = New_ForeColor
   PropertyChanged "ForeColor"
End Property


"WARNING! DO NOT REMOVE OR MODIFY THE FOLLOWING COMMENTED LINES!
"MappingInfo=UserControl,UserControl,-1,Enabled
Public Property Get Enabled() As Boolean
Attribute Enabled.VB_Description = "Returns/sets a " & _
   "value that determines whether an object can respond " & _
   "to user-generated events."
Attribute Enabled.VB_ProcData.VB_Invoke_Property = ";Behavior"
```

```
Attribute Enabled.VB_UserMemId = -514
    Enabled = UserControl.Enabled
End Property

Public Property Let Enabled(ByVal New_Enabled As Boolean)
    UserControl.Enabled() = New_Enabled
    PropertyChanged "Enabled"
End Property

"WARNING! DO NOT REMOVE OR MODIFY THE FOLLOWING COMMENTED LINES!
"MappingInfo=UserControl,UserControl,-1,BackStyle
Public Property Get BackStyle() As Integer
Attribute BackStyle.VB_Description = "Indicates whether a Label or the
background of a Shape is transparent or opaque."
Attribute BackStyle.VB_ProcData.VB_Invoke_Property = ";Appearance"
Attribute BackStyle.VB_UserMemId = -502
    BackStyle = UserControl.BackStyle
End Property

Public Property Let BackStyle(ByVal New_BackStyle As Integer)
    UserControl.BackStyle() = New_BackStyle
    PropertyChanged "BackStyle"
End Property

"WARNING! DO NOT REMOVE OR MODIFY THE FOLLOWING COMMENTED LINES!
"MappingInfo=UserControl,UserControl,-1,BorderStyle
Public Property Get BorderStyle() As Integer
Attribute BorderStyle.VB_Description = "Returns/sets " & _
  "the border style for an object."
Attribute BorderStyle.VB_ProcData.VB_Invoke_Property = _
  ";Appearance"
Attribute BorderStyle.VB_UserMemId = -504
    BorderStyle = UserControl.BorderStyle
End Property

"WARNING! DO NOT REMOVE OR MODIFY THE FOLLOWING COMMENTED LINES!
"MappingInfo=UserControl,UserControl,-1,Refresh
Public Sub Refresh()
Attribute Refresh.VB_Description = _
  "Forces a complete repaint of an object."
Attribute Refresh.VB_UserMemId = -550
    UserControl.Refresh
End Sub

"WARNING! DO NOT REMOVE OR MODIFY THE FOLLOWING COMMENTED LINES!
"MappingInfo=WebBrowser,WebBrowser,-1,GoSearch
Public Sub GoSearch()
```

```
Attribute GoSearch.VB_Description = "Go Search Page."
    On Error Resume Next
    WebBrowser.GoSearch
    If Err.Number <> 0 Then Beep
End Sub


"WARNING! DO NOT REMOVE OR MODIFY THE FOLLOWING COMMENTED LINES!
"MappingInfo=WebBrowser,WebBrowser,-1,GoHome
Public Sub GoHome()
Attribute GoHome.VB_Description = "Go home/start page."
    On Error Resume Next
    WebBrowser.GoHome
    If Err.Number <> 0 Then Beep
End Sub


"WARNING! DO NOT REMOVE OR MODIFY THE FOLLOWING COMMENTED LINES!
"MappingInfo=WebBrowser,WebBrowser,-1,GoForward
Public Sub GoForward()
Attribute GoForward.VB_Description = _
  "Navigates to the next item in the history list."
    On Error Resume Next
    WebBrowser.GoForward
    If Err.Number <> 0 Then Beep
End Sub


"WARNING! DO NOT REMOVE OR MODIFY THE FOLLOWING COMMENTED LINES!
"MappingInfo=WebBrowser,WebBrowser,-1,GoBack
Public Sub GoBack()
Attribute GoBack.VB_Description = _
  "Navigates to the previous item in the history list."
    On Error Resume Next
    WebBrowser.GoBack
    If Err.Number <> 0 Then Beep
End Sub


"WARNING! DO NOT REMOVE OR MODIFY THE FOLLOWING COMMENTED LINES!
"MappingInfo=WebBrowser,WebBrowser,-1,LocationURL
Public Property Get LocationURL() As String
Attribute LocationURL.VB_Description = _
  "Gets the full URL/path currently viewed."
    LocationURL = WebBrowser.LocationURL
End Property


"WARNING! DO NOT REMOVE OR MODIFY THE FOLLOWING COMMENTED LINES!
"MappingInfo=WebBrowser,WebBrowser,-1,LocationName
Public Property Get LocationName() As String
```

```
Attribute LocationName.VB_Description = _
  "Gets the short (UI-friendly) name of the " & _
  "URL/file currently viewed."
    LocationName = WebBrowser.LocationName
End Property


"WARNING! DO NOT REMOVE OR MODIFY THE FOLLOWING COMMENTED LINES!
"MappingInfo=WebBrowser,WebBrowser,-1,Navigate
Public Sub Navigate(Url As String, Optional Flags As _
  Variant, Optional TargetFrameName As Variant, _
  Optional PostData As Variant, Optional Headers _
  As Variant)
Attribute Navigate.VB_Description = _
  "Navigates to a URL or file."
    On Error Resume Next
    WebBrowser.Navigate Url, Flags, TargetFrameName, PostData, Headers
    If Err.Number <> 0 Then Beep
End Sub


Public Property Get ShowStatus() As BRStatusType
Attribute ShowStatus.VB_Description = _
  "Set to True if browser should show status messages"
Attribute ShowStatus.VB_ProcData.VB_Invoke_Property = _
  ";Appearance"
    ShowStatus = Status.Visible
End Property


Public Property Let ShowStatus(ByVal New_ShowStatus As _
  BRStatusType)
    Status.Visible = New_ShowStatus
    PropertyChanged "ShowStatus"
End Property


Private Sub WebBrowser_TitleChange(ByVal Text As String)
    RaiseEvent TitleChange(Text)
End Sub


"Initialize Properties for User Control
Private Sub UserControl_InitProperties()
    End Sub


"Load property values from storage
Private Sub UserControl_ReadProperties(PropBag As PropertyBag)

    UserControl.BackColor = PropBag.ReadProperty("BackColor", &H80000005)
    UserControl.ForeColor = PropBag.ReadProperty("ForeColor", &H80000008)
```

```
    UserControl.Enabled = PropBag.ReadProperty("Enabled", True)
    UserControl.BackStyle = PropBag.ReadProperty("BackStyle", 1)
    Status.Visible = PropBag.ReadProperty("ShowStatus", True)
End Sub

"Write property values to storage
Private Sub UserControl_WriteProperties(PropBag As PropertyBag)

    Call PropBag.WriteProperty("BackColor", UserControl.BackColor, _
        &H80000005)
    Call PropBag.WriteProperty("ForeColor", UserControl.ForeColor, _
        &H80000008)
    Call PropBag.WriteProperty("Enabled", UserControl.Enabled, True)
    Call PropBag.WriteProperty("BackStyle", UserControl.BackStyle, 1)
    Call PropBag.WriteProperty("ShowStatus", Status.Visible, True)
End Sub
```

Making It Work

Making the control work is perhaps the easiest part of the whole process. The buttons all correspond to simple methods in the WebBrowser control (see Table 6.2 and Listing 6.1). The only odd things to implement are the URL entry bar near the top, the logo that changes color to indicate progress, and the status bar. I'll show you how the logo works after we talk about resources. The other interface elements are trivial.

The URL bar examines keystrokes using the **Url_KeyPress** event handler. If the key is equal to 13 (the enter key), the code calls the **WebBrowser.Navigate** method, passing the contents of the URL bar. It also sets the key to 0 so that the control doesn't generate a beep to indicate that it doesn't know what to do with the key.

The status bar requires a bit more work. The WebBrowser control generates **StatusTextChange** events when it has updated status text. Sometimes this text is empty, so the event handler in the component ignores empty text. This always keeps the last message in the status bar, which is often useful. Otherwise, the code just copies the text passed with the event into the status bar's caption.

Using Resources

How can you handle the pictures used for the buttons and the progress logo? It would be a bad idea to require the component's users to have bitmap files. Instead, you want to build the bitmaps into the control. You can do this with resources.

Table 6.2   Available WebBrowser members.

Member	Type	Description
Application	Property	Returns automation object for containing application or WebBrowser
Busy	Property	True when browser is busy
Container	Property	Object containing browser, if any
Document	Property	Automation object of current document, if any
Height	Property	Height of control
Left	Property	Left side of control
LocationName	Property	Name of current location
LocationURL	Property	URL of current location
Parent	Property	Parent object (container or InternetExplorer object)
Top	Property	Top coordinate of control
TopLevelContainer	Property	True if this is the top container
Type	Property	Type of document displayed
Width	Property	Width of control
GoBack	Method	Go to previous location in history
GoForward	Method	Go to next location in history
GoHome	Method	Go to home page
GoSearch	Method	Go to search page
Navigate	Method	Go to a different URL
Refresh	Method	Refresh current URL
Refresh2	Method	Refresh current URL with caching options
Stop	Method	Stop current transfer
BeforeNavigate	Event	Fires before navigation occurs
CommandStateChange	Event	Indicates a change in the status of Forward/Back buttons
DownloadBegin	Event	Fires when downloading of document commences
DownloadComplete	Event	Fires when downloading is complete
FrameBeforeNavigate	Event	Fires before navigation to a frame occurs
FrameNavigateComplete	Event	Fires after navigation to a frame is complete
FrameNewWindow	Event	Fires when a new frame window is needed
NavigateComplete	Event	Fires when navigation is complete
NewWindow	Event	Fires when a new (non-frame) window is needed
ProgressChange	Event	Indicates progress of current download
StatusTextChange	Event	Fires when status text changes
TitleChange	Event	Fires when document title changes

Resources are nothing more than binary data attached to a program file (in this case, an ActiveX control in a DLL). Resources may be icons, bitmaps, dialog boxes, strings, or even user-defined data. In this case, you want to store bitmaps.

The first step to adding a resource is to build an RC file using a text editor. The RC file in this case is quite simple (see Listing 6.2). Each line defines a relationship between a number and an ordinary bitmap file. You'll use the number in your program to retrieve the picture as a Picture object.

Once you have the RC file completed, you have to run RC (a Microsoft program) to create a RES file. Just name the RC file on RC's command line. For example:

```
RC PICS.RC
```

This will create PICS.RES. The RES file contains a binary representation of the RC file and all of the data in each BMP file, as well. You add the RES file to your control project using *Add File* on the *Project* menu. Now your project contains the bitmaps (and any other resources mentioned in the RC file).

How do you access the pictures? Simple: use **LoadResPicture**. You'll need to pass it the number of the image and **vbResBitmap** to indicate that you want a bitmap. The **vbResBitmap** constant is necessary because it is possible to have an icon, for example, that uses the same number as a bitmap. This call returns a *Picture* object that you can use just like any other picture object. The code in Listing 6.1 loads all the pictures into the buttons (and the logo control) during the **UserControl_Initialize** event.

LISTING 6.2   THE RC FILE.

```
10 BITMAP home.bmp
11 BITMAP stop.bmp
12 BITMAP search.bmp
13 BITMAP refresh.bmp
14 BITMAP lhand.bmp
15 BITMAP rhand.bmp
20 BITMAP logor.bmp
21 BITMAP logog.bmp
22 BITMAP logob.bmp
```

There are many other kinds of resources you can add to an RC file (see Table 6.3). There are also many editors designed to permit you to create and edit RC files graphically. Practically every Windows C++ environment comes with such a tool. You can also find resource editors available as separate products.

Table 6.3 Types of resources.

Keyword	Meaning
Bitmap	Standard Windows bitmap
Cursor	Standard cursor
Font	Text font
Icon	Ordinary icon
StringTable	Collection of strings (useful when localizing programs for different languages)
VersionInfo	Information about the program's version and copyright (may be displayed by shell programs)
MessageTable	Special string table used for event log messages
RCData	Raw data
AniIcon	Animated icon
AniCursor	Animated cursor
Dialog	Dialog box template (usually not very useful with VB programs)
DialogEx	Extended dialog box (usually not very useful for VB)
Menu	Menu bars, popup menus, etc. (not often used with VB)
MenuEx	Extended menu (extra attributes for help IDs, etc.; rarely used with VB)
Accelerators	Keyboard shortcut table (usually not very useful for VB)

Of course, you only use **LoadResPicture** for icons, bitmaps, and cursor images (**vbResIcon**, **vbResBitmap**, and **vbResCursor**, respectively). Use **LoadResString** to read strings from your resources. You can also use **LoadResData** to load nearly anything from your resources to a byte array (see Table 6.4). Of course, it isn't very useful to load a bitmap as a byte array in most cases.

Notice that the code also resizes the buttons to match the size of the picture. Doing this requires a little understanding about the **Width** and **Height** parameters that different components support under VB. By default, forms and user controls always specify units in TWIPS (1/20 of a point or 1/1440 of an inch). Buttons and similar controls use whatever value their container uses. Pictures, however, are different. The Picture object's measurements are always in HIMETRIC units (Windows slang for 1/100 of a millimeter). Although you could convert HIMETRIC to TWIPS, it is easier to just change the user control to use millimeters. You can do this by changing the **ScaleMode** property on the user control itself. Then it is a simple matter to divide the Picture's HIMETRIC values by 100 to obtain millimeter measurements (remember, **Height** and **Width** don't have to be integers). You can find the code in the **SetButton** subroutine.

Table 6.4 Types used with LoadResData.

Setting	Description
1	Cursor
2	Bitmap
3	Icon
4	Menu
5	Dialog box
6	String
7	Font directory
8	Font
9	Accelerator table
10	User-defined resource
12	Group icon
14	Group cursor

This simple function reads the bitmap from the resources, and sets the button size to match (after scaling millimeters to HIMETRIC).

Another time the code uses **LoadResPicture** is when it creates the color-changing logo. When the WebBrowser control fires a **ProgressChange** event, the component loads a different color bitmap from the resources into the Logo control. When the **DownloadComplete** event occurs, it resets the logo back to its original state. The code also uses **DownloadComplete** (along with **DownloadBegin**) to disable (and enable) the **StopCmd** button.

More About Resources

Once you know how to include resources in your VB programs, you'll find many uses for them. For example, you can easily create conditional resources that contain different language strings:

```
STRINGTABLE
BEGIN
#if defined(ENGLISH)
  10 "Hello"
  11 "Goodbye"
#endif
#elif defined(SPANISH)
  10 "Hola"
  11 "Adios"
#endif
```

Assuming you have the above resource script, you can use -DENGLISH or -DSPANISH on the RC command line to select a language of your choice. Also, placing strings in the resource table makes it fairly simple to translate your strings into another language. Of course, you still may have problems with the size of fields, as well as other problems, but it is a good first step to making all your VB code usable in international markets.

By the way, for strings, you have to use a numeric ID. However, for other resources, you can use a string, if you prefer. However, using strings makes your resources a bit larger compared to those that use numbers.

For example, the browser's RC file (Listing 6.2) might look like this:

```
HomeBMP BITMAP home.bmp
StopBMP BITMAP stop.bmp
   .
   .
   .
```

Then you'd load the bitmap like this:

```
HomeCMD.Picture = LoadResPicture("HomeBMP",vbResBitMap)
```

Notice that you don't use quotes to surround the string in the RC file. C programmers often use **#define** statements to use an easy-to-read name for resources, while still keeping the efficiency of numbers. However, this doesn't work well for VB since VB doesn't understand **#define**. You can get a similar effect like this:

```
#define HomeBMP 10
HomeBMP BITMAP home.bmp
```

and:

```
const HomeBMP = 10
HomeCmd.Picture = LoadResPicture(HomeBMP,vbResBitMap)
```

This is somewhat inconvenient, however, since you have to keep the **#define** and **const** statements in sync.

Handling Errors

One important facet of creating a new control is properly handling errors. Just try something as an experiment. Find the **GoBack** method and comment out the **On Error Resume Next** statement. Then comment out the **Command StateChange** event handler. Next, run the sample program (included on line) and immediately press the back button. Not very pretty (see Figure 6.8) and certainly something an end user should never see.

The **On Error Resume Next** statement prevents the user from seeing the error dialog. Instead, your code has to check the Err object (unless you just want to ignore the error). If **Err.Number** is zero, no error occurred. By the way, Err is a global object. You don't need to create it or worry about it in any way. Just use it.

The Err object has several other members, but only the *Description* is usually useful in this context. The *Description* field, as you might guess, has the text that describes the error ready to display.

In many cases, you just want to ignore the error anyway. If you wanted to be a stickler for detail, you could note each error code you expect, and report only errors you don't expect. However, in this case, just beeping in every case is sufficient.

There is another way you can use **On Error** that you might prefer if you have a large procedure with many possible errors. However, it involves the use of the dreaded **GoTo** statement.

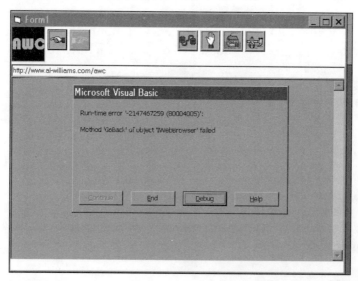

Figure 6.8 A runtime error.

Instead of writing:

```
On Error Resume Next
Some_Operation
If Err.Number <> 0 Then ...
Another_Operation
If Err.Number<> 0 Then ...
  . . .
End Sub
```

you can write:

```
On Error GoTo ErrHandle
Some_Operation
Another_Operation
Exit Sub
ErrHandle:
   " Put Error code here
End Sub
```

Of course, many people don't like to use **GoTo**. Use your own judgment, but VB will let you write **On Error GoTo** if you decide you like that method. If for some reason you want to turn the original error handling back on, use **On Error GoTo 0**. Of course, this will cause the ugly error dialog in Figure 6.8 to reappear if you encounter an error.

Distributing Components

You'll find an example program that uses the browser control in Listing 6.3. It is really nothing more than a form that contains the control and resizes it when the user resizes the form. Since I created both projects, I had no trouble using the control. However, if you distribute a control like this one, watch out for legal pitfalls. Of course, your control needs the Visual Basic runtime DLLs. However, in this case, it also needs Internet Explorer. You can just tell your users that they have to get a copy themselves. You can also arrange with Microsoft (or whatever vendor you've used) to distribute the software with your own. Oddly, you can easily get an arrangement with Microsoft to distribute IE, but not everyone will accommodate you.

You'll find more about using the VB Application Setup Wizard in Chapter 8. Meanwhile, just be aware that controls that use other ActiveX controls might need OCXs that you can't redistribute.

LISTING 6.3   USING THE COMPONENT.

```
VERSION 5.00
Object = "{9B0FF261-6FC8-11D0-A7B2-444553540000}#5.0#0"; "browser.ocx"
Begin VB.Form Form1
    ClientHeight    =   5628
    ClientLeft      =   48
    ClientTop       =   312
    ClientWidth     =   7992
    LinkTopic       =   "Form1"
    ScaleHeight     =   5628
    ScaleWidth      =   7992
    StartUpPosition =   3   "Windows Default
    Begin CBrowser.Browser Browser1
        Height      =   5652
        Left        =   120
        TabIndex    =   0
        Top         =   0
        Width       =   7812
        _ExtentX    =   13780
        _ExtentY    =   9970
        BackColor   =   16777215
        ForeColor   =   -2147483630
        ShowStatus  =   0   "False
    End
End
Attribute VB_Name = "Form1"
Attribute VB_GlobalNameSpace = False
Attribute VB_Creatable = False
Attribute VB_PredeclaredId = True
Attribute VB_Exposed = False
Option Explicit


" Resize browser to fill form
Private Sub Form_Resize()
Browser1.Left = 0
Browser1.Top = 0
Browser1.Width = ScaleWidth
Browser1.Height = ScaleHeight
End Sub

" Set Title
Private Sub Browser1_TitleChange(ByVal Text As String)
Form1.Caption = Text
End Sub
```

Licensing

Speaking of redistributing controls, what happens when you want to create a control and sell it to other programmers? You'd like to allow programmers to redistribute your control, but you don't want to simply give it away to other programmers.

Consider the following scenario: you create a reusable word processing component. You sell your component to other developers for $99.99. A programmer buys your control and uses it to make another control. The new control is identical to your original control except it displays the time of day in the status bar. If this time-conscious programmer sells your control to other programmers, what do you do? He hardly has any effort invested in it, so he can sell it for $29.99. It is just like your control (in fact, it has extra features), so who will pay you 100 bucks for yours?

Or suppose you write a spell checking control that you sell for $999. A major word processing vendor buys your control and uses it. A programmer buys the word processor ($49.95) and notices your control is doing the spell checking. What prevents the programmer from using your control?

Of course, you could require a fee for each copy distributed. However, programmers using your control in ordinary projects won't like that—especially if the fee is high. To prevent this problem, Microsoft allows you to provide a license key with your control. This license key takes the form of a special file with a .VBL extension. When you sell your control to a developer, you include a copy of the license key which gets installed on the developer's system registry. You grant the developer the right to redistribute your control, but not the license file or registry keys.

How does this work? When a developer uses a tool like Visual Basic, it reads information from the registry and passes it to the control. If the control doesn't recognize the special information, it refuses to create itself. When Visual Basic writes the control to an executable file, it also encodes the license information in the program. The program then uses the embedded license to create the control, bypassing the registry.

Suppose the program ships to another programmer. The programmer notices your control and decides to use it. When this programmer tries to create the control using VB, VB refuses because it can't find the license keys in the registry. However, the program, which has the license key embedded, still works fine.

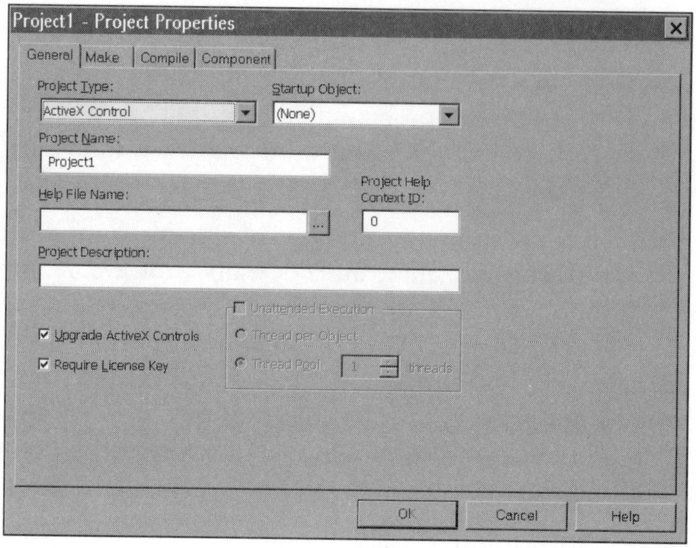

Figure 6.9 Using a license key.

So, how do you set all of this up? Easy. Simply check the **Require License Key** check box in the project options for the control (see Figure 6.9). That's all there is to it. VB will create a VBL file and make all necessary changes. In Chapter 8, you'll see how the installation program will install this file.

You might argue that this system isn't very secure. That's true. It isn't designed to foil anyone who really wants to steal your control. For example, if a licensed developer gives someone else your VBL file (or the registry entries it contains), they can use your control. Also, it isn't inconceivable that someone could reverse engineer a legitimate program and learn your license key. Then they could reconstruct the VBL file. However, anyone going to these extremes clearly knows they are doing something wrong and are opening themselves to legal liability.

Listing 6.4 shows a simple control that displays the current date and time. Just for practice, I checked the project option to require a license key. The control itself could hardly be simpler. A timer ticks every quarter of a second. The code uses **Now** to set a label's caption. That way, the label always contains the current time and date.

The only tricky part to the control is determining how big the label's font should be. Since the label fills the ActiveX control area, you don't want the defaultfont size. On the other hand, if you make the font large enough to fill the label vertically, it is probably too large to fit inside the label. As a compromise, I elected to set the font height to 1/50 of the total label's height. This isn't ideal in every case, but it works surprisingly well. Of course, it would be very little trouble to expose the font as a property for the programmer to set. You might want to try to add such a font property just for the practice.

If you install the control (run REGSVR32 on the TODCTL.OCX file), you'll be able to run the companion example program. However, you won't be able to add the control to VB and use it in any programs. To get that to work, you also need to copy the VBL file. Then run REGEDIT and import the VBL file. You can see the contents of the VBL file in Listing 6.5. Notice that it is just an ordinary REG file that REGEDIT normally imports and exports.

It is worth noting that VB only creates the VBL file when you actually make the OCX file (using the **Make** command on the *File* menu). During development, you won't see the VBL file unless you've made the OCX file at least once.

LISTING 6.4   A LICENSED CONTROL.

```
VERSION 5.00
Begin VB.UserControl TodControl
    ClientHeight    =    720
    ClientLeft      =    0
    ClientTop       =    0
    ClientWidth     =    3192
    PropertyPages   =    "todctrl.ctx":0000
    ScaleHeight     =    720
    ScaleWidth      =    3192
    Begin VB.Timer Timer1
        Interval        =    250
        Left            =    240
        Top             =    120
    End
    Begin VB.Label Tod
        Alignment       =    2    "Center
        BeginProperty Font
            Name            =    "Arial Black"
            Size            =    7.8
            Charset         =    0
            Weight          =    400
            Underline       =    0    "False
            Italic          =    0    "False
            Strikethrough   =    0    "False
        EndProperty
        Height          =    216
        Left            =    1776
        TabIndex        =    0
```

```
        Top             =    120
        Width           =     60
    End
End
Attribute VB_Name = "TodControl"
Attribute VB_GlobalNameSpace = False
Attribute VB_Creatable = True
Attribute VB_PredeclaredId = False
Attribute VB_Exposed = True
Option Explicit

Private Sub Timer1_Timer()
Tod.Caption = Now
End Sub

Private Sub UserControl_Resize()
Tod.Top = 0
Tod.Left = 0
Tod.Width = ScaleWidth
Tod.Height = ScaleHeight
Tod.Font.Size = ScaleHeight / 50
End Sub
```

LISTING 6.5   A VBL LICENSE KEY FILE.

```
REGEDIT
HKEY_CLASSES_ROOT\Licenses = Licensing: Copying the keys may be a
violation of established copyrights.
HKEY_CLASSES_ROOT\Licenses\417A13A2-7131-11D0-A7B2-444553540000 =
kghgnghnlgmginngohjglgngshvhjnmglgth
```

Other Changes

You might find it instructive to make a few changes to the browser control. One nice feature would be properties that set the pictures to use for each button. If the properties are empty you could use the original bitmaps. This would be a bit tricky for the logo since it is actually several bitmaps. You also might want to try exposing more of the **WebBrowser** events to allow the container more options when interacting with the browser.

Another interesting addition would be to make a more traditional progress bar. Currently, as a file downloads, the logo in the top left corner changes color. While that's flashy, it doesn't really tell you how much of the file is on your computer, and how much is still on the remote host.

More About The Web

While we're talking about the Web, it is worth pointing out that you don't need the entire WebBrowser control in many cases. Suppose you just want to read HTML files from inside a program. You don't need the overhead that **WebBrowser** carries to display ActiveX objects, manage links, and so forth.

Microsoft provides an ActiveX control that you can use, however, called the Microsoft Internet Transfer control. It can read Web pages (and their headers), submit data to Web servers (like a form submits data), and do FTP transactions. When the control submits data, it can use standard HTTP or a secure protocol (HTTPS).

If you want to use this control, you'll need to add the component to your project (it is in the MSINET.OCX file). Just select *Components* from the *Project* menu (or press Control+T). If you just want basic transfers, you'll find the control is very easy to use. If you need to submit data, or monitor the transfer's progress, you'll still find it relatively easy, but there is a bit more to do.

In the next chapter, you'll see an invisible control that uses the Internet transfer control. Until then, look at the program in Figure 6.10. It lets you enter a URL and see the resulting headers and raw data. This is often useful for debugging your HTML and HTML-related programs.

The Transfer Control

The transfer control offers you a vast array of properties, a few methods, and only one event. For many simple uses, you won't use the event, only one or two key methods.

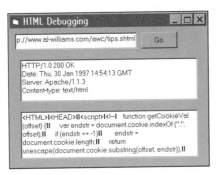

Figure 6.10 The HTMLDBG application.

Table 6.5 shows the members the control exposes to the outside world. If you only want to read a URL, you only really need **OpenURL**. This method takes a URL as an argument (you can also specify if you want the data returned as a string or as a byte array). The default is to return the data as a string. This call literally does all the work.

Many of the members you see in Table 6.5 aren't used very often. For example, **hInternet** is only useful if you plan to make WinInet calls directly. You usually don't want to specify if the control should connect directly or via a proxy, either.

Table 6.5 Internet Transfer Control members.

Member	Type	Description
AccessType	Property	Indicates whether Internet connection is direct or via a proxy
Document	Property	Sets the file name to be used with the Execute method
hInternet	Property	The underlying HINTERNET handle for the connection (used to directly call WININET functions only)
Password	Property	User's password for login, if any (see UserName)
Protocol	Property	Selects HTTP, HTTPS, or FTP protocol
Proxy	Property	Returns or sets the name of the proxy used to access the Internet (see also AccessType)
RemoteHost	Property	Selects remote host computer
RemotePort	Property	Selects port to connect to on host computer
RequestTimeout	Property	Sets timeout in seconds (0 means no timeout)
ResponseCode	Property	Error code (when state is icError; see Table 6.8)
ResponseInfo	Property	Description of error (when state is icError; see Table 6.8)
StillExecuting	Property	Boolean flag that is True while a transfer is in progress
URL	Property	Current URL; changing this property may change other properties (e.g., Protocols, RemoteHost, RemotePort, Document); changing other properties may affect URL, as well
UserName	Property	The user's name, if any (see Password)
Cancel	Method	Cancel current transaction
Execute	Method	Perform FTP command or HTTP Get/Post
GetChunk	Method	Retrieve data when state is icResponseReceived or icResponseCompleted (see Table 6.8)
GetHeader	Method	Get specific header or all headers
OpenURL	Method	Completely retrieves an HTTP document or FTP file
StateChanged	Event	Indicates a change in the download status (see Table 6.8)

Instead, you'll want it to use the default for the current system. Luckily, that is exactly what the control will do if you don't change the **AccessType** property.

Another oddity about some properties is their interrelationship with the **URL** property. In particular, the **Document, Protocol, RemoteHost,** and **RemotePort** properties change to match what you put in the **URL** property. Conversely, if you change those properties, the control alters the **URL** property. The **OpenURL** and **Execute** methods also change these properties. In practice, you won't really use the properties as much as you'll simply make calls to **OpenURL** and, perhaps, **Execute.**

You can access HTTP headers using the **GetHeader** method (see Table 6.6 for typical header values). If this method receives a header name as an argument, it returns the value of that header. If you don't pass any arguments, the function returns all the available headers. You can read the HTTP response code from the **ResponseCode** property (see Table 6.7).

For HTTP and anonymous FTP, you don't need to bother about the **User** and **Password** properties. However, if you want to connect to a host that requires you to log in, you may need these. When you don't specify a user name or password, the control will use anonymous FTP. Of course, you could also set up anonymous FTP by setting the **UserName** property to anonymous and the **Password** property to the user's email address.

If you want to execute FTP commands, or submit data to a Web server, you'll need to use the control's **Execute** method. You can actually use **Execute** instead of **OpenURL**. **Execute** can do everything **OpenURL** does, and then some. However, **Execute** is a bit trickier to use, so you'll only want to resort to it when you can't use **OpenURL**.

Table 6.6 Typical HTTP headers.

Header	Description
Date	Returns the time and date of the document's transmission. The format of the returned data is Wednesday, 27-April-98 19:34:15 GMT.
MIME-version	Returns the MIME protocol version (currently 1.00)
Server	Returns the name of the server
Content-length	Returns the length in bytes of the data
Content-type	Returns the MIME Content-type of the data
Last-modified	Returns the date and time of the document's last modification. The format of the returned data is Wednesday, 27-April-98 19:34:15 GMT.

Table 6.7   HTTP ResponseCodes.

Value	Keyword	Description
200	OK	Everything is OK
201	Created	Successful POST
202	Accepted	Request accepted, but not completed
203	Partial Information	Information returned may not be complete
204	No Response	Don't display any data; stay in current document
301	Moved	Requested document moved
302	Found	Document redirected
303	Method	Try alternate URL
304	Not Modified	Requested document has not changed
400	Bad Request	Improper client request
401	Unauthorized	Document protected
402	Payment Required	Client needs ChargeTo: header
403	Forbidden	No one can access this document
404	Not Found	Document not found
500	Internal Error	Server blew up
501	Not Implemented	Serve doesn't do this
502	Service Overloaded	Too busy to service request
503	Gateway Timeout	A gateway (e.g., CGI script) did not respond

The control's sole event, **StateChanged**, passes a number to your code to indicate what is happening (see Table 6.8). If you use **OpenURL**, you won't get many events since the component handles them internally. However, when you use **Execute**, you'll get enough events that you can track every step of the download process. The **icResponseReceived** indicates that some data is available, and you can read it with **GetChunk**. If you prefer to wait until all data is available, you can wait for the **icResponseComplete** code.

Most of the other members are either self-explanatory or obscure. If you are trying to write a really sophisticated application, you can control almost everything. You can even get the underlying handle that represents the Internet connection and use it, if you like.

You don't have to know how to connect to the Internet, look up host names, or any other obscure details, just like you don't have to know these things to use the **WebBrowser** control. Just drop the control on a form, call **OpenURL**, and you're loading data from the Internet. These kinds of controls really show off the power of ActiveX controls. Imagine if you had to write this from scratch.

Table 6.8 StateChanged constants.

Value	Numeric Value	Description
icNone	0	No state to report
icHostResolvingHost	1	The control is looking up the IP address of the specified host computer
icHostResolved	2	The control successfully found the IP address of the specified host computer
icConnecting	3	The control is connecting to the host computer
icConnected	4	The control successfully connected to the host computer
icRequesting	5	The control is sending a request to the host computer
icRequestSent	6	The control successfully sent the request
icReceivingResponse	7	The control is receiving a response from the host computer
icResponseReceived	8	The control successfully received a response from the host computer
icDisconnecting	9	The control is disconnecting from the host computer
icDisconnected	10	The control successfully disconnected from the host computer
icError	11	An error occurred in communicating with the host computer
icResponseCompleted	12	The request has been completed and all data has been received

An Example

Listing 6.6 shows a simple application (not an ActiveX control) that reads Internet data and displays it (see Figure 6.10). Simply enter a URL in the topmost edit control, and press the Go button. The Go button will dim until the control reads your data into the two multiline edit controls. The upper edit box shows the headers. The lower box shows the raw HTML (the funny looking characters are line breaks, by the way).

Listing 6.6 The HTML debugger.

```
VERSION 5.00
Object = "{48E59290-9880-11CF-9754- _
  00AA00C00908}#1.0#0"; "MSINET.OCX"
```

```
Begin VB.Form Form1
    Caption         =   "HTML Debugging"
    ClientHeight    =   3195
    ClientLeft      =   60
    ClientTop       =   345
    ClientWidth     =   4680
    LinkTopic       =   "Form1"
    ScaleHeight     =   3195
    ScaleWidth      =   4680
    StartUpPosition =   3   "Windows Default
    Begin VB.TextBox HTML
        Height          =   1095
        Left            =   240
        MultiLine       =   -1  "True
        TabIndex        =   3
        Top             =   1920
        Width           =   4215
    End
    Begin VB.TextBox Headers
        Height          =   975
        Left            =   240
        MultiLine       =   -1  "True
        TabIndex        =   2
        Top             =   720
        Width           =   4215
    End
    Begin VB.CommandButton Go
        Caption         =   "Go"
        Height          =   375
        Left            =   3120
        TabIndex        =   1
        Top             =   120
        Width           =   855
    End
    Begin VB.TextBox URL
        Height          =   375
        Left            =   120
        TabIndex        =   0
        Top             =   120
        Width           =   2895
    End
    Begin InetCtlsObjects.Inet Inet1
        Left            =   3960
        Top             =   120
        _ExtentX        =   1005
        _ExtentY        =   1005
    End
End
```

```
Attribute VB_Name = "Form1"
Attribute VB_GlobalNameSpace = False
Attribute VB_Creatable = False
Attribute VB_PredeclaredId = True
Attribute VB_Exposed = False
Private Sub Go_Click()
  Dim aURL As String
" Ignore errors
  "On Error Resume Next
  Go.Enabled = False
  aURL = URL.Text
  HTML.Text = Inet1.OpenURL(aURL)
  Headers.Text = Inet1.GetHeader
  Go.Enabled = True
End Sub
```

Here's something to think about: This control has a lot of extra functionality that you really don't need for this application. Also, the interface doesn't make good use of properties. Think about it. For simple applications, you'd like to just set the URL property, and the control would go to work. Once the transfer is complete, you'd like to read the HTML right out of a property. For headers, you could use a parameterized property. For example, I'd like to write something like this:

```
SimpleHTTP.URL="http://www.al-williams.com/awc"
HTML.Text=SimpleHTTP.HTML
nrBytes=SimpleHTTP.Header("Content-length")
```

It should be obvious that you could write a wrapper around this control, just like the one that wraps WebBrowser. However, there is a problem. Your new control would be visible. The original transfer control doesn't show up at run time.

You'll find the solution to this problem in the next chapter. In fact, you'll find the SimpleHTTP control wrapper there too. Of course, the standard transfer control is much more powerful, but you often don't need that much power.

Summary

OK, so I didn't invent the Web. I didn't even write a Web browser. Thanks to ActiveX and VB5, I can still pretend that I did. Simple components can combine to create fantastic creations. Just look at Tinkertoys or Unix shell programming. Even better, you can drop in really complex components (like the Internet Transfer Control) and build some amazing things with almost no effort.

The project in this chapter shows you some of the real world considerations you need to think about when distributing your controls: error handling, resource management, licensing, and—of course—the inevitable legal concerns. You'll find yourself worrying about these issues with every control you write for distribution.

7 Unusual Controls

The art of our necessities is strange,
That can make vile things precious.

—King Lear

've always enjoyed offbeat movies—in general, the stranger the better. Of course, unusual doesn't have to mean bad. *Dr. Strangelove* was unusual, and also a great movie. *Darkstar* was very unusual, and managed to be better than many movies of its genre that were trying to be normal movies. On the other hand, *Attack of the Killer Tomatoes* or *Plan Nine from Outer Space* were just strange. *Top Secret* (with an unknown Val Kilmer playing Nick Rivers) comes somewhere in between.

I've always wondered how you learn to make movies like that. Do you suppose that if you major in film at a major university they offer *Making B Movies?* Of course, some movies are accidentally offbeat (I think). Dino DeLaurentis's *Flash Gordon* comes to mind. A great comedy—except I don't think they meant it to be.

I suspect it might be more fun to make *Darkstar* or *Top Secret* than it is to make a serious movie. It is hard to imagine that the director of *Dr. Zhivago* had more fun than the director of *Dr. Strangelove.* In fact, you have to wonder if well-known directors don't occasionally sneak off to make offbeat movies under different names.

I can relate. I enjoy offbeat programming. I *like* programming device drivers in assembly. I enjoy writing programs that modify other programs at run time. There are few things better than writing compilers and interpreters. Once, to win a bet, I wrote a Basic compiler for the TRS-80 in Basic. Now that's weird.

Perhaps that's why I wanted a chapter on odd, offbeat controls. In the previous two chapters, you've learned how to write good old-fashioned visual components. But what about something strange? In this chapter, you'll see how to write invisible components, components that behave differently at different times, components that manipulate their containers, and components that can contain other components.

Will you ever need these oddball components? Maybe not. But if you do, it is good to know how to build them. Luckily, VB makes creating many kinds of odd components simple if you know how. Of course, as always, there are some pitfalls that you'll see on the way.

An Invisible Control

Think about the standard timer control. Could you build something similar? The problem with the timer control is that it is invisible. Or is it? You can see it on your form when you design your interface. That's good, because it is easy to select it to work with its properties and events. However, at run time, the control disappears. Even if it is on top of another control, it just vanishes.

Luckily, creating a control like this is quite simple. The key is to set the **InvisibleAtRuntime** property to **True**. Is that it? Practically. The only problem is, you still need to draw some visible representation for developers using the control at design time. Also, you'll often want to fix the control's size since it usually doesn't make sense to resize a control that will be invisible at run time.

Usually, the easiest way to make the control visible at design time is to add a picture box or an image control. Image controls use fewer resources, but it doesn't matter much since they won't have anything to do at run time anyway. You can also draw something directly on the surface of the control (some text, for example).

The hard part about this is making changes to the control itself. For example, suppose you want to alter the standard timer control. You place the timer component in your control, place a picture box on the control to hold a design-time image, and make the control's size that of a regular timer component. The problem is, both the timer and the picture box are the same size and they are sitting on top of each other. This is simply inconvenient since you can also directly select an object in the property browser window.

Adapting To Design Time

Occasionally, you'll want to have your control respond differently in design mode. For example, you might want to display some debugging information. Another example is design-time behavior. Have you noticed the controls in previous chapters all continue to work during design? The LEDBAR scans even on your form designer. The Web browser control loads its homepage (or tries to) the moment you drop it on a form. In some cases, it'd be nice to inhibit this sort of behavior.

You can easily do this by checking the **UserMode** property of the **Ambient** object. If this property is **True**, you are in a run-time environment, and should do what you normally do. If the value is **False**, you are in a design mode.

There is one thing you should be aware of, however. You can't examine this property (or any ambient property) during **Initialize**, which is where you would usually want to know the mode. However, you can read it practically anywhere else, including during **InitProperties** and **ReadProperties**.

You generally don't need to worry about the **UserMode** property for invisible controls, since the control is invisible and will prevent a picture box or image control from working. However, I like to set the picture's **Visible** property to **False** when **UserMode** is **False** just to document the behavior.

Another thing you may have noticed: when you use the interface Wizard to define properties, you can specify whether a property is available at design time and at run time. You can, for example, create a property that is read/write during design, but read-only at run time. You can do this only for custom properties (those you don't hook up to other controls).

Making Controls A Fixed Size

It isn't difficult to make controls a fixed size. Just write a **UserControl_Resize** event handler and add a single line of code. Suppose you want your control to be 720×720 TWIPS (1/2 inch both ways). You'd write this:

```
Private Sub UserControl_Resize()
Size 720, 720
End Sub
```

You'll always specify the size of the control in TWIPS (1/20 of a point or 1/1440th of an inch).

An Example: OneShot

In electronic design, a common component is a retriggerable one shot. This is a logic device that takes a binary input. When the input pulses (goes from zero to one to zero again), the one shot begins a countdown period. When the period expires, the one shot produces a pulse of its own. If the one shot sees a pulse before the timer runs down to zero, the one shot starts counting all over again.

One shots are useful in communication systems as missing pulse detectors, in timing circuits to ensure events occur in the appropriate sequence, and in many other applications.

VB doesn't have a control that models a one shot, but it does have the timer control, which almost fits the bill. A one shot component would need to be invisible, like the timer control.

The one shot control has one property, one method, and one event. The single property (**Interval**) sets the timeout period (in milliseconds). The method, **Start**, presents a single pulse to the input of the one shot. The **Timer** event fires one time for the last pulse received after counting off the **Interval**.

The code is quite simple (see Listing 7.1). There is a single timer control. The finished control exposes the timer's **Interval** property and **Timer** event directly. The timer begins in the disabled state. When the **Start** method occurs, the control disables the timer (which has no effect) and then enables it. If another **Start** call happens while the timer is running, disabling the timer will force it to restart.

The interface Wizard writes an event handler to transfer the timer's **Timer** control to the external **Timer** event. The procedure looks like this:

```
Private Sub Timer1_Timer()
  RaiseEvent Timer
End Sub
```

The one shot control makes one change to this procedure:

```
Private Sub Timer1_Timer()
    Timer1.Enabled = False ' clear one shot
    RaiseEvent Timer
End Sub
```

This makes certain that the event only fires once.

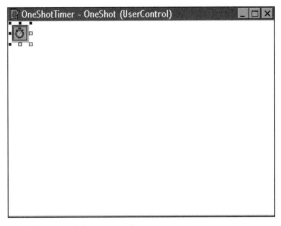

Figure 7.1 Designing the invisible control.

The control also incorporates a picture box for the sole purpose of displaying something at design time. Figure 7.1 shows the control as you'll see it while creating it. Notice all of the controls are on top of one another, making it difficult to work with. You may want to make the control bigger until it is debugged, and then set the size for the finished product. In either event, programmers using the control are unaffected.

LISTING 7.1 THE ONE SHOT.

```
VERSION 5.00
Begin VB.UserControl OneShot
   ClientHeight    =   408
   ClientLeft      =   0
   ClientTop       =   0
   ClientWidth     =   408
   InvisibleAtRuntime=   -1  'True
   PropertyPages   =   "OneShot.ctx":0000
   ScaleHeight     =   408
   ScaleWidth      =   408
   ToolboxBitmap   =   "OneShot.ctx":0004
   Begin VB.PictureBox Picture1
      AutoSize        =   -1  'True
      Height          =   384
      Left            =   0
      Picture         =   "OneShot.ctx":0316
      ScaleHeight     =   336
      ScaleWidth      =   348
      TabIndex        =   0
      Top             =   0
      Width           =   396
   End
```

```
    Begin VB.Timer Timer1
        Enabled         =   0      'False
        Left            =   0
        Top             =   0
    End
End
Attribute VB_Name = "OneShot"
Attribute VB_GlobalNameSpace = False
Attribute VB_Creatable = True
Attribute VB_PredeclaredId = False
Attribute VB_Exposed = True
Option Explicit
'Event Declarations:
Event Timer() 'MappingInfo=Timer1,Timer1,-1,Timer


'WARNING! DO NOT REMOVE OR MODIFY THE FOLLOWING COMMENTED LINES!
'MappingInfo=Timer1,Timer1,-1,Interval
Public Property Get Interval() As Long
Attribute Interval.VB_Description = "Returns/sets " & _
  "the number of milliseconds between calls to a Timer " & _
  "control's Timer event."
    Interval = Timer1.Interval
End Property

Public Property Let Interval(ByVal New_Interval As Long)
    Timer1.Interval() = New_Interval
    PropertyChanged "Interval"
End Property

Private Sub Timer1_Timer()
    Timer1.Enabled = False ' clear one shot
    RaiseEvent Timer
End Sub

Public Sub Start()
Attribute Start.VB_Description = "Starts (or restarts) the one shot"
    Timer1.Enabled = False
    Timer1.Enabled = True
End Sub

'Load property values from storage
Private Sub UserControl_ReadProperties(PropBag As PropertyBag)
    If Ambient.UserMode Then Picture1.Visible = False
    Timer1.Interval = PropBag.ReadProperty("Interval", 0)
End Sub
```

```
Private Sub UserControl_Resize()
Size 408, 408
End Sub

'Write property values to storage
Private Sub UserControl_WriteProperties(PropBag As PropertyBag)
    Call PropBag.WriteProperty("Interval", Timer1.Interval, 0)
End Sub
```

You'll find a simple example program in the project group. It counts the number of **Timer** events it receives from the one shot. A button on the form triggers the one shot by calling **Start**.

To see the one shot in action, press the command button and wait five seconds. Notice the count increases by one. Then press the button again but only wait one or two seconds. Press it again. Repeat this for a while. Notice that as long as you keep pressing the button, the count remains the same. When you quit pressing the button, five seconds will pass and the count will increase by one. If you don't press the button, nothing happens to the count.

Alternatives To Invisible Controls

Do you really need an invisible control? Maybe not. Remember ActiveX DLLs? These can often serve as invisible processing blocks and they have much less overhead compared to invisible controls.

Some invisible controls can be quite complex. Consider the case where you want to use a perceptron (a form of neural network) in a VB program. Sure, you could just write the perceptron code in your main program. However, it would be great if you could transform your perceptron into a reusable ActiveX component.

Perceptron Basics

A perceptron is a simple form of neural network. The perceptron takes a fixed number of inputs. These inputs are real numbers and represent the input's level or degree of confidence. The perceptron uses a matrix to transform the inputs to a fixed number of outputs. The output with the highest value is the output the perceptron assigns for that input pattern. The transform matrix has as many rows as there are inputs and a column for each possible output. To calculate an output value, multiply each input value by the corresponding row in the output column and sum the values (see Figure 7.2). Repeat this procedure for each output column.

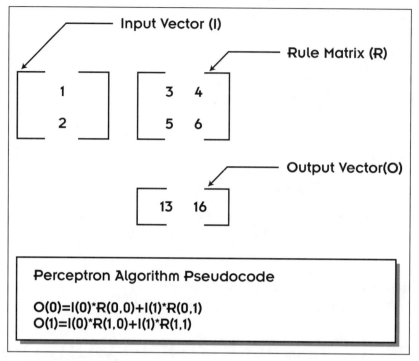

Figure 7.2 Perceptron basics.

If the matrix contains zeros or random values, you won't get the results you want from the perceptron. However, you can train the matrix to produce the results you want. The procedure is simple. Given a set of inputs, compare the perceptron's output with the desired output. If they are the same, you don't need to take any action. If they are different, you subtract the inputs from the column in the matrix that corresponds to the wrong result and add the inputs to the correct result's column. Eventually, the matrix will converge on the proper values.

Perceptrons have several limitations, but they are appropriate for many simple pattern-matching tasks. In particular, the perceptron can't solve problems unless they are linearly separable. That is to say, if each input value is a dimension in an n-dimensional space, you must be able to draw hyperplanes that separate all the output values. For example, a two-input and gate are linearly separable; a two-input XOR gate is not (see Figure 7.3).

Writing The Class

The **Discriminate** class isn't very complex (see Listing 7.2). It contains two arrays of unspecified dimensions: **in_ary**() holds the input pattern and **Rules**()

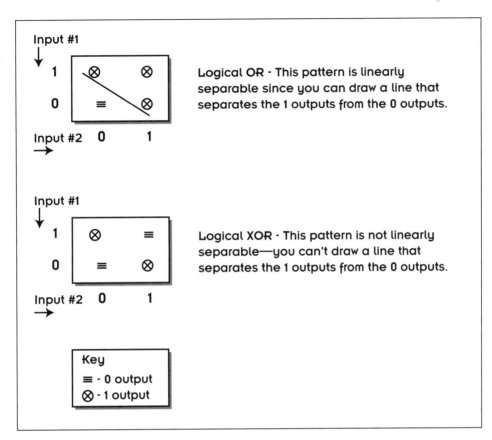

Figure 7.3   Linear separability.

holds the perceptron vector. The **Setup** subroutine takes two parameters: the number of possible results and the number of inputs. **Setup** redimensions the two arrays and sets the **maxx** and **maxy** parameters.

LISTING 7.2   THE DISCRIMINATOR CLASS.

```
VERSION 1.0 CLASS
BEGIN
  MultiUse = -1  'True
END
Attribute VB_Name = "Discriminate"
Attribute VB_GlobalNameSpace = False
Attribute VB_Creatable = True
Attribute VB_PredeclaredId = False
Attribute VB_Exposed = True
Private in_ary() As Single
Private Rules() As Single
Private maxx, maxy As Integer
```

```
Property Get Calc() As Integer
ReDim Res(maxx) As Single
For x = 0 To maxx
For y = 0 To maxy
  Res(x) = Res(x) + in_ary(y) * Rules(x, y)
Next y
Next x
Max = -3.4E+38
maxi = -1
For x = 0 To maxx
  If Res(x) >= Max Then Max = Res(x): maxi = x
Next x
Calc = maxi
End Property

Sub Setup(x As Integer, y As Integer)
maxx = x - 1
maxy = y - 1
ReDim in_ary(maxy)
ReDim Rules(maxx, maxy)
End Sub

Sub Load(fn As String)
On Error Resume Next
Open fn For Input As #1
If Err <> 0 Then
 MsgBox "Can't open file", vbOKOnly, "Warning"
 Err.Clear
Else
 Input #1, maxx
 Input #1, maxy
 Setup maxx + 1, maxy + 1
 For y = 0 To maxy
 For x = 0 To maxx
  Input #1, Rules(x, y)
 Next x
 Next y
 Close 1
End If
End Sub

Sub Save(fn As String)
Open fn For Output As 1
Write #1, maxx
Write #1, maxy
For y = 0 To maxy
```

```
For x = 0 To maxx
  Write #1, Rules(x, y)
Next x
Next y
Close 1
End Sub

Sub Train(n As Integer)
Dim r As Integer
Dim y As Integer
r = Calc()
If r <> n Then
  For y = 0 To maxy
    Rules(r, y) = Rules(r, y) - in_ary(y)
    Rules(n, y) = Rules(n, y) + in_ary(y)
  Next y
End If
End Sub

Property Get Value(n As Integer) As Single
  Value = in_ary(n)
End Property


Property Let Value(n As Integer, val As Single)
in_ary(n) = val
End Property
```

The class exposes a **Value** property that you use to fill the **in_ary**. This is an example of an array property—you can pass any number of parameters of any type to the **Property Get** routine. Then the **Property Let** routine takes the same parameters plus one extra parameter that specifies the value. Since the arguments can be of any time, you can easily create pseudo-arrays that take non-integer indices. The class also exposes a read-only property, **Calc**, that computes the result based on the current input pattern. This routine implements the simple logic required to multiply the input array by each column of the rule matrix and score the results. The return value is an integer (starting with 0) that indicates which column scored highest.

Rounding out the class are the **Train**, **Load**, and **Save** subroutines. **Train** compares its single argument to the current **Calc** property. If the values are not equal, the routine performs the training algorithm described above. The **Load** and **Save** routines read and write a disk file that contains the rule matrix.

By itself, this class isn't particularly useful. However, it is quite general-purpose. By avoiding any specific knowledge of a particular problem, the discriminator class is useful in many programs. Using Visual Basic's dynamic memory allocation (the **ReDim** statement) allows the class to handle any size problem without waste.

Representing The Game

There are several ways you might represent a Tic Tac Toe game using a perceptron. Usually, when you select a representation, the input represents the "strength" of the input. For example, a signal processor might use values from 0-255 to represent signal strength. A medical diagnostic program might use values from -1000 to 1000 to represent the certainty of a symptom. In this case, -1000 means the symptom is not present, 1000 means the symptom is present, and values in between signify various levels of uncertainty. Then, 0 means you don't know if the patient has the symptom. This is important, since multiplying by 0 results in another 0. You shouldn't use 0 as a meaningful value in the input vector.

For Tic Tac Toe, I elected to use 18 input values. The first nine are set to 1 if the corresponding square contains an X. The last nine are set to 1 if the corresponding square contains an O. The program knows what is in each square so each value is always 1 or 0. There are nine possible outputs—one for each square on the board. Given a particular input pattern, the discriminator should select the best move as an output.

The Training Programs

The problem with perceptrons and neural networks is that you have to train them. This can be a tedious process. Training for a particular case is easy, but training for the next case may upset the original training. Then retraining that case may upset the second one. Eventually, the rule matrix will converge on stable values, but this can take some time, especially with many training cases.

To make training more manageable, I decided to always allow the computer to go first. It always moves to the same square. You could change this, but if you do, it makes for more training. To further simplify training, I assume the opponent will always make a good move. With this strategy, if you make crazy random moves, you can beat the computer. You could train for all of these cases, but again, it is more time consuming.

In Listing 7.3, you'll find a program that allows you to interactively train the rule matrix. While this is fun, you'll probably lose patience before the matrix converges. Instead, you'll want to use the batch training program (see Listing 7.4). This program takes a simple ASCII file that specifies the possible board positions and the correct response for each. The batch training program checks each case, calling the discriminator's **Train** subroutine as needed. The program tries the cases over and over until it can run through the entire file without any training. Then it writes the rule matrix out to RULEBASE.DAT.

LISTING 7.3   THE INTERACTIVE TRAINER.

```
VERSION 5.00
Object = "{A8B3B723-0B5A-101B-B22E-00AA0037B2FC}#1.0#0"; "GRID32.OCX"
Begin VB.Form Form1
   Caption         =   "Tic Tac Toe Trainer"
   ClientHeight    =   5292
   ClientLeft      =   300
   ClientTop       =   1980
   ClientWidth     =   9288
   LinkTopic       =   "Form1"
   PaletteMode     =   1  'UseZOrder
   ScaleHeight     =   5292
   ScaleWidth      =   9288
   Begin VB.CheckBox TrainOn
      Caption      =   "Train next move"
      Height       =   495
      Left         =   240
      TabIndex     =   4
      Top          =   120
      Width        =   1695
   End
   Begin VB.CommandButton ResetCmd
      Caption      =   "Reset Board"
      Height       =   375
      Left         =   3240
      TabIndex     =   3
      Top          =   120
      Width        =   2775
   End
   Begin VB.CommandButton SaveButton
      Caption      =   "Save"
      Height       =   495
      Left         =   3600
      TabIndex     =   1
      Top          =   4560
      Width        =   1815
   End
```

```
Begin MSGrid.Grid Grid1
    Height          =    3615
    Left            =    240
    TabIndex        =    0
    Top             =    720
    Width           =    8775
    _Version        =    65536
    _ExtentX        =    15478
    _ExtentY        =    6376
    _StockProps     =    77
    BackColor       =    16777215
    BeginProperty Font {0BE35203-8F91-11CE-9DE3-00AA004BB851}
        Name            =    "Arial"
        Size            =    48.04
        Charset         =    0
        Weight          =    700
        Underline       =    0        'False
        Italic          =    0        'False
        Strikethrough   =    0        'False
    EndProperty
    Rows            =    3
    Cols            =    3
    FixedRows       =    0
    FixedCols       =    0
    ScrollBars      =    0
    HighLight       =    0         'False
End
Begin VB.Label Label1
    Caption         =    "Next X move:"
    Height          =    255
    Left            =    240
    TabIndex        =    5
    Top             =    4440
    Width           =    1215
End
Begin VB.Label playdisp
    Height          =    375
    Left            =    1680
    TabIndex        =    2
    Top             =    4560
    Width           =    1335
End
End
Attribute VB_Name = "Form1"
Attribute VB_GlobalNameSpace = False
Attribute VB_Creatable = False
Attribute VB_PredeclaredId = True
```

```
Attribute VB_Exposed = False
Dim rulebase As New Percep.Discriminate
Dim NextPlay As String
Dim XorO As String
Dim play, pctr, right As Integer

Sub Reset()
 Dim y As Integer
 For y = 0 To 8
   Grid1.Row = y Mod 3
   Grid1.Col = Fix(y / 3)
   Grid1.Text = ""
 Next y
 pctr = 0
XorO = "X"
   Grid1.Row = 0
   Grid1.Col = 0
   Grid1.Text = "X"
   pctr = 1
   playdisp.Caption = ""
End Sub

Private Sub Form_Load()
rulebase.Setup 9, 18
rulebase.Load "RULEBASE.DAT"
right = 0
play = 0
XorO = "X"
Reset
End Sub

Private Sub Grid1_Click()
Dim xy As Integer, i As Integer
If Grid1.Text = "" Then
  If (pctr Mod 2) = 1 Then
    Grid1.Text = "O"
  End If
  Row = Grid1.Row
  Col = Grid1.Col
  For i = 0 To 8
    Grid1.Row = i Mod 3
    Grid1.Col = Fix(i / 3)
    rulebase.Value(i) = -1
    rulebase.Value(i + 9) = -1
    If Grid1.Text = "X" Then rulebase.Value(i) = 1
    If Grid1.Text = "O" Then rulebase.Value(i + 9) = 1
```

```
    Next i
    n = rulebase.Calc
    If (pctr Mod 2) = 0 Then
      n1 = Col * 3 + Row
      If (n <> n1) And (pctr > 1) And (TrainOn.Value = 1) Then
rulebase.Train (n1)
      Grid1.Row = Row
      Grid1.Col = Col
      Grid1.Text = "X"
      playdisp.Caption = ""
    Else
      playdisp.Caption = "(" + Str(Fix(n / 3) + 1) + "," +_
      Str$((n Mod 3) + 1) + ")"
    End If


    pctr = pctr + 1
End If
End Sub


Private Sub ResetCmd_Click()
Reset
End Sub


Private Sub SaveButton_Click()
rulebase.Save ("RULEBASE.DAT")
End Sub
```

LISTING 7.4   THE BATCH TRAINER.

```
Attribute VB_Name = "Module1"


Dim Rulebase As New Percep.Discriminate
Sub main()
Dim i As Integer
Dim d As String
Dim Train As Integer
Dim n As Integer
Dim n1 As Integer
MsgBox "Begin Training"
' Create rulebase
Rulebase.Setup 9, 18
' This flag will equal 0 when all cases
' are successful
Train = 1
Do While Train = 1
 Train = 0
```

```
Open "Train" For Input As 1
Do While Not EOF(1)
  Input #1, d
  ' Ignore comments
  If Left(d, 1) <> ";" Then
   For i = 0 To 17
     If Mid(d, i + 1, 1) = " " Then
     Rulebase.Value(i) = -1
     Else Rulebase.Value(i) = 1
   Next i
   n = Val(Mid(d, 19, 1))
   n1 = Rulebase.Calc
  ' If not right, train and set Train flag
   If (n <> n1) Then
     Rulebase.Train n
     Train = 1
   End If
  End If
 Loop
Close 1

Loop
Rem training complete!
MsgBox "Training complete"
Rulebase.Save "RULEBASE.DAT"
End Sub
```

The important thing to notice here is that the logic for both of these programs is in the discriminator component. Each program shares this single ActiveX component. You don't need an entire visual component in this case, because there are no user interface elements associated with the reusable code.

The Main Program

The main program (TICTAC.BAS, in Listing 7.5) also uses the exact same discriminator class. The user interface is simplistic (see Figure 7.4). It uses a grid control as the Tic Tac Toe board. The program first reads the rule matrix from RULEBASE.DAT file (if present). Then it begins playing. When you click on an empty square, the program places an O in the space. It then calls the **Win** function to see if you won the game. If the game is still going, it uses the discriminator to compute the next move. In case the training is bad, the program makes sure that the proposed square is empty. If it isn't empty, the program just searches for the next available square. When TICTAC finds an empty square, it places an X and checks for a win again.

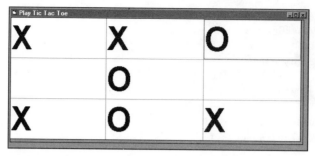

Figure 7.4 Tic Tac Toe in action.

The only other logic in the TICTAC program is a routine to reset the board. The game playing logic is all in the rule matrix. You can certainly improve the user interface, but that isn't the point. The point is that the discriminator learns to play Tic Tac Toe without any traditional programming.

LISTING 7.5 THE MAIN GAME PROGRAM.

```
VERSION 5.00
Object = "{A8B3B723-0B5A-101B-B22E-00AA0037B2FC}#1.0#0"; "GRID32.OCX"
Begin VB.Form Form1
    Caption         =   "Play Tic Tac Toe"
    ClientHeight    =   3732
    ClientLeft      =   240
    ClientTop       =   1488
    ClientWidth     =   8868
    LinkTopic       =   "Form1"
    PaletteMode     =   1   'UseZOrder
    ScaleHeight     =   3732
    ScaleWidth      =   8868
    Begin MSGrid.Grid Grid1
        Height      =   3615
        Left        =   0
        TabIndex    =   0
        Top         =   0
        Width       =   8775
        _Version    =   65536
        _ExtentX    =   15478
        _ExtentY    =   6376
        _StockProps =   77
        BackColor   =   16777215
        BeginProperty Font {0BE35203-8F91-11CE-9DE3-00AA004BB851}
            Name    =   "Arial"
            Size    =   48
            Charset =   0
```

```
          Weight         =    700
          Underline      =    0    'False
          Italic         =    0    'False
          Strikethrough  =    0    'False
       EndProperty
       Rows        =    3
       Cols        =    3
       FixedRows   =    0
       FixedCols   =    0
       ScrollBars  =    0
       HighLight   =    0    'False
    End
End
Attribute VB_Name = "Form1"
Attribute VB_GlobalNameSpace = False
Attribute VB_Creatable = False
Attribute VB_PredeclaredId = True
Attribute VB_Exposed = False
' Rule matrix
Dim rulebase As New Percep.Discriminate
' Cell Types
Dim NextPlay
Dim XorO
'Play Counter
Dim pctr As Integer

'Reset board
Sub Reset()
  For y = 0 To 8
    Grid1.Row = y Mod 3
    Grid1.Col = Fix(y / 3)
    Grid1.Text = ""
  Next y
  pctr = 0
  XorO = "X"   ' This version always plays X
  Grid1.Row = 0
  Grid1.Col = 0
  Grid1.Text = "X"
  pctr = 1
End Sub


'Check for a win or draw
Function Win()
  Dim c(2) As String
  Win = 0
  For x = 0 To 2
```

```
    Grid1.Col = x
    For y = 0 To 2
      Grid1.Row = y
       c(y) = Grid1.Text
    Next y
  If c(0) <> "" And c(0) = c(1) And c(1) = c(2) Then
    Win = -1
    Exit Function
  End If
  Next x
  For y = 0 To 2
    Grid1.Row = y
    For x = 0 To 2
      Grid1.Col = x
       c(x) = Grid1.Text
    Next x
  If c(0) <> "" And c(0) = c(1) And c(1) = c(2) Then
    Win = -1
    Exit Function
  End If
  Next y
  Grid1.Row = 1
  Grid1.Col = 1
  c(0) = Grid1.Text
  Grid1.Row = 0
  Grid1.Col = 0
  c(1) = Grid1.Text
  Grid1.Row = 2
  Grid1.Col = 2
  c(2) = Grid1.Text
  If c(0) <> "" And c(0) = c(1) And c(1) = c(2) Then
    Win = -1
    Exit Function
  End If
  Grid1.Row = 2
  Grid1.Col = 0
  c(1) = Grid1.Text
  Grid1.Row = 0
  Grid1.Col = 2
  c(2) = Grid1.Text
  If c(0) <> "" And c(0) = c(1) And c(1) = c(2) Then
    Win = -1
    Exit Function
  End If

End Function
```

```
'Create a new rulebase and read in file
Private Sub Form_Load()
rulebase.Setup 9, 18
rulebase.Load "RULEBASE.DAT"

Reset

End Sub

'Player clicked on a square
Private Sub Grid1_Click()
Dim xy As Integer, i As Integer
If Grid1.Text = "" Then ' Can't move to full sq
   NextPlay = "0"
   Grid1.Text = NextPlay
  Rem check for win
  If Win() Then
    MsgBox "You Win!"
    Reset
    Exit Sub
    End
  End If

  Rem set up state for our move
  For i = 0 To 8
    Grid1.Row = i Mod 3
    Grid1.Col = Fix(i / 3)
    rulebase.Value(i) = -1
    rulebase.Value(i + 9) = -1
    If Grid1.Text = Xor0 Then rulebase.Value(i) = 1
    If Grid1.Text = NextPlay Then rulebase.Value(i + 9) = 1
  Next i
  n = rulebase.Calc
  Rem check n for legal move
  Do
   Grid1.Row = n Mod 3
   Grid1.Col = Fix(n / 3)
   If Grid1.Text <> "" Then
     Rem try again
     n = n + 1
     If n = 9 Then n = 0
    End If
  Loop While Grid1.Text <> ""
  Grid1.Text = Xor0
  pctr = pctr + 2
  Rem check for win
  If Win() Then
```

```
    MsgBox "I Win!"
    Reset
    Exit Sub
  End If
  If pctr = 9 Then
    MsgBox "Draw Game!"
    Reset
    Exit Sub
  End If
 End If
End Sub
```

Training Tips

The RULEBASE.DAT file included on the CD-ROM plays a good game if you make sensible moves. However, you could train the game to play better or even just differently, if you like. If you use the manual training program, be sure to have a consistent plan. For any given board configuration, you should train the same response. Otherwise, the matrix may never converge. Also, be sure to test as many cases as possible. Remember, just because a case worked once doesn't mean it will work after further training.

The manual training program is entertaining. You play both X and O in the trainer. The computer guesses your X moves and displays its forecast. If you move to a different square (and there is a check in the training button), the program trains using the move you make. There is no win detection—you'll press the reset button when you want to restart the game. When you press the save button, the trainer writes the updated rule matrix to a file. It is interesting to watch the program project your moves. However, you may tire of waiting for the matrix to converge.

If you want to create your own batch input data file, just place each case on a single line. The first 18 spaces of the line correspond to the 18 elements of the pattern input. A space in a slot sets the corresponding pattern input to 0. Any other character sets the input to 1. The 19th character is a single digit from 0 to 8 that specifies the desired output for the pattern. Figure 7.5 shows how the positions relate to the Tic Tac Toe board.

Another Place For Invisible Controls

If you are using Microsoft's IIS 3.0 (Internet Information Server) as a Web server, you can create ActiveX components from within Active Server Page

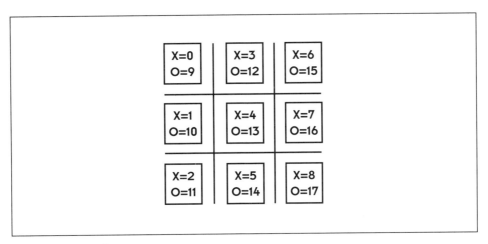

Figure 7.5 Board positions.

(ASP) files. These files use Visual Basic Script to create HTML. The server has many predefined ActiveX components that you can use to connect to databases, rotate advertisements, and perform other tasks that would be difficult or impossible using only VB Script. What happens if you would like a component that Microsoft doesn't supply?

You'll see in a later chapter that you can create your own components for use with ASP, but since they run on the server, they must be invisible. Any output would show up on the Web server, not the client machine. Again, ActiveX DLLs are usually the best way to make these invisible controls.

VB Meets C++: ISAPI With VB

If you want to create active Web pages, the traditional answer is to write a CGI program. A CGI program can accept input (from a form or URL) and send output to a web browser. For example, a CGI program might accept your name and email address, look up your account in a database, and display your current bill.

If you use Microsoft's IIS server, you can write CGI programs, but there is another way: ISAPI. An ISAPI DLL actually becomes part of the server and is generally more efficient than a classic CGI program. I've written ISAPI DLLs in C and using MFC. Neither way is that difficult. Recently, a friend of mine called me and asked if he could write ISAPI extensions in VB. My first answer was no, because VB can't make traditional DLLs (only ActiveX DLLs).

I fired up a Web search engine, looked around, and found that Microsoft has a sample, OLEISAPI that allows VB ISAPI. However, judging from the traffic on the Web, it didn't work well. Sure enough, after trying to make it work for two days, we gave up. Besides, OLEISAPI didn't encapsulate ISAPI in an object-oriented way. One of the advantages to ActiveX is OOP. It also didn't allow you to fully access ISAPI features. A few days later, I finished CBISAPI, an ISAPI module that allows you to write ActiveX ISAPI extensions. Although I wrote it with VB5 in mind, you can use it with any ActiveX-capable language.

The Plan

My idea was simple: Write an ISAPI extension DLL that calls an ActiveX server. The DLL passes the server an ActiveX object that it uses to read the HTTP information and manipulate the HTTP output (usually an HTML file). This is a bit odd: the DLL is both an ISAPI DLL and an ActiveX server. It, in turn, serves an object to another ActiveX server (the VB ISAPI extension). In truth, the VB ISAPI extension doesn't really have to be an OLE server, but that is the only kind of DLL VB can make.

Table 7.1 shows the members of the object the VB server uses to interact with IIS (the Internet Information Server). The VB server's **SUB** may have any name, but it must take an object as an argument:

```
Public Sub VBISAPI(server as Object)
. . .
End Sub
```

You use the object (**server** in this case) in the VB code by using the members in Table 7.1.

A May-December Marriage

Although VB5 makes it easy to create an ActiveX DLL, it doesn't have a good way to make an ISAPI DLL. Therefore, the main ISAPI DLL uses MFC (ISERVER.CPP; Listing 7.6A). Although MFC has special provisions for creating ISAPI DLLs, this server doesn't use them since they try to add another layer on top of ISAPI. Instead, the DLL is just an ordinary MFC DLL with the correct ISAPI entry points. You can find the supporting DLL code (CBISAPI.CPP and some header files) on line.

Table 7.1 CBISAPI Object Members.

Member	Type	Description
RetVal	Property	Sets ISAPI return value
StatCode	Property	Sets HTTP response code
Method	Property (R/O)	Method ("GET" or "POST," for example)
QueryString	Property (R/O)	Entire query string
PathInfo	Property (R/O)	Virtual path to script
PathTranslated	Property (R/O)	Translated path to script
Content	Property (R/O)	Data submitted by client
ContentType	Property (R/O)	Type of data in Content property
ContentLength	Property (R/O)	Length of data in Content property
Write	Method	Write a string to the client (terminates on NULL byte)
WriteLine	Method	Write a string terminated by a new line (not a <P>)
WriteByte	Method	Write a single byte to the client
ServerVariable	Method	Retrieves a standard CGI server variable (see Table 7.3)
ServerDoneSession	Method	Indicates extension is complete during asynchronous operations
Redirect	Method	Redirects browser to a different URL
SendUrl	Method	Sends an alternate URL
SendHeaders	Method	Sends HTTP headers
MapURL2Path	Method	Maps a local URL to a full path name

LISTING 7.6A THE ISERVER C++ CODE.

```
// IServer.cpp : implementation file
//

#include "stdafx.h"
#include "cbisapi.h"
#include "IServer.h"
#include <malloc.h>
#include <afxconv.h>   // BSTR conversions

#ifdef _DEBUG
#define new DEBUG_NEW
#undef THIS_FILE
static char THIS_FILE[] = __FILE__;
```

```
#endif

/////////////////////////////////////////
// CIsapiServer

IMPLEMENT_DYNCREATE(CIsapiServer, CCmdTarget)

CIsapiServer::CIsapiServer()
{
  EnableAutomation();
}

CIsapiServer::~CIsapiServer()
{
}


void CIsapiServer::OnFinalRelease()
{
  CCmdTarget::OnFinalRelease();
}


BEGIN_MESSAGE_MAP(CIsapiServer, CCmdTarget)
  //{{AFX_MSG_MAP(CIsapiServer)
  // NOTE - the ClassWizard will add and remove mapping macros here.
  //}}AFX_MSG_MAP
END_MESSAGE_MAP()

BEGIN_DISPATCH_MAP(CIsapiServer, CCmdTarget)
  //{{AFX_DISPATCH_MAP(CIsapiServer)
  DISP_PROPERTY(CIsapiServer, "RetVal", m_retVal, VT_I4)
  DISP_PROPERTY(CIsapiServer, "StatCode", m_statCode, VT_I4)
  DISP_PROPERTY_EX(CIsapiServer, "Method", GetMethod,
    SetNotSupported, VT_BSTR)
  DISP_PROPERTY_EX(CIsapiServer, "QueryString",
    GetQueryString, SetNotSupported, VT_BSTR)
  DISP_PROPERTY_EX(CIsapiServer, "PathInfo", GetPathInfo,
    SetNotSupported, VT_BSTR)
  DISP_PROPERTY_EX(CIsapiServer, "PathTranslated",
    GetPathTranslated, SetNotSupported, VT_BSTR)
  DISP_PROPERTY_EX(CIsapiServer, "ContentLength",
    GetContentLength, SetNotSupported, VT_I4)
  DISP_PROPERTY_EX(CIsapiServer, "Content", GetContent,
    SetNotSupported, VT_BSTR)
  DISP_PROPERTY_EX(CIsapiServer, "ContentType",
```

```
      GetContentType, SetNotSupported, VT_BSTR)
    DISP_FUNCTION(CIsapiServer, "Write", Write, VT_BOOL,
      VTS_VARIANT)
    DISP_FUNCTION(CIsapiServer, "ServerVariable",
      ServerVariable, VT_BOOL, VTS_VARIANT VTS_PVARIANT)
    DISP_FUNCTION(CIsapiServer, "WriteLine", WriteLine,
      VT_BOOL, VTS_VARIANT)
    DISP_FUNCTION(CIsapiServer, "WriteByte", WriteByte,
      VT_BOOL, VTS_VARIANT)
    DISP_FUNCTION(CIsapiServer, "ServerDoneSession",
      ServerDoneSession, VT_BOOL, VTS_NONE)
    DISP_FUNCTION(CIsapiServer, "Redirect", Redirect,
      VT_BOOL, VTS_VARIANT)
    DISP_FUNCTION(CIsapiServer, "SendURL", SendURL,
      VT_BOOL, VTS_VARIANT)
    DISP_FUNCTION(CIsapiServer, "SendHeaders", SendHeaders,
      VT_BOOL, VTS_VARIANT VTS_VARIANT)
    DISP_FUNCTION(CIsapiServer, "MapURL2Path", MapURL2Path,
      VT_BOOL, VTS_PVARIANT)
    //}}AFX_DISPATCH_MAP
END_DISPATCH_MAP()


// Note: we add support for IID_IIsapiServer to support
// typesafe binding from VBA. This IID must match the
// GUID that is attached to the dispinterface in the .ODL
// file. Not really used in any meaningful way, but the
// wiz puts it here.

// {A3B7D305-647C-11D0-A7B2-444553540000}
static const IID IID_IIsapiServer =
{ 0xa3b7d305, 0x647c, 0x11d0, { 0xa7, 0xb2, 0x44, 0x45,
  0x53, 0x54, 0x0, 0x0 } };


BEGIN_INTERFACE_MAP(CIsapiServer, CCmdTarget)
  INTERFACE_PART(CIsapiServer, IID_IIsapiServer, Dispatch)
END_INTERFACE_MAP()

/////////////////////////////////////////////////
// CIsapiServer message handlers

// Write to client
BOOL CIsapiServer::Write(const VARIANT FAR& idata)
{
  COleVariant data=idata;
  USES_CONVERSION;
  data.ChangeType(VT_BSTR);  // Force to BSTR
```

```
    if (data.vt!=VT_BSTR)
        return FALSE;
    char *s=W2A(data.bstrVal);  // switch to ANSI
    DWORD siz=strlen(s);
    return ecb->WriteClient(ecb->ConnID,s,&siz,0); // out!
}


// This fetches a Server Variable into a VARIANT
// Be careful. Since the second argument is a variant
// by reference, the formal argument must really be
// a variant. In other words, NO:
//    dim x as string
//    server.ServerVariable "SCRIPT_NAME",x
// YES:
//    dim x as variant
//    server.ServerVariable "SCRIPT_NAME",x
// Probably should have been a function returning VARIANT, but then
// again...
BOOL CIsapiServer::ServerVariable(const VARIANT FAR& Variable,
                    VARIANT FAR* Result)
{
    COleVariant var;
    var=Variable;
    var.ChangeType(VT_BSTR);
    if (var.vt!=VT_BSTR) return FALSE;

    USES_CONVERSION;
    char *v=W2A(var.bstrVal);
    CString res;
    DWORD siz=1024;
    BOOL rv;
    rv=ecb->GetServerVariable(ecb->ConnID,v,
        (char *)res.GetBufferSetLength(siz),&siz);
    res.ReleaseBuffer(siz-1);
    VariantClear(Result);
    Result->vt=VT_BSTR;
    Result->bstrVal=res.AllocSysString();
    return rv;
}

// R/O Property — these all look the same
BSTR CIsapiServer::GetMethod()
{
    CString strResult=ecb->lpszMethod;
    BSTR rv;
    rv=strResult.AllocSysString();
```

```
    return rv;
}


// Another R/O Property
BSTR CIsapiServer::GetQueryString()
{
  CString strResult=ecb->lpszQueryString;
  BSTR rv;
  rv=strResult.AllocSysString();
  return rv;
}


// R/O Property
BSTR CIsapiServer::GetPathInfo()
{
  CString strResult=ecb->lpszPathInfo;
  BSTR rv;
  rv=strResult.AllocSysString();
  return rv;
}


// R/O Property
BSTR CIsapiServer::GetPathTranslated()
{
  CString strResult=ecb->lpszPathTranslated;
  BSTR rv;
  rv=strResult.AllocSysString();
  return rv;
}


// R/O Property
long CIsapiServer::GetContentLength()
{
  return ecb->cbTotalBytes;
}


// R/O Property with a twist
// Apparently sometimes the server calls the
// extension without having all the content
// data (does this really happen?)
// This function reads it all so it is available
// BTW, the docs say that if the count is
// 0xFFFFFFFF then MORE than 4G of data
// is forthcoming and you should call ReadClient
// until it is empty.
// NEWS BULLETIN: If you expect 4G or more in
// a request, don't use these functions!
```

```
BSTR CIsapiServer::GetContent()
{
  CString strResult;
  char *p=strResult.GetBufferSetLength(ecb->cbTotalBytes);
  // put available bytes in CString
  memcpy(p,ecb->lpbData,ecb->cbAvailable);
  // Read excess
  if (ecb->cbAvailable!=ecb->cbTotalBytes)
    {
    DWORD siz=ecb->cbTotalBytes-ecb->cbAvailable;
    ecb->ReadClient(ecb->ConnID,p+ecb->cbAvailable,&siz);
    }
  strResult.ReleaseBuffer(ecb->cbTotalBytes);
  BSTR rv;
  rv=strResult.AllocSysString();
  return rv;
}


// Another R/O
BSTR CIsapiServer::GetContentType()
{
  CString strResult=ecb->lpszContentType;
  BSTR rv;
  rv=strResult.AllocSysString();
  return rv;
}


// Simple Method to write a line
// Note that HTML doesn't care one
// whit about the \r\n — it just
// makes the HTML source nicer
// Use <P> or <BR> to get a newline in HTML
BOOL CIsapiServer::WriteLine(const VARIANT FAR& idata)
{
  BOOL rv=Write(idata);
  DWORD siz=2;
  if (rv) rv=ecb->WriteClient(ecb->ConnID,"\r\n",&siz,0);
  return rv;
}


// Write a byte out
BOOL CIsapiServer::WriteByte(const VARIANT FAR& byte)
{
  COleVariant num=byte;
  num.ChangeType(VT_UI1);
  if (num.vt!=VT_UI1)
    return FALSE;
```

```
    char s=num.bVal;
    DWORD siz=1;
    return ecb->WriteClient(ecb->ConnID,&s,&siz,0);
}


// Wrap ServerSupportFunction Done with Session
BOOL CIsapiServer::ServerDoneSession()
{
    return ecb->ServerSupportFunction(ecb->ConnID,
        HSE_REQ_DONE_WITH_SESSION,NULL,NULL,NULL);
}

// Redirect to another URL (wrap ServerSupportFunction)
BOOL CIsapiServer::Redirect(const VARIANT FAR& url)
{
    COleVariant var;
    var=url;
    var.ChangeType(VT_BSTR);
    if (var.vt!=VT_BSTR) return FALSE;

    USES_CONVERSION;
    char *v=W2A(var.bstrVal);
    DWORD siz=strlen(v);
    return ecb->ServerSupportFunction(ecb->ConnID,
        HSE_REQ_SEND_URL_REDIRECT_RESP,v,&siz,NULL);
}


// Send alternate URL (wrap ServerSupportFunction)
BOOL CIsapiServer::SendURL(const VARIANT FAR& url)
{
    COleVariant var;
    var=url;
    var.ChangeType(VT_BSTR);
    if (var.vt!=VT_BSTR) return FALSE;

    USES_CONVERSION;
    char *v=W2A(var.bstrVal);
    DWORD siz=strlen(v);
    return ecb->ServerSupportFunction(ecb->ConnID,
        HSE_REQ_SEND_URL,v,&siz,NULL);
}
```

```
// Send headers (wrap ServerSupport Function)
BOOL CIsapiServer::SendHeaders(const VARIANT FAR& Status,
                  const VARIANT FAR& Headers)
{
  COleVariant var,var2;
  var=Status;
  var2=Headers;
  var.ChangeType(VT_BSTR);
  if (var.vt!=VT_BSTR) return FALSE;
  var2.ChangeType(VT_BSTR);
  if (var.vt!=VT_BSTR) return FALSE;

  USES_CONVERSION;
  char *status=W2A(var.bstrVal);
  char *hdr=W2A(var.bstrVal);
  return ecb->ServerSupportFunction(ecb->ConnID,
    HSE_REQ_SEND_RESPONSE_HEADER,status,NULL,(DWORD *)hdr);
}

// Map Virtual Path to Real Path (wrap ServerSupportFunction)
BOOL CIsapiServer::MapURL2Path(VARIANT FAR* urlpath)
{
  BOOL rv;
  COleVariant var,var2;
  var=urlpath;
  var.ChangeType(VT_BSTR);
  if (var.vt!=VT_BSTR) return FALSE;
  USES_CONVERSION;
  char *varin=W2A(var.bstrVal);
  DWORD siz=1024;
  CString url(varin);
  rv=ecb->ServerSupportFunction(ecb->ConnID,
    HSE_REQ_MAP_URL_TO_PATH,
    url.GetBufferSetLength(siz),&siz,NULL);
  url.ReleaseBuffer(siz-1);
  // set up return value
  VariantClear(urlpath);
  urlpath->vt=VT_BSTR;
  urlpath->bstrVal=url.AllocSysString();
  return rv;
}
```

LISTING 7.6B THE MAIN FILE THAT HANDLES DLL FUNCTIONS.

```cpp
// cbisapi.cpp : Defines the initialization routines for the DLL.
//

#include "stdafx.h"
#include "cbisapi.h"
#include "IServer.h"
#include <malloc.h>
#include <afxconv.h>

#ifdef _DEBUG
#define new DEBUG_NEW
#undef THIS_FILE
static char THIS_FILE[] = __FILE__;
#endif

/////////////////////////////////////////////////////////
// CCbisapiApp

BEGIN_MESSAGE_MAP(CCbisapiApp, CWinApp)
  //{{AFX_MSG_MAP(CCbisapiApp)
  // NOTE - the ClassWizard will add and remove mapping macros here.
  // DO NOT EDIT what you see in these blocks of generated code!
  //}}AFX_MSG_MAP
END_MESSAGE_MAP()

/////////////////////////////////////////////////////////
// CCbisapiApp construction

CCbisapiApp::CCbisapiApp()
{
  // TODO: add construction code here,
  // Place all significant initialization in InitInstance
}

/////////////////////////////////////////////////////////
// The one and only CCbisapiApp object

CCbisapiApp theApp;

/////////////////////////////////////////////////////////
// CCbisapiApp initialization

BOOL CCbisapiApp::InitInstance()
{
```

```
  // Register all OLE server (factories) as running. This enables the
  // OLE libraries to create objects from other applications.
  COleObjectFactory::RegisterAll();
  return TRUE;
}


//////////////////////////////////////////////////////
// Special entry points required for inproc servers

STDAPI DllGetClassObject(REFCLSID rclsid, REFIID riid, LPVOID* ppv)
{
  AFX_MANAGE_STATE(AfxGetStaticModuleState());
  return AfxDllGetClassObject(rclsid, riid, ppv);
}


STDAPI DllCanUnloadNow(void)
{
  AFX_MANAGE_STATE(AfxGetStaticModuleState());
  return AfxDllCanUnloadNow();
}


// by exporting DllRegisterServer, you can use regsvr.exe
STDAPI DllRegisterServer(void)
{
  AFX_MANAGE_STATE(AfxGetStaticModuleState());
  COleObjectFactory::UpdateRegistryAll();
  return S_OK;
}


// ISAPI Functions
 BOOL WINAPI GetExtensionVersion (HSE_VERSION_INFO *pVer)
  {
  pVer->dwExtensionVersion
      =MAKELONG(HSE_VERSION_MINOR,HSE_VERSION_MAJOR);
  lstrcpyn(pVer->lpszExtensionDesc,
    "OLE object ISAPI Gateway. Copyright 1997 by Al Williams",
    HSE_MAX_EXT_DLL_NAME_LEN);
  return TRUE;
  }

 DWORD WINAPI HttpExtensionProc(EXTENSION_CONTROL_BLOCK *lpEcb)
  {
  // create IsapiServer object
  USES_CONVERSION;
  CoInitialize(NULL);
  CIsapiServer svr;
  svr.SetECB(lpEcb);
```

```
// create user's object
COleDispatchDriver obj;
COleException x;
DWORD siz;
CString str;
OLECHAR *name;
char *plus,*colon;
colon=strchr(lpEcb->lpszQueryString,':');
plus=strchr(lpEcb->lpszQueryString,'+');
if (plus) *plus='\0';
if (colon)
  {
  *colon='\0';
  name=A2W(colon+1);
  }
else
  name=L"ISAPI";
if (!obj.CreateDispatch(lpEcb->lpszQueryString,&x))
  {
  str.Format("Can't create %s %x",lpEcb->lpszQueryString,x.m_sc);
  siz=str.GetLength();
  lpEcb->WriteClient(lpEcb->ConnID,(LPVOID)(LPCSTR)str,&siz,0);
  return HSE_STATUS_SUCCESS;
  }
if (plus) *plus='+';
*colon=':';
// call user's object ISAPI method passing IsapiServer object
DISPID dispid;
static BYTE params[]= VTS_DISPATCH;
IDispatch * dsptch=svr.GetIDispatch(FALSE);
if (FAILED(obj.m_lpDispatch->GetIDsOfNames(IID_NULL,&name,1,
      LOCALE_SYSTEM_DEFAULT,&dispid)))
  {
  str.Format("Can't find method %s",colon?colon+1:"ISAPI");
  siz=str.GetLength();
  lpEcb->WriteClient(lpEcb->ConnID,(LPVOID)(LPCSTR)str,&siz,0);
  return HSE_STATUS_SUCCESS;
  }
try
  {
  obj.InvokeHelper(dispid,DISPATCH_METHOD,VT_EMPTY,NULL,params,dsptch);
  }
catch (COleException *e)
  {
  str.Format("COleException: &H%x",  e->m_sc);
  siz=str.GetLength();
  lpEcb->WriteClient(lpEcb->ConnID,(LPVOID)(LPCSTR)str,&siz,0);
  }
```

```
catch (COleDispatchException *e)
  {
  str.Format("COleDispatchException: %s",  e->m_strDescription);
  siz=str.GetLength();
  lpEcb->WriteClient(lpEcb->ConnID,(LPVOID)(LPCSTR)str,&siz,0);
  }
catch (...)
  {
  str.Format("Unknown Exception!");
  siz=str.GetLength();
  lpEcb->WriteClient(lpEcb->ConnID,(LPVOID)(LPCSTR)str,&siz,0);
  }
// return status
CoUninitialize();
return svr.GetRV(); // init
  }
```

My example ISAPI extension uses VB, but really any language that can create a comparable OLE server will work. In this case, however, I'll call the OLE extension server a VB server to distinguish it from the C++ ISAPI extension DLL. How do you write a URL that calls your code? It is a two-step process. First, you have to get ISAPI to call the C++ DLL (CBISAPI.DLL). Then, you name the VB server in the URL's query string (the part following a question mark). Finally, you add a colon, and the name of the OLE method you want to call. For example:

```
<A HREF=http://www.al-williams.com/awc/scripts/
cbisapi.dll?hilo.dll:Guess+newgame> Click to begin </A>
```

What does all that mean? The part before the question mark invokes the ISAPI DLL. When you create an OLE server with VB, the server's name will be the project name, a period, and the name of the VB Class module that contains the object you want to work with. In this example, the HILO project (I'll show it to you later in this chapter) has all of its code in a class module named DLL. Inside that module is a SUB named **Guess**. The plus sign signifies the end of the OLE server name. Everything after that is part of the query string the server sends to the program. Notice that the C++ server doesn't change the query string—it is up to your code to skip the first part, parse HTTP escape sequences, and otherwise process the query string.

A Quick Look At ISAPI

ISAPI programs are not too difficult to write in C or C++. There are two types. The extension DLL (the one we will look at here) generates output dynamically. Another type of extension, a filter, can handle certain requests for data. We won't examine filters.

For the type of DLL we want to write, you need two functions: **GetExtensionVersion** and **HttpExtensionProc**. The **GetExtensionVersion** informs the server what version of IIS your DLL expects and provides a description string. You can copy this code directly from the help—it is mindless. The **HttpExtensionProc** function is where all the work occurs. It receives a single argument, but that argument is a pointer to an **EXTEN SION_CONTROL_BLOCK** (Table 7.2) that contains quite a bit of data.

Table 7.2 Extension Control Block members.

Member	Description
cbSize	Size of structure
dwVersion	Version number of structure
ConnID	Connection ID identifies particular request (passed back to many IIS functions)
dwHttpStatusCode	HTTP result code
lpszLogData	Extension-specific log data
lpszMethod	Method of request ("POST" or "GET," for example)
lpszQueryString	Query String
lpszPathInfo	Path to script
lpszPathTranslated	Translated path
cbTotalBytes	Total amount of content
cbAvailable	Amount of content already read
lpbData	Content (cbAvailable bytes)
lpszContentType	Data type of content
GetServerVariable	Function pointer used to retrieve server variables (see Table 7.3)
ServerSupport	Function pointer used to call special functions that redirect, send URLs, map virtual paths, etc.
WriteClient	Function pointer used to write data to client
ReadClient	Function pointer used to read excess data from client (cbTotalBytes-cbAvailable bytes)

Table 7.3 Server variables.

Name	Description
ALL_HTTP	All HTTP headers
AUTH_PASS	This will retrieve the password corresponding to REMOTE_USER as supplied by the client (if available)
AUTH_TYPE	Contains the type of authentication used, if any
CONTENT_LENGTH	The number of bytes which the script can expect to receive
CONTENT_TYPE	The content type of the information supplied in the body of a POST request, if known; often empty since application/x-www-formurlencoded is implied
GATEWAY_INTERFACE	The revision of the CGI specification to which this server complies
HTTP_ACCEPT	MIME types browser can accept
PATH_INFO	Additional path information, if any
PATH_TRANSLATED	Complete path translated to a local name
QUERY_STRING	The information which follows the '?' in the URL that referenced this script
REMOTE_ADDR	The IP address of the client
REMOTE_HOST	The host name of the client, if known
REMOTE_USER	This contains the user name supplied by the client and authenticated by the server, if any
REQUEST_METHOD	The HTTP request method ('POST' or 'GET,' for example)
SCRIPT_NAME	The name of the script program being executed
SERVER_NAME	The server's host name (or IP address) as it should appear in self-referencing URLs
SERVER_PORT	The TCP/IP port on which the request was received
SERVER_PROTOCOL	The name and version of the information retrieval protocol relating to this request
SERVER_SOFTWARE	The name and version of the Web server under which the CGI program is running

Compare Table 7.1 and Table 7.2. You'll notice that the members in Table 7.1 generally encapsulate the **EXTENSION_CONTROL_BLOCK** in an object-oriented way.

You have to be careful when writing an extension DLL. Just as DLLs that you use in a program become part of your process, your extension DLL will become part of IIS. If you crash, you could crash the server. If you throw an exception, the server will quietly continue and terminate your DLL. CBISAPI is careful to run the VB code inside a *try* block. It reports any exceptions it finds to the HTML stream.

Writing The HILO.DLL Server

This project is just another ActiveX DLL. From the starting screen, simply select ActiveX DLL as usual. You'll want to be sure to rename the project and the class module—these will make up the name of the server.

For a CBISAPI server, you only need to define a **Public Sub** that takes an **Object** as an argument. The HILO.DLL class module (Listing 7.7) has several private **Subs** to handle internal processing. These are strictly for the benefit of the **Guess** subroutine—the one the HTML code calls.

Listing 7.7   HILO VB ISAPI class.

```
VERSION 1.0 CLASS
BEGIN
  MultiUse = -1  'True
END
Attribute VB_Name = "DLL"
Attribute VB_GlobalNameSpace = False
Attribute VB_Creatable = True
Attribute VB_PredeclaredId = False
Attribute VB_Exposed = True
Option Explicit
Private Sub svrerr(server As Object, errstr As String)
server.WriteLine "Error: " & errstr
server.statcode = 400
server.retval = 4
End Sub


Private Sub Win(server As Object)
server.WriteLine "<HTML><HEAD><TITLE>I Win</TITLE></HEAD><BODY>"
server.WriteLine "I got it right!</BODY></HTML>"
End Sub


Private Sub GuessAgain(server As Object, Hi As Long, Lo As Long)
Dim servername As Variant
Dim script As Variant
server.WriteLine "<HTML><HEAD><TITLE>HiLo!</TITLE></HEAD><BODY>"
server.WriteLine "My guess is" & CInt((Hi + Lo) / 2) & "<P>"
server.ServerVariable "SERVER_NAME", servername
server.ServerVariable "SCRIPT_NAME", script
server.WriteLine "Is my guess:<P>"
```

```
server.Write "<FORM ACTION=http://" & servername
server.Write "/" & script
server.WriteLine "?HILO.DLL:Guess+HI=" & Hi & "+LO=" &_
  Lo & " METHOD=POST>"
server.WriteLine "High <INPUT TYPE=RADIO NAME=ANSWER VALUE=HI><P>"
server.WriteLine "Correct <INPUT TYPE=RADIO NAME=ANSWER VALUE=OK><P>"
server.WriteLine "Low <INPUT TYPE=RADIO NAME=ANSWER VALUE=LO><P>"
server.WriteLine "<INPUT TYPE=SUBMIT>"
server.WriteLine "</FORM>"
server.WriteLine "</BODY></HTML>"
End Sub


Public Sub Guess(server As Object)
 Dim Guess As Long
 Dim Hi As Long
 Dim Lo As Long
 Dim pos As Long
 Dim ans As String
 pos = InStr(1, server.QueryString, "HI=", vbTextCompare)
 If pos = 0 Then
   svrerr server, "Can't find HI"
   Exit Sub
 End If
 Hi = Val(Mid(server.QueryString, pos + 3))
 pos = InStr(1, server.QueryString, "LO=", vbTextCompare)
 If pos = 0 Then
   svrerr server, "Can't find LO"
   Exit Sub
 End If
 Lo = Val(Mid(server.QueryString, pos + 3))
 If server.ContentLength = 0 Then
  GuessAgain server, Hi, Lo
 Else
  Guess = (Hi + Lo) / 2
  pos = InStr(1, server.Content, "ANSWER=", vbTextCompare)
  If pos = 0 Then
    svrerr server, "Form error"
    Exit Sub
  End If
 ans = Mid(server.Content, pos + 7, 2)
 If ans = "OK" Then Win server
 If ans = "LO" Then GuessAgain server, Hi, Guess
 If ans = "HI" Then GuessAgain server, Guess, Lo
 If ans <> "OK" And ans <> "LO" And ans <> "HI" Then
    svrerr server, "Unknown Response: " & server.Content
End If
End Sub
```

Although this class server only has one public entry point, there is no reason you couldn't have multiple ones in a server. You can add more class modules too. This would allow you to group related functions together in each class and group related classes in one DLL.

You can see the finished product in Figure 7.6. The game is actually a simple binary search. It will always guess correctly within ten tries. Of course, you could always cheat. If the content (the data submitted by a form) is empty, the program assumes you are just starting the game. It expects the query string to have two variables: **HI** and **LO** that specify the range of numbers. The program just calls the private **GuessAgain** routine to generate a form that displays the current guess and offers three radio buttons that specify if the guess is high, low, or correct. The form submits back to the same *Guess* method via CBISAPI. The program sets the query string to reflect the current high and low values.

On subsequent calls, the content will contain the status of the form buttons. The code detects that content is present and recalculates the high and low limits. It then calls **GuessAgain** to generate a new form. Of course, if the guess is correct, the code doesn't generate the form. Instead, it calls the **Win** routine to generate an appropriate message.

Listing 7.8 shows the HTML file that starts the whole thing running. Of course, you could embellish this if you like. Also, the guessing form in Figure 7.6 could be fancier. For example, you might put some JavaScript in the form so that when you click a radio button it automatically submits the form. Still, the existing code does the job and is enough to show how the ISAPI interface works.

Figure 7.6 The HILO Web page.

LISTING 7.8   THE INITIAL HILO.HTM FILE.

```
<HTML>
<HEAD>
<TITLE>Play Hi-Lo!</TITLE>
</HEAD>
<BODY>
I'll guess your number.<BR>
Think of a number between 1 and 1024 and I'll guess it.<BR>
Think of your number and
<A HREF=http://www/scripts/cbisapi.dll?HILO.DLL:GUESS+HI=1024+LO=1>
   click here to play</A>
</BODY>
</HTML>
```

Installation And Distribution

The C++ DLL has to create an ActiveX object. However, it does so on the behalf of an anonymous Internet user. Therefore, the default Internet user must have privileges to create ActiveX objects. For NT 4.0, you can set this by running DCOMCNFG (a program in your SYSTEM32 directory). Select the default security tab and add IUSR_xxx (where xxx is your server's name) to the Default Access Permissions and Default Launch Permissions sections. When you first click the Add button on each choice, you'll only see group names. Click the Show Users button to show individual users (including IUSR_xxx).

Of course, all the DLLs required by each piece of the puzzle must be on the server. If you build CBISAPI to use the MFC DLLs, then they must be present (preferably in the \WINNT\SYSTEM32 directory). The VB portion requires the VB run-time DLLs, also.

One other thing that should be obvious: you must register your VB server on the Internet server machine using REGSVR32 for DLLs or by running the executable. Registering the server on a different machine only affects that machine's registry. If you fail to do this, you'll get an exception with an error code of **REGDB_E_CLASSNOTREG** (0x80040154).

By the way, even though CBISAPI provides an ActiveX object, it doesn't require registration. That's because no other program ever creates its object. It creates the object itself and passes it to another ActiveX program. Of course, that means the object has no type information, preventing VB from validating your calls at compile time. Instead, you'll find out any type mismatches or misspelled names at run time.

Inside The C++ DLL

The C++ DLL is a fairly straightforward MFC OLE DLL. The CBISAPI.CPP file (see the online listings) contains entry points required for ActiveX (provided by MFC's App Wizard) and the ISAPI entry points. The standard HTTPEXT.H prototypes the functions as C entry points so the C++ compiler won't alter the names. However, this same header doesn't declare the functions as exportable (using __declspec(dllexport)). Therefore, you must mention the functions in the **EXPORTS** section of the DEF file so that IIS can locate them.

The **HttpExtensionProc** routine isn't very sophisticated. It parses the query string to find the name of the server and the method name. This name must be the first thing in the query string. The parsing ends at the end of the query string or at the first plus sign the code encounters. If you omit the method name, CBISAPI tries to call the **ISAPI** method.

Notice the use of UNICODE characters for the member name. If you pass in a name, the program uses the *A2W* function to convert the string to UNICODE. Otherwise, it uses the string literal *L"ISAPI"* (the L indicates a UNICODE constant). This is the first (but not the last) place this problem rears its ugly head. IIS supports HTTP, of course. HTTP uses ANSI characters (the normal characters we all know and love). However ActiveX uses UNICODE (a two-byte character) strings for everything. In theory, the whole world will eventually switch to UNICODE. In theory, the U.S. will switch to the metric system— one day. In the meantime, you have to resort to conversions.

There are many ways to convert ANSI and UNICODE characters. I elected to use the MFC functions from AFXCONV.H. See MFC's Technical Note #59 for more about these macros. By the way, the note inaccurately states that you need AFXPRIV.H for the macros; this used to be true, but now you should use AFXCONV.H.

Once the code knows what object to create, it uses the MFC class **CDispatchDriver** class to represent it. A simple call to **CreateDispatch** will create the object. Next, a call to **GetIDsOfNames** converts the member name to a dispatch ID (DISPID). DISPIDs are function codes that ActiveX automation objects use to identify members (and properties, too). Armed with the DISPID, a call to **InvokeHelper** calls the VB code. A previous call to **GetIDispatch** retrieves the pointer you need to pass to the VB code so that it can access the server object.

Notice that CBISAPI protects the **InvokeHelper** call with a **try** statement. This ensures that any exceptions return to CBISAPI. CBISAPI reports errors by printing to the HTML stream. This works as long as the VB extension hasn't started writing some non-HTML data type before causing the exception.

The server object (see Listing 7.6) is where all the real work occurs. This class is easier to construct than you might expect. First, I used Class Wizard to create a **CCmdTarget**-derived class. All ActiveX automation objects in MFC derive from **CCmdTarget**. Then I used Class Wizard's OLE Automation tab to add the properties and methods (see Figure 7.7). The only hard part is writing the code.

The only odd part about the code is the conversion between **BSTRs** (ActiveX UNICODE strings) and **char *** (IIS ANSI strings). In several places I used the MFC conversion functions I mentioned earlier. However, in several cases I had the data in an MFC **CString** and decided to use **CString::AllocSysString**() to create a **BSTR**. That's where I ran into a little trouble.

BSTRs are not C (or C++) strings. They may contain embedded **NULL** characters. To facilitate this, each **BSTR** has a count of characters. Usually, the string ends in a **NULL** out of consideration for C/C++ programmers (and the Windows API), but the terminal **NULL** isn't usually part of the string. For example, a **BSTR** that contains the string "WD5GNR\0" should have a count of 6 unless your intent is to embed the **NULL** character inside the string. However, the size returned by ISAPI includes the **NULL** character. Who

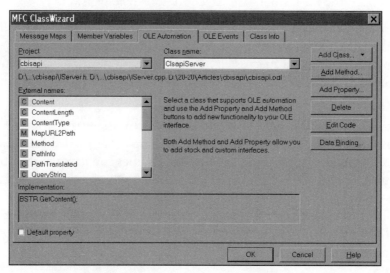

Figure 7.7 Using Class Wizard.

cares? Well, VB cares. Consider the **ServerVariable** property in the CBISAPI server object. If it creates a **BSTR** that contains the **NULL**, what happens? Consider this VB code:

```
Dim x as Variant
server.ServerVariable "HOST_NAME",x
server.Write x
server.ServerVariable "SCRIPT_NAME",x
server.Write x
```

In this code, everything works fine, and the trailing zero byte is innocuous. However, consider this:

```
Dim x as Variant
Dim y as Variant
server.ServerVariable "HOST_NAME",x
server.ServerVariable "SCRIPT_NAME",y
server.Write x & y
```

Suppose the value of **HOST_NAME** is "www.al-williams.com\0" and the value of **SCRIPT_NAME** is "ztest.dll\0." VB dutifully forms the string "www.al-williams.com\0ztest.dll\0." However, the C code that drives the **Write** method stops at the first **NULL**.

To prevent this problem, don't forget to subtract one from the size that ISAPI returns. Alternately, you could allow **CString** to recalculate the size. Either way, you must not set the size to include the **NULL** byte.

Debugging Tips

Debugging ISAPI extensions is an unpleasant business at best. To debug the C++ portion, you can fudge IIS to run as a user process and run it under a debugger. You can find complete instructions for how to do this in MFC Technical Note #63.

Debugging the VB portion is even worse. The easiest thing to do is pepper your code with temporary **WriteLine** commands so you can see things in your HTML stream. Not ideal, but it works. Luckily, CBISAPI will report any exceptions that occur, so you only need to worry about logical errors.

Another annoyance is that you usually have to shut down IIS so you can copy over (or relink) your files. You can set the **HKEY_LOCAL_MACHINE/SYSTEM/CurrentControlSet/Services/W3SVC/Parameters/CacheExtensions** registry key to zero to make IIS release the files more quickly. Also, each time you recreate the VB server, you must reregister it on the IIS machine.

Future Directions

There are many enhancements you could make to the C++ DLL CBISAPI. One welcome change would be automatic parsing of the query string and of content. For example, you could create a parameterized property named **ParsedQueryString**. It could take the name of an argument and return the string value, like this:

```
Dim s as String
s=server.ParsedQueryString("HI")
```

I also toyed with adding a debugging mode you could turn on with a query string option. Another idea would be to make a debugging version of CBISAPI.DLL (perhaps CBISAPID.DLL). This version would print debugging information out to the HTML stream. There are two problems with this. First, if the extension you are writing wants to set headers, it must do so before any output (including your debugging output). Second, what about extensions that output something other than an HTML file (for example, a GIF file)?

Finally, it would probably be a good idea to disallow remote users from creating arbitrary ActiveX servers on your machine. Of course, the risk is minimal because the ActiveX server would have to have an entry point that expects a single object, too. Still, it would be simple to make CBISAPI read a configuration file on the server that defined symbolic names for ActiveX servers. If the request specifies a name that isn't on the list, CBISAPI could reject the command.

The Internet Revisited

Do you remember the HTML debugging application in Chapter 6? It used the Internet transfer control to read a Web page and its headers. I mentioned then that you'd really like a simpler interface to the transfer control. The problem is that if you make a wrapper control around the transfer control, the wrapper control is visible.

Now that you know how to make invisible controls, it is trivial to convert the HTMLDBG application into a control. This illustrates an important point. Just because your control is invisible doesn't mean you can't use visible components to perform work. However, in this case, converting the application is a naïve approach, since you really don't need the edit fields to hold the data. Instead, you can directly interact with the transfer control.

You'll find the code for the first approach—a direct conversion from the original application—in Listing 7.9. The improved code is in Listing 7.10. Really, there isn't much difference between these two versions. However, you have to suspect that the second incarnation is more efficient.

LISTING 7.9   A DIRECT CONVERSION FROM APPLICATION TO CONTROL.

```
VERSION 5.00
Object = "{48E59290-9880-11CF-9754-00AA00C00908}#1.0#0"; "MSINET.OCX"
Begin VB.UserControl SimpleHTTP
   ClientHeight    =   3492
   ClientLeft      =   0
   ClientTop       =   0
   ClientWidth     =   5052
   InvisibleAtRuntime=   -1  'True
   PropertyPages   =   "SimHTTP.ctx":0000
   ScaleHeight     =   3492
   ScaleWidth      =   5052
   Begin VB.TextBox URLctl
      Height       =     375
      Left         =     120
      TabIndex     =     2
      Top          =     240
      Width        =    2895
   End
   Begin VB.TextBox HeadersCtl
      Height       =     975
      Left         =     120
      MultiLine    =      -1  'True
      TabIndex     =       1
      Top          =     840
      Width        =    4215
   End
   Begin VB.TextBox HTMLCtl
      Height       =    1095
      Left         =     120
      MultiLine    =      -1  'True
      TabIndex     =       0
      Top          =    2040
      Width        =    4215
   End
   Begin InetCtlsObjects.Inet Inet1
      Left         =    3840
      Top          =     240
      _ExtentX     =     995
      _ExtentY     =     995
   End
```

```
End
Attribute VB_Name = "SimpleHTTP"
Attribute VB_GlobalNameSpace = False
Attribute VB_Creatable = True
Attribute VB_PredeclaredId = False
Attribute VB_Exposed = True


'WARNING! DO NOT REMOVE OR MODIFY THE FOLLOWING COMMENTED LINES!
'MappingInfo=URLctl,URLctl,-1,Text
Public Property Get URL() As String
Attribute URL.VB_Description = "Returns/sets the text " & _
  "contained in the control."
    URL = URLctl.Text
End Property


Public Property Let URL(ByVal New_URL As String)
  URLctl.Text() = New_URL
' Ignore errors
  On Error Resume Next
  HTMLCtl.Text = Inet1.OpenURL(URLctl.Text)
  HeadersCtl.Text = Inet1.GetHeader
  PropertyChanged "URL"
End Property


'WARNING! DO NOT REMOVE OR MODIFY THE FOLLOWING COMMENTED LINES!
'MappingInfo=HTMLCtl,HTMLCtl,-1,Text
Public Property Get HTML() As String
Attribute HTML.VB_Description = "Returns/sets the text " & _
  "contained in the control."
    HTML = HTMLCtl.Text
End Property


Public Property Let HTML(ByVal New_HTML As String)
    'Err.Raise 382
End Property


Public Property Get Header(ByVal n As Variant) As Variant
Attribute Header.VB_Description = "Get a specific header"
Attribute Header.VB_MemberFlags = "400"
    Header = Inet1.GetHeader(n)
End Property


Public Property Let Header(ByVal n As Variant, ByVal _
  New_Header As Variant)
    ' Err.Raise 382 ' Never change!
End Property
```

```
'WARNING! DO NOT REMOVE OR MODIFY THE FOLLOWING COMMENTED LINES!
'MappingInfo=HeadersCtl,HeadersCtl,-1,Text
Public Property Get Headers() As String
Attribute Headers.VB_Description = "Returns/sets the text " & _
   "contained in the control."
    Headers = HeadersCtl.Text
End Property


Public Property Let Headers(ByVal New_Headers As String)
  'Err.Raise 382
End Property


'Initialize Properties for User Control
Private Sub UserControl_InitProperties()
End Sub


'Load property values from storage
Private Sub UserControl_ReadProperties(PropBag As PropertyBag)
    URLctl.Text = PropBag.ReadProperty("URL", "")
    PropertyChanged "URL"
End Sub


'Write property values to storage
Private Sub UserControl_WriteProperties(PropBag As PropertyBag)
    Call PropBag.WriteProperty("URL", URLctl.Text, "")
End Sub
```

LISTING 7.10   A BETTER SIMPLEHTTP CONTROL.

```
VERSION 5.00
Begin VB.UserControl SimpleHTTP
    ClientHeight    =    2880
    ClientLeft      =    0
    ClientTop       =    0
    ClientWidth     =    3840
    PropertyPages   =    "simhttp.ctx":0000
    ScaleHeight     =    2880
    ScaleWidth      =    3840
End
Attribute VB_Name = "SimpleHTTP"
Attribute VB_GlobalNameSpace = False
Attribute VB_Creatable = True
Attribute VB_PredeclaredId = False
Attribute VB_Exposed = True
Option Explicit
'Default Property Values:
Const m_def_URL = ""
```

```vb
'Property Variables:
Dim m_URL As String
Dim m_HTML As String


Public Property Get URL() As Variant
    URL = m_URL
End Property

Public Property Let URL(ByVal New_URL As Variant)
    m_URL = New_URL
    UpdateProps
    PropertyChanged "URL"
End Property

Public Property Get HTML() As Variant
Attribute HTML.VB_MemberFlags = "400"
    HTML = m_HTML
End Property

Public Property Let HTML(ByVal New_HTML As Variant)
    If Ambient.UserMode = False Then Err.Raise 382
    If Ambient.UserMode Then Exit Property
End Property

Public Property Get Headers() As Variant
Attribute Headers.VB_MemberFlags = "400"
    Headers = Inet1.GetHeader
End Property

Public Property Let Headers(ByVal New_Headers As Variant)
    If Ambient.UserMode = False Then Err.Raise 382
    If Ambient.UserMode Then Exit Property
End Property

Public Property Get Header() As Variant
Attribute Header.VB_MemberFlags = "400"
    Header = "Not Impl"
End Property

Public Property Let Header(ByVal New_Header As Variant)
    If Ambient.UserMode = False Then Err.Raise 382
    If Ambient.UserMode Then Exit Property
End Property
```

```
'Initialize Properties for User Control
Private Sub UserControl_InitProperties()
    m_URL = m_def_URL
End Sub
Private Sub UpdateProps()
If m_URL <> "" Then m_HTML = Inet1.OpenURL(m_URL)
End Sub

'Load property values from storage
Private Sub UserControl_ReadProperties(PropBag As PropertyBag)
    m_URL = PropBag.ReadProperty("URL", m_def_URL)
    UpdateProps
End Sub

'Write property values to storage
Private Sub UserControl_WriteProperties(PropBag As PropertyBag)
    Call PropBag.WriteProperty("URL", m_URL, m_def_URL)
End Sub
```

Notice that in both cases, the control is set to be invisible at run time. You
might wonder what the advantage is to creating these simple wrappers. Two
things come to mind: First, a simplified interface allows less experienced
programmers to utilize the new control. Second, if you eventually change how
the control works, no one will know the difference.

I manually modified a good bit of the code in Listing 7.9. For this control,
saving properties like **HTML** and **Headers** doesn't make sense. Instead, you
want to save the **URL** property. When the **URL** property loads, you'll want to
reread the other data. Also, many of the properties mapped to constituent
controls should be read-only. It isn't hard to change the existing **Property Let**
routines to raise an error at run time.

For example, suppose you start using the wrapper control to create a product
that scans the user's favorite Web sites and notes which ones have changed.
The product becomes very popular, but users complain it takes too much
memory and disk space. The current design of the **SimpleHTTP** control
requires the Microsoft Internet Transfer control. But this control does many
things you don't need. You could—with some effort—reengineer the
SimpleHTTP control to make it more efficient.

Container Controls

You may not have noticed, but not all VB controls behave the same way with respect to other controls. Try an experiment:

1. Create a new standard EXE program
2. Create a rather large button on the blank form
3. Create a new button that overlaps the first button (see Figure 7.8)
4. Drag the first button away from the second button

Nothing very interesting happens, right? Delete the buttons, and try this:

1. Create a frame control
2. Create a button on top of the frame control by clicking on the button icon once and dragging a button over the frame; **do not double click the button icon** (see Figure 7.9)
3. Drag the frame

Frames are special components that can contain other components. You doubtless noticed that the button in the frame moves with the frame. Also, hiding the frame will hide the button. A container control can contain many components. If you stop to think about it, a form is also a container control, right?

One caution: Don't double click a component to add it to a frame (or other container). When you double click, VB places the component on the form, even if it physically appears on top of the container. Also, you can only place a control in a container by drawing it that way to begin with. Moving it on top of the container later doesn't work.

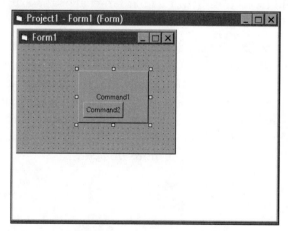

Figure 7.8 Two overlapping buttons.

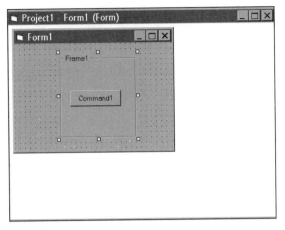

Figure 7.9 A frame and button.

Can you make your own containers? Of course. All you need to do is set the **ControlContainer** property in **UserControl** to **True**. That will create a basic container. However, you'll often want to manipulate the controls in a container. That's what the **ContainedControls** array (or collection) is for. Don't confuse this with the **Controls** array. The **Controls** array contains components you used to build an ActiveX control. **ContainedControls** references components the developer placed on top of your container.

For example, in the one shot component (earlier in this chapter), the **Controls** array would contain a timer component and a picture box. In the above example (the one with the frame and the button), the frame's **ContainedControls** array would contain a single button. Of course, you don't have access to the frame's array, but if you did, that's what it would contain.

Why do you need custom containers? Well, you might want to customize the look of a frame container. For example, you might want to draw a custom border around a bunch of controls. How about a container that selectively makes one of its contained components visible? Each component's **Tag** property would contain an ID, and the frame would accept an ID for the component to make visible. When you change the ID, the frame hides all the components, searches for the correct **Tag** (using **ContainedControls**), makes that component visible, and optionally changes its size to fill the frame.

Another interesting idea is layout managers. Some programming systems (in particular, Java and Motif) have the idea of a window that controls the layout of other windows. For example, you might have a layout manager that centers all windows. You can easily create layout manager controls using VB control containers.

An Example: CornerLayout

As an example of this, consider the program in Figure 7.10. This program has four buttons in a container. The container arranges for the buttons to always be in the four corners of the container. It also resizes the buttons to fill the available space.

The component that creates this effect is very simple (see Listing 7.11). It contains no components and only exports one property: **NoResize**. When **NoResize** is **True**, the layout manager won't resize its components to fit. It simply places them in the corners with their size unchanged.

LISTING 7.11　THE EXAMPLE LAYOUT CONTROL.

```
VERSION 5.00
Begin VB.UserControl CornerLayout
    ClientHeight    =    2880
    ClientLeft      =    0
    ClientTop       =    0
    ClientWidth     =    3840
    ControlContainer=    -1   'True
    PropertyPages   =    "CLayOut.ctx":0000
    ScaleHeight     =    2880
    ScaleWidth      =    3840
End
Attribute VB_Name = "CornerLayout"
Attribute VB_GlobalNameSpace = False
Attribute VB_Creatable = True
Attribute VB_PredeclaredId = False
Attribute VB_Exposed = True
Option Explicit
'Default Property Values:
Const m_def_NoResize = 0
'Property Variables:
Dim m_NoResize As Boolean

Private Sub UserControl_Click()
Print ContainedControls.Count
End Sub

Private Sub UserControl_Resize()
Dim i As Integer
Dim n As Integer
Dim ctl As Object
For n = 0 To ContainedControls.Count - 1
  On Error Resume Next
```

```
    Set ctl = ContainedControls(n)
    i = 3 - ctl.Tag
    If Err.Number <> 0 Or i < 0 Or i > 3 Then i = n
    If m_NoResize = False Then
      ctl.Height = ScaleHeight / 2
      ctl.Width = ScaleWidth / 2
    End If
    If i >= 2 Then
      ctl.Top = 0
    Else
      ctl.Top = ScaleHeight - ctl.Height
    End If
    If i = 0 Or i = 2 Then
      ctl.Left = ScaleWidth - ctl.Width
    Else
      ctl.Left = 0
    End If
  Next n
End Sub
Public Property Get NoResize() As Boolean
Attribute NoResize.VB_Description = "Set to true to prevent the layout
manager from resizing controls"
    NoResize = m_NoResize
End Property

Public Property Let NoResize(ByVal New_NoResize As Boolean)
    m_NoResize = New_NoResize
    PropertyChanged "NoResize"
End Property

'Initialize Properties for User Control
Private Sub UserControl_InitProperties()
    m_NoResize = m_def_NoResize
End Sub

'Load property values from storage
Private Sub UserControl_ReadProperties(PropBag As PropertyBag)

    m_NoResize = PropBag.ReadProperty("NoResize", m_def_NoResize)
End Sub

'Write property values to storage
Private Sub UserControl_WriteProperties(PropBag As PropertyBag)

    Call PropBag.WriteProperty("NoResize", m_NoResize, m_def_NoResize)
End Sub
```

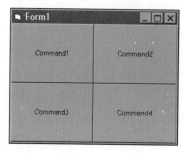

Figure 7.10 The CornerLayout control.

The only important piece of code in the control is during **UserControl_Resize**. This recalculates the size and position of every control. Experience shows that controls in the **ContainedControls** array are in reverse order. That is, the control you added last to the container is in array element zero. The first control is in the last element. You can learn exactly how many elements the array has by writing the expression: **ContainedControls.Count**. Of course, for this control, it doesn't make sense to have more than four contained controls (one for each corner).

To help you position your controls relatively, you can place a number between 0 and 3 in the **Tag** field of each control. If the code finds this tag, it uses the number to determine the position of the control (see Table 7.4). If it doesn't find the tag (or it isn't a legal number), the container uses its position in the array, instead.

Notice that this presents a problem. The control in question may not even have a **Tag** property. In addition, the tag might be a string or empty. That's why the code starts with **On Error Resume Next**. After it reads the tag, the program examines the **Err** object. If an error occurs, the program resorts to using the array position instead of the tag.

The remainder of the procedure is straightforward. If the programmer wants resizing, the container changes the size of the controls before it moves them.

Table 7.4 Show tag positions.

Value	Position
0	Top-left
1	Top-right
2	Bottom-left
3	Bottom-right

The corner calculations to follow need to know the final size of the controls, so it is important to do this step first.

There is no end to the kinds of layout managers you can create using this type of technique. Just be sure the **ControlContainer** property is set, and you are ready to go.

A Selective Container

For another example, look at Listing 7.12. This container has a property **ShowTag** that accepts a tag name. The container scans its components until it finds one with the specified tag name. It makes this component visible and hides all the others.

LISTING 7.12   THE SELECTING CONTAINER.

```
VERSION 5.00
Begin VB.UserControl ShowTag
   ClientHeight    =    2880
   ClientLeft      =    0
   ClientTop       =    0
   ClientWidth     =    3840
   ControlContainer=   -1  'True
   PropertyPages   =    "showtag.ctx":0000
   ScaleHeight     =    2880
   ScaleWidth      =    3840
End
Attribute VB_Name = "ShowTag"
Attribute VB_GlobalNameSpace = False
Attribute VB_Creatable = True
Attribute VB_PredeclaredId = False
Attribute VB_Exposed = True
Option Explicit
'Default Property Values:
Const m_def_ShowTag = ""
'Property Variables:
Dim m_ShowTag As Variant
Dim m_CurrentObj As Object

'WARNING! DO NOT REMOVE OR MODIFY THE FOLLOWING COMMENTED LINES!
'MappingInfo=UserControl,UserControl,-1,Enabled
Public Property Get Enabled() As Boolean
Attribute Enabled.VB_Description = "Returns/sets a value " & _
   "that determines whether an object can respond to user-" & _
   "  generated events."
      Enabled = UserControl.Enabled
End Property
```

```vb
Public Property Let Enabled(ByVal New_Enabled As Boolean)
    UserControl.Enabled() = New_Enabled
    PropertyChanged "Enabled"
End Property


Public Property Get ShowTag() As Variant
Attribute ShowTag.VB_Description = "Enter the tag of the " & _
  "contained control you want to be visible"
Attribute ShowTag.VB_MemberFlags = "400"
    ShowTag = m_ShowTag
End Property
Private Sub ShowIt()
  Dim i As Integer
  For i = 0 To ContainedControls.Count - 1
    If ContainedControls(i).Tag = m_ShowTag Then
      ContainedControls(i).Visible = True
      Set m_CurrentObj = ContainedControls(i)
    Else
      ContainedControls(i).Visible = False
    End If
  Next i
End Sub
Public Property Let ShowTag(ByVal New_ShowTag As Variant)
    If Ambient.UserMode = False Then Err.Raise 382
    m_ShowTag = New_ShowTag
    ShowIt
    PropertyChanged "ShowTag"
End Property


'Initialize Properties for User Control
Private Sub UserControl_InitProperties()
    m_ShowTag = m_def_ShowTag
    ShowIt
End Sub


'Load property values from storage
Private Sub UserControl_ReadProperties(PropBag As PropertyBag)

    UserControl.Enabled = PropBag.ReadProperty("Enabled", True)
    m_ShowTag = PropBag.ReadProperty("ShowTag", m_def_ShowTag)
    ShowIt
End Sub


'Write property values to storage
Private Sub UserControl_WriteProperties(PropBag As PropertyBag)
```

```
    Call PropBag.WriteProperty("Enabled", _
      UserControl.Enabled, True)
    Call PropBag.WriteProperty("ShowTag", m_ShowTag, m_def_ShowTag)
End Sub
```

All the important work is in the **ShowIt** procedure. If you step through this with the debugger, you'll see that the first time VB calls **ShowIt**, the container is empty. That's why the included example programs start with everything hidden. Until the entire form loads, the container is empty.

This container doesn't resize its components, but it could. It wouldn't be difficult to write a **Resize** event handler similar to the one in the previous example. For practice, you might like to add the handler yourself.

Think about the advantage of a container like this. Sure, you could do the same thing by writing code. But the advantage to a visual program is that it's—well—visual. By using this container, you can drop any number of controls in and select them simply by setting a property.

The example program included in the project group is just a simple test framework. You have to enter "Button" or "Picture" and press the button (case matters, by the way). However, a real program that uses this container might set the tag based on some state. For example, you might show one control if the user has a dial-up network connection active, and another if the connection is not active.

Controls That Know Their Container

As a general rule, your control shouldn't know anything about its container. This is a good idea, since if you know about the container, your control can only work inside the particular container you designed for (or one that emulates that container).

Does this mean you should never use the **Extender** object? The **Extender** object makes available various properties that the container creates for your object (see Table 7.5). Users of your object think the properties belong to your control, but they really belong to the container. For example, the **Name**, **Tag**, and **Visible** properties are extended properties managed by the container. Every time you access the **Extender** object, you should ask yourself if you really need to do it.

Table 7.5 VB Extender members.

Member	Type	Description
Name	Property	Name of control
Visible	Property	True if control is visible
Parent	Property	Control's owner
Cancel	Property	True if control is a cancel button
Default	Property	True if control is a default button
Container	Property	Control's visual container
DragIcon	Property	Icon to use during dragging
DragMode	Property	Determines if VB automatically drags control
Enabled	Property	True if control responds to user input
Height	Property	Height of control
HelpContextID	Property	ID for context-sensitive help
Index	Property	Control array index
Left	Property	Left coordinate of control
TabIndex	Property	Order that tab key visit this control
TabStop	Property	True if tab key stops on this control
Tag	Property	User-defined data
Top	Property	Top coordinate of control
WhatsThis Help	Property	Determines if help appears in pop up window
Width	Property	Width of control
SetFocus	Method	
DragDrop	Event	
DragOver	Event	
GotFocus	Event	
LostFocus	Event	

That being said, there are times when it is invaluable to access the **Extender** object. For example, you might want to write a control that needs its own name. Another specialized case is when you want to control or manipulate your own container. You might also want to alter other components on the same form.

Of course, this violates all hope of remaining ignorant about your container. If you write a control like this, it will only work in the container that you design it for (or a very similar container).

As an example, consider managing a complex user interface. One popular option you see in some commercial software is to use a Details button. At first, the program shows a dialog box with a minimal set of useful information. If you want to know more, you push the Details (or Advanced) button. Immediately, the dialog box grows and more controls become visible. You can often press the button again to hide the new controls. VB uses this scheme in several places, including the **Procedure Attributes** dialog (under the **Tools** menu).

It isn't hard to imagine how to write something like this. You can simply write an event handler for the Details button that knows which controls to show (or hide) and how big to resize the form that contains it. However, the whole point of components is to quit writing code wherever possible. The question is: Can you create an ActiveX control that can resize its own form and show (or hide) other controls on the form?

You can write such a control (see Figure 7.11). The control looks and acts like a regular button. In addition to the properties buttons usually have, this special button also has a **State** property. This property shows you if the extra controls are currently visible or invisible.

When you click the button, it automatically finds its form and resizes it to dimensions you specify (you can disable this behavior by setting **ResizeForm** to **False**). Then the button uses the form's **Controls** collection to visit each component the form owns. If the component has a **Tag** property equal to *Detail*, the button hides or shows the component as necessary. Any control that doesn't have *Detail* in the tag remains as it was. You can find the code that implements this logic in Listing 7.13.

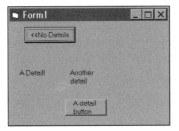

Figure 7.11 An application showing detail.

LISTING 7.13   THE DETAIL BUTTON.

```
VERSION 5.00
Begin VB.UserControl DButton
   ClientHeight    =   624
   ClientLeft      =   0
   ClientTop       =   0
   ClientWidth     =   1152
   PropertyPages   =   "dbutton.ctx":0000
   ScaleHeight     =   624
   ScaleWidth      =   1152
   Begin VB.CommandButton Command1
      Appearance   =   0  'Flat
      Caption      =   "Details>>"
      Height       =   492
      Left         =   0
      TabIndex     =   0
      Top          =   0
      Width        =   1092
   End
End
Attribute VB_Name = "DButton"
Attribute VB_GlobalNameSpace = False
Attribute VB_Creatable = True
Attribute VB_PredeclaredId = False
Attribute VB_Exposed = True
Option Explicit
'Default Property Values:
Const m_def_ResizeForm = False
Const m_def_OnWidth = 0
Const m_def_OnHeight = 0
Const m_def_OffWidth = 0
Const m_def_OffHeight = 0
Const m_def_OnCaption = "<<No Details"
Const m_def_OffCaption = "Details>>"
Const m_def_State = 0
'Property Variables:
Dim m_ResizeForm As Boolean
Dim m_OnWidth As Variant
Dim m_OnHeight As Variant
Dim m_OffWidth As Variant
Dim m_OffHeight As Variant
Dim m_OnCaption As String
Dim m_OffCaption As String
Dim m_State As Boolean
```

```
Private Sub Command1_Click()
Toggle
End Sub
'WARNING! DO NOT REMOVE OR MODIFY THE FOLLOWING COMMENTED LINES!
'MappingInfo=Command1,Command1,-1,BackColor
Public Property Get BackColor() As OLE_COLOR
Attribute BackColor.VB_Description = "Returns/sets the " & _
   "background color used to display text and graphics in " & _
   "an object."
Attribute BackColor.VB_UserMemId = -501
    BackColor = Command1.BackColor
End Property


Public Property Let BackColor(ByVal New_BackColor As OLE_COLOR)
    Command1.BackColor() = New_BackColor
    PropertyChanged "BackColor"
End Property


'WARNING! DO NOT REMOVE OR MODIFY THE FOLLOWING COMMENTED LINES!
'MappingInfo=UserControl,UserControl,-1,Enabled
Public Property Get Enabled() As Boolean
Attribute Enabled.VB_Description = "Returns/sets a value " & _
   "that determines whether an object can respond to user-" & _
   "generated events."
Attribute Enabled.VB_UserMemId = -514
    Enabled = UserControl.Enabled
End Property


Public Property Let Enabled(ByVal New_Enabled As Boolean)
    UserControl.Enabled() = New_Enabled
    PropertyChanged "Enabled"
End Property


'WARNING! DO NOT REMOVE OR MODIFY THE FOLLOWING COMMENTED LINES!
'MappingInfo=Command1,Command1,-1,Appearance
Public Property Get Appearance() As Integer
Attribute Appearance.VB_Description = "Returns/sets " & _
   "whether or not an object is painted at run time with " & _
   "3-D effects."
Attribute Appearance.VB_UserMemId = -520
    Appearance = Command1.Appearance
End Property
'WARNING! DO NOT REMOVE OR MODIFY THE FOLLOWING COMMENTED LINES!
'MappingInfo=Command1,Command1,-1,DownPicture
Public Property Get DownPicture() As Picture
```

```
Attribute DownPicture.VB_Description = "Returns/sets a " & _
  "graphic to be displayed when the button is in the down " & _
  "position, if Style is set to 1."
    Set DownPicture = Command1.DownPicture
End Property


Public Property Set DownPicture(ByVal New_DownPicture As Picture)
    Set Command1.DownPicture = New_DownPicture
    PropertyChanged "DownPicture"
End Property


'WARNING! DO NOT REMOVE OR MODIFY THE FOLLOWING COMMENTED LINES!
'MappingInfo=Command1,Command1,-1,DisabledPicture
Public Property Get DisabledPicture() As Picture
Attribute DisabledPicture.VB_Description = "Returns/sets " & _
  "a graphic to be displayed when the button is disabled, " & _
  "if Style is set to 1."
    Set DisabledPicture = Command1.DisabledPicture
End Property


Public Property Set DisabledPicture(ByVal New_DisabledPicture As Picture)
    Set Command1.DisabledPicture = New_DisabledPicture
    PropertyChanged "DisabledPicture"
End Property


'WARNING! DO NOT REMOVE OR MODIFY THE FOLLOWING COMMENTED LINES!
'MappingInfo=Command1,Command1,-1,MaskColor
Public Property Get MaskColor() As Long
Attribute MaskColor.VB_Description = "Returns or sets a " & _
  "color in a button's picture to be a 'mask' (that is, " & _
  "transparent), if Style is set to 1."
    MaskColor = Command1.MaskColor
End Property


Public Property Let MaskColor(ByVal New_MaskColor As Long)
    Command1.MaskColor() = New_MaskColor
    PropertyChanged "MaskColor"
End Property


'WARNING! DO NOT REMOVE OR MODIFY THE FOLLOWING COMMENTED LINES!
'MappingInfo=Command1,Command1,-1,MouseIcon
Public Property Get MouseIcon() As Picture
Attribute MouseIcon.VB_Description = "Sets a custom mouse icon."
    Set MouseIcon = Command1.MouseIcon
End Property
```

```
Public Property Set MouseIcon(ByVal New_MouseIcon As Picture)
    Set Command1.MouseIcon = New_MouseIcon
    PropertyChanged "MouseIcon"
End Property


'WARNING! DO NOT REMOVE OR MODIFY THE FOLLOWING COMMENTED LINES!
'MappingInfo=Command1,Command1,-1,MousePointer
Public Property Get MousePointer() As Integer
Attribute MousePointer.VB_Description = "Returns/sets the " & _
  "type of mouse pointer displayed when over part of an " & _
  "object."
    MousePointer = Command1.MousePointer
End Property


Public Property Let MousePointer(ByVal New_MousePointer As Integer)
    Command1.MousePointer() = New_MousePointer
    PropertyChanged "MousePointer"
End Property


'WARNING! DO NOT REMOVE OR MODIFY THE FOLLOWING COMMENTED LINES!
'MappingInfo=Command1,Command1,-1,Picture
Public Property Get Picture() As Picture
Attribute Picture.VB_Description = "Returns/sets a " & _
  "graphic to be displayed in a CommandButton, " & _
  "OptionButton or CheckBox control, if Style is " & _
  "set to 1."
    Set Picture = Command1.Picture
End Property


Public Property Set Picture(ByVal New_Picture As Picture)
    Set Command1.Picture = New_Picture
    PropertyChanged "Picture"
End Property


'WARNING! DO NOT REMOVE OR MODIFY THE FOLLOWING COMMENTED LINES!
'MappingInfo=Command1,Command1,-1,Style
Public Property Get Style() As Integer
Attribute Style.VB_Description = "Returns/sets the " & _
  "appearance of the control, whether standard (standard " & _
  "Windows style) or graphical (with a custom picture)."
    Style = Command1.Style
End Property


'WARNING! DO NOT REMOVE OR MODIFY THE FOLLOWING COMMENTED LINES!
'MappingInfo=Command1,Command1,-1,ToolTipText
```

```vb
Public Property Get ToolTipText() As String
Attribute ToolTipText.VB_Description = "Returns/sets the " & _
  "text displayed when the mouse is paused over the " & _
  "control."
    ToolTipText = Command1.ToolTipText
End Property


Public Property Let ToolTipText(ByVal New_ToolTipText As String)
    Command1.ToolTipText() = New_ToolTipText
    PropertyChanged "ToolTipText"
End Property


'WARNING! DO NOT REMOVE OR MODIFY THE FOLLOWING COMMENTED LINES!
'MappingInfo=Command1,Command1,-1,UseMaskColor
Public Property Get UseMaskColor() As Boolean
Attribute UseMaskColor.VB_Description = "Returns or sets " & _
"a value that determines whether the color assigned in " & _
  "the MaskColor property is used as a 'mask.' (That is, " & _
  "used to create transparent regions.) Applies only if " & _
  "Style is set to 1."
    UseMaskColor = Command1.UseMaskColor
End Property


Public Property Let UseMaskColor(ByVal New_UseMaskColor As Boolean)
    Command1.UseMaskColor() = New_UseMaskColor
    PropertyChanged "UseMaskColor"
End Property


'WARNING! DO NOT REMOVE OR MODIFY THE FOLLOWING COMMENTED LINES!
'MappingInfo=Command1,Command1,-1,WhatsThisHelpID
Public Property Get WhatsThisHelpID() As Long
Attribute WhatsThisHelpID.VB_Description = "Returns/sets " & _
  "an associated context number for an object."
    WhatsThisHelpID = Command1.WhatsThisHelpID
End Property


Public Property Let WhatsThisHelpID(ByVal New_WhatsThisHelpID As Long)
    Command1.WhatsThisHelpID() = New_WhatsThisHelpID
    PropertyChanged "WhatsThisHelpID"
End Property


Public Property Get State() As Boolean
Attribute State.VB_Description = "Set/read the current " & _
  "state of the detail controls (True=visible). Note: " & _
  "detail controls have *Detail* in their Tag field"
    State = m_State
End Property
```

```
Public Property Let State(ByVal New_State As Boolean)
    m_State = New_State
    PropertyChanged "State"
End Property


Public Sub Toggle()
Attribute Toggle.VB_Description = "Call to simulate Detail button
push\r\n"
Dim TheForm As form
Dim i As Integer
Dim aControl As Object
Set TheForm = UserControl.Extender.Parent
m_State = Not m_State
If m_ResizeForm Then
  If m_State Then
    TheForm.Height = OnHeight
    TheForm.Width = OnWidth
  Else
    TheForm.Height = OffHeight
    TheForm.Width = OffWidth
  End If
End If
For i = 0 To TheForm.Controls.Count - 1
  Set aControl = TheForm.Controls(i)
  If aControl.Tag = "*Detail*" Then
    aControl.Visible = m_State
  End If
Next i
If m_State Then
  Command1.Caption = m_OnCaption
Else
  Command1.Caption = m_OffCaption
End If
End Sub


'Initialize Properties for User Control
Private Sub UserControl_InitProperties()
    m_State = m_def_State
    m_OnCaption = m_def_OnCaption
    m_OffCaption = m_def_OffCaption
    m_ResizeForm = m_def_ResizeForm
    m_OnWidth = m_def_OnWidth
    m_OnHeight = m_def_OnHeight
    m_OffWidth = m_def_OffWidth
    m_OffHeight = m_def_OffHeight
End Sub
```

```vb
'Load property values from storage
Private Sub UserControl_ReadProperties(PropBag As PropertyBag)

  Command1.BackColor = PropBag.ReadProperty("BackColor", &H8000000F)
  UserControl.Enabled = PropBag.ReadProperty("Enabled", True)
  Command1.Caption = PropBag.ReadProperty("Caption", "Detail>>")
  Set DownPicture = PropBag.ReadProperty("DownPicture", Nothing)
  Set DisabledPicture = PropBag.ReadProperty("DisabledPicture", Nothing)
  Command1.MaskColor = PropBag.ReadProperty("MaskColor", 12632256)
  Set MouseIcon = PropBag.ReadProperty("MouseIcon", Nothing)
  Command1.MousePointer = PropBag.ReadProperty("MousePointer", 0)
  Set Picture = PropBag.ReadProperty("Picture", Nothing)
  Command1.ToolTipText = PropBag.ReadProperty("ToolTipText", "")
  Command1.UseMaskColor = PropBag.ReadProperty("UseMaskColor", False)
  Command1.WhatsThisHelpID = PropBag.ReadProperty("WhatsThisHelpID", 0)
  m_State = PropBag.ReadProperty("State", m_def_State)
  m_OnCaption = PropBag.ReadProperty("OnCaption", m_def_OnCaption)
  m_OffCaption = PropBag.ReadProperty("OffCaption", m_def_OffCaption)
  m_ResizeForm = PropBag.ReadProperty("ResizeForm", m_def_ResizeForm)
  m_OnWidth = PropBag.ReadProperty("OnWidth", m_def_OnWidth)
  m_OnHeight = PropBag.ReadProperty("OnHeight", m_def_OnHeight)
  m_OffWidth = PropBag.ReadProperty("OffWidth", m_def_OffWidth)
  m_OffHeight = PropBag.ReadProperty("OffHeight", m_def_OffHeight)
End Sub

Private Sub UserControl_Resize()
Command1.Top = 0
Command1.Left = 0
Command1.Height = ScaleHeight
Command1.Width = ScaleWidth
End Sub

'Write property values to storage
Private Sub UserControl_WriteProperties(PropBag As PropertyBag)

  Call PropBag.WriteProperty("BackColor", Command1.BackColor, &H8000000F)
  Call PropBag.WriteProperty("Enabled", UserControl.Enabled, True)
  Call PropBag.WriteProperty("Caption", Command1.Caption, "Detail>>")
  Call PropBag.WriteProperty("DownPicture", DownPicture, Nothing)
  Call PropBag.WriteProperty("DisabledPicture", DisabledPicture, Nothing)
  Call PropBag.WriteProperty("MaskColor", Command1.MaskColor, 12632256)
  Call PropBag.WriteProperty("MouseIcon", MouseIcon, Nothing)
  Call PropBag.WriteProperty("MousePointer", Command1.MousePointer, 0)
  Call PropBag.WriteProperty("Picture", Picture, Nothing)
  Call PropBag.WriteProperty("ToolTipText", Command1.ToolTipText, "")
```

```
   Call PropBag.WriteProperty("UseMaskColor", Command1.UseMaskColor, False)
   Call PropBag.WriteProperty("WhatsThisHelpID",_
     Command1.WhatsThisHelpID, 0)
   Call PropBag.WriteProperty("State", m_State, m_def_State)
   Call PropBag.WriteProperty("OnCaption", m_OnCaption, m_def_OnCaption)
   Call PropBag.WriteProperty("OffCaption", m_OffCaption, m_def_OffCaption)
   Call PropBag.WriteProperty("ResizeForm", m_ResizeForm, m_def_ResizeForm)
   Call PropBag.WriteProperty("OnWidth", m_OnWidth, m_def_OnWidth)
   Call PropBag.WriteProperty("OnHeight", m_OnHeight, m_def_OnHeight)
   Call PropBag.WriteProperty("OffWidth", m_OffWidth, m_def_OffWidth)
   Call PropBag.WriteProperty("OffHeight", m_OffHeight, m_def_OffHeight)
End Sub

Public Property Get OnCaption() As String
Attribute OnCaption.VB_Description = "Caption to display " & _
   "when details are on"
   OnCaption = m_OnCaption
End Property

Public Property Let OnCaption(ByVal New_OnCaption As String)
   m_OnCaption = New_OnCaption
   PropertyChanged "OnCaption"
End Property

Public Property Get OffCaption() As String
Attribute OffCaption.VB_Description = "Caption to display " & _
   "when details are hidden"
   OffCaption = m_OffCaption
End Property

Public Property Let OffCaption(ByVal New_OffCaption As String)
   m_OffCaption = New_OffCaption
   PropertyChanged "OffCaption"
End Property

Public Property Get ResizeForm() As Boolean
Attribute ResizeForm.VB_Description = "Set to TRUE if " & _
   "button should resize parent form (be sure to set " & _
   "OnWidth, OnHeight, OffWidth, and OffHeight properties " & _
   "too)"
   ResizeForm = m_ResizeForm
End Property

Public Property Let ResizeForm(ByVal New_ResizeForm As Boolean)
   m_ResizeForm = New_ResizeForm
   PropertyChanged "ResizeForm"
End Property
```

```
Public Property Get OnWidth() As Variant
Attribute OnWidth.VB_Description = "Width of parent form " & _
  "when details are on"
  OnWidth = m_OnWidth
End Property


Public Property Let OnWidth(ByVal New_OnWidth As Variant)
  m_OnWidth = New_OnWidth
  PropertyChanged "OnWidth"
End Property


Public Property Get OnHeight() As Variant
Attribute OnHeight.VB_Description = "Height of parent " & _
  "form when details are off"
  OnHeight = m_OnHeight
End Property


Public Property Let OnHeight(ByVal New_OnHeight As Variant)
  m_OnHeight = New_OnHeight
  PropertyChanged "OnHeight"
End Property


Public Property Get OffWidth() As Variant
Attribute OffWidth.VB_Description = "Width of parent form " & _
  "when details are off"
  OffWidth = m_OffWidth
End Property


Public Property Let OffWidth(ByVal New_OffWidth As Variant)
  m_OffWidth = New_OffWidth
  PropertyChanged "OffWidth"
End Property


Public Property Get OffHeight() As Variant
Attribute OffHeight.VB_Description = "Height of parent " & _
  "form when details are off"
  OffHeight = m_OffHeight
End Property


Public Property Let OffHeight(ByVal New_OffHeight As Variant)
  m_OffHeight = New_OffHeight
  PropertyChanged "OffHeight"
End Property
```

There are two things you should realize about this approach. First, if you place this button in another container (for example, a Web browser) it won't work. Second, notice in Listing 7.13 that when the code examines the controls, it uses the generic **Object** type. This works well, because you can't assume what kind of control you'll examine. A single form may contain buttons, text boxes, and other kinds of controls. However, that means VB can't check for errors until you run the code. It also means that when you press the period key in the VB environment, it won't bring up a list of members you can type. How could it? VB doesn't know at that time what type of object you are working with.

Should you write controls that know about containers? Generally, no. However, in some cases, there is practically no other way to accomplish your task. Just be careful when writing controls like this to clearly document the behavior they depend on from their container. Also, it wouldn't hurt to liberally use **On Error Resume Next** and check the **Err** variable.

Summary

Although the controls in this chapter don't fall into the regular ActiveX control category, you'll find them useful additions to your tool-building arsenal. Control containers offer the possibility of hybrid components. That is, a component that has behavior of its own but also contains other controls.

The challenge to these unusual controls is to think of them. When you think of ActiveX controls, you usually think of a visible widget that you can see. Once you start thinking about invisible controls and containers, you'll probably find many uses for them.

8

ActiveX And The Internet

O brave new world,
That has such people in't!

—The Tempest

Have you ever wondered about the Nobel Peace Prize? I always wonder about odd things that no one else seems to pay much attention to. For instance, it always bothered me that there is an Absorbine Jr. What the heck is Absorbine Sr.? It turns out plain Absorbine is horse liniment.

I recently had a chance to ask a rabbi why you always see signs in Baskin Robbins stores that say "All of our products are kosher except for those containing miniature marshmallows." Oddly, no one I've asked at Baskin Robbins over the years seemed to know. There seems to be no end to the amount of odd trivia I wonder about. Years ago I heard about the Nobel winners on the news, and it got my curiosity going.

Alfred Nobel, the man who set up the prize, invented dynamite (no kidding, look it up at http://www.nobel.se). Poor Alfred. He thought he had assured the destruction of the world, and was quite depressed. He set up his awards to encourage acts of peace to atone for his invention. Of course, in retrospect, dynamite isn't so bad. Truthfully, it can be used for good and ill. Dynamite is neither good nor bad; people are.

The World Wide Web isn't inherently good or bad. There are many interesting, informative sites. There are even more bland, mediocre sites. There are plenty of sites most folks would find offensive. There are even more sites that announce the creator's preferences as far as pizza, movies, and music (as though we care).

When is the last time you saw a Web site that you thought was culturally important? Have you seen a site that fosters greater international understanding and world peace? I'm sure there must be some sites like this, but not many.

Perhaps a Web "Nobel" award would be in order. The Web can be a powerful tool for social change, or a powerful waste of telecommunications bandwidth. I suppose it is up to us as Web developers.

No matter what kind of Web site you are creating, you can enhance it with ActiveX controls. Microsoft's Internet Explorer can embed ActiveX controls in Web pages. Netscape can too with the right plug-in. Also, Netscape is likely to directly support ActiveX soon.

Sure, you can put ActiveX controls on your Web pages, but how can you expect users to have that control? After all, for an ActiveX control to work, it needs to be on the user's hard disk and the correct entries must be in the registry. It isn't reasonable to expect users to manually download and install software just to see your spinning pepperoni pizza control.

Luckily, ActiveX-aware Web browsers can automatically download and install your controls. There are several methods you can use, but the best way is to let VB's Application Setup Wizard do the work for you.

ActiveX And HTML

Before you worry too much about setup, how do you use an ActiveX control in a Web page to begin with? If you aren't familiar with HTML, you might want to read Appendix B. Once your HTML page is ready, you'll want to use the **<OBJECT>** tag to insert the ActiveX control.

For example, here is the code you'll use to insert the LEDBAR control into a page:

```
<HTML>
<BODY>
<OBJECT CLASSID="clsid:5220cb21-c88d-11cf-b347-00aa00a28331">
</OBJECT>
</BODY>
</HTML>
```

If you need to pass parameters, you can use the **<PARAM>** tag in between the **<Object>** and **</Object>** tags, as in:

```
<OBJECT CLASSID = "clsid:5220cb21-c88d-11cf-b347-00aa00a28331">
    <PARAM NAME="LPKPath" VALUE="tod.lpk">
</OBJECT>
```

You don't necessarily have to do this by hand (although you certainly can). Some HTML editors (Microsoft's Control Pad, for example) will automatically generate these tags for you, if you like.

What about browsers that don't understand ActiveX? You can insert plain HTML between the **<Object>** and **</Object>** tags. Browsers that understand ActiveX also know to ignore this HTML:

```
<OBJECT . . .>
Hey! <I>Get a new browser!</I><P>
<A HREF=getnew.htm>Download a new browser now.</A>
</OBJECT>
```

A non-object-aware browser will ignore the **<OBJECT>** tags and unwittingly display the HTML you include after the tag. Newer browsers know to skip the HTML.

Licensing Controls

What happens if the control you want to use requires a license key? Normally, if your control requires a key, the programming language you use (VB, for example) embeds the key into the program. Where do you put the key for an HTML page?

The solution is far from automatic and requires more intervention on your part than in other languages. For any HTML file that requires licensed ActiveX controls, you have to construct an LPK file. This file contains an ASCII legal warning, and the keys for all the licensed controls used on the page. Whether the HTML file uses one control or 100 controls, you use a single LPK file.

To create the LPK file, you use Microsoft's LPK_TOOL program (see Figure 8.1). Simply select all the controls you want to use, and save the resulting LPK file. Of course, you must have the appropriate development license on your machine to make this work. You can't use LPK_TOOL to circumvent the normal licensing arrangement.

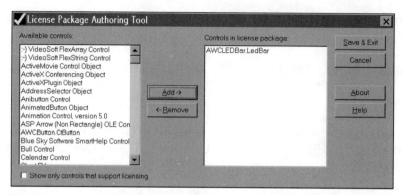

Figure 8.1 Microsoft's LPK_TOOL program.

If you examine the LPK file, you'll see that it is just a garbled-looking text file (see Listing 8.1). Don't be alarmed about the odd looking CLSID at the beginning. That identifies the version of the LPK format in use and doesn't have anything to do with your controls.

LISTING 8.1 AN LPK FILE.

```
LPK License Package
////////////////////////////////////////////////////////////////////////////
//  WARNING: The information in this file is protected by copyright law    //
//  and international treaty provisions. Unauthorized reproduction or       //
//  distribution of this file, or any portion of it, may result in severe  //
//  criminal and civil penalties, and will be prosecuted to the maximum    //
//  extent possible under the law. Further, you may not reverse engineer,  //
//  decompile, or disassemble the file.                                    //
////////////////////////////////////////////////////////////////////////////
{3d25aba1-caec-11cf-b34a-00aa00a28331}
IYRiGl14OBGnskRFU1QAAA=

AQAAAA=

oBN6QTFxOBGnskRFU1QAABIAAAB
xAG4AdwBuAG4AbQBuAGwAeABuAHUAbgBrAGkAbwBuAHQAbAA=
```

How do you make your HTML file use a particular LPK? You have to create an instance of the Microsoft License Manager control before you create any licensed ActiveX controls. As an argument, you pass the name of the LPK file as a relative URL. You can find an example HTML file that uses the licensed TOD control from Chapter 7 in Listing 8.2.

LISTING 8.2   USING THE LICENSED CONTROL.

```
<HTML>
<BODY>
<OBJECT CLASSID = "clsid:5220cb21-c88d-11cf-b347-00aa00a28331">
<PARAM NAME="LPKPath" VALUE="tod.lpk">
<EMBED SRC="tod.lpk">
</OBJECT>

<OBJECT CLASSID="clsid:417A13A0-7131-11D0-A7B2-444553540000">
</BODY>
</HTML>
```

If you are worried about users that use the NCompass plug-in from Netscape to view ActiveX controls, you should include an **<EMBED>** tag that names your LPK file in the **SRC** attribute inside the **<OBJECT>** tag.

Is the LPK scheme foolproof? No. Like ordinary licensing, it doesn't really prevent anyone from using your control. What it does do is ensure that if anyone does steal your control, they did it on purpose and with the knowledge that you did not want them to take it. Presumably, this would make it easier to pursue legal remedies. You should use a relative URL for the LPK file. That way if someone simply copies your HTML file, your ActiveX controls will fail to work. Still, anyone could copy the LPK file, too. They could also make a copy from their browser's cache. Again, this isn't rock solid security, but it does stop the casual or accidental copying of your valuable control.

Be sure to test your licensing on a machine that doesn't already have a license for the control. Your development machine, for example, will always allow you to use the control even if the LPK file isn't correct.

If you can't get the LPK file to work, here are a few things you might check:

1. The LPK file type should have a mime type of text/plain
2. Be sure the client machine has Microsoft's License Key Manager control installed (it should install with the Web browser)
3. If the browser fails to create the control once, I've found it will continue to fail, even if you fix the problem; exit the browser and try again
4. Make sure the control you select in LPK_TOOL is really the same control you specify in the HTML file's **<OBJECT>** tag; this is a problem if you have controls floating around with the same (or similar) names
5. Be sure you create the Microsoft License Key Manager before any other licensed controls

6. Be sure the control is really installed on the client machine for debugging purposes, I often install the control by hand (using REGSVR32) instead of depending on an automatic download (see below)

Distributing Controls On The Net

All the above HTML works if your machine already has the ActiveX control. But most Internet users probably won't. What's the answer? The **CodeBase** attribute allows you to specify a URL that contains the control you want to use. You also specify the version of the control. The browser then checks to see if the machine already has this control (or a newer version) in its registry. If it doesn't, the browser will download it, install the control, and continue.

You can directly specify your OCX file in a **CodeBase** statement. However, you'll almost never do that. There are two reasons for this: First, you usually have more than one file to install (the VB run time, for example); Second, you'd like to compress your files that the user will download.

To solve these problems, Microsoft allows you to use a cabinet file (one with a .CAB extension). This compressed file contains all the files required to install your control. In addition, it can contain an INF file that controls the installation.

ActiveX defines a mechanism for a browser to load and install an ActiveX control when it first encounters it. Doing this requires the control designer to specify where the control resides, the current version, and other information. A system administrator (or user) can specify where the browser should look for a control. In this way, you can search local libraries of controls (perhaps on a LAN) first. You can also prevent downloading any code, if you like.

Remember the **<OBJECT>** HTML tag? This is the tag you use to create an ActiveX object on a Web page. One of the attributes of this tag is the **CODEBASE** parameter. This is how the designer of a Web page specifies where an ActiveX control resides.

When a Web browser encounters an **<OBJECT>** tag, it searches for the object's **CLSID** in the system registry. If the object is already there (and at least the same version as the object specified in the **CODEBASE** parameter), the browser simply uses the existing object. If the object isn't already in the system registry, the browser searches for the control in a special search path. In this search path, the administrator can specify any number of URLs. The administrator can also indicate that the system should download the control from the URL specified in the **CODEBASE** parameter. Then the system downloads the control, checks its digital signature (see *Trust Verification*, later in this chapter), and installs the control.

Naturally, this process uses URL monikers, so the process is asynchronous. You don't have to wait for the objects on a page to download before you can proceed. This is a good idea, since users may not want to watch the browser lock up while you download a few dozen ActiveX controls.

The file argument can specify a normal ActiveX control file (usually with the extension .OCX), an INF file, or a CAB file. Which one you should use depends on what your control requires in the way of support.

The easiest, and least useful, option is to specify an OCX file directly. This is usually not satisfactory, because there is no file compression, and if you need any supporting files (perhaps the VB DLL), the system won't check for them.

A cabinet, or CAB file, is a special archive that can contain multiple files in a compressed format. This is good if you need several files, or if you want to compress the files (almost always a good idea). The disadvantage of CAB files is that you have to download everything in the CAB file. Imagine you have an ActiveX control that uses one of the VB DLLs. If you place the control and the DLL in the same CAB file, the system must load everything, even if the target computer already has the VB DLLs. Also, if you want to support multiple platforms, you won't want to download versions for all platforms on each machine.

Within the CAB file, you place an INF file that tells the system how to install the files in the cabinet. You can also specify an INF file directly. Using an INF file by itself is the most general method since it can point to other files (including CAB files). The INF file won't benefit from compression, but INF files are usually small, so this isn't a problem. Of course, you may compress the files that the INF file calls for by using a cabinet.

Writing An INF File

VB makes it easy to create simple INF files by running the Application Setup Wizard. However, sometimes you'll need to make your own, if you want to do anything complicated. First, I'll show you how to manually assemble an INF file, then I'll show you the easier Wizard method.

The INF file format is quite simple. INF files resemble ordinary Windows INI files. The first section is the [**Add.Code**] section. In that section, you place a line that specifies a tag and a section name for each file you need to install. Then you create the sections that contain commands for each file.

For example:

```
[Add.Code]
FILE1.OCX=FILE1.OCX
FILE2.DLL=FILE2.DLL
[FILE1.OCX]
  .
  .
```

You don't have to use the file name for the section name, but it is common practice. Besides, it helps keep things straight.

In each file section, you can place the following lines:

FILE=url	Specifies where the system can download the control.
FILE=thiscab	Informs the system that the file is in this cabinet (only applies to INF files in a cabinet).
FILEVERSION=a,b,c,d	Version numbers for the control.
FILE-WIN32-X86=url	Indicates URL to use for downloading a version of code for Win32 platforms using an x86 processor. You can also use MAC in place of WIN32 for the Macintosh. In place of X86, you can also specify PPC, MIPS, or ALPHA.
FILE-WIN32-X86=ignore	Informs the system that the file is not required (or not available) for the target platform specified. Again, you may specify MAC, PPC, ALPHA, or MIPS.
CLSID={...}	The CLSID for the control in the usual registry format.
DESTDIR=10	This command places the file in the \WINDOWS directory (or whatever is the equivalent location for this machine). If there is no DESTDIR command, the system places the file in a special object cache directory.
DESTDIR=11	If you use this DESTDIR command, the system will place the file in the \WINDOWS\SYSTEM directory (or its equivalent).

You can find a simple example INF file in Listing 8.3. Listing 8.4 shows a similar INF file that handles multiple platforms.

LISTING 8.3 AN EXAMPLE INF FILE.

```
; Sample INF File
[Add.Code]
Sample.OCX=Sample.OCX
MFC40.DLL=MFC40.DLL

[Sample.OCX]
File=http://www.coriolis.com/not_real/sample.ocx
CLSID={12345678-1234-1234-123456789abc}
FileVersion=1,0,0,1
```

```
[MFC40.DLL]
File=http://www.coriolis.com/not_real/mfc40.dll
FileVersion=4,0,0,5
```

Note that you can handle multiple platforms without using INF files. The system adds an HTTP Accept header when it queries the server for a control file. By interpreting this header it is possible to send the correct executable or CAB file for the given platform. However, using the INF file is a much easier solution and easier to keep straight.

LISTING 8.4   AN EXAMPLE MULTIPLATFORM **INF** FILE.

```
; Sample INF File
[Add.Code]
Sample.OCX=Sample.OCX

[Sample.OCX]
file-win32-x86=http://www.coriolis.com/not_real/x86/sample.ocx
file-win32-alpha=http://www.coriolis.com/not_real/a/sample.ocx
file-mac-ppc=ignore ; no mac!
CLSID={12345678-1234-1234-123456789abc}
FileVersion=1,0,0,1
```

One important advantage to using INF files is that the system can selectively download only the files that are not on the system already. For example, if the INF file contains a reference to a control, and a reference to the MFC DLL that it requires, the system need only load the files that are not already present.

Building A CAB File

For reasons known only to Microsoft, CAB files are often known as Diamond files. Therefore, to build one, you must construct a Diamond directive file (DDF). This file has a very simple format:

```
.Option Explicit
.Set CabinetNameTemplate=dummy.CAB
.Set Cabinet=on
.Set Compress=on
file1
    .
    .
    .
fileN
```

In the previous example, you will create a cabinet named DUMMY.CAB (of course, you could name it anything you like). The cabinet will contain file1, filen, and whatever other files you name in between.

When you want to create the cabinet file, run the DIANTZ utility:

```
DIANTZ /f xxx.DDF
```

Of course, substitute the name of your DDF file in the above command line.

The Simple Way

To create a simple CAB file, just run VB's Application Setup Wizard (see Figures 8.2, 8.3, 8.4, 8.5, and 8.6). First the Wizard will prompt you for a project name (see Figure 8.2). You can ask the Wizard to rebuild the project before proceeding, if you like. This makes sure that you will distribute the latest code. For the purposes of this chapter, you'll want to check the Create Internet Download Setup checkbox before clicking the Next button.

The next screen (Figure 8.3) prompts you to enter a destination directory. This is where the Wizard will create the CAB file (and some other related files). This doesn't have to be a directory on your server, although you will need the CAB file on your server eventually.

Now the Wizard asks you where you want the users to get the VB5 run time (Figure 8.4). The users can download it from Microsoft's Internet server, or

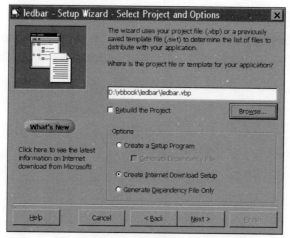

Figure 8.2 Starting the Setup Wizard.

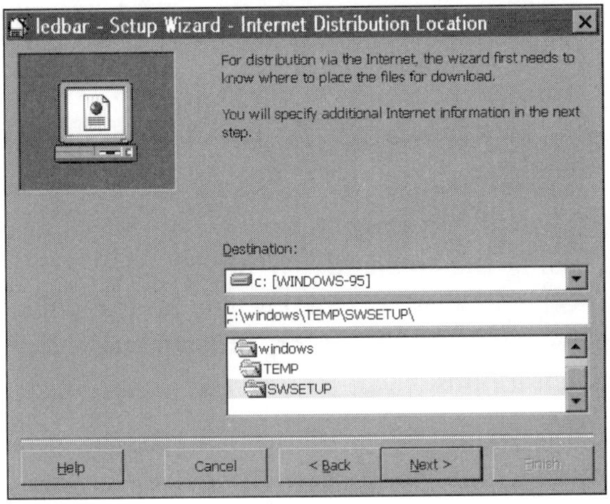

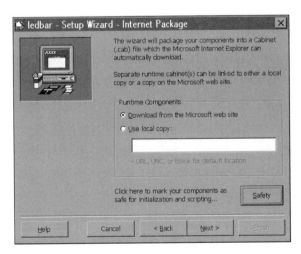

Figure 8.3 Selecting a directory.

you can arrange for them to download it from your Web site by specifying a URL. The other choice on this dialog is the Safety button. Click this button to tell the Wizard you want registry entries that indicate your control is safe for initialization and scripting. Without these entries, the browser may warn the user that your control is unsafe. Setting the control as safe for initialization indicates that the HTML which uses your control can set parameters using the **<PARAM>** tag. Setting your control as safe for scripting allows HTML to reference your control using script (i.e., JavaScript or VBScript).

Figure 8.4 Setup options.

Notice that this is not the same kind of safety afforded by digital code signing. Digital code signing (discussed below) assures the user that your control is from a trusted source and hasn't been modified since you signed it. The safety controls here only indicate that you believe it is safe for programmers to set your control's values.

For the next step, you'll see a list of any files the Wizard determines you are using (not including the standard VB run time). You can use this screen (Figure 8.5) to add more files, if you know you need any that VB didn't detect. Adding files may cause VB to find more files you need. If this is the case, VB will show you what it finds.

Eventually, you'll see a summary of all the files you'll be installing (Figure 8.6). You can add any other files you'd like to have installed and view the information about the files.

On the final Wizard screen, you have the opportunity to save your choices to a template file. You can load this template file back into the Wizard later, if you like. This will save you the effort of typing it all again. Finally, you can click the Finish button and the Wizard will generate your CAB and INF files.

While this is much simpler than rolling it all by hand, you'll find times that you want more control. In these cases, you have a choice. You can simply write the entire DDF file by hand, or you can start with the files the VB Wizard writes for you. If you examine the SWSETUP directory, you'll find a subdirectory called SUPPORT. In this directory, the Wizard places

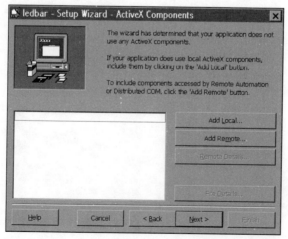

Figure 8.5 Files in use.

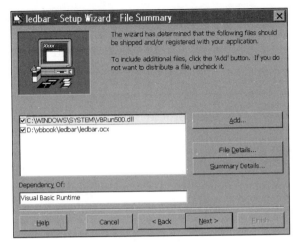

Figure 8.6 The setup summary.

the DDF file along with other important files that it uses to create your CAB and INF files.

Seeking Components

Just because a Web page designer specifies a certain **CODEBASE** parameter doesn't mean that the browser will automatically download from that location. Instead, the browser refers to a special registry key to decide where to search for the component.

For Microsoft's browser, the key in question is under **HKEY_ CURRENT_USER\Software\Microsoft\InternetExplorer\CodeBaseSearchPath**. This key's value is a list of URLs separated by semicolons. If a URL has a special value (**CODEBASE**) then the browser will search the location specified by the **CODEBASE** parameter in the Web page. Consider these examples:

```
CodeBaseSearchPath=http://m1;http://m2;CODEBASE
```

Search local object stores first, then specify URL

```
CodeBaseSearchPath=CODEBASE
```

Always look where specified

```
CodeBaseSearchPath=http://m1;http://m2
```

Never download code from the specified location

This gives the system administrator a great deal of control over the search for components. The first case tries to optimize performance by searching local object stores. The third case forbids downloading except from certain known servers.

You might think that the third search path would allow a certain amount of security. That's true, although it is a bit draconian. If this were the sole method of controlling access, only controls on the trusted servers would be usable. If you are especially paranoid, that might be a good idea. However, you'd like a better solution. That's why the trust verification services exist.

Trust Verification

Every time you download a piece of code from the Internet, you risk infecting your system with a virus. That's a problem when you consciously transfer a file. Now that ActiveX can automatically download, install, and run an ActiveX component, the problem increases many times over. How can you be sure that the code that runs won't wipe out your hard disk or play other malicious tricks on you?

ActiveX provides trust verification services that allow you to control what code gets to execute on your machine. Here's the basic idea:

1. A software developer gets a certificate file from a trusted certificate authority. The authority verifies that the developer is legitimate.
2. The developer encrypts a digest of a file (similar to a checksum, but much longer than a traditional checksum) and combines it with the certificate to form a signature block.
3. The developer finally stores the signature block in the file.

When ActiveX downloads your file, it checks the signature block. It scans the certificate to see if it comes from a certificate authority that the system administrator trusts. It also checks the digest to verify that the file is unmodified. If there is no signature, the certificate is not trustworthy, or the file appears modified, the system considers the file unsafe. If everything checks out, the system proceeds with the file's installation.

Each certificate knows about the authority that issued it, and the authority that certified the originating authority. That means your machine can trust authorities that it doesn't know about directly. Suppose that authority "A" trusts authority "B" and authority "B" issues the Coriolis Group a code certificate. When you download a Coriolis control, your machine notes that the certificate originates from authority "B." Your machine doesn't know about authority

"B," but by tracing the certificate chain, the system discovers that authority "B" has a certificate from authority "A." The trust verification service will conclude that the code is trustworthy, in this case.

If the system doesn't trust code, one of several things may happen depending on the settings you use in the browser (see Figure 8.7). For most users, the machine will refuse to load the offending component. However, you can elect to have the browser warn you that the code is not trustworthy. Then you can elect to load it or not. Finally, you can tell the browser to always load code regardless of its trust status (a dangerous proposition).

This raises some interesting questions: Who trusts the authorities? Microsoft? A third party? If your machine becomes infected, who is liable? Will small-time developers be able to get certificates? How much will they cost? The answers to these questions are far from clear today. Only time will tell how safe—or how sinister—trust verification is.

Using Trust Verification

You can use the **MAKECERT** program to generate your keys and certificate file. Here's a typical command line:

```
MAKECERT -C -u:keyset -k:keyfile.pvk -n:"CN=CertName" mycert.cer
```

The arguments, in no particular order, are:

-u	The keyset file used for the developer's public/private key pair. If this keyset does not exist, it is created
-U	Use existing certificate and keys

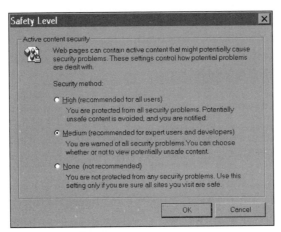

Figure 8.7 Browser security settings.

-k	The PVK file that contains the key pair. If this file doesn't exist, it is created
-n	The name of the developer's certificate (the name must begin with CN= as in "CN=AWC")
-s	The issuer's key file (default to the test root key)
-i	The issuer's certificate
-l	A URL to the policy information about this certification
-I	Marks certificate as an individual certificate
-C	Marks certificate as a commercial developer certificate (use :f to set financial criteria)
-S	Set session
-P	Set purpose for certificate (default is code signing)
-x	Set crypto provider
-y	Set crypto provider type
-K	Type of key (S=signature; E=exchange)
-B	Start of valid period (defaults to now)
-D	Number of months certificate is valid
-E	End date of valid period (default is 2039)
-h	Sets maximum number of child certificates this certificate may have
-t	Certificate type (E=end of hierarchy; C=potential root; may use both)
-g	Create a glue certificate for encapsulating multiple certificates
-r	Create a self-signed (no root) certificate
-m	Use MD5 hashing (default)
-a	Use SHA1 hashing
-N	Include Netscape client authorization extension
-#	Override default serial number (not recommended)

Once you have a certificate file, you have to generate a signature block (sometimes known as credentials) by combining it with your trusted certificate. To test, you may use the ROOT.CER file that Microsoft provides. Run CERT2SPC to make your signature block:

```
CERT2SPC \inetsdk\bin\root.cer my.cer my.spc
```

The output of this command is the my.spc file. This file contains all of the certificates listed in the input (you can specify as many as you like).

Finally, you'll need to run the SIGNCODE wizard to add the spc file to your code. Although this program has a Wizard-style interface, you may prefer to provide command line options if you are running it as part of a lengthy build:

-prog	Program name
-spc	Credential file
-pvk	Public/private key file or keyset name
-name	Program name
-info	URL or file for more information
-nocerts	No certification
-provider	Specifies which crypto provider to use
-providerType	Specifies what type of crypto provider to use
-individual	Mark as an individual developer (default)
-commercial	Mark as a commercial developer
-md5	Encrypt using MD5 hashing (default)
-sha	Encrypt using SHA1 hashing
-gui	Use GUI to gather any additional arguments (without this option, incomplete command line options cause the operation to fail)

You can see the results by running the CHKTRUST utility. This program checks your trust in the same way a user's browser will. Don't forget: every time you change your code, you must re-sign your code.

To summarize, here are the steps you must take along with example command lines:

1. Run MAKECERT to create a pair of keys (public and private keys) and associate the keys with a readable name.

```
MAKECERT -u:mykeys -n:CN=Coriolis newcert.cer
```

2. Run CERT2SPC to place the root certificate (presumably from a third party) and the user certificate (from step 1) into a signature block.

```
CERT2SPC root.cer newcert.cer coriolis.spc
```

3. Execute SIGNCODE to add the signature block to your executable file. If you just run the SIGNCODE program, you can fill in a Wizard-like form to specify arguments. You may also use command line arguments.

```
SIGNCODE -prog myprogram.exe -spc coriolis.spc -pvk mykeys
```

Once these steps are complete, you can verify that the certificate is present by running PESIGMGR (Portable Executable SIGnature ManaGeR):

```
PESIGMGR -l myprogram.exe
```

You can also specify a variety of arguments to PESIGMGR to manually add and delete certificates (use PESIGMGR /? to find out more). Usually, you'll let SIGNCODE do all the work for you.

You can also manually check the file for trustworthiness by running CHKTRUST. Just specify your executable file name as an argument to this program. For practice, try making a copy of solitaire (or any other small program), run CHKTRUST on it, and then sign it with your own signature. If you do this, try changing the file with a binary editor and note the results. The signature is only valid if the file is intact. There is some small possibility that you could alter a file in such a way that the digest (basically a very long checksum) would not detect it, but the chances of that are astronomically slim.

If you ever want to write a program to manually check a signature, you can call **WinVerifyTrust**. This API call finds the signature, validates it, and tells you if the code is trustworthy or not.

The browser has a special setup dialog that allows you to confer trustworthy status to particular agencies or types of developers (see Figure 8.8). Also, if the browser prompts you for an unsafe component, you can ask it to consider other components from the same source as trustworthy.

ActiveX And VBScript

If you write VBScript in your Web pages, you'll be glad to know you can manipulate your controls via script. Just be sure to use the **ID** attribute in the **OBJECT** statement. This sets the object's name you'll use in your scripts.

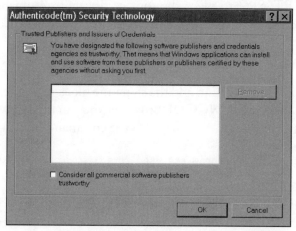

Figure 8.8   A security warning dialog.

Once your object has a name, you can call methods and set properties. You can also write VBScript code to handle events that your control fires. This allows you to extend VBScript in any way you like by supplying ActiveX controls.

Consider Listing 8.5. This is a simple button control with a twist. Each time you click the button, it sends a special event (**ClickN**) that has the number of times you've clicked the button. You can set the caption using a property and reset the count using the **Reset** method.

LISTING 8.5   A SIMPLE BUTTON CONTROL.

```
VERSION 5.00
Begin VB.UserControl CtButton
   ClientHeight    =    792
   ClientLeft      =    0
   ClientTop       =    0
   ClientWidth     =    1308
   PropertyPages   =    "CtButton.ctx":0000
   ScaleHeight     =    792
   ScaleWidth      =    1308
   Begin VB.CommandButton Command1
      Caption      =    "Command1"
      Height       =    492
      Left         =    120
      TabIndex     =    0
      Top          =    120
      Width        =    972
   End
End
Attribute VB_Name = "CtButton"
Attribute VB_GlobalNameSpace = False
Attribute VB_Creatable = True
Attribute VB_PredeclaredId = False
Attribute VB_Exposed = True
Option Explicit
'Event Declarations:
Event ClickN(n)
Private count As Integer

'WARNING! DO NOT REMOVE OR MODIFY THE FOLLOWING COMMENTED LINES!
'MappingInfo=Command1,Command1,-1,Caption
Public Property Get Caption() As String
Attribute Caption.VB_Description = "Returns/sets the text " & _
  "displayed in an object's title bar or below an " & _
  "object's icon."
    Caption = Command1.Caption
End Property
```

```
Public Property Let Caption(ByVal New_Caption As String)
    Command1.Caption() = New_Caption
    PropertyChanged "Caption"
End Property

Public Sub Reset()
Attribute Reset.VB_Description = "Resets the buttons count"
    count = 0
End Sub

Private Sub Command1_Click()
count = count + 1
RaiseEvent ClickN(count)
End Sub

'Load property values from storage
Private Sub UserControl_ReadProperties(PropBag As PropertyBag)
    Command1.Caption = PropBag.ReadProperty("Caption", "Command1")
End Sub

Private Sub UserControl_Resize()
Command1.Top = 0
Command1.Left = 0
Command1.Width = Width
Command1.Height = Height
End Sub

'Write property values to storage
Private Sub UserControl_WriteProperties(PropBag As PropertyBag)

    Call PropBag.WriteProperty("Caption", Command1.Caption, "Command1")
End Sub
```

One major difference between ordinary VB and VBScript is that VBScript only recognizes the **Variant** data type. That means you must use a **Variant** argument to **RaiseEvent** in the **Command1.Click** handler. If you try to pass an integer, for example, IE will see that as an error.

Now look at Listing 8.6. This HTML script uses the special button object. The VBScript code is inside the **<SCRIPT>** tag. You have to specify the **LANGUAGE** attribute as **VBScript** or **VBS**; otherwise the browser will use JavaScript.

It isn't strictly necessary, but it is customary to surround the script with HTML comments (<!-- and -->). This prevents older browsers that don't understand script from displaying your code to the user.

Notice that the script sets the button's caption in two ways. The initial caption comes from a <PARAM> tag. However, each time the user pushes the button, the code changes the caption from inside the VBScript event handler.

LISTING 8.6   HTML SCRIPT WITH EVENTS.

```
<HTML>
<BODY>
<OBJECT WIDTH=85 HEIGHT=30 ID=Btn1
        CLASSID="clsid:701ada71-78eb-11D0-A7B2-444553540000">
<PARAM NAME="Caption" VALUE="Click Me 1">
</OBJECT>
<SCRIPT LANGUAGE=VBS>
<!--
Sub Btn1_ClickN(n)
  Alert "Click " & n
  if n=3 then
    Btn1.Reset
    n=0
  end if
  Btn1.Caption = "Click Me " & n+1
End Sub
-->
</SCRIPT>
</BODY>
</HTML>
```

To handle the event, you simply write a Sub in the VBScript code that contains the name of the control, an underscore, and the name of the event. VB is smart enough to figure out what you want to do.

This opens up many possibilities. You can write ActiveX controls to handle animation, special text effects (like scrolling), or user interface items that HTML doesn't provide.

Note that you don't have to use VBScript with objects. Any scripting language may handle objects if it chooses to do so. The above example could use JavaScript, for example, just as easily.

Built-In ActiveX Objects

Internet Explorer provides many objects that VBScript code can use to manipulate the browser itself. These objects are ActiveX objects, but you don't have to specify them using the **<OBJECT>** tag. Instead, they are always present and ready to use.

These objects constitute the scripting object model (see Table 8.1). At the root of the model is the **Window** object. You don't actually need to name the **Window** object if you want to work with the current **Window**. You can find the members of **Window** in Table 8.2.

Notice that one of the members of **Window** is an array named **frames**. This is an array of **Window** objects, each of which represents a frame in the current **Window**. These windows may further contain other windows if you have nested frames.

Another important member of **Window** is **Document**. This object represents the document in the window. You can find the **Document** object's members in Table 8.3. You'll notice the **Document** object has several arrays that allow you to access the links, anchors, and forms in the document. Before you get too excited about some of these properties, you should know that many of them are read-only. Others can only be set before the browser displays the document ("parse time").

You'll find information about the other objects available in Tables 8.4 to 8.9. By the way, some Microsoft documentation has a flaw you should know about: When you access an array (like **Document.Frames**) you should use VB syntax when using VBScript, although some documentation always uses Java notation, that is, if the documentation suggests writing:

```
Document.Frame[0]
```

Table 8.1   The Scripting object model (client-side).

Object	Description
Window	The browser's window or a frame
History	Record of browser's history list
Navigator	Information about the browser (named for compatibility with Netscape Navigator)
Location	The current URL, both as a URL and parsed into component pieces
Document	The HTML document
Link	An **<A HREF=>** tag in the document
Anchor	An **<A>** tag in the Document (Anchor objects only contain one property, **Name**)
Form	An HTML form in a Document
Element	An HTML intrinsic control or ActiveX control in a form

You should write:

```
Document.Frame(0)
```

Look again at Listing 8.6 (the example script that uses an object). Notice that in the event handler, the code uses **Alert** to display a dialog box. Now look carefully at Table 8.2. Notice that **Alert** is a member of **Window**. However, the code doesn't explicitly reference a **Window** object since it wants to use the current window. Nevertheless, looking in the standard VBScript documentation for **Alert** will not yield anything useful. You must look in the Scripting Object Model documentation (part of the ActiveX SDK).

Table 8.2 Window object members.

Member	Type	Description
name	Property	Name of window
parent	Property	Parent window
opener	Property	Window that opened this window
self	Property	Reference to this window
top	Property	Reference to topmost browser window
location	Property	Location object for this window
defaultStatus	Property	Default status bar text
status	Property	Status bar text
frames	Property	Array of Window objects, one for each frame
history	Property	History object tracks URLs visited
navigator	Property	Navigator object provides information about browser
document	Property	Document object provides information about HTML document
alert	Method	Displays message in a dialog box
confirm	Method	Displays message and receives OK or Cancel status from user
prompt	Method	Prompts user for a string
open	Method	Opens a new window
close	Method	Closes a window
setTimeout	Method	Calls a function after a number of milliseconds expire
clearTimeout	Method	Cancels timeout function
Navigate	Method	Go to a new URL
onLoad	Event	Fires when window loads
onUnload	Event	Fires when window unloads

Table 8.3 Document object members.

Member	Type	Description
linkColor	Property	The color of document links
aLinkColor	Property	Active link color (not used in IE)
vLinkColor	Property	Visited link color
bgColor	Property	Color of background
fgColor	Property	Foreground color
anchors	Property	Array of Anchor objects
links	Property	Array of Link objects
forms	Property	Array of Form objects
location	Property	The location object that shows where the document originated
lastModified	Property	Last modified date of current page
title	Property	Document's title
cookie	Property	The raw cookie string (only available if document came from server via http)
referrer	Property	The referring Web page
write	Method	Write string to output
writeLn	Method	Write string and new line to output (Note: outputs a real new line, not a <P> tag)
open	Method	Clears document data and begins buffering subsequent write and writeln statements
close	Method	Closes open document, writing all buffered write statements
clear	Method	Writes buffered output without closing open document

Table 8.4 The Form object's members.

Member	Type	Description
action	Property	URL to submit form to
encoding	Property	Form data encoding method
method	Property	How to submit form (e.g., Get, Post)
target	Property	Target frame for form results
elements	Property	Array of element objects
submit	Method	Submit form
onSubmit	Event	Fires before form is submitted

Table 8.5 Location object properties.

Properties	Description
href	The entire URL
protocol	The protocol portion of the URL
host	URL's host name field and port field
hostname	URL's host name field (without port)
pathname	Path from URL
search	Search string (portion after "?")
hash	Hash field from URL

Table 8.6 The Link object's members.

Member	Type	Description
href	Property	Target URL
target	Property	Frame to target
protocol	Property	The protocol portion of the URL
host	Property	URL's host name field and port field
hostname	Property	URL's host name field (without port)
pathname	Property	Path from URL
search	Property	Search string (portion after "?")
hash	Property	Hash field from URL (portion after "#")
onMouseMove	Event	Mouse is moving over link
onMouseOver	Event	Mouse is standing still over link
onClick	Event	Link clicked

Table 8.7 Element object members.

Member	Type	Description
form	Property	Form that element belongs to
name	Property	Name of element
value	Property	Element's current value
defaultValue	Property	Element's default value
checked	Property	Element's current check state
defaultChecked	Property	Element's default check state
length	Property	Length of element
options	Property	<Select> options
selectedIndex	Property	Selected item

continued

Table 8.7 Element object members (continued).

Member	Type	Description
click	Method	Activate element
focus	Method	Shift focus to element
blur	Method	Move focus away from element
select	Method	Select contents
onClick	Event	Element activated
onFocus	Event	Element received focus
onBlur	Event	Element lost focus
onChange	Event	Element changed
onSelect	Event	Element contents selected

Note: Not all members apply to every possible element type.

Table 8.8 History members.

Member	Type	Description
length	Property	Number of items in history object
back	Method	Go backward specified number of pages
forward	Method	Go forward specified number of pages
go	Method	Go to specific page in history list

Table 8.9 Navigator properties.

Property	Description
appCodeName	Code name of application
appName	Name of application
appVersion	Version of application
userAgent	User agent identification (e.g., Mozilla/2.0)

ActiveX And Server-Side Scripting

If you use Microsoft's Internet Information Server 3.0 (IIS3), you know that you can also write VBScript at the server side. This is not much like the client-side scripting in the previous section. With client-side scripting, you send Basic code to the client browser where it executes on the client machine. Contrast this with server-side scripting which executes a Basic program on the server. The Basic program outputs HTML that the server sends to the client.

Notice that this isn't an either/or proposition. You can certainly write a server script that outputs client script as part of its HTML output. In fact, for many effects, this is necessary. However, server scripts can't directly access client variables and objects. By the same token, client scripts can't directly access server variables and objects.

Writing server side scripts is easy. You put your code in a file with a .ASP extension. This file looks like HTML except for a few special cases. First, you can use server-side include statements to insert another file into the ASP file. For example, suppose I have a file named GREET.INC that contains the string "Good Day." Then, this ASP file:

```
I want to wish you
<!#include file=greet.inc>
<P>And nothing more
```

is the same as if the file contained:

```
I want to wish you
Good Day
<P>And nothing more
```

That's not terribly exciting. The exciting part comes from two new HTML-like tags: <% and <%=. The first tag starts a server-side VBScript program. The second tag executes some VBScript and places the result of the code into the HTML output stream. For example:

```
<% LogTime = Now %>
You started your session at <%= LogTime %>
```

What could be easier? You can also insert code into script by using the **<SCRIPT RUNAT=SERVER>** tag, although you'll rarely do that unless you are writing an event handler.

A nice feature of the <% tag is that you can intermix it with HTML code, like this:

```
<% Validated = IsValidUser(UserName)
      if Validated = True then %>
Welcome to our world!<P>
<%   else %>
<B>You are not authorized to proceed!</B>
<% end if %>
```

What's this got to do with ActiveX objects? You can create ActiveX objects on the server and use them for processing. These can be true controls or just ActiveX DLLs. The most common way to create these objects is to use **Server.CreateObject**. The Server object is built in to IIS (you'll find out more about **Server** and other built-in objects shortly). Here is an example you might use to create an object whose ProgID is **IISExample.Test**:

```
set TestObj = Server.CreateObject("IISExample.Test")
```

Once you create an object, you can use it like you'd expect, accessing methods and properties. To handle events, you have to write an event handler subroutine (much like you do in client-side script). Just be sure to use **RUNAT=SERVER** in your **<SCRIPT>** tag.

One important thing you should notice about server-side ActiveX components: They must not have a user interface. Suppose your ActiveX component creates a window. That window will be on the server, not on the user's browser. Worse still, what if your component waits for user input? Not a good idea since someone physically at the server will have to provide that input.

Of course, you can write invisible components or DLLs (see Chapter 7). These work very well as server-side components. Also, IIS gives you a variety of controls with IIS that do many useful things (see Table 8.10). Notice that these aren't built into IIS. They are just ActiveX components that ship with IIS.

Table 8.10 IIS components.

Components	ProgID	Description
Ad Rotator	MSWC.AdRotator	Selects ads based on a scheduling file
Browser Capabilities	MSWC.BrowserType	Looks up browser's User Agent string in a server database and reports that agent's known capabilities
Content Linking	MSWC.NextLink	Allows you to create next/previous page links
File	Scripting.FileSystemObject	Represents an open file
Text Stream	N/A	A text stream in a file system object
Database Connection	ADODB.Connection	Connection to an ODBC database
Record Set	ADODB.Recordset	Records in database

Built-in IIS Components

However, IIS does provide its own set of built-in objects. These objects allow server-side scripts to interact with the server (see Table 8.11). You've already seen one of these objects, **Server**. The **Server** object allows you to affect the IIS server program (see Table 8.12).

Another object, **Application**, represents your virtual directory (see Table 8.13). The first time a user loads a file from your virtual directory, the server creates the **Application** object. You can write event handling script for the **Application** object in a special file, GLOBAL.ASA.

Table 8.11 Server-side scripting objects.

Object	Description
Server	Represents the entire server
Application	Object that controls your application (all files in a virtual directory)
Session	Object that tracks a user session
Request	Allows access to incoming data
Response	Represents the HTML output stream

Table 8.12 Server object members.

Member	Type	Description
ScriptTimeout	Property	Sets maximum time a script may run
CreateObject	Method	Creates an ActiveX object
HTMLEncode	Method	Encodes a string using HTML escapes
MapPath	Method	Converts a relative or virtual path name to an absolute path name suitable for access via the server's filesystem
URLEncode	Method	Encode a string using URL-style escapes

Table 8.13 Members of application.

Member	Type	Description
OnStart	Event	Application started (initial user loaded a page)
OnEnd	Event	Application terminating
Lock	Method	Locks application variables
Unlock	Method	Unlocks application variables

GLOBAL.ASA also contains handlers for the **Session** object (Table 8.14). The server creates this object the first time a user downloads a page from your application. The **Session** object remains active until a certain time expires (usually 20 minutes or more). If the same host loads another file before that time expires, the server uses the same **Session** object. This is useful for keeping information that applies to an entire session (a shopping cart, for example).

You can create objects that last for the entire session or application lifetime by using the **Session** and **Application** objects as collections. For example, to create an object that lasts for the entire session, you'd write:

```
<% Set Session("UsrObj")=Server.Create("SDemo.Obj1") %>
```

If you use the **Application** object instead of the **Session** object, then the object will exist from the time a user first loads a page from your virtual directory until IIS shuts down. However, be sure to call **Application.Lock** before setting the variable and **Application.Unlock** afterwards. Since all sessions share the same **Application** object, you must do this to ensure consistency. Using the **Application** object allows you to create a single object that all your server-side scripts access.

The **Request** object (see Table 8.15) contains the data sent by the client to the Web server. This data may be from the query string (the part of the URL that appears after a question mark), a form, a certificate, or cookies. In addition, you can access standard CGI variables using the **Request** object. You can access the request data easily by just treating the **Request** object as a collection. Then, the server searches for the data in the query string. If it isn't there, the server looks at form data, then cookies, then the client's certificate, and finally in the server variables.

Table 8.14 Session object details.

Member	Type	Description
OnStart	Event	Session opening (new user)
OnEnd	Event	Session closing
SessionID	Property	User's ID for this session
Timeout	Property	ID expires after this many minutes of server inactivity (default=20 minutes)
Abandon	Method	Terminate user's session now

Table 8.15 Request members.

Member	Type	Description
QueryString	Property	Collection containing query string variables
Form	Property	Collection holding form variables
Cookies	Property	Collection that contains cookie-based variables
ClientCertificate	Property	Collection containing SSL certificate (https only)
ServerVariables	Property	Standard CGI-style environment variables

Assume the server receives a request with this URL:

```
http://www.al-williams.com/awc/rtest.html?name=Al
```

Then:

```
<%= Request.QueryString("name") %>
```

and

```
<%= Request("name") %>
```

will both place "Al" in the output HTML.

Table 8.16 shows the members available in the **Response** object. This object allows you to write headers to the client. You can also manipulate the output HTML stream. In fact, <%= is really just shorthand for **Response.Write**. You'll often see error messages refer to **Response.Write** when you actually used <%=.

Asynchronous Data

Surely by now you've viewed a Web page sometime in your life. I can say this with confidence, because my parents have and I think they were the last two people who had not seen a Web page. Did you ever notice how browsers handle graphics? Since graphics tend to be large (and Internet connections tend to be slow) the browser just puts a placeholder where the image should go and continues its other work. Meanwhile, it downloads the image, filling it in as it arrives.

This works well for several reasons. First, it lets the user see all the text right away. If the page isn't interesting, users can move on without waiting for the graphics to load. On the converse side, users won't get bored waiting for a

Table 8.16 About the Response object.

Member	Type	Description
Cookies	Property	Collection that sets cookies
Buffer	Property	Indicates if server should buffer output to client
ContentType	Property	Sets output content type
Expires	Property	Sets expiration time for page relative to current time
ExpiresAbsolute	Property	Sets absolute expiration time for page
Status	Property	HTTP status code
AddHeader	Method	Output a header to the client
AppendToLog	Method	Write to server's log
BinaryWrite	Method	Write binary data to output stream
Clear	Method	Clear buffered response data (except headers)
End	Method	Write buffered response data and stop buffering
Flush	Method	Write buffered response data and continue buffering
Redirect	Method	Reroute request to a different URL
Write	Method	Write text string to output

graphic and surf over to another page. Besides, all the graphics load concurrently. Depending on the network and the location of the graphics, this might speed things up a bit.

The ActiveX specification allows you to create asynchronous properties that work in a similar fashion. The control can initialize itself and then load the data it needs over the Web in an asynchronous fashion. The program continues, as usual.

Of course, you'll only use asynchronous properties where you have a large amount of data (usually, but not always, an image of some kind). There's no law that says you can't load nearly all of your properties asynchronously, but it doesn't make much sense.

If you've ever tried to make asynchronous properties with C++, you know it isn't easy. You have to understand asynchronous monikers, ready states, and handle a lot of protocol. As usual, VB makes it almost trivial to pull this off—within certain limits.

Here are the basic steps:

1. In your **UserControl** object, call **AsyncRead** to start loading your data. You'll usually make the call in the **Initialize** event handler, but you could

call it from anywhere. You specify the URL where the control can find the data, the type of data, and an optional name. The name is only necessary if you need to handle multiple properties.

2. When the control fires an **AsyncReadComplete** event, it passes you the downloaded data in an **AsyncProp** object (see Table 8.17). Set the appropriate property with the passed data item.

3. Refresh any controls that need repainting.

Is that all? In a nutshell, yes. However, there is one fine point you might want to consider. Remember that the program will run even when your data is not available yet. In many cases, you'll want to export a read-only **Ready** property, or a **Ready** event (you can name it to whatever makes sense). This property starts out in the **False** state. When all the data you need is available, you can change the **Ready** property to **True**. This tells the rest of the program that you have all of your data. If you use an event, you can fire it when the data is available.

You can choose among three data types for your asynchronous property (see Table 8.18). Usually, you'll use **vbAsyncTypePicture**. Then the **AsyncProp.Value** you receive in the **AsyncReadComplete** event will contain a standard VB picture. You can also elect to get a byte array (**vbAsyncTypeByte**) or a file (**vbAsyncTypeFile**). In all cases, you use **AsyncProp.Value** to extract the data.

The **AsyncProp** object has two other useful members. One is **AsyncType**. This is the value you passed in as the type of the data (for example, **vbAsyncTypePicture**). The other data member is **PropertyName**. This item has the same value as the optional property name you pass to **AsyncRead**.

Table 8.17 The AsyncProp Object.

Property	Description
AsyncType	Type specified in read request
PropertyName	User-defined name for this request
Value	Actual data

Table 8.18 Values for AsyncType.

Value	Description
vbAsyncTypePicture	Standard VB picture
vbAsyncTypeByte	Byte array
vbAsyncTypeFile	VB-created file

The only purpose for this value is to allow you to distinguish between multiple properties. For example, suppose you were loading two picture properties. Your **Initialize** event might look like this:

```
Private Sub UserControl_Initialize()
' Start async read — fire AsyncReadComplete when done
  AsyncRead "http://www/al.gif", vbAsyncTypePicture, _
    "pix1"
AsyncRead "http://www/jeff.gif", vbAsyncTypePicture, _
    "pix2"
End Sub
```

Then, the event handler might look something like this:

```
Private Sub UserControl_AsyncReadComplete(AsyncProp As AsyncProperty)
  if AsyncProp.PropertyName = "pix1" Then
    Set LeftPix.Picture = AsyncProp.Value
    LeftPix.Refresh
else
    Set RightPix.Picture = AsyncProp.Value
    RightPix.Refresh
end if
End Sub
```

If you've tried to handle asynchronous properties in other languages (say, C++) you might wonder why they are so easy in VB. Don't forget that VB restricts your asynchronous properties to some extent. For example, in C++, you can get data as it arrives, even if it is incomplete. In VB, you get all the data at once. That wouldn't be good if you were streaming large amounts of audio or video, for example. Still, for most cases, the VB model works quite well and it certainly is simpler to use.

An Example

Consider Figure 8.9. This control loads a handsome picture from my Web server. OK, so maybe it isn't that handsome, but at least it loads it asynchronously from the Web. You can find the source code for the control in Listing 8.7.

Figure 8.9 An asynchronous control.

LISTING 8.7 THE ASYNCHRONOUS PICTURE CONTROL.

```
VERSION 5.00
Begin VB.UserControl Leader
   ClientHeight    =    2880
   ClientLeft      =    0
   ClientTop       =    0
   ClientWidth     =    3840
   PropertyPages   =    "leader.ctx":0000
   ScaleHeight     =    2880
   ScaleWidth      =    3840
   Begin VB.PictureBox Picture1
      Height       =    1812
      Left         =    120
      ScaleHeight  =    1764
      ScaleWidth   =    2964
      TabIndex     =    0
      Top          =    120
      Width        =    3012
   End
   Begin VB.Label Label1
      Caption      =    "Our Fearless Leader"
      Height       =    492
      Left         =    120
      TabIndex     =    1
      Top          =    2280
      Visible      =    0    'False
      Width        =    3492
```

```
    End
End
Attribute VB_Name = "Leader"
Attribute VB_GlobalNameSpace = False
Attribute VB_Creatable = True
Attribute VB_PredeclaredId = False
Attribute VB_Exposed = True
Option Explicit


Private Sub UserControl AsyncReadComplete(AsyncProp As AsyncProperty)
Set Picture1.Picture = AsyncProp.Value
Label1.Visible = True
End Sub

Private Sub UserControl_Initialize()
AsyncRead "http://www.al-williams.com/awc/al_sm.gif", vbAsyncTypePicture
End Sub

Private Sub UserControl_Paint()
Line (0, 0)-(ScaleWidth, ScaleHeight), 0, B
End Sub

Private Sub UserControl_Resize()
Picture1.Left = 20
Picture1.Top = 20
Picture1.Width = ScaleWidth * 0.9
Picture1.Height = ScaleHeight * 0.8
Label1.Left = 20
Label1.Top = 20 + Picture1.Height
Label1.Width = Picture1.Width
End Sub
```

The control fires an event to tell the remainder of the program that data is available. It also hides the text control until the data is present. In this case, the surrounding Web page doesn't care if the picture is visible or not, but it is still a good idea to build in the event.

Why not just use a simple <IMG> tag to load this picture? There are several advantages to using this control. Most notably, the control fires an event when the picture loads. The HTML author could catch this event by using VBScript (or JavaScript). Another advantage is that the control could be significantly more sophisticated. For example, it could draw on the image or otherwise manipulate it. The control could also load multiple images and switch between them using interesting visual effects. In short, you could do most anything with the control.

Summary

When Microsoft changed the old-style OLE controls (OCX) to ActiveX controls, they aimed almost all the changes and improvements at the Internet. Microsoft knows that the Internet is the battlefield to win today and they want ActiveX to win that battle.

There are certainly some important competitors to ActiveX in the Web arena. Chief among those is Java. Many things that a Java applet can do, you could also do with ActiveX. Which is better? That depends.

Java is another language to learn, and arguably more difficult to learn than VB. Also, even though it is similar to C++, it isn't nearly as efficient as C++. You can create ActiveX controls in VB, for ease of development, or in C++ for efficiency—the choice is yours.

On the plus side, Java is platform-independent. A properly constructed Java applet can run on many different computers. Although Microsoft promises cross-platform ActiveX, you can only wonder how successful that will be. Another plus for Java is that it is safe. Java interpreters embedded in Web browsers prevent you from doing things that might harm the system (for example, writing to files or making most network connections). Of course, this can be a minus if you need to do those things.

So, which way will the wind blow? There's no way to tell. Each side has its proponents and advantages. Neither side lacks detractors or problems, either. You'll have to wait and see what the future brings. You can read more about what I think, by the way, in the final chapter of this book.

In any event, VB controls can let you easily activate your Web pages using technology that is simple to grasp. Web browsers can download your control from the Internet, verify its contents, install it, and even provide a license key for the control. Once the browser creates the control, your code can asynchronously download large blocks of data from your server. Very impressive for some simple VB code.

Look for Microsoft to make constant improvements to VB (and ActiveX). I would not be very surprised to see better tools for creating LPK files, for example. There also should be a better way to generate complex CAB files, too. This is certainly an area to watch.

INTERFACE BESTIARY

9

*Here comes a pair of very strange beasts,
which in all tongues are called fools.*

—As You Like It

There's an old joke about a man who lives in the woods. He goes into town and the dry goods salesman talks him into taking a chain saw. "If it doesn't work out, just bring it back and there's no charge," the salesman says. "You'll be able to do a week's worth of cutting in a single day."

A few days later, the man returns to the store. "This thing's no good," he drawls. "I've been cutting down the same tree for three days and I'm only halfway done!"

The salesman can't believe it. He says, "Let me see that thing. There must be something wrong with it."

The man hands over the saw. The salesman throws the choke, pulls the cord, and starts up the saw. The startled man looks up and asks, "What's that awful noise?"

OK, so you've heard that one before. Pretend you haven't so I don't tell another one. The point is that what we know about ActiveX is just a tool. What makes the tool do useful things?

The real power of ActiveX is writing objects that interact with the system (or other programs) via predefined interfaces. Remember, if an object contains an interface, it is polymorphic with all other objects that also expose the same interface. ActiveX provides several objects that you'll use. If you want to interact with ActiveX, you must provide certain interfaces in your objects, too.

A bestiary, by the way, is an old type of book that contained descriptions of animals. Although the bestiary was billed as scientific fact, many of the animals in it were mythical. This bestiary contains interfaces. Some you'll find inside ActiveX. Others are almost mythical—you'll have to write them yourself.

Interfaces And Visual Basic

Usually you don't worry about writing interfaces in VB. After all, VB does a perfectly good job of providing the interfaces you need to create controls. It also handles creating **IDispatch** when you write ActiveX servers. You can't readily implement most standard interfaces using VB because of type conversions and other limitations. However, you can create your own interfaces and use them in the same way standard ActiveX programs use them.

True, in many VB programs you'll never need to know about interfaces. Still, to have a complete understanding of ActiveX, you must know what an interface is and you must understand a handful of crucial interfaces.

If you are satisfied writing the kinds of controls you've seen in the last few chapters, you might want to skip this chapter for now. But later, as you try to do more intricate things with ActiveX, you'll want this information. Also, if you are trying to decipher ActiveX documentation, a knowledge of interfaces is most useful.

Creating Interfaces With VB

VB has some support for interfaces, but that support is in conjunction with the usual **IDispatch** mechanism (see Chapter 5). Although VB5 interfaces don't exactly mimic the standard ActiveX implementation, they do give VB5 classes a whole different dimension compared to VB4 classes.

Every time you create an ActiveX class module in a VB program, you are creating an **IDispatch** (or an automation) interface. By default, your object has a default interface that is based on the class name. If your class is named **MyObj**, the default interface is **_MyObj**. Of course, VB hides this from you. You have to hunt through the type library manually to see this.

However, VB allows you to create other interfaces by using the **Implements** keyword. All **Implements** does is copy another class' members into your new class and treat them as a separate interface. Then you write **Private** functions to handle each of the imported members. For example, suppose class **Vehicle** has this method:

```
Public Sub Drive(dist as Integer)
. . .
End Sub
```

Now further assume that you create an **Auto** class like this:

```
Implements Vehicle
Public Sub LoadPassengers(n as Integer)
. . .
End Sub

Private Sub Vehicle_Drive(dist as Integer)
. . .
End Sub
```

Now if some piece of code is expecting a **Vehicle**, you can pass it an **Auto** instead. Everything will work and your **Vehicle_Drive** subroutine will handle requests for the **Drive** function. Notice that this function is private (and named **Vehicle_Drive**). VB handles rerouting requests for **Drive** in the **Vehicle** class to the correct place. Of course, you can have as many **Implements** as you like, and each class is free to contain multiple methods and properties.

An important thing to realize is that the **Implements** statement doesn't bring in any code. If your **Vehicle_Drive** routine doesn't do anything, then neither does your object. You can either write your own code to handle the semantics of driving, or you can reuse the existing code in the **Vehicle** module. To reuse **Vehicle**, you'll have to create a private copy of the **Vehicle** object and delegate the call to it. Of course, you could execute your own code before and after the delegated call. For example, assuming **PrivateV** is an instance of a **Vehicle** object:

```
Private Sub Vehicle_Drive(dist as Integer)
' Auto-specific code here
PrivateV.Drive(dist)  ' delegate
' More Auto-specific code here
End Sub
```

In case you are wondering, this is the same as the containment reuse strategy you saw in earlier chapters. VB doesn't support aggregation, the other reuse strategy that ActiveX allows you to use.

It isn't uncommon to define abstract classes. These are classes that define an interface, but supply no code. Then it is up to classes that implement the interface to define their own behavior. Unlike other languages, however, VB doesn't enforce abstraction. You are free to make objects with no code in them.

However, as you might expect, their usefulness is limited. The value of an abstract class is that you can use it as a template to define a particular behavior.

Why can't VB create standard interfaces? First, most standard interfaces are not automation-aware. Second, the data types you need to work with in some interfaces are not usable from VB—at least not easily. However, understanding ActiveX still requires you to know something about the standard interfaces you'll encounter.

IMalloc And IMallocSpy

IMalloc is an interface that ActiveX provides for you. You can use it to allocate memory that is thread-safe. You don't have to stop using **malloc** or **new** for memory that you use within your own program. Why should you? However, sometimes when you need to pass data around to another process, you'll have to use **IMalloc**.

You should never have occasion to write your own implementation of **IMalloc**. Instead, you obtain a pointer to the built-in one by calling **CoGetMalloc**. Table 9.1 shows the functions you can call via **IMalloc**. When you no longer need the interface, be sure to call its **Release** function.

If you need to debug allocation, you can call **CoRegisterMallocSpy** and **CoRevokeMallocSpy**. To use these functions, you have to create an object that exposes **IMallocSpy** (see Table 9.2). When you pass a pointer to this interface to **CoRegisterMallocSpy**, the default **IMalloc** will call your spy functions at key points in the allocation process. What you do with this information is up to you.

Table 9.1   The IMalloc interface.

Function	Description
Alloc	Allocates a block of memory
Realloc	Changes the size of a block of memory
Free	Frees a block of memory
GetSize	Returns the size in bytes of a memory block
DidAlloc	Determines if this instance of IMalloc allocated a particular memory block
HeapMinimize	Minimizes the heap by releasing unused memory to the operating system

Table 9.2 The IMallocSpy interface.

Function	Description
PreAlloc	Called before invoking IMalloc::Alloc; this function may extend or modify the allocation's size in order to store debug information
PostAlloc	Called after invoking IMalloc::Alloc
PreFree	Called before invoking IMalloc::Free
PostFree	Called after invoking IMalloc::Free
PreRealloc	Called before invoking IMalloc::Realloc
PostRealloc	Called after invoking IMalloc::Realloc
PreGetSize	Called before invoking IMalloc::GetSize
PostGetSize	Called after invoking IMalloc::GetSize
PreDidAlloc	Called before invoking IMalloc::DidAlloc
PostDidAlloc	Called after invoking IMalloc::DidAlloc
PreHeapMinimize	Called before invoking IMalloc::HeapMinimize
PostHeapMinimize	Called after invoking IMalloc::HeapMinimize

A few other entities might supply an **IMalloc** interface. The new-style shell is a good example of this. The shell has its own memory allocator, and supplies its own **IMalloc** interface so that other programs can use the same memory allocation scheme.

IEnum

IEnum is an abstract interface that allows you to walk over a list of items. There is no actual **IEnum** interface. Instead, there are different types of enumerators (like **IEnumIDList**, for example) that enumerate different types.

You can find the functions that all **IEnum** interfaces support in Table 9.3. The only unusual thing is that the **Next** function takes different parameters depending on the type of data the enumerator returns.

Table 9.3 The IEnum pseudo-interface.

Function	Description
Clone	Creates a new enumerator having the same contents and state (see text)
Next	Retrieves one or more items in the enumeration
Reset	Resets the current position within the enumeration
Skip	Skips over one or more items in the enumeration

Sometimes you'll use an enumerator (like **IEnumIDList**). Other times, you'll have to provide an enumerator for a particular list inside an object you create. Luckily, many types of enumerators have built-in support. You can simply delegate calls to an ActiveX-provided function or ask ActiveX to create the enumerator for you. For example, you can ask ActiveX to create an **IEnumOLEVERB** enumerator from your registry information by calling **OleRegEnumVerbs**. You'll find a list of common enumeration interfaces in Table 9.4.

IStorage And IStream

ActiveX provides two interfaces that create a pseudo-file system for storing data in some underlying medium (like a file, for example). You can think of a storage (**IStorage**) as a directory and a stream (**IStream**) as a file. As you might expect, a storage can contain any number of streams. A storage can also contain substorages (similar to a subdirectory). That's really all there is to it. You can find the **IStorage** and **IStream** interfaces in Tables 9.5 and 9.6.

Table 9.4 Common Enumerator interfaces.

Object	Enumerates
IEnumFORMATETC	An array of FORMATETC structures
IEnumMoniker	The components of a moniker, or the monikers in a table (discussed later)
IEnumOLEVERB	The different verbs available for an object, in order of ascending verb number
IEnumSTATDATA	An array of STATDATA structures which contain advisory connection information for a data object
IEnumSTATSTG	An array of STATSTG structures which contain information about a storage, a stream, or a ILockBytes object (discussed later)
IEnumString	Strings
IEnumUnknown	Enumerates IUnknown interface pointers
IEnumVARIANT	A collection of VARIANT structures (discussed later)

Table 9.5 The IStorage interface.

Function	Description
CreateStream	Creates and opens a stream object with the specified name
OpenStream	Opens an existing stream object
CreateStorage	Creates and opens a new storage object

continued

Table 9.5 The IStorage interface (continued).

Function	Description
OpenStorage	Opens an existing storage object
CopyTo	Copies the entire contents of this open storage into another storage
MoveElementTo	Copies or moves a substorage or stream from this storage to another
Commit	Reflects changes for a transacted storage to the parent level
Revert	Discards all changes that have been made to the storage object since the last commit
EnumElements	Returns an enumerator for all storage and stream objects contained within this storage
DestroyElement	Removes the specified element
RenameElement	Renames the specified element
SetElementTimes	Sets the modification, access, and creation times of the storage element, if supported by the underlying file system
SetClass	Assigns the specified CLSID to this storage
SetStateBits	Associates up to 32 bits of state information for this storage; currently, Microsoft defines no state bits and reserves them all
Stat	Returns the STATSTG structure for this open storage (see Table 9.9)

Table 9.6 The IStream Interface.

Function	Description
Read	Reads from stream to memory starting at the current position
Write	Writes from memory to stream starting at the current position
Seek	Changes the current position
SetSize	Changes the size of the stream; useful to truncate or preallocate space
CopyTo	Copies bytes from the current position in the stream to the current position in another stream
Commit	Ensures that any changes made to the stream are reflected in the parent storage (not supported for compound files)
Revert	Discards all changes made to a transacted stream since the last commit call (no effect for compound files)
LockRegion	Restricts access to a specified range of bytes in the stream (not supported for compound files)
UnlockRegion	Removes the access restriction on a range of bytes previously restricted with LockRegion (not supported for compound files)
Stat	Retrieves the STATSTG structure for this stream
Clone	Creates a new stream that is identical to the current stream but has a separate current position

Don't get too carried away with the storage/stream/file system analogy. A main storage is often a single file. Inside that file is data that corresponds to individual substorages and streams. From the user's point of view, there is one operating system file that contains all the data. However, you can construct storages and streams in other ways. For example, it is easy to create a stream in memory. You could also create a stream in a database field, if you needed to do that. The point is that **IStorage** and **IStream** are simply interfaces to objects that store data. Where the objects store the data is up to them.

ActiveX provides code (the compound file system) that can expose **IStorage** and **IStream**. This default implementation stores everything inside one operating system file. To create a compound file, you call **StgCreateDocfile** (see Table 9.7). This call uses the archaic name *Docfile* instead of the more modern term, compound file. If you want to open an existing compound file, call **StgOpenStorage** (see Table 9.8). In either case, you pass a Unicode file name and an access mode. The calls return an **IStorage** pointer. You use this pointer to create substorages and streams within the storage. It is noteworthy that regardless of some versions of the online help, **StgOpenStorage** *cannot* open an ordinary directory or an ordinary file.

Table 9.7   Arguments to StgCreateDocfile.

Parameter	Type	Description
pwcsName	WCHAR	Unicode path name
grfMode	DWORD	Access mode (see Table 9.10)
reserved	DWORD	Not used
ppstgOpen	IStorage **	Pointer to created IStorage

Table 9.8   Arguments to StgOpenStorage.

Parameter	Type	Description
pwcsName	WCHAR	Unicode path name
pstgPriority	IStorage *	Storage to reopen in priority mode (used instead of pwcsName)
grfMode	DWORD	Access mode (see Table 9.10)
snbExclude	SNB	List of elements to exclude
reserved	DWORD	Not used
ppstgOpen	IStorage **	Pointer to created IStorage

You can also create a stream on a block of memory by calling **Create Stream OnHGlobal**. You pass this function a handle to memory and a flag. If the flag is set, the system will free the memory block when you release the underlying object. The function passes you an **IStream** pointer that you can use.

Streams In Detail

As you can see from Table 9.6, streams do pretty much what you'd expect them to do. The only functions that deserve special comment are **Stat** and **Clone**. **Stat** fills in a **STATSTG** structure for the stream (see Table 9.9). You can find out a great deal about the stream by examining this structure. The name of the stream appears in the **pwcsName** field. You are responsible for freeing the memory this points to by using the **IMalloc** interface you obtain by calling **CoGetMalloc**.

If you pass **STATFLAG_NONAME** to the **Stat** call, the stream doesn't return its name, and you don't have to free the memory in that case.

Table 9.9 Members of the STATSTG structure.

Member	Type	Description
pwcsName	LPWSTR	Name of a stream or a storage
type	DWORD	Type of item (STGTY_STORAGE or STGTY_STREAM; see the STGTY enumeration)
cbSize	ULARGE_INTEGER	Size of item (64 bits); 0 for storage items
mtime	FILETIME	Last modification time
ctime	FILETIME	Time item was created
atime	FILETIME	Time of last access
grfMode	DWORD	Access mode
grfLocksSupported	DWORD	Type of stream locking allowed (see LOCKTYPES enumeration); not applicable to storage items
clsid	CLSID	ActiveX object associated with a storage (not valid for streams)
grfStateBits	DWORD	Current state bits (only valid for storages); currently, Microsoft defines no state bits and reserves them all
dwStgFmt	DWORD	Storage format (see STGFMT enumeration)

There are a few other things you should know about the **STATSTG** structure. This structure is valid for streams and storages. The **atime**, **clsid**, **ctime**, **mtime**, **clsid**, **dwStgFmt**, and **grfStateBits** fields are only valid for storages. The **grfLocksSupported** field is only for streams.

The **Clone** function duplicates a stream, but not the stream's data. That is to say, the duplicate refers to the same file (or other, underlying data storage). However, it has a separate seek pointer. This allows you to easily copy data from one point in the stream to another point in the same stream. You can even use the **CopyTo** function to accomplish this.

Stream names can contain up to 32 Unicode characters. All characters are legal except for '/,' '\,' ':,' and '!'. ActiveX reserves names that begin with characters '\x00' to '\x1F'.

Storages In Detail

Storages come in two flavors: root storages and substorages. For the purposes of compound files, a root storage always corresponds to an operating system file. That means it suffers from the same name limitations as an operating system file. A root storage can contain streams and substorages. Of course, substorages may also contain other substorages and streams.

Given a storage interface, you can use member functions to create, delete, copy, move, enumerate, or open elements (that is, substorages or streams). You can call **Stat** to fill in a **STATSTG** structure to learn about the storage. When you want to enumerate the storage's elements, you call **EnumElements**. This returns an **IEnumSTATSTG** interface (this is an **IEnum** interface). Then, when you call **Next** on the enumerator, it will fill in a **STATSTG** structure.

You can open a storage in several modes (see Table 9.10). Most of these are common-sense. Keep in mind that you may select, at most, one flag from each group. For example, you can't mix the **STGM_DIRECT** and **STGM_TRAN-SACTED** flags because they are from the same group. If you don't specify any Group I flags, the default (**STGM_DIRECT**) takes effect.

The sharing flags operate as you might expect. The **STGM_FAILIFTHERE** flag only works when creating a storage. This prevents you from creating a new storage on top of an old one. If you want to create a new empty storage, even at the expense of an existing storage, specify **STGM_CREATE**.

The **STGM_TRANSACTED** mode allows you to open a storage, modify it, and then elect to commit the changes or roll them back. If you call **Commit**, your changes become permanent. If you call **Revert** (or **Release** the object without calling **Commit**), you lose all changes. The default mode,

STGM_DIRECT, works more like an ordinary file. Changes are always permanent. **STGM_TRANSACTED** files can greatly simplify undo commands and revert to saved commands.

Table 9.10 Storage modes.

Name	Description
Group I: Type	
STGM_DIRECT*	Allows changes to the item to take effect immediately
STGM_TRANSACTED	Prevents changes from taking effect until a commit call
STGM_SIMPLE	Limited, more efficient mode (see online help); must combine with STGM_CREATE, STGM_READWRITE, and STGM_SHAREEXCLUSIVE
Group II: Access Mode	
STGM_READ*	Opens for reading only
STGM_WRITE	Opens for writing only
STGM_READWRITE	Opens for reading and writing
Group III: Share Mode	
STGM_SHARE_DENY_NONE	Allow others to open object
STGM_SHARE_DENY_READ	Allows others to open object for writing
STGM_SHARE_DENY_WRITE	Allows others to open object for reading
STGM_SHARE_EXCLUSIVE	Disallows others from opening object
Group IV: Disposition	
STGM_CREATE	Always creates a new, empty item
STGM_CONVERT	Creates a new item while preserving the old contents in a stream named CONTENTS; useful for converting old file structures to compound files
STGM_FAILIFTHERE*	Fails if item already exists
Group V: Miscellaneous	
STGM_NOSCRATCH	For Windows 95 only; allows transacted storages to use dead space in the storage instead of a separate scratch file
STGM_PRIORITY	Opens for semi-exclusive access (others can't commit changes); must combine with STGM_DIRECT and STGM_READ
STGM_DELETEONRELEASE	Instructs the system to delete the item after its final release

You may select only one flag from each group except Group V. You may use any number of flags from Group V. You may also omit any group's flag in which case the system uses the default value.

* Indicates default value

Table 9.11   Commit options.

Option	Description
STGC_DEFAULT	No options
STGC_OVERWRITE	Allow commit to overwrite existing data—this may lead to data loss if the operation fails
STGC_ONLYIFCURRENT	Prevents commits if other users of the storage have outstanding changes
STGC_DANGEROUSLY–COMMITMERELYTODISKCACHE	This commits changes only to the file system cache which presumably will write the changes to disk sometime in the future

When you call **Commit**, you have several options (see Table 9.11). Usually, you'll use the **STGC_DEFAULT** option. However, if you have special requirements, there are other choices available. For example, if you share elements between processes or threads, you can specify **STGC_ONLYIFCURRENT**. This forces an error (**STG_E_NOTCURRENT**) if another process or thread already committed the element. Then your program has to reconcile the changes and commit again without this flag. If you are low on memory, you might specify **STGC_OVERWRITE**. This uses less memory, but can be risky since the operation destroys some old data before the new data is in place.

Another special mode is the **STGM_CONVERT**. This mode allows you to open a normal file as a root storage (using **StgOpenStorage**). The storage will have a single stream named **CONTENTS**. This stream will contain all the bytes of the original file. The conversion rewrites the file, so you must include **STGM_WRITE** with this mode. If you don't want the conversion to be permanent, you'll want to open the file with the **STGM_TRANSACTED** flag, too. That way you can revert the file to its original state before you exit.

The **STGM_PRIORITY** mode allows you to quickly open a direct, read-only storage or stream. You won't often use this mode since it bypasses nearly all buffering and locks out other users. However, it does allow for rapid "save as" operations.

Remember, the root storage of a compound file always corresponds to an operating system file. If you want to know if a file is a compound file root storage, call **StgIsStorageFile**. You can also set the element times of the root storage by calling **StgSetTimes**. This is similar to calling **SetElementTimes** except you don't need to open the storage.

Practical Considerations

The compound file implementation has several limitations. These aren't limits inherit to arbitrary **IStorage** and **IStream** interfaces. They are limits to the internal code for compound files.

1. Compound files can only contain 4 gigabytes of data (the interface specification allows 264 bytes).

2. Streams don't support transactioning. Streams inside a transactioned storage work as you expect, but you can't transaction a single stream.

3. Streams grow in increments of 512 bytes.

4. **IStorage::SetStateBits** doesn't do anything.

5. Some operations (e.g., backward seeking, **IStorage::EnumElements**, etc.) may not perform very rapidly.

6. You can't lock stream objects.

7. **STGM_PRIORITY** mode is only available for root storages.

8. You may not open one storage multiple times via the same parent storage.

Be particularly careful of the 512-byte granularity for streams. It would be a bad idea, for example, to create 100 streams that each contain two integers. That would use 5,120 bytes to store 800 bytes of information. It is better to try to group small data elements together.

Another concern is the performance of **EnumElements**. Microsoft recommends that you avoid enumerating a storage's elements where possible. This usually means maintaining a stream that contains the names of the other streams you create in a storage. Then you can open the directory stream and read from it instead of enumerating the elements directly.

ILockBytes

What happens if you want a structured storage to exist on a non-file medium? For example, you might want to store data in a database instead of a file. Or perhaps you need to allow structured storage to coexist in a file with an existing format. The answer to these problems is to implement an object with the **ILockBytes** interface that knows how to manage your storage needs.

ILockBytes is a simple interface that knows how to read from and write to some array of bytes. Where that array resides is strictly up to you. Table 9.12 shows the handful of functions **ILockBytes** requires. You usually won't create your own **ILockBytes** interface since ActiveX provides perfectly good implementations for files and for managing a block of memory. If you do provide

Table 9.12 The ILockBytes interface.

Function	Description
ReadAt	Reads a specified number of bytes starting at a given offset
WriteAt	Writes a specified number of bytes to a given offset
Flush	Writes any buffers that the ILockBytes implementation may maintain
SetSize	Changes the size of the object
LockRegion	Restricts access to a specified range of bytes
UnlockRegion	Removes the access restriction on a range of bytes
Stat	Retrieves a STATSTG structure for this object (see Table 9.9)

your own, you'll probably want to add marshalling to your object, since the system doesn't automatically know how to marshal your objects.

If you want to manage a block of memory as a structured storage, you can call **CreateILockBytesOnHGlobal** to return an **ILockBytes** on a global memory handle. Once you have any **ILockBytes** interface, you can create or open a storage in it by calling **StgCreateDocfileOnILockBytes** or **StgOpenStorageOnILockBytes**.

Why would you need a block of memory to look like structured storage? Consider the case where some external object wants to save its state in a structured storage. However, you want to incorporate the object's storage in your own file format. You could create an **ILockBytes** interface to manage your file format, but that's a lot of work. Instead, you might allocate some memory, create an **ILockBytes** interface on it, and create a storage on the **ILockBytes** interface. Then you pass the new storage to the object, it saves itself, and you can copy the memory to your file format. Reading it back is essentially the opposite: read the memory in, convert it to a storage, and pass the storage to the external object.

There is no guarantee that ActiveX won't change your memory handle in certain cases. Therefore, if you need the memory handle after you create the **ILockBytes** object, call the **GetHGlobalFromILockBytes** function to recover the memory handle. Don't use the same handle you passed into **CreateILockBytesOnHGlobal**.

IPersistFile, IPersistStream, And IPersistStorage

If you have some ActiveX object and you want it to save its state to a storage, a stream, or a file, how do you proceed? All objects that have persistent state support one or more of the persistence interfaces: **IPersistFile** (Table 9.13), **IPersistStream** (Table 9.14), **IPersistStreamInit** (Table 9.14), and **IPersistStorage** (Table 9.15). Each interface supports persistence on different media.

These interfaces share their first four functions. The first three are, of course, the **IUnknown** functions. The fourth function is **GetClassID**. You'll often hear these four functions called the **IPersist** interface (although no objects expose just an **IPersist** interface). Of course, you can treat any of the persistence interfaces as an **IPersist** interface. There are also some specialized variations on **IPersist**, such as **IPersistMemory** or **IPersistPropertyBag**. However, for the most part, you'll deal with persistent files, streams, and storages.

IPersistFile

An **IPersistFile** interface (Table 9.13) allows you to work with an ordinary file of indeterminate format. The file may or may not be structured. You don't know. The functions, as you'd expect, are simple. You can find out if the object requires saving (**IsDirty**), save or load the object (with **Save** or **Load**), or learn the file's full path (**GetCurFile**).

Loading the file is straightforward. The **Load** function informs the object of its file name. The object may leave the file open and write to it if it wishes. In

Table 9.13   The IPersistFile interface.

Function	Description
GetClassID	Returns the CLSID for the server that handles this file
IsDirty	Checks an object for changes since it was last saved to its current file
Load	Opens the specified file and initializes the object from the contents of the file
Save	Saves the object into the specified file
SaveCompleted	Notifies the object that saving is complete (see text)
GetCurFile	Gets the current file name

other words, when the load completes, there is no assurance that the object is finished with the file—only that the object is ready.

Saving a file is a bit more complex than it might appear. The **Save** function takes a file name and a flag named **fSameAsLoad**. If the file name is **NULL**, then the save operation saves the object to the current file (presumably passed in the **Load** function or a prior **Save**). Then the object ignores the **fSameAsLoad** flag and clears its dirty bit (the bit that **IsDirty** returns). However, if the file name is not **NULL**, the object can't determine if you are renaming the existing file or just copying it.

The **fSameAsLoad** flag allows the object to differentiate between these cases. If the flag is **TRUE**, the object is free to keep the file open and alter it. The object clears the dirty flag and considers the new file name to be the current file. If the flag is **FALSE**, however, the object must completely write the entire file. Then it must close the file until it receives a **SaveCompleted** call. This allows the object's user to manipulate the file without fear of sharing violations or other interference.

IPersistStream And IPersistStreamInit

The **IPersistStream** interface allows you to save an object to a structured storage stream. **IPersistStreamInit** is identical to **IPersistStream** except it has one additional member function, (**InitNew**). The functions (see Table 9.14) are all as you would expect with two exceptions: **GetSizeMax** and **InitNew**.

It is possible that an object's user may need to preallocate storage for the object (in a database field, for example). Therefore, **GetSizeMax** must return the absolute maximum number of bytes the object might need to save itself. This is especially important if an object's user wants to store several objects in the same stream.

Table 9.14 The IPersistStream and IPersistStreamInit interfaces.

Function	Description
GetClassID	Returns the CLSID for the server that handles this object
IsDirty	Checks the object for changes since it was last saved
Load	Reads the stream into the object
Save	Saves the object to a stream
GetSizeMax	Returns the maximum number of bytes required to save (see text)
InitNew	Initializes an object to a default state (IPersistStreamInit only)

Because it is possible for multiple objects to coexist in a single stream, the object must not hold the stream open. When the object receives a **Load** or **Save** call, it can use the stream pointer provided until it returns from the function. After that, it must not access the stream. It also must start using the stream at the current seek position and not use more bytes than **GetSizeMax** returns.

Some objects may have significant initialization to perform when you first create them. Performing the initialization is a waste, if the first thing you call is **Load** to restore the state from a stream. That's where the **IPersistStreamInit** interface comes into play. This interface is identical to **IPersistStream** except that a client can call **InitNew** to cue the object to initialize a new object.

If you write an object that provides **IPersistStreamInit**, you may be able to use the same interface to handle **IPersistStream**. Just make your **QueryInterface** implementation recognize that these interfaces are the same. If a client requests **IPersistStream**, the fact that there is an extra function is unimportant. Of course, this assumes that you don't need special initialization semantics that differ between the interfaces.

IPersistStorage

The **IPersistStorage** interface (Table 9.15) is the most powerful (and most difficult) of the persistence interfaces. An object that exposes **IPersistStorage** can save itself to a storage object. Within that storage, it can create new substorages and streams at its whim. This effectively gives an object its own private file system for storing its persistent state.

The functions for **IPersistStorage** are similar to those of the other persistence interfaces. As usual, the protocol for saving a file is the most complex. When

Table 9.15   The IPersistStorage interface.

Function	Description
GetClassID	Returns the CLSID for this object
IsDirty	Indicates whether the object has changed since it was last saved to its current storage
InitNew	Initializes a new storage object
Load	Reads the storage into the object
Save	Saves the object and any nested objects that it contains into the specified storage object
SaveCompleted	Notifies the object that a save operation is finished (see text)
HandsOffStorage	Instructs object to close all open elements (see text)

you open or initialize an object that uses **IPersistStorage**, you call **Load** or **InitNew**. In either case, the object is free to hold a pointer to the storage and use it during normal operations. This is a good idea since you should be able to save even if memory is low. If memory is low, you might not be able to reopen the storage or any elements you need opened. Most objects open everything first and then hold them open.

When the client wants to save the object, it calls **Save**. This is similar to the case for **IPersistFile**. The only difference is that the object need not release any open elements it is using. However, it can't write to the storage after the save. The object can only resume writing to storage after a call to **SaveCompleted**. If the client requires the object to release the storage (so it can rename the storage, for example), then it must call **HandsOffStorage** in between the **Save** and **SaveCompleted** calls.

Notice that the object must not call **Commit** on the main storage managed through **IPersistStorage**. The client decides when and if to make that call.

Associating CLSIDs With Storage

The only unique function in **IPersist** (the effective base class for all persistence interfaces) is **GetClassID**. As you might suspect, this function returns the CLSID of an ActiveX server that knows how to interpret the file or storage. The **WriteClassStg** function writes this value into a storage, and the **WriteClassStm** function writes it into a stream. You can then use the corresponding read functions to recover the CLSID. That means that to read a compound file, you can learn its associated CLSID, call **CoCreateInstance** to create the object (which presumably supports an **IPersist**-derived interface), and call the interface's **Load** function.

If you are using a transacted storage, you can often call **OleSave** to keep you from doing so much work. Here's what **OleSave** does:

1. Calls the **IPersistStorage::GetClassID** method to get the object's CLSID
2. Writes the CLSID to the storage object using the **WriteClassStg** function
3. Calls the **IPersistStorage::Save** method to save the object
4. Calls the **IStorage::Commit** method to commit the changes if there were no errors

As you might expect, there is a corresponding **OleLoad** function. Here's what it does:

1. If necessary, performs an automatic conversion of the object (that is, it uses the **OleDoAutoConvert** function to interpret the **TreatAs** and **AutoTreatAs** registry entries; see Chapter 4)

2. Gets the **CLSID** from the open storage object by calling the **IStorage::Stat** method

3. Calls the **CoCreateInstance** function to create an instance of the handler

4. Calls the **IOleObject::SetClientSite** method with the *pClientSite* parameter to inform the object of its client site

5. Calls the **QueryInterface** method for the **IPersistStorage** interface. If successful, the **IPersistStorage::Load** method is invoked for the object

6. Queries and returns the desired interface pointer

Wait a minute! What's this **SetClientSite** function in the **IOleObject** interface? It turns out that this function is for traditional object linking and embedding. Certain ActiveX controls also use it. These objects always have an **IOleObject** interface. Since the objects in this chapter don't have **IOleObject** interfaces, you can't use **OleLoad** with them. Still, it is interesting to see what **OleLoad** does. You can easily perform all of these steps as they pertain to your situation.

IMoniker And IOleItemContainer

File names, in the traditional sense, are not very object-oriented. A file name has no meaning in of itself. The functions that manipulate it have to have explicit knowledge of what to do with a file name. This causes grief when file name formats change (for example, long file names or UNC file names) and the functions do not.

An object-oriented file name would not only include the file's name but also the operations that you might want to perform on it (open, for one). Imagine this partial class (named **SmartFileName**):

```
Public name as String
Public Sub Open
  . . .
End Sub
  .
  .
  .
```

So long as **SmartFileName** knows how to open a file, no one cares what actions it takes. That's the idea behind a moniker. It returns an open storage or stream that refers to some object. What object? Who knows? Who cares? If you have a moniker that refers to, say, a document file, just ask it for the corresponding storage. If you have a moniker that refers to a section of a drawing object, you can open that, too. Monikers can refer to things as generic as files or as specific as a word inside a word processing document. Monikers can also refer to Internet URLs—a type of moniker you'll examine later.

You'll rarely, if ever, need to create monikers from scratch (although you can). Instead, you'll build monikers using predefined moniker types. There are four atomic moniker types. They all expose the **IMoniker** interface (selected portions of this interface appear in Table 9.16). You can use these to build composite monikers, monikers made up of different types of atomic monikers.

Table 9.17 shows the four atomic monikers and the functions you use to create them. Only file and pointer monikers have any usefulness by themselves. Item and anti monikers are only useful inside composite monikers.

Table 9.16   Selected IMoniker member functions.

Function	Description
BindToObject	Binds to the object named by the moniker
BindToStorage	Binds to the object's storage
Reduce	Reduces the moniker to simplest form
ComposeWith	Composes with another moniker
Enum	Enumerates component monikers
IsEqual	Compares with another moniker
IsRunning	Checks whether object is running
GetTimeOfLastChange	Returns time the object was last changed
Inverse	Returns the inverse of the moniker
CommonPrefixWith	Finds the prefix that the moniker has in common with another moniker
RelativePathTo	Constructs a relative moniker between the moniker and another
GetDisplayName	Returns the display name
ParseDisplayName	Converts a display name into a moniker
IsSystemMoniker	Checks whether this moniker is one of the system-supplied types

Table 9.17   Atomic monikers.

Moniker	Usage
File	Refers to a file
Item	Refers to an item which is just a string that the server interprets (see text)
Pointer	Refers to an object
Anti	Destroys the previous component moniker in a composite

As you might expect, a file moniker encapsulates a file name. When you ask the moniker to open its contents (binding the moniker, in ActiveX parlance), it finds a CLSID associated with the file, creates an object of that class, finds the object's **IPersistFile** interface, and calls **IPersistFile::Load**. Pointer monikers are convenient because they allow you to treat an existing ActiveX object just as you would a file that uses that object.

Item monikers are only useful inside a composite. You specify a delimiter character (usually an exclamation point) and a string. This string has no intrinsic meaning to the moniker. Hopefully, the string means something to the target object. The string must not contain the delimiter character. Suppose we have an ActiveX object that manages a database that resides in a file. A client might form a composite moniker that contains a file moniker (for the database file), an item moniker to specify the record key, and another item moniker to specify a field.

When it is time to bind this composite moniker, the moniker code will create an instance of our ActiveX server to load the database file (our CLSID is in the file). Our server must support **IOleItemContainer** (see Table 9.18). Next, the system will call **IOleItemContainer::GetObject** or **IOleItemContainer:: GetObjectStorage** to convert the item string in the first item moniker to another **IOleItemContainer** (representing the database record). The record **IOleItemContainer** then resolves the second item string to produce whatever interface is necessary to represent the database fields. You'll usually see this type of moniker written with the delimiter (often the exclamation point) between the atomic monikers. For example:

```
file!record!field
```

You'll often hear this called the moniker's display name. Monikers know how to parse a display name or convert their contents into display names.

Table 9.18 The IOleItemContainer interface.

Function	Description
ParseDisplayName	Parses object's display name to form a moniker
EnumObjects	Enumerates objects in this container
LockContainer	Keeps container running until explicitly released
GetObject	Returns a pointer to a specified object
GetObjectStorage	Returns a pointer to an object's storage
IsRunning	Checks whether an object is running

Anti monikers destroy the previous moniker in a composite. Adding an anti moniker to the above example (file!record!field), would result in a moniker that refers to the file and record. Adding two anti monikers would result in just a file moniker.

You can create a composite moniker one piece at a time by calling **CreateGenericComposite**. This function takes two **IMoniker** pointers and returns a third pointer. In effect, this function merges the two input monikers to form the output. If you need more pieces, you simply call the function again using the output from the first call as one of the inputs. You can repeat this until the entire moniker is complete.

IMoniker is derived from **IPersistStream**. As you might guess, file monikers store their file names and item monikers store their strings. The other atomic monikers have no persistent state. A composite moniker's state is a stream that contains the state of each constituent moniker.

IConnectionPoint And IConnectionPointContainer

Some ActiveX objects need to notify another object of an event. To put it another way, a server may ask a client to support a particular interface that the server will call when something interesting happens. This is contrary to the usual model of a client calling a server.

Some older ActiveX interfaces hardwire the logic to do this into the server. Part of the protocol for using a certain server might be to provide a "sink" interface to the server. Then, when the server wants to call the client, it calls prearranged functions in the sink interface.

This works well when there is a one-to-one relationship between client and server. However, it is inflexible and not a very general method. To fix these problems, Microsoft introduced the concept of connectable objects. A connectable object is one that provides the **IConnectionPointContainer** (see Table 9.19). The two functions in this interface allow you to query an object to see if it supports a particular sink interface or enumerate all supported sink interfaces. Note that these are not interfaces the server implements (you'd find those with **QueryInterface**), but rather interfaces the client must supply.

If you call **IConnectionPointContainer::FindConnectionPoint** it returns an **IConnectionPoint** interface pointer you can use to register your sink interface (see Table 9.20). Here's some typical pseudo-code that registers a fictitious **IID_OurSinkInterface** sink:

```
if (QueryInterface on server fails for IID_IConnectionPoint)
   error("No connections");
if (FindConnectionPoint for IID_OurSinkInterface fails)
   error("Server doesn't support our sink interface");
call the connection point's Advise function passing our interface pointer-
this call returns a 32-bit magic number that identifies the connection;
When the client no longer wants to use the sink, call Unadvise, passing
the 32-bit magic number from the Advise call.
```

From the server's point of view, you maintain a list of connections. You add pointers to the list during **Advise** and remove them during **Unadvise**. When you want to call a particular sink function, you walk through the list, calling the function on each sink interface in the list. This allows one server to successfully service multiple clients.

IProvideClassInfo

Objects that expose the **IProvideClassInfo** interface can return their type library information (see Chapter 4 for more on type libraries). This interface is

Table 9.19   The IConnectionPointContainer interface.

Function	Description
EnumConnectionPoints	Returns an enumerator for all the connection points associated with this object
FindConnectionPoint	Returns a pointer to the IConnectionPoint interface for a specified connection point

Table 9.20   The IConnectionPoint interface.

Function	Description
GetConnectionInterface	Returns the IID of the sink interface managed by this connection point
GetConnectionPointContainer	Returns the parent object's IConnectionPointContainer interface pointer
Advise	Creates a connection between a connection point and a client's sink where the sink implements the outgoing interface supported by this connection point
Unadvise	Terminates a notification previously set up with Advise
EnumConnections	Returns an enumerator for the current connections maintained by this connection point

very simple since it only contains a single (non-**IUnknown**) function that is easy to implement. This function is the **GetClassInfo** function.

This function is easy to implement since you can just load your type information from the TLB library (using **LoadRegTypeLib** or **LoadTypeLib**) and then call the type library's **GetTypeInforOfGuid** function to get the **ITypeInfo** interface that **IProvideClassInfo::GetClassInfo** returns.

The End Of The Bestiary?

There are an endless number of interfaces, with new ones defined all the time. Of course, you can define your own interface specifications, too. However, the interfaces in this chapter are the most important ones for ActiveX controls. There are many more interfaces that are specific to controls, but the ones in this chapter form a foundation on which many ActiveX technologies build.

When you encounter a new interface, try finding it in the ActiveX documentation. Be sure to notice if it derives from another interface. Then try to understand what each function does. Also see if the specification allows you to not implement certain portions of the interface. For many interfaces, you can simply return **E_NOTIMPL** from functions you elect not to provide.

Interfaces can be simple, like **IProvideClassInfo**, or complex, like **IMoniker**. The interaction between clients and servers via complicated interfaces is where ActiveX programming gets its bad reputation. If you try to understand each interface a little at a time, you'll have no problems.

ActiveX Documents

'Tis in my memory lock'd,
And you yourself shall keep the key of it.

— Hamlet

My daughter Amy hates to be alone. I mean she ***really*** hates to be alone. When she lived at home, she'd occasionally baby-sit her little brother Patrick for us. Invariably, we'd come home to find that after Patrick went to bed, Amy would have company over.

One night a few years ago, we went out for the evening. When we came home around 11 p.m., we noticed that there were no strange cars in our driveway. Foolishly, we thought she had toughed it out by herself.

When we walked in, we saw one of the neighbors' sons was keeping her company—she wasn't alone after all. The young man—I'll call him Joe Frank—had some exciting news. He had just gotten a tattoo (just wait until your kids are this age). He removed his shirt to show me his bicep sporting "FRANK" in big bold letters.

I said, "You know, if someone doesn't know you, they are going to think that's odd."

"Why?" he asked.

I replied, "Most folks with tattoos have the name of their girlfriend on their arm. If I didn't know you, I'd think your girlfriend was named Frank." A look of sudden panic swept over his face. Obviously he hadn't thought this through.

Maybe sometimes, it is better to be alone. However, that certainly isn't the case when it comes to ActiveX programs. ActiveX programs need each other. Controls can't function without containers. Many containers hardly do anything without controls. Tattoos, however, are optional.

ActiveX controls give you one way to write a program that coexists with another program. You can drop an ActiveX control in a VB program, on a Web page, inside a Delphi form, or on a C++ dialog box. As you've seen throughout this book, ActiveX controls are very powerful and allow you to create complex applications with minimal coding.

However, what if you want more? As powerful as controls are, they aren't full-blown applications. For example, they don't have menus. They also can't conveniently offer multiple windows and other features you expect of an application.

Do you remember the scenario I painted in Chapter 1? In Chapter 1, I painted a picture of you composing email, working with charts, and running Quicken all from inside your Web browser. ActiveX controls are powerful, but it'd be quite difficult to use them to implement complex applications like Word, Excel, or Quicken.

Microsoft's answer to these problems is ActiveX documents (sometimes called OLE doc objects or just doc objects). These are programs that exist only to operate inside a doc object container. Not every ActiveX container can host doc objects and not every ActiveX object is a doc object.

What's more, you don't always need or want a doc object. Whereas controls are little bite-sized nuggets of functionality you can reuse, a doc object is the whole meal. Doc objects implement an entire application that you want to integrate with a doc object container like Internet Explorer or Office Binder.

Like most things, VB makes doc objects relatively painless. Better still, VB doc objects are almost exactly like ActiveX controls. However, there are a few pitfalls you should know about. Also, there are a few special techniques you only use with doc objects.

Getting Started

You start an ActiveX document project like most any other VB project. You can select an EXE file or a DLL. For most purposes, a DLL will offer better performance since it is an inproc server. However, many containers don't support modeless forms from a DLL document. To be safe, if you expect to display modeless forms, you should use the EXE form of the document object.

The project starts with a single **UserDocument** object. This object is suspiciously like a **UserControl** object (see Table 10.1). There are a few minor differences, but if you understand the **UserControl** object, you shouldn't have any problems with **UserDocument**. There are many other members available with **UserDocument**. You'll find nearly all of these duplicate members in forms and ordinary ActiveX controls.

The important difference between a **UserDocument** and a **UserControl** is what you can do with a **UserDocument**. For example, later in this chapter, you'll see that you can use menus with a **UserDocument**.

Don't let the word "document" throw you. The **UserDocument** object is just like a control and similar to a form. Just throw the usual controls on the object and you are ready to go.

Table 10.1   Selected UserDocument members.

Member	Type	Description
AsyncRead	Method	Begin asynchronous read
AsyncReadComplete	Event	Asynchronous read completed; data available
CancelAsyncRead	Method	Cancel pending asynchronous read
ContinuousScroll	Property	True if program wants to update while scrolling is in progress
HScrollSmallChange	Property	Horizontal scroll size
VScrollSmallChange	Property	Vertical scroll size
HyperLink	Property	Hyperlink object used to navigate to another document
MinHeight	Property	Height of actual document
MinWidth	Property	Width of actual document
Picture	Property	Picture to display
ReadProperties	Event	Read properties as appropriate
WriteProperties	Event	Write properties as appropriate
SetViewPort	Method	Set view port
ViewPortHeight	Property	Current view port height
ViewPortWidth	Property	Current view port width
ViewPortTop	Property	Current view port top coordinate
ViewPortLeft	Property	Current view port left coordinate

Viewing The Document

Once you have your document built, you can use Internet Explorer (or any other doc object container) to view your work. VB creates a VBD file in the same directory as your project. IE can open this file and display your document. However, be careful to type the file name directly into the browser. It isn't likely that your machine associates VBD files with any application. If you double click the VBD file (or make any other attempt to open it directly) the system will probably complain.

By the way, you don't have to stick with the VBD file extension once your project is complete. You can rename the document.

If the doc object has a menu, it merges with the container's menus. The user sees a combination of the two menus. If the doc object doesn't have a menu, the container only displays a subset of its usual menu.

Populating The Document

There are several odd things you should realize about ActiveX documents. First, you can't control the size of your workspace. The container (and, perhaps, the user) sets that. Another oddity is that you can't control how users enter your application. If you only have one document object, that isn't a problem. However, what if you have multiple documents that comprise one application?

As an example, suppose you've written a document object that asks for information about the user's mortgage. The user presses a button and jumps to another document object that displays information based on the input (you'll see how to jump to another document soon). You have to be aware that the user may bookmark the second document and return to it three months later (for example). Just be sure each document is self-contained and you shouldn't have a problem with this.

The size problem is a little more complex. When you design a **UserDocument**, the height and width you use in the designer are important. This is the true size of the document. However, the container will arrange for the user to view the document through a view port. The view port size is the size of the container's visual display of the document.

Obviously, if the view port is larger than the document size, there's no big problem. However, if the view port is smaller, the **UserDocument** object automatically supplies scroll bars that allow the user to scroll around the document. You can find out where you are scrolled (if you care) by examining the

ViewPortLeft, **ViewPortTop**, **ViewPortWidth**, and **ViewPortHeight** members of **UserDocument**.

If you need to change the true size of the document dynamically, you can do that too. Just set the **MinHeight** and **MinWidth** properties. You can also cause the view port to scroll by calling **SetViewPort**. This method lets you change **ViewPortLeft** and **ViewPortTop** so that a different portion of the document is visible. For example, to reset the document to the top left corner, write:

```
SetViewPort 0,0
```

If you want to scroll 50% of the way vertically, you could write:

```
SetViewPort ViewPortLeft,MinHeight/2
```

One final note about scrolling: The **UserDocument** object has to decide how much to scroll your document with each click of the scroll bars. If you don't like the default, you can change it by setting **HScrollSmallChange** and **VScrollSmallChange**.

Bringing Up A Form

ActiveX documents can bring up forms. Keep in mind that some containers don't allow DLL servers to fire modeless forms, however. If you want to use modeless forms, you'll want to stick with EXE servers.

Bringing up a form is trivial. Just add a form to your project in the usual way. When you want to load it, just use the **Show** method as usual. You can specify the **vbModal** argument for a modal form or omit it for modeless.

Later, if you want to remove the form from the screen, just call **Unload**. This is exactly the same way you handle forms in a regular VB program. Keep in mind, however, that the form will have its own window. It won't be contained in the Internet Explorer (or wherever).

Using Menus

ActiveX documents can have menus just like any other VB program. Just use the VB menu editor (see Figure 10.1) to create menu objects, and handle the events they generate. Of course, the document object has no frame, so no menu items are visible. The key is that your top level menu items have to have negotiation turned on (see Figure 10.1). Then, the container merges the menu items with its own menus.

Figure 10.1   The VB Menu Editor.

Exactly how the menu appears in the container depends on the container. IE, for example, merges any unique top level menu items with its own menus. If you name a submenu with the same name that an IE menu has, your menu will appear as a submenu of the IE menu (see Figure 10.2).

Linking To Other Documents

What happens if you want to link to another ActiveX document? That's where you use the **UserDocument**'s **HyperLink** object property. This property contains an object with three methods: **NavigateTo**, **GoForward**, and **GoBack**. The most useful, in this context, is **NavigateTo**. Just provide the name of the ActiveX document you want the browser to display.

You might guess that you could use the **HyperLink** object to navigate the browser to any URL. That's correct. Of course, if the container doesn't know how to display the file the URL references, you might not like the results.

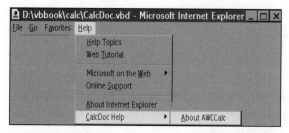

Figure 10.2   Nested submenus.

Saving And Loading Data

How can you make your data persistent? The **UserDocument** object has two events to help you make this happen: **WriteProperties** and **ReadProperties**. Here's the basic idea:

1. When anything changes in your document, call **PropertyChanged** (a member of **UserDocument**).

2. When you receive the **WriteProperties** event, it will convey a **PropertyBag** object to your code. You can use the **WriteProperty** method of the **PropertyBag** object to write your data into the document.

3. When your code sees a **ReadProperties** event, you'll get another **PropertyBag**. This time, use **ReadProperty** to read the results.

That sounds simple, and it mostly is. However, there are a few things you should consider. First, if you are running your document server under the VB environment, it recreates your document every time you restart. This wipes out any data you saved. Until you figure this out, you'll think the code isn't working. It probably is.

Another thing to worry about is that some containers don't support saving data. In that case, you'll have to devise your own scheme to open a file and save your data.

Both **ReadProperty** and **WriteProperty** require you to supply a default value. This is similar to the **UserControl** object. The idea is that if you are saving the default value, VB doesn't waste space in the file actually writing it. Of course, if the **ReadProperty** method doesn't find the data, it just returns the default value.

Converting Existing Applications

VB supplies an add-in that allows you to convert your existing forms to ActiveX documents (see the ActiveX Document Migration Wizard in Figure 10.3). All you need to do is specify your project, make a few selections, and it converts your existing forms into ActiveX documents.

Of course, there are a few things you might do in a form that you can't do in an ActiveX document. When the Wizard finds these, it just comments out your code.

This isn't really rocket science, but it is helpful. Just don't expect your forms to convert 100% with no effort on your part. Of course, if they do, that's just that much better.

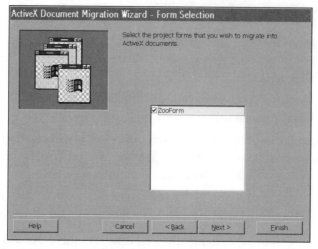

Figure 10.3 The ActiveX Document Migration Wizard.

Debugging ActiveX Documents

Debugging ActiveX documents isn't much harder than debugging a regular program. The only thing you have to do is run your project before you load the ActiveX document. Then you can set breakpoints and do all the other things you want to do using VB's built-in debugger.

You should be aware that Internet Explorer caches documents, and this can lead to trouble when you try to stop debugging. If you attempt to end debugging, you may see a message that tells you that your document is in use. Of course, if the document is really open, that's one thing. But often you'll see this message when your document is nowhere to be seen on your monitor.

The problem is that IE keeps your document open in its cache. The trick is to navigate to some other documents (or URLs) until the cache is empty. Microsoft says that this is currently four documents. Then you can safely stop your debugging session.

According to Microsoft, IE will also clear its ActiveX document cache if you scan the root directory of a drive. In other words, type in "C:\" in the URL address box. However, they also warn that this behavior may not be true in future versions of IE, so don't be surprised if it doesn't work in versions later than 3.01.

An Example

Just to exercise the capabilities of ActiveX documents, I wrote a calculator program (see Figure 10.4). The calculator is simple: four functions are executed in the order you enter them. Also, you must use the mouse to push the buttons. Still, this is a full-blown ActiveX document.

You can find the code for the calculator document in Listing 10.1. Notice that it really doesn't look different from a form or an ActiveX control. Since the calculator saves its value, the edit control that holds the value calls **PropertyChanged** when it detects a change. Also, the **WriteProperties** and **ReadProperties** events do the correct actions.

Beyond that, the program is quite ordinary. Load the CalcDoc.VBD file and try it. Then resize your browser so that the calculator doesn't fit. You'll see scroll bars (Figure 10.5) appear automatically. The code really doesn't care. Everything works the same.

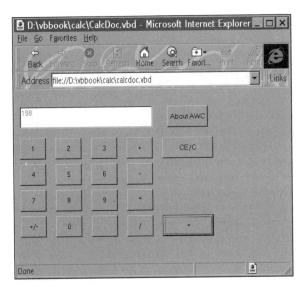

Figure 10.4 The Calculator document.

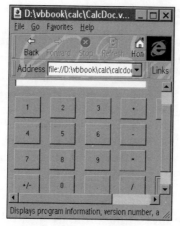

Figure 10.5   The Calculator document with scroll bars.

LISTING 10.1   THE CALCULATOR DOCUMENT.

```
VERSION 5.00
Begin VB.UserDocument CalcDoc
    ClientHeight    =    3600
    ClientLeft      =    0
    ClientTop       =    0
    ClientWidth     =    4800
    HScrollSmallChange=  225
    ScaleHeight     =    3600
    ScaleWidth      =    4800
    VScrollSmallChange=  225
    Begin VB.CommandButton Negate
        Caption         =    "+/-"
        Height          =    492
        Left            =    120
        TabIndex        =    19
        Top             =    2880
        Width           =    612
    End
    Begin VB.CommandButton Opkey
        Caption         =    "="
        Height          =    492
        Index           =    4
        Left            =    3480
        TabIndex        =    18
        Top             =    2880
        Width           =    1212
    End
```

```
Begin VB.CommandButton Opkey
   Caption         =    "/"
   Height          =    492
   Index           =    3
   Left            =    2640
   TabIndex        =    17
   Top             =    2880
   Width           =    612
End
Begin VB.CommandButton Opkey
   Caption         =    "*"
   Height          =    492
   Index           =    2
   Left            =    2640
   TabIndex        =    16
   Top             =    2280
   Width           =    612
End
Begin VB.CommandButton Opkey
   Caption         =    "-"
   Height          =    492
   Index           =    1
   Left            =    2640
   TabIndex        =    15
   Top             =    1680
   Width           =    612
End
Begin VB.CommandButton Opkey
   Caption         =    "+"
   Height          =    492
   Index           =    0
   Left            =    2640
   TabIndex        =    14
   Top             =    1080
   Width           =    612
End
Begin VB.CommandButton Clear
   Caption         =    "CE/C"
   Height          =    492
   Left            =    3480
   TabIndex        =    13
   Top             =    1080
   Width           =    1212
End
Begin VB.CommandButton Point
   Caption         =    "."
   Height          =    492
```

```
        Left          =    1800
        TabIndex      =    12
        Top           =    2880
        Width         =    612
     End
     Begin VB.CommandButton Number
        Caption       =    "9"
        Height        =    492
        Index         =    9
        Left          =    1800
        TabIndex      =    11
        Top           =    2280
        Width         =    612
     End
     Begin VB.CommandButton Number
        Caption       =    "8"
        Height        =    492
        Index         =    8
        Left          =    960
        TabIndex      =    10
        Top           =    2280
        Width         =    612
     End
     Begin VB.CommandButton Number
        Caption       =    "7"
        Height        =    492
        Index         =    7
        Left          =    120
        TabIndex      =    9
        Top           =    2280
        Width         =    612
     End
     Begin VB.CommandButton Number
        Caption       =    "6"
        Height        =    492
        Index         =    6
        Left          =    1800
        TabIndex      =    8
        Top           =    1680
        Width         =    612
     End
     Begin VB.CommandButton Number
        Caption       =    "5"
        Height        =    492
        Index         =    5
        Left          =    960
        TabIndex      =    7
```

```
         Top             =    1680
         Width           =    612
      End
      Begin VB.CommandButton Number
         Caption         =    "4"
         Height          =    492
         Index           =    4
         Left            =    120
         TabIndex        =    6
         Top             =    1680
         Width           =    612
      End
      Begin VB.CommandButton Number
         Caption         =    "3"
         Height          =    492
         Index           =    3
         Left            =    1800
         TabIndex        =    5
         Top             =    1080
         Width           =    612
      End
      Begin VB.CommandButton Number
         Caption         =    "2"
         Height          =    492
         Index           =    2
         Left            =    960
         TabIndex        =    4
         Top             =    1080
         Width           =    612
      End
      Begin VB.CommandButton Number
         Caption         =    "0"
         Height          =    492
         Index           =    0
         Left            =    960
         TabIndex        =    3
         Top             =    2880
         Width           =    612
      End
      Begin VB.CommandButton Number
         Caption         =    "1"
         Height          =    492
         Index           =    1
         Left            =    120
         TabIndex        =    2
         Top             =    1080
         Width           =    612
      End
```

```
      Begin VB.CommandButton Command1
         Caption         =    "About AWC"
         Height          =    492
         Left            =    3600
         TabIndex        =    1
         Top             =    360
         Width           =    972
      End
      Begin VB.TextBox Accum
         Alignment       =    1   'Right Justify
         Enabled         =    0   'False
         Height          =    492
         Left            =    120
         TabIndex        =    0
         Text            =    "0"
         Top             =    360
         Width           =    3132
      End
      Begin VB.Menu mnuHelp
         Caption         =    "&Help"
         NegotiatePosition=   3   'Right
         Begin VB.Menu mnuAbout
            Caption      =       "&About AWCCalc"
         End
      End
   End
End
Attribute VB_Name = "CalcDoc"
Attribute VB_GlobalNameSpace = False
Attribute VB_Creatable = True
Attribute VB_PredeclaredId = False
Attribute VB_Exposed = True
Option Explicit
Private Operand
Private Op
Private DataEntry
Private DP


Private Sub Accum_Change()
PropertyChanged
End Sub

Private Sub Clear_Click()
If DataEntry = False Then
  Op = Empty
  Operand = Empty
```

```
End If
Accum.Text = 0
DP = 0
DataEntry = False
End Sub

Private Sub Command1_Click()
Hyperlink.NavigateTo "http://www.al-williams.com/awc"

End Sub

Private Sub mnuAbout_Click()
MsgBox "AWCCalc is an example ActiveX Document Object using VB5"
End Sub

Private Sub Negate_Click()
Accum.Text = -Accum.Text
End Sub

Private Sub Number_Click(Index As Integer)
If DataEntry = True Then
  If DP = 0 Then
    Accum.Text = Accum.Text * 10 + Index
  Else
    Accum.Text = Accum.Text + Index / 10 ^ DP
    DP = DP + 1
  End If
Else
  DataEntry = True
  Accum.Text = Index
End If
End Sub

Private Sub Opkey_Click(Index As Integer)
If Not IsEmpty(Operand) And Not IsEmpty(Op) Then
  Select Case Op
    Case 0
    ' + is ambiguous since it is a string op too!
      Accum.Text = CDbl(Operand) + Accum.Text
    Case 1
      Accum.Text = Operand - Accum.Text
    Case 2
      Accum.Text = Operand * Accum.Text
    Case 3
      If Accum.Text = 0 Then
        ' our error code goes here
        Div0.Show vbModal, Me
```

```
          Else
             Accum.Text = Operand / Accum.Text
          End If
      End Select
   End If
   If Index = 4 Then
     Op = Empty
     Operand = Empty
   Else
     Op = Index
     Operand = Accum.Text
   End If
   DataEntry = False
   DP = 0
   End Sub


   Private Sub Point_Click()
   If DataEntry = False Then
     Accum.Text = 0
     DataEntry = True
   End If
   If DP = 0 Then DP = 1
   End Sub



   Private Sub UserDocument_ReadProperties(PropBag As PropertyBag)
   Accum.Text = PropBag.ReadProperty("Accum", "0")
   End Sub


   Private Sub UserDocument_WriteProperties(PropBag As PropertyBag)
   PropBag.WriteProperty "Accum", Accum.Text, "0"
   End Sub
```

Effective Use Of Doc Objects

How can you most effectively leverage your effort when constructing an application that uses doc objects? Consider Internet Explorer. If you look at IE's executable, it is only about 40K (38.4K on my machine). How can this be? I certainly couldn't write a program that connects over the network, parses HTML, creates ActiveX controls, interprets VBScript and JavaScript, and does all the other tasks that IE performs in 40K.

As you may have guessed, IE's executable is really just an ActiveX container that can load documents. SHDOCVW contains the Web browsing portion of the code. The key is that you can use the Web browsing with or without IE.

This is a smart strategy. A bad idea would be to write two separate pieces of code: a regular application and a document object. This would be an endless maintenance nightmare.

When do you use a control and when do you use a doc object? Those are good questions. There's no hard and fast rule. However, if you think of your program as an application, you should probably write a doc object. If, on the other hand, it is just a part of an application—especially one that will be the object of programming commands—you should consider a control.

Summary

Doc objects aren't much different from ActiveX controls. There are a few minor things that differ, but most of what you know about ActiveX applies to doc objects too.

Today there aren't many places to use doc objects. Internet Explorer and the Microsoft Office binder are the two best known examples. However, you can also write VB add-ins as doc objects. In the future, you can expect many more document containers to appear.

In the meantime, you can easily write your applications in two parts: a document object container (easy to do with VB) and a document object. Then you'll be ready to take advantage of new doc object containers.

11

THE END?

No epilogue, I pray you, for your play needs no excuse.
Never excuse.

—A Midsummer-Night's Dream

Who knows what the future will hold? Over the long haul, nobody really knows. However, for the foreseeable future, it's clear that Microsoft will be a big part of that future. And, for good or ill, Microsoft wants ActiveX to succeed.

Why fight it? Overall, ActiveX is a very versatile protocol for working with binary objects. It can be as efficient as you like or as feature-rich as you need (although not always at the same time). With the proper tools (like VB5), ActiveX doesn't even have to be all that difficult.

Do you remember the imaginary scenario in Chapter 1, the example where you (disguised as a Herman Miller salesman) send me some flaming email? That future is not very far off. ActiveX (and technologies layered on top of ActiveX) will make it possible.

If you go out a bit further, you'll see even more changes. Imagine a workspace that allows you to plug in modules that you need to perform certain jobs. A word processor is a great example of that. As a business owner, I need a word processor that types letters, packing lists, and proposals. As an author, I need a word processor that handles huge documents, does indexing, and word counting. As a programmer, I need a word processor that handles inserting code snippets and graphics as well as producing RTF for my help files.

Today, when you buy a word processor, you get all of this and more. For example, I never use the features aimed at producing legal pleading papers (thank goodness). You wind up with a giant program that is hard to learn and use.

What if you had a general-purpose frame into which you could drop a universal text component? The text component would do basic text manipulation. Since I need indexing and style management compatible with a publishing program, I could drop in those modules (maybe from two different vendors). The text component might have a spell checker that is horrible at spell checking computer-related documents, so I'd buy a computer-literate spell checker from someone else.

When programming, I might use the same text component for writing code. Then I'd use the compiler module and the help file module to compile, debug, and create help all in the same environment. We'd have the ultimate customizable programming environment.

Another example would be a high-end graphics program. You can easily imagine various graphics converters, filters, and drawing tools forming a mix and match environment. Of course, if you did it right, the same tools from the graphics program would drop right into the word processor and vice versa.

Will this come to pass? I think so. The obstacles are more legal and diplomatic than technological. If the industry can agree on how components integrate their functionality with a controlling frame and meaningfully share content, then this sort of application is right around the corner. Things like ActiveX controls approach this, but they still lack an easy way to share content. For example, how does the spell checker control cooperate with the frame that contains text?

The Future Of The Internet

Don't forget: The ActiveX controls in this book just scratch the surface of Microsoft's Internet strategy. There are server scripting tools that can allow Web servers to store preferences, tally votes, and run code either on the server or on the host.

Once there is some uniform way to provide active content, look for more plug-in tools that will extend Web pages. You can already build 3D Web sites, or include sophisticated presentation graphics. What will be next? Interactive games? Live stock quotes? Real-time video from concerts? Some of these exist already. More are on their way.

The Future Of Java

Java has an unusual position in the PC world. It started the idea of active content on the Internet. While Java works well at those tasks for which it was explicitly designed, it falls short in areas where people have pushed it. Java is largely interpreted and often lacks sophisticated development tools that the C++ industry has spent years building. Java code can't easily communicate with other Java programs (or applets). It also can't easily communicate with its container (the Web browser).

Besides, many people already know how to program in Basic, C++, or some other standard language. If these languages can provide the same features as Java, then why learn Java and switch?

About the only compelling argument for Java today is its cross-platform nature. Java will run on nearly any kind of computer with any operating system: Windows PCs, Macs, Unix boxes, and more. Today, ActiveX is primarily a Windows phenomenon (although there is supposedly a Mac version now). Microsoft promises that ActiveX will move to other platforms rapidly, however. Only time will tell how successful these ActiveX ports will be. On the other hand, the basic ideas behind ActiveX are quite simple and similar to RPC. It is easy to imagine how other machines and operating systems could incorporate ActiveX technology.

Microsoft recently released Visual J++, a Java environment that works like Microsoft's Visual C++ environment. This certainly gives Java a world-class development environment (whether you like the environment or not, you have to admit that there's plenty of it). It also telegraphs an odd strategy for Microsoft: straddling the fence. It is clear that Microsoft wants ActiveX to be the long-term answer for active Web content. But Microsoft also realizes that for the immediate future, Java was there first. In particular, until ActiveX successfully demonstrates its ability to cross platforms seamlessly, Java will still have its proponents. Besides, it doesn't have to be an either/or proposition. Java interfaces and ActiveX interfaces are quite similar. Products like Microsoft's Visual J++ can successfully integrate Java and ActiveX, perhaps giving you the best of both worlds.

A recent innovation is Java Beans—a direct attempt to challenge ActiveX controls. Java Beans is an emerging standard that allows Java programs to act as components and communicate between themselves. Will this really matter to everyone using ActiveX today? Time will tell, but I suspect ActiveX has too wide a head start. Judge for yourself. You can find out more about Java Beans at **http://www.javasoft.com/beans**.

The Future Of Other Object Standards

When it comes to building reusable objects, ActiveX has plenty of competition. There are many competing standards that attempt to define binary object compatibility guidelines (for example, DSOM or CORBA). However, these standards have not gained widespread acceptance—at least, not in the Windows world.

Why these other standards can't gain a foothold isn't clear. Of course, Microsoft's full weight behind ActiveX hasn't hurt it any. Also, instead of one cohesive standard, there are a half-dozen different "standards." This limits the possibility of any serious competition to ActiveX, because Microsoft doesn't need a lot of cooperation to set a standard.

The Future Of Windows

There's an old saying in the engineering world: I don't know what language engineers will be using to write programs in the year 2020, but I know they will call it "Fortran." You could make the same observation about operating systems: I don't know what the desktop operating system will be in the year 2020, but I know it will be named Windows. Granted, it is possible that some brilliant company will find a way to break the Microsoft stranglehold on the desktop operating system market. However, how that would happen is far from clear (if you know, then put down this book, go out, and get rich).

For developers, this isn't necessarily a bad thing. Having an operating system that runs on the vast majority of computers makes things easier for us. There are fewer new things to learn, large markets for our software, and greater protection of our investments (both time and money) in hardware, software, and code.

However, Windows is not set in stone. In the last decade, we've seen Windows move from a very sophisticated DOS shell to an operating system that has more in common with Unix and the Macintosh (shudder) than it does with DOS. You can look for even more changes as Windows embraces object orientation.

The good news is that ActiveX provides a very flexible, extensible framework within which future Windows enhancements can work. If you know ActiveX, you already know how many new features work in a general sort of way. You only need learn the specifics. I expect new Windows technology to be ActiveX-based for the foreseeable future.

The Future Of Programming

Many nay-sayers tell me that traditional programming is a thing of the past. They say that soon, blissful programmers will drop little modules on forms and create wonderful applications in hours. That's probably true. But who is writing these modules? To get rid of the low-level programmers, you need a collection of perfect modules, as well as a very efficient way to tie them together. You also need a set of basic modules from which you can do anything. That strikes me as unlikely, at least in our lifetime.

True, the market for high-tech programmers may shrink—many programs are best written using high-level constructs. Many programs are not sensitive to efficiency. Still, there will always be room for some number of people who build the tools and modules that others use to create their programs.

How do you hedge your bets? Be flexible. Don't be too quick to dismiss tools like Visual C++, Delphi, and the like. You don't have to use them, but you owe it to yourself to keep abreast of them. Many workaday programmers will be using these tools to generate the thousands of everyday programs that run the world. And since these languages can incorporate ActiveX controls and objects, they represent a huge market for your controls. Just be careful not to let the market shrink to where you no longer fit in it.

Another oddity I've noticed is that while Visual Basic programmers, for example, are eager to embrace components, C++ programmers tend to turn their noses up at them. Yet C++ programs can use your ActiveX components and controls quite easily. Few people refuse to use the standard I/O library. Why shouldn't they use off-the-shelf components where they are available? Your mission—should you decide to accept it—is to convince these programmers to buy and use your controls.

Where To Go?

Do you remember the movie *The Graduate*? In that movie, there was a scene where somebody told a young Dustin Hoffman the one-word secret to succcss: "plastics."

Imagine if you had invested in plastics before it exploded. What about buying Intel or Microsoft stock when you could afford it? Success in the computer business is not too different. If you guess the right place to be, you can be wildly successful. Witness all the fortunes made by oddballs who were staking out the Internet first. Microsoft itself can be accused of being at the right place (IBM) at the right time (pre-1980) with the right product (MSDOS, which they bought from another company).

If you guess wrong—well, that's another story. Look at the fortunes lost on sure things like OS/2, artificial intelligence, and even the PC Jr. So the trick is to guess the right technology and get there before anyone else.

I'd like to tell you that I know where the future lies. But the truth is, I haven't any more of a clue than anyone else. The trick here is to not get too stuck in one rut. If you know Java, learn ActiveX. If you know VB, try C++ for a change. I know it is distasteful, but the different perspective will do you good. I'm not saying to drop VB (or whatever you are currently using). I'm simply saying you can afford to broaden your point of view a bit. Programmers—like weight lifters—have to cross train to stay limber.

Magazines are a good way to stay current on trends. However, you have to be careful about editorial bias. Many magazines, for example, stayed committed to OS/2 long after the programming community at large had drifted away from it. Conferences are another good way to see what some groups of people believe is the wave of the future.

In the end, nothing is better than simply talking to other people in the computer business. In the past, that meant going to user group meetings, conferences, and even job interviews. I've known people who go on interviews just to see what other companies are doing. Today, you need only log into the Internet.

There are many ways to interact with people over the Net. Subscribe to a mailing list or participate in a Usenet group. Both are excellent ways to stay abreast of the industry trends in a real way. If you are like me, you find most Usenet groups a bit noisy. That's not a problem anymore. Simply use one of the search services that index news groups (www.altavista.digital.com and www.dejanews.com come to mind).

End Of The Soapbox

Okay, that's all of the preaching for today. Whatever course you should take, you'll find ActiveX all along it. At least that seems true for the foreseeable future.

Just as today's Windows bears only a passing resemblance to the older versions, there is no telling what ActiveX will look like in, say, five years. However, it is a good bet that ActiveX will still exist in five years, too. All that's left is to wish you good luck!

ActiveX Thesaurus

One of the things that makes learning ActiveX so much fun is that Microsoft scrambles up all the names every six months. If you find some of the jargon from other sources confusing, check out this list of ActiveX synonyms. Entries with an asterisk are the words this book usually uses to express a concept.

*ActiveX Component
An ActiveX server that provides one or more tables of function pointers (interfaces) that other programs can use to request services.

*ActiveX Control
A special class of ActiveX component that understands how to work like an ordinary Windows control. This type of component replaces older standards like Visual Basic Extensions (VBX). Notice that Microsoft currently calls almost any ActiveX server a control, but I prefer to call them components. Controls specifically know how to interact with a window.

*ActiveX Object
Another word for ActiveX component.

*Advanced Template Library
A library, based on C++ templates, that allows you to create ActiveX interfaces in a simplified fashion. As this book was being written, the library was still in beta form.

*Ambient Property
A property that a container exposes to its controls.

*Asynchronous Moniker
A moniker that returns from a binding call before the bound object is completely ready. The object binding completes while program execution continues.

*ATL
The Advanced Template Library.

*Base Control
An example shipped with Visual C++ that you can use as a starting point for ActiveX controls.

*BSTR
A counted string such as used by Visual Basic.

CA
Certification Authority.

*CATID
A UUID that identifies a component category.

Certification Authority
A trusted entity that makes a statement (represented by an X.509 certificate) about the authenticity of another certificate.

CGI
Common Gateway Interface.

*Client
Any program that uses ActiveX components.

*CLSID
A UUID that identifies a class.

*COleControl
The MFC class that represents all OCX-style ActiveX controls. This class derives from **CWnd**.

COM
Component Object Model; older term for ActiveX.

COM Object
An ActiveX object.

Common Gateway Interface
The traditional way to activate Web pages. This is a means for Web pages to send data back to a host machine, which can then select or generate a page on the fly.

Component Object Model
An older name for ActiveX. Usually, COM refers to OLE technology outside the scope of document linking and embedding.

Compound Documents
See Structured Storage System.

*Container
A program that can hold an ActiveX control or DocObject.

Cryptographic Digest
A one-way hash function that takes a variable-length input string and converts it to a fixed-length output string (called a cryptographic digest). This fixed-length string is similar to a checksum (albeit, a large checksum) for the file.

*CString
An MFC class that represents a string.

*CWnd
The class that MFC uses to represent all windows.

*Data Bound Property
A property that can request permission to change from its container and notify the container when a change takes place.

*Dispatch Interface
An IDispatch interface that translates **DISPIDs** into method calls or property accesses.

*DISPID
An integer that identifies the function requested of a dispatch interface.

*DocObject
An ActiveX server that can supply a document to link or embed in a container. This is the same thing that OLE documents have always been.

*Enumerator
An ActiveX object that provides a way to walk through some list of items.

*Event
A message that a control sends to its container.

*Form View
An MFC view that uses a dialog template to simulate a form.

*GUID
Globally Unique Identifier. This is another name for a UUID.

*HTML
The markup language ("Hypertext Markup Language") used to build Web pages.

*Interface
A table of function pointers. Clients make requests of an object by calling functions from an interface. An object may have more than one interface.

*IDL
Interface Description Language.

*IID
Interface Identifier. This is a UUID that identifies an interface.

*Interface Description Language
A script language that allows you to describe interfaces so that the IDL compiler can automatically create marshaling code. Newer versions of the IDL compiler can accept scripts that can also create type libraries.

Local Registration Authority
An intermediary between a publisher and a CA. The LRA can, for example, verify a publisher's credentials before sending them to the CA.

LRA
Local Registration Authority.

*Marshalling
A technique that allows programs in one process to transparently call interfaces that reside in another process. The processes need not be on the same machine.

*Method
A function that an ActiveX control exposes to its container.

*MFC
Microsoft Foundation Classes.

*Microsoft Foundation Classes
A C++ library designed to simplify many Windows programming tasks, including ActiveX programming.

*Moniker
An ActiveX object that encapsulates a data item's name, location, and the operations required to open it. For example, a moniker might contain a file name or a URL.

Object Application
A server.

OLE Control
An ActiveX control.

OLE Control Extension
An OCX or OLE Control.

OLE Automation
Scripting.

OCX
An ActiveX control.

*Object Description Language
A script that describes objects for the purpose of creating type libraries. Newer versions of the IDL compiler can accept a mixed IDL/ODL file so that you can maintain one single IDL file for both purposes.

*ODL
Object Description Language.

*Persistence
Any means of writing an object to some external data storage so that a program can later recreate the object with all of its internal state intact.

PKCS#7 Signed Data
A Public Key Certificate Standard #7 (PKCS#7) signed-data object encapsulates the information used to sign a file. It usually includes the signer's certificate, the root certificate, and the signer's public key.

*Property
A pseudo-variable that an ActiveX control allows containers to access. The property may correspond to a variable in the control, or may trigger a function call to set or retrieve the value.

*Property Sheet
A dialog page, typically used in a tabbed dialog, that allows users to read and set properties.

Protocol
Interface.

*Proxy
A function that works with a stub to transparently handle calls between processes. You can automatically generate proxies from an IDL script.

Recursion
See "recursion."

*Regedit
A program (first shipped with Windows 95) that allows you to manually view and manipulate the registry.

*Regedt32
A Windows NT version of REGEDIT.

*Registry
A system-wide database that contains configuration information in a hierarchical database.

*SAFEARRAY
An array type that ActiveX defines to facilitate sharing of array data between clients and servers.

*Scripting
The ability for a program to control objects from other programs without prior knowledge of those programs. This used to be known as OLE automation.

*Server
Any DLL or EXE that provides ActiveX Components. DLL servers are also known as InProc servers.

Software Publishing Certificate
A PKCS#7 signed-data object containing X.509 certificates and public key signatures.

SPC
Software Publishing Certificate.

*Synchronous Moniker
A moniker that doesn't return from a binding call until the bound object is completely ready.

Trust Provider
The portion of Windows that decides whether or not a given file is trusted. This decision is based on the certificate associated with the file.

*Stock Events
Events that have a common meaning defined by ActiveX.

*Stock Property
A standard property. That is, a property whose meaning is predefined by ActiveX.

*Storage
A portion of the structured storage system that most resembles a directory. It may contain substorages or streams.

*Stream
A portion of the structured storage system that most resembles a file. Contrast with storage.

*Structured Storage System
A way for an ActiveX object to treat some form of storage (e.g., a file or a database record) in a way that is conducive to saving objects.

*Stub
A function that works with a proxy to transparently handle calls between processes. You can automatically generate stubs from an IDL file.

*Test Container
A special program provided by the Microsoft Visual C++ environment for testing ActiveX controls. The container can alter properties, call methods, change ambient properties, monitor events, and perform other testing functions.

*Type Library
Data about the interfaces and types provided by an ActiveX component.

*URL
A Uniform Resource Locator. This is an address used to specify items (particularly Web pages). It consists of a data type, a server name, and a path.

*UUID
Universally Unique Identifier. This is a 128 bit number that you can generate so that they are unique. These numbers identify interfaces (IIDs), classes (CLSIDs), and categories (CATIDs). Sometimes UUIDs are known as GUIDs.

*VARIANT
A data structure that contains a union and a type field. Programs must use the type field to determine what portion of the union to read. ActiveX defines this structure to help facilitate data sharing between clients and servers.

VBX
Visual Basic Extension.

*VIEW
An MFC class responsible for displaying data and accepting input.

Visual Basic Extension
A packaged piece of code usable by Visual Basic and certain other 16-bit programming environments. Visual Basic Extensions (VBXs) were superseded by OCX controls.

WIN_CERTIFICATE

A Win32 data structure that contains either a PKCS#7 signed-data object or an X.509 certificate.

X.509 Certificate

A cryptographic certificate that contains a vendor's unique name and the vendor's public key.

Just Enough HTML

HTML (Hypertext Markup Language) is the *lingua franca* of the Web. Web content, from the simplest personal home page to a state-of-the art virtual reality extravaganza, uses HTML to define the appearance of the page.

Of course, HTML (by itself) isn't powerful enough to build virtual reality venues, but it is powerful enough to contain objects (such as ActiveX objects) that can do anything you can dream up.

There have been entire books written on how to create HTML, but in this appendix, I want to show you enough HTML to get started and try a few things. You'll need to create some HTML to test your ActiveX creations on the Web.

If you are really interested in creating high-quality Web pages, stop! Your best bet is to get a tool that creates Web content automatically. For example, you can get the Internet Assistant for Microsoft Word (or PowerPoint or several other products), that allows you to layout Web pages without knowing much about HTML.

Still, if you want to do anything out of the ordinary, you'll need to know HTML, so you might as well dig right in and get started. Even the best tools won't do everything you need. It also isn't unusual to have to tweak automatically-generated HTML to get the results you want.

By the way, HTML started as a subset of SGML (the Standard Generalized Markup Language) designed to transfer documents between systems. If you know SGML, you might find you practically know HTML already.

The Basic Structure

HTML files are really just ASCII text files. By convention, they use the .HTML extension unless MS-DOS is involved, in which case, the .HTM extension is the standard.

Ordinary text in an HTML file appears as ordinary text in the produced document. What could be easier? The magic comes into play when you add tags to produce special formatting. Most tags come in pairs, so that they affect the text between them. For example, to indicate boldface, you'll use the **<B>** and **</B>** tags:

```
<B>This is bold text</B> This is not!
```

The starting tag has no slash, while the ending one does. In a few special cases, you can omit the ending tag, but usually you do need it. For instance, the above line needs the **</B>** tag so that the remaining text is not in bold. By the way, tags are not case sensitive. You could just as well use **** and **** in the above example.

Some tags take parameters which appear *inside* the angle brackets. Others are required by the HTML specification, but not required by common browsers. Like most other things involving computers, HTML is subject to some interpretation.

An HTML Document

An HTML document has several standard elements. Some of them are optional some of the time, but all of them are available if you want to use them. Here is the structure of a correctly-formatted HTML document:

```
<HTML>
<!-- A comment - these can go anywhere-->
<HEAD>
<!-- Header information (the page title, for example)-->
</HEAD>
<BODY>
<!-- Main text which consists of headings, paragraphs, and images-->
```

```
</BODY>
</HTML>
```

Notice that the entire content appears between the **<HTML>** and **</HTML>** tags. While this is officially correct, most browsers will display any file with a .HTM or .HTML extension as HTML, even if it doesn't contain this tag.

The first portion of the HTML document appears between the **<HEAD>** tags. This is for special information pertaining to the entire document. You can use the **<TITLE>** tag, for example, to set a title for your page. Keep it 64 characters or less if you expect it to be visible in its entirety.

Another tag that can appear in the **<HEAD>** section is the **<BASE>** tag. This tag has no closing tag; it appears by itself. You can use it to specify the address of the page. This is helpful if someone copies your page (to a local machine, for example). If someone tries to follow a link and the browser can't find it, it will search relative to the address specified in the **<BASE>** tag. Any time you need to specify a URL in a tag, you'll use the **HREF** parameter, as in:

```
<BASE HREF=http://www.coriolis.com/made_up.html>
```

It isn't strictly necessary, but some pages place an **<ADDRESS>** tag pair after the **</BODY>** tag. The intent of this tag is to place information about the page's authorship, revision date, and so forth at the bottom of the page. When you see a line at the bottom of the page that reads

```
Last modified: April 1, 1996. Send comments to webmaster@coriolis.com
```

that text is probably inside a pair of **<ADDRESS>** tags.

You can enter special characters by using an ampersand. This is especially important for the '<', '>', and '&' characters, as well as currency symbols and other non-ASCII characters. You can use a letter name followed by a semi-colon (for example, **<** is the '<' character and **>** is the '>' character). Alternately, you can use the sequence **&#nnn;** where **nnn** is a decimal character code from the ISO Latin-1 character set. You can find a list of common key names in Table B.1. Key names, by the way, are one place where HTML is case-sensitive.

Table B.1 Common key names.

Name	Key
amp	Ampersand (&)
copy	Copyright sign ©
gt	Greater than sign (>)
lt	Less than sign (<)
nbsp	Non breaking space
quot	Quotation mark (")
reg	Registered trademark ®
shy	Soft hyphen

Inside The Body (With Apologies To Asimov)

Within the body of the document, the browser will wrap all normal words into one long paragraph—unless you tell it otherwise. This makes sense, because you can't know how wide the user's screen is. It would be a bad idea, but you could put one word on each line of your HTML source and the browser would take care of wrapping it into a paragraph.

When you want to start a new paragraph, use the **<P>** tag. Technically, you use this tag to start a paragraph, and the **</P>** tag to end it. However, very few people actually use the **</P>** tag since it is optional.

Sometimes, you just want a line break inside the same paragraph. Then you can use the **
** tag to start a new line. This tag has no corresponding ending tag. For example, to format an address, you might write:

```
Coriolis Group Books<BR>
14455 N. Hayden Road, #220<BR>
Scottsdale, AZ 85260<BR>
```

You can format text in a variety of ways. The best way is to use a logical formatting attribute. You tell the browser what you want to do, and it figures out how to represent that format. For example, if you tell the browser you want strong emphasis (using the **<STRONG>** tag), it will probably render the text in bold face. Table B.2 shows the common logical attributes and common ways that browsers render them. Notice that the browser may elect to show different items in different colors, or use a user-defined style, so don't count on

Table B.2 Logical attributes.

Tag	Name	Use	Often rendered as...
<CITE>	Citation	References to books	Italic
<CODE>	Code	Source code	Monospaced
<DFN>	Definition	Definition of a word	Italic
<EM>	Emphasis	Special emphasis	Italic
<KBD>	Keyboard	Text the user should type (for example, in a procedure document)	Bold and monospaced
<SAMP>	Sample	Sample output	Monospaced
<STRONG>	Strong	Strong emphasis	Bold
<VAR>	Variable	Placeholder text	Italic

the appearance of these items to be consistent. Naturally, all of these tags have a corresponding closing tag.

Sometimes you want more control over the appearance of your text. Then you can use the physical attribute tags shown in Table B.3. These allow you to specify exactly how the text should look.

You can nest attributes. For example, if you wanted bold underlined text, you might use:

```
Try <B><U>ActiveX</U></B>
```

Be sure to place the closing tags in the reverse order of the starting tag. Otherwise, some browsers may get confused.

In addition to normal paragraphs, HTML can create paragraphs in six different styles for headings. The intent is for you to use these as headings for different sections of the document. In truth, you can use them for anything you like.

Table B.3 Physical attributes.

Tag	Name	Description
<B>	Bold	Heavy face text
<I>	Italic	Italic type face
<U>	Underline	Line drawn beneath text
<TT>	Teletype	Monospaced text

You can also use them in any order. You don't have to use them at all. The tags are <H1> through <H6> (and, of course, the usual closing tags).

Often you'd like to place a line between sections of your documents. Printers call these lines *rules*. HTML allows you to use the <HR> tag (by itself) to insert a horizontal rule in the text. This is better than drawing a line with ASCII characters (or even a graphic), since you don't know how wide the user's screen is.

In addition to the header styles, HTML also provides the <BLOCKQUOTE> and <PRE> paragraph tags. The <BLOCKQUOTE> style sets off text in some way (usually by using indentation and italics). The <PRE> style implies that the text is preformatted. The browser does *not* wrap text in a <PRE>-style paragraph. It shows it exactly as it is in the HTML file. This is useful for source code. Usually, a <PRE> paragraph appears in monospaced type. You can specify the width of the text in characters by using the **WIDTH** parameter to the <PRE> tag. Don't forget the closing tags </BLOCKQUOTE> and </PRE>.

Images And Objects

Of course, the big selling point to the Web is graphics. The <IMG> tag is the ordinary way to insert a graphic in your document. However, the <OBJECT> tag (discussed in Chapter 6) will also insert graphics in a more general way. Since the <OBJECT> tag is new, however, most pages still use the <IMG> tag for simple graphics. Many browsers don't support <OBJECT> yet, and those that do may not support it completely.

Each <IMG> tag requires a **SRC** parameter to name the file that contains the image. This file name can be a full-blown URL, or just a file name if the file is in the same location as the Web page (or its base address). Since some browsers don't show graphics (or users will turn graphics off), it is a good idea to specify the **ALT** parameter, too. This parameter specifies some text to show in case the image does not display. Here's a typical image statement:

```
<IMG SRC="PIX1.GIF" ALT="The first picture">
```

Normally, an image acts like a single character in your text. If you don't want things to appear after your image, you'll need a <BR> or <P> tag following it. You can also control the alignment of text around the image by using the **ALIGN** parameter. This parameter can take one of three values: **TOP**, **BOTTOM**, or **MIDDLE**. If you don't use an **ALIGN** parameter in your <IMG> tag, the text will line up with the bottom of the image.

Of course, you could also insert the same image with:

```
<OBJECT DATA="PIX1.GIF">
</OBJECT>
```

The **<OBJECT>** tag is more flexible because it can insert typed data (like a .GIF file) or an object (see Chapter 6). Table B.4 shows a summary of parameters the **<OBJECT>** tag accepts.

The **WIDTH** and **HEIGHT** parameters allow you to specify the desired size (which need not match the actual size). This allows you to scale up a small image (which transfers faster). You can specify sizes in pixels or in the units found in Table B.5. For example, to make an image 2 inches square, you would specify "2in" in both parameters.

Lists

HTML supports several types of lists. These are similar to paragraph styles. The most common types of lists use the **<LI>** tag to denote the beginning of a list element. To create a numbered list, use the **<OL>** ("ordered list") tag. For example:

```
<OL>
<LI> Item 1
<LI> Item 2
</OL>
```

produces

```
1. Item 1
2. Item 2
```

If you prefer a bulleted list, use the **<UL>** ("un-numbered list") tag. You can also get a more compact list by using **<MENU>** or **<DIR>**. Items in a menu list should not exceed one line of text. The **<DIR>** list items shouldn't exceed 20 characters so that the browser can form columns, if it has that capability.

There is another kind of list that HTML supports: the description list. This type of list uses text instead of a bullet and may be used for lexicons or encyclopedia-style entries. The **<DL>** tag starts the list. You begin each text "bullet" with the **<DT>** tag. After the text, place a **<DD>** tag (not a **</DT>** tag). Then follow with the text that goes with that pseudo-bullet. There is no **</DD>** tag; just start another **<DT>** entry or end with **</DL>**. Some browsers will attempt to place short text "bullets" on the same line as the other text if you specify the **COMPACT** parameter to the **<DL>** tag.

Table B.4   Object tag parameters.

Parameter	Description
ID	Name of object
DECLARE	Don't create object until referenced
CODEBASE	Location to find object
DATA	Data to use with object (object may be implied by type)
TYPE	Type of data (if not implied by extension)
CODETYPE	Type of object
STANDBY	Message to display while loading
ALIGN	Alignment properties
HEIGHT	Height of object
WIDTH	Width of object
BORDER	Size of border (0=no border)
HSPACE	Horizontal space to leave around object
VSPACE	Vertical space to leave around object
USEMAP	Use an image map to create anchors
SHAPES	Use a client-side image map to create anchors
NAME	Name used in forms

Table B.5   Unit suffixes.

Suffix	Description
%	Percentage of display area
pt	Points (72 points==1 inch)
pi	Picas (6 picas==1 inch)
in	Inches
cm	Centimeters

Hyperlinks

The H in HTML stands for hypertext, and the Web wouldn't be the same without links, would it? Each link has two parts: a presentation part (text or graphics) and an invisible portion (the *anchor* that specifies where to go).

The <A> tag inserts anchors. The presentation portion can be any mix of text or graphics that you like. This allows you to create very sophisticated links since you can use any text or HTML commands you like in the presentation.

Here is a simple link:

```
To continue click <A HREF="http://www.coriolis.com/nextpage.htm">here</A>
```

When you click the word "here" the browser jumps to the correct URL. Usually, the browser will show the link word underlined (and possibly in a special color). Of course, you can use graphics as the presentation portion, too:

```
<A HREF="http://www.coriolis.com/p1.htm"><IMG SRC="clickme.gif"></A>
```

You can also use anchors to name a spot in your document. For example:

```
<A NAME="Summary">My Conclusions</A>
```

This line creates an anchor named "Summary". You can jump to it by using a '#' character in the **HREF** portion of another anchor tag. For example:

```
<A HREF="#Summary">Jump directly to summary</A>
```

or

```
<A HREF="http://www.coriolis.com/report.html#Summary">See summary</A>
```

The first example jumps to the Summary anchor on the same page. The second example jumps to a new page and finds the Summary anchor on that page.

Image Maps, Forms, And More

There is much more to HTML. For example, you can divide up a single graphic into multiple anchors or use a background graphic. You can use tables and multiple windows (frames). You can create forms and process them on your server, you can add sounds, scrolling marquees, and—well, you get the idea.

With each new browser release, there are new HTML features. One of the best ways to get information about HTML is from the Web itself. There are technical specifications, tutorials, and even software to help you create HTML. Look at **http://www.w3.org** for the latest specifications for HTML. After all, what better place to find information about the Web than on the Web?

TOP 10 SURPRISES FOR NON-VB PROGRAMMERS

Basic has a reputation for being easy to learn—and it is. However, if you are accustomed to using a different language (perhaps C++, or Pascal, for example), you might find a few surprising things along the way. Here, in no particular order, are my top 10 surprises you'll trip over when using Visual Basic.

10. Subroutine calls only use parenthesis when using Call.

Assume you have the following definitions:

```
Function f(n as Integer) as Integer
.
.
.
Sub s(n as Integer)
```

When calling these routines, you have several choices:

```
n=f(10) ' call function; parenthesis required
s 10 ' call sub; parenthesis not allowed
call s(10)  ' call sub (as above); parenthesis required
```

This is maddening if you are a C/C++ programmer where everything is really a function and you always use the parenthesis.

351

9. Use Set to assign objects to variables.

Technically, the Basic keyword **Let** introduces an assignment. For example:

```
Let I=0
```

However, most everyone omits the **Let** because it is optional, leading to the more common form:

```
I=0
```

When working with objects, you must use the **Set** keyword:

```
Dim sheet as Object
Set sheet = CreateObject("SpreadSheet.Worksheet")
```

8. To delete an object, assign nothing to the variable that contains it.

Basic performs garbage collection automatically for you. It frees memory that your program no longer uses. What about times when you want an object to go away now? Just assign the special value **nothing** to the object reference. Continuing with the example from item 9, above:

```
Set Sheet = nothing
```

7. Strings start at index 1; arrays begin at index 0.

John Kemeny and Thomas Kurtz (from Dartmouth College) designed Basic to appeal to ordinary people, not programmers. Ordinary people (unlike us) begin counting at 1, not 0. The end result is that the first letter in a string is at position 1. To manipulate a portion of a string, use the **Mid** function. It takes three arguments: the string, the starting position, and the length. You can use it on either side of an assignment:

```
x = Mid(aString,2,1) ' the second character in the string
Mid(aString,5,2)="xx" ' two characters @ pos 5 now "xx"
```

Arrays do start at zero, however. The catch is that Basic is afraid you might not know that, so it adds an extra array element for good measure. For example, suppose in C++ you were to write:

```
int x[10];  /* almost the same as Dim x(10) as Integer */
```

This generates an array of integers ranging from **x[0]** to **x[9]**. That is a total of ten elements, with the tenth element having an index of 9. In VB, you might write:

```
Dim x(10) as Integer
```

This statement results in an array with elements ranging from 0 to 10 for a total of 11 elements. This prevents people who start counting at 1 from becoming confused. However, it does waste one element of the array if you are not careful. There are four ways to approach this problem: a) ignore it and waste one element; b) convince yourself to use the maximum array index in **Dim** statements instead of the count of elements; c) use the **Option Base** statement to set the starting element of arrays to 1 instead of 0; or d) use the **To** keyword to explicitly specify the upper and lower bounds of the array.

6. Strings can contain the null character, but most components can't.

VB doesn't use a null-terminated string format like many other languages. That means a string can legitimately contain zero bytes. For example:

```
x="Hello" & Chr(0) & "Goodbye"
```

However, most components (being C-language based somewhere down the road) don't understand this. For example, suppose you have a text box named **Text1** and you execute the following code:

```
x="Hello" & Chr(0) & "Goodbye"
Text1.Text=x
x=Text1.Text
```

If you examine x, you'll see it was summarily truncated at the **Chr(0)**.

5. Basic programs can dynamically allocate memory.

Older versions of Basic couldn't dynamically allocate memory the way other languages can. VB, however, allows you to create arrays you can resize on the fly. The trick is the **Redim** statement. First, you use **Dim** to specify an array, but you omit the size information in the parenthesis. Then, when you know the size you want (which could be in a variable) you call **Redim**. If you change your mind, you can call **Redim** again. Just be careful. Each time you call **Redim**, VB destroys the previous contents of the array *unless* you specify the **Preserve** keyword. Here's some example code:

```
Dim msg() as String ' Dynamic array
' later we find out how many lines are in msg
' old contents destroyed, but nothing there!
Redim msg(linecount)
 ' even later we add a line to msg
linecount = linecount+1
' Preserve contents this time
Redim Preserve msg(linecount)
```

4. VB can't create ordinary DLLs—only ActiveX DLLs.

Without resorting to third-party tools, you can't create an ordinary Windows DLL using Visual Basic. You can, however, create an ActiveX DLL (see Chapter 5).

3. VB can call most DLLs, including Windows internal DLLs.

Although VB can't create ordinary DLLs, it is very good at calling them. You have to write a **Declare** statement to define the name of each DLL function you want to call and the arguments it expects. You can't call functions with the C calling convention (most DLL functions use the Pascal calling method). You also can't pass certain arguments (notably pointers to functions). To pass pointers to items, you must specify them as **ByRef** in the **Declare**. To pass the unadorned object, use **ByVal**.

Don't forget that the Windows API is just a set of DLLs. Therefore, VB can call most of the API with no trouble. In fact, VB supplies the API Text Viewer application that will automatically write **Declares** for most API functions. You can find out more in Appendix E.

2. Integers are 16 bits wide.

For historical reasons, VB maintains 16-bit wide integers as the default integer type. If you want a 32-bit integer, you must use **Long**. Don't forget: the default variable type is a **Variant** and can hold either type of integer. You only need to worry when you explicitly declare variables of a certain type.

1. You can create controls at runtime using control arrays.

The way VB allows you to create controls at design time is very simple and straightforward. However, sometimes you want to create items on the fly at run time. Fortunately, VB allows you to do this with control arrays. Given a control array, you can call **Load** and **Unload** to dynamically create and destroy controls in the array.

More Tips For Non-VB Programmers

Here are a few other questions you may be asking yourself about VB if you are more familiar with a different language.

Q: What kind of variable should I use?

It is good practice to start each program with **Option Explicit** and then use **Dim** (or a similar statement) to precisely define your variables. Without **Option Explicit**, you could write code like this:

```
Receive=10
. . .
if Receiv=10 then …
```

VB assumes **Receiv** is just a new variable, and doesn't complain. With **Option Explicit** set, VB will complain since there is no **Dim** (or similar) statement declaring the variable **Receiv**. Using **Variant** arguments (the default type) is convenient, but wasteful. Variants are larger than most standard data types, so you probably should avoid them unless you really need a typeless variable. This is especially true when you construct large arrays.

```
Dim x(10000) ' variant
Dim x(10000) as Integer ' 16-bit integer
```

Q: Isn't VB interpreted and how will that affect performance?

VB5 can produce two different types of code: P-Code and native code. P-Code is an abstract assembly language that a special DLL interprets at run time. This can be slower than executing true assembly language in some cases. Also, your program can't run without the special P-Code interpreter and support libraries. Native code generation is similar to the output of traditional C or Pascal compiler. Although it isn't necessarily as efficient as well-written assembly language, it is usually much faster than interpreted code.

VB/C++ Rosetta Stone

The Rosetta stone was found by Napoleon's men in Egypt. It was a stone containing a message in Egyptian hieroglyphics and Greek. Until scholars had this stone, no one could read hieroglyphs. However, since many people speak Greek (not the least of whom are Grecians), it became possible to learn the ancient Egyptian language (at least, the written language).

Sometimes you know what you want to do in C++, but you can't quite come to grips with the Basic syntax. Table C.1 shows some C++ idioms and their equivalent VB form, to help you out.

Like the real Rosetta stone, this table won't help you "speak" Basic, but it will help you encode your C++ thoughts into VB (or vice versa). Like real languages, of course, you'll have to practice if you want to think native VB.

Luckily, VB is simple to learn. If you have experience with most any other language, you may be able to pick up VB just from working the examples in this book. There are also many excellent books on general VB programming that you'll want to check out. For example, you might want to read *Visual Basic 5 Programming EXplorer* by Peter Aitken or *Visual Basic 5 Object-Oriented Programming* by Gene Swartzfager (both from The Coriolis group, of course).

Table C.1 Visual Basic equivalents of C++ constructs.

C++	VB
`short n;`	`Dim n as Integer`
`long n;`	`Dim n as Long`
`char p[10];`	`Dim p as String`

`struct t1 {`
`  int a;`
`  int b;`
`  };`
	`Type t1`
	`    a as Long`
	`    b as Long`
	`End Type`

`for (I=0;I<10;I++)`
`  {`
`  foo(I);`
`  }`
	`For I=0 to 9`
	`    foo I`
	`Next I`

`for (I=0;I<10;I+=2)`
`  {`
`  foo(I);`
`  }`
	`For I=0 to 9 step 2`
	`    foo I`
	`Next I`

`if (x==0) foo(0);`	`If x=0 Then foo 0`

`if (x==0)`
`  {`
`  foo(0);`
`  foo(1);`
`  }`
	`If x=0 Then`
	`    foo 0`
	`    foo 1`
	`End If`

`while (x!=0)`
`  {`
`  x=foo();`
`  }`
	`Do While x<>0`
	`    x = foo`
	`Loop`

`do {`
`  x=foo();`
`  } while (x!=0);`
	`Do`
	`    x = foo`
	`Loop While x<>0`

continued

Table C.1   Visual Basic equivalents of C++ constructs (continued).

C++	VB

```
int foo(int x)          Function foo(x as LongInt) as LongInt
  {                         . . .
  . . .                     if x<0 then
  if (x<0) return -1;         foo = -1
  . . .                       Exit Function
  return 10;                End If
  }                         . . .
                            foo=10
                          End Function
```

```
void foo(int &x)        Sub foo(ByRef x as Long)
  {                         . . .
  . . .                   End Sub
  }
```

```
for (I=0;I<10;I++)      For I=0 to 9
  {                         . . .
  . . .                     If x=0 Then Exit For
  if (x==0) break;        Next I
  }
```

JUST A LITTLE C++

You might wonder why there is an appendix about C++ in a Visual Basic book. That's a good question. This appendix won't teach you to use C++. If you want to write ActiveX using C++, I've written another book for that (*Developing ActiveX Web Controls* from Coriolis). However, it is a fact of life that much of the ActiveX documentation along with many books and magazine articles about ActiveX have a distinct C++ bias. This appendix will show you a little about C++ syntax so you can decipher documents. Sort of a C++ Rosetta stone; at least for ActiveX programming purposes.

C++'s philosophy centers around classes. These are similar (and perhaps more powerful than) VB's class modules. A class is a collection of code and data that behaves as a unit. Here is a simple C++ class declaration:

```
class InputRecord
  {
  private:
  int lock_count;
  CString name;
  CString phonenum;
  public:
  InputRecord();
  InputRecord(char *name, char *num);
  ~InputRecord();
  BOOL AddToDatabase(Database *db);
  int MatchInDatabase(Database *db);
  };
```

What does this mean? First, it means there is a class named **InputRecord**. Notice that there isn't any variables named

InputRecord. Instead, **InputRecord** is like a new user-defined type. To make an integer variable **I** in C++, you'd write:

```
int I;
```

To make a new **InputRecord** named **irec** you'd write:

```
InputRecord irec;
```

CString and **Database** are other classes that represent a string and a database. The Microsoft Foundation Classes (MFC; a popular C++ library) provide a **CString** class for strings. I just made the **Database** class up for this example. Table D.1 shows some common built-in C++ types and their equivalent Basic types. Of course, **lock_count** is a simple integer variable.

The class has three private variables (**lock_count**, **name**, and **phonenum**). Actually, the **private:** keyword is redundant. Everything at the beginning of a class is private until you use the **protected:** or **public:** keyword (you'll see more about **protected:** shortly). Then everything will be public or protected until you use the **private:** keyword again.

The class also has two functions (**AddToDatabase** and **MatchInDatabase**). These functions (whose code resides somewhere else) perform operations on the class. Since they are public, other pieces of code can call them. Suppose you've declared the **irec** variable as an **InputRecord**. You could call **AddToDatabase** like this:

```
irec.AddToDatabase(db);
```

Table D.1   Common types.

C++ Type	VB Type
short	Integer
int	Long
long	Long
char[]	String (see text)
char	Byte
BOOL	Boolean
float	Single

These two functions return a **BOOL** (similar to a **Boolean** type) and an integer (similar to a **Long**). Just to make the comparison, comparable functions in VB might look like this:

```
Public Function AddToDatabase (ByRef db as Database) as Boolean
Public Function MatchInDatabase(ByRef db as Database) as Integer
```

The other two items that look like functions are **InputRecord** and **~InputRecord**. Notice anything odd about these names? The first one is the same as the class name. That makes it a constructor. There are two versions of the constructor: one that takes no arguments and one that takes two character pointers (more about pointers later). If you create an **InputRecord** like this:

```
InputRecord irec;
```

C++ calls the first (default) constructor. If, on the other hand, you write:

```
InputRecord irect(nam,num);
```

C++ calls the second constructor using the arguments you specify.

By the way, it is a common practice in C++ to have two or more functions with the same name. The only way to tell the difference is by the argument lists. This is known as function overloading.

The **~InputRecord** function is a destructor. C++ calls it every time an **InputRecord** variable goes out of scope. For example, if you define an **InputRecord** inside a function, when the function ends, C++ calls the destructor. For global variables, the system calls the constructor before the program begins and calls the destructor after the program terminates.

When you look up an interface in the ActiveX documentation, you'll often see it described in C++ terms. In the above example, for instance, you'd refer to the **MatchInDatabase** function as **InputRecord::MatchInDatabase**. The double colon signifies that the function is a part of the class. This is also how you usually write code for the function, as in:

```
int InputRecord::MatchInDatabase(Database * db)
  {
// Code goes here
  }
```

What About Pointers?

One thing many new C++ programmers have difficulty with is pointers. Pointers serve at least two purposes in a C++ program: they allow you to pass values by reference and they allow you to pass arrays to functions.

The first usage corresponds closely to VB's **ByRef** keyword. Consider this Basic example:

```
Public Function doubleit(n as Integer) as Integer
   n = n * 2
   doubleit = n
End Function
```

This is roughly equivalent to the following C++ code:

```
int AnObj::doubleit(int n)
   {
   n = n * 2;
   return n;
   }
```

In both cases, the value passed to the function isn't changed. Only the function's copy of the variable changes. For example:

```
Dim x as Integer
Dim y as Integer
x=10
y=doubleit(x)
' x= 10, y=20
```

However, suppose your wrote:

```
Public Function doubleit(ByRef n as Integer) as Integer
   n = n * 2
   doubleit = n
End Function
```

Or, in C++:

```
int AnObj::doubleit(int *n)
   {
   *n = *n * 2;
   return *n;
   }
```

Now the value **x** in the example code will change. The answer will be 20. Notice that in C++, you have to use the asterisk to dereference the pointer. That also means you have to convert the variable to an address using the address-of operator (the ampersand). Suppose you have a variable **someobj** which is an instance of **AnObj**. Your code might look like this:

```
y=someobj.doubleit(&x);  // address of x
```

Pointers used in this way are a throwback to the original C language. C++ has a better way to do this called references. Here is what the same code snippets look like using references:

```
int AnObj::doubleit(int &n)
  {
  n = n * 2;
  return n;
  }


y=someobj.doubleit(x);
```

Notice that the syntax is more natural. Still, you'll see pointers in a great deal of code, even where references would be more appropriate.

The other place where pointers come into play is when you have to pass an array to a function. In C++, the name of an array is a pointer to the array, and it is almost impossible to distinguish pointers from arrays. For example, this is legal in C++:

```
void init_array(int *ary,int ct)
  {
  int I;
  for (I=0;I<ct;I++)
    {
// treat pointer as an array
    ary[I]=0;
    }
  }
int x[10]; // array of 10 integers
// treat array as a pointer!
init_array(x,10);
```

C++ programs often use the same trick when passing large classes or structures (user-defined types) to functions. It is more economical to pass a 4 byte pointer (or reference) to a structure, than it is to pass the entire structure, even if the function doesn't really want to modify the structure.

Strings

Speaking of arrays, standard C++ represents strings as arrays of characters. The end of the string contains a zero byte. This has two important ramifications: first, you can't have a zero byte in the middle of a string. Second, you have to make your array one byte longer than your string. C++ is smart enough to automatically convert string literals (constant strings in double quotes) into zero terminated string arrays of the proper length. You might see code like this:

```
char name[]="Jose Jimenez"; //no need to specify length
char real[22]="Bill Dana"; // extra space at end
```

You can also treat a string literal as a pointer to the string, which is as good as an array (as long as you don't need to modify the string):

```
char *host="Ed Sullivan";
```

If that were all there was to it, you wouldn't have much problems with strings. However, strings have become such a nightmare, that even most C++ programmers have trouble with some of the nuances.

With Windows 3.1, there was only one kind of character: an 8-bit ASCII character from the ANSI character set. These ANSI strings closely model the strings you find on most other operating systems, and everyone used them comfortably. Everyone, that is, except for programmers and users using non-English characters.

Windows tried to adapt by using double byte characters. In this scheme, some 8-bit characters act as a flag, signifying that the next byte is an extended character. This has several advantages. First, it can be relatively compact. Also, it means that if you don't see any non-English characters, nothing is different, so old data files, strings, and so on are still usable. The downside is that functions that count characters (for example) have to know when two bytes are the same as two characters, and when they are the same as one character.

International standards committees worked on this problem for a while. After all, this isn't a Windows-specific problem. The answer eventually agreed to was Unicode. All Unicode characters are 16-bits wide. That makes it easy to count characters and allows plenty of characters for each language.

Windows NT and ActiveX use Unicode internally. Windows NT can also translate ANSI strings for you automatically (of course, with some performance degradation). ActiveX doesn't translate for you, but VB automatically does. C++ however, doesn't do any conversions for you for a variety of reasons.

To make matters worse, the C++ headers and documentation use different names to refer to the same kind of string. For example a **char** * is the same as an **LPSTR**, both of which are ANSI strings. Of course, that doesn't account for **OLESTR**s, **BSTR**s, and the MFC-specific **CString**. Some strings are ANSI and some are Unicode. All OLE strings use Unicode (even if something like VB makes you unaware of that). Mass confusion. Just be aware that C++ programs spend a lot of effort converting ANSI strings to Unicode and vice versa. You might wonder why C++ programmers don't just use Unicode. The answer is simple. Windows 95 has virtually no support for Unicode (outside of ActiveX and a few other special areas). That means that if you want your code to run on Windows 95 and Windows NT, you've got to stick with ANSI for now.

MFC (the class library that many C++ Windows programmers use) supplies a **CString** class that handles many of these problems. In fact, you might notice it looks a great deal like a VB string. The **CString** class can convert between ANSI and Unicode without much intervention from the programmer. Of course, it might not be as efficient as a pure string.

About The Preprocessor

The last area you should know about is the C++ preprocessor. The preprocessor, in theory, is a program that scans C++ code before it is compiled. This special program substitutes commands and macros in the source code with other text. Then the translated result moves to the compiler. Today's compilers generally do preprocessing themselves without using a different program, but the principle is the same. C++ programmers get a variety of effects from the preprocessor. If you don't know about the preprocessor, you can quickly go insane trying to figure out some C++ source.

The most important use of the preprocessor is to include other files into another file. This is often used to read in predefined class definitions, constants, etc. For example, constants and declarations used by Windows are in WINDOWS.H. It isn't uncommon to see the following line at the start of a C++ program:

```
#include <windows.h>
```

The sharp symbol (#, or pound sign if you are an American) identifies the line as a preprocessor command (known as a directive). The **include** keyword asks the preprocessor to search for the mentioned file, read it, and insert its contents at this point in the file. It is customary to put system headers (that might be a system-defined directory) in angle brackets (like the above example). Your private includes usually go in double quotes.

The confusing part of the preprocessor is its ability to perform macro expansion. C++ programmers may use this to provide constant values, enumerated values, and efficient, small functions. You should note that C++ actually provides better ways to do these things, but C didn't and old habits persist for one reason or another.

Here is a C++ constant:

```
#define MAX_NAME_LEN 1024
```

It is customary, but not necessary, to make the name of a preprocessor macro all upper case. You'll see why in a few moments. Somewhere in the code you might find lines like these:

```
char name[MAX_NAME_LEN];
strncpy(iobuf,name,MAX_NAME_LEN);
```

That's not too hard to understand. The problem is when you find programmers writing pseudo-functions using macros that take arguments. For example:

```
#define doubleit(n) ((n)*2)
```

This makes a very efficient version of the **doubleit** function you saw earlier. However, if you look at a line of code like this,

```
x=doubleit(10)
```

it could drive you crazy trying to find where the program defines **doubleit**. Again, a good idea to make preprocessor macros upper case and most programmers do.

Summary

This short appendix isn't going to turn you into a C++ programmer. Besides, you probably don't want to be a C++ programmer. However, having seen a bit about how C++ works, you'll be better prepared to wade through the Windows API and ActiveX documentation.

If you want to learn more, there are many resources available. Why learn more? C++ trades design-time efficiency for potential run-time efficiency. If you write good code, C++ will let you write programs that execute quickly, reside in small files, and use little memory. Of course, you can write lousy code in any language. Using ActiveX, you can even merge VB and C++ and write powerful systems.

Luckily, C++ has been around for awhile, so there is no shortage of books and courses available. You might also check out my *Windows Commando* column in each issue of *Visual Developer Magazine*. *Windows Commando* deals almost exclusively with C++ Windows programming. You can find a special trial offer for *Visual Developer Magazine* in the back of this book, or go online at **http://www.coriolis.com** to find out more.

CALLING THE WINDOWS API

E

V B can easily call functions stored in DLLs. Since the Windows API is nothing more than a collection of DLLs, VB can directly make API calls. The CONSTANT.BAS file (See Listing E.1) contains the declarations required to call the registry functions from VB. I used the API Text Viewer program (that ships with VB5) to create most of this file.

Because the API is so large, it would slow VB down to know about every API call each time you ran your program. Instead, Microsoft provides the API Text Viewer. Using the viewer, you select the calls you are interested in and the viewer exports them to a file of your choice.

This is handy, but there are a few problems. The viewer doesn't understand dependencies. Depending on how you create the output file, you may have errors when you try to run your program. For example, you might get an error on the following line:

```
Public Const KEY_EXECUTE = (KEY_READ)
```

Examining the file, you'll find that **KEY_READ** is defined later in the file. You'll have to manually move the **KEY_READ** definition to precede **KEY_EXECUTE**.

The other problem is similar. You may export a function only to find that it depends on a data type that you'll need to export.

Then you'll discover that the data type requires several **Const** definitions. This can go on for some time before you unearth all the dependencies.

If you need to call DLLs that don't belong to the Windows API, you can do that too. Just manually construct the same type of **Declare** statements that the API viewer creates for you. For example:

```
Declare Function RegOpenKey Lib "advapi32.dll" Alias    "RegOpenKeyA"
(ByVal hKey As Long, ByVal lpSubKey As String, phkResult As Long) As Long
```

This defines a function named **RegOpenKey**. It is really a reference to the **RegOpenKeyA** function in the **ADVAPI32.DLL** library. It takes 3 arguments (**hKey**, **lpSubKey**, and **phkResult**). The **ByVal** keyword indicates that those values are not passed as pointer types. The final argument doesn't use **ByVal** (**ByRef** is the default), therefore it is passed as a pointer to the variable. The final **As Long** clause denotes that the function returns a long integer.

If you read C, a corresponding C definition might be:

```
LONG RegOpenKeyA(LONG hKey, char *lpSubKey, LONG *phkResult);
```

or

```
LONG RegOpenKeyA(HKEY hKey, LPSTR lpSubKey, LPLONG phkResult);
```

In the second example, constant definitions (like **HKEY** and **LPSTR**) appear, but make no difference to VB. It isn't uncommon for VB programs to use a **LONG** to represent other 32-bit quantities (**HKEY, HRESULT, HWND**, etc.).

Listing E.1 CONSTANT.BAS.

```
Attribute VB_Name = "Module1"
' Autogenerated by API Viewer

Public Const STANDARD_RIGHTS_ALL = &H1F0000
Public Const REG_BINARY = 3
Public Const REG_CREATED_NEW_KEY = &H1
Public Const REG_DWORD = 4
Public Const REG_DWORD_BIG_ENDIAN = 5
Public Const REG_DWORD_LITTLE_ENDIAN = 4
Public Const REG_EXPAND_SZ = 2
Public Const REG_NOTIFY_CHANGE_ATTRIBUTES = &H2
Public Const REG_NOTIFY_CHANGE_LAST_SET = &H4
Public Const REG_NOTIFY_CHANGE_NAME = &H1
Public Const REG_NOTIFY_CHANGE_SECURITY = &H8
```

```
Public Const REG_OPTION_RESERVED = 0
Public Const REG_OPTION_VOLATILE = 1
Public Const REG_OPTION_BACKUP_RESTORE = 4
Public Const REG_OPTION_CREATE_LINK = 2
Public Const REG_OPTION_NON_VOLATILE = 0
Public Const REG_FULL_RESOURCE_DESCRIPTOR = 9
Public Const REG_LEGAL_CHANGE_FILTER = (REG_NOTIFY_CHANGE_NAME _
  Or REG_NOTIFY_CHANGE_ATTRIBUTES Or REG_NOTIFY_CHANGE_LAST_SET Or _
  REG_NOTIFY_CHANGE_SECURITY)
Public Const REG_LEGAL_OPTION = (REG_OPTION_RESERVED Or _
  REG_OPTION_NON_VOLATILE Or REG_OPTION_VOLATILE Or _
  REG_OPTION_CREATE_LINK Or REG_OPTION_BACKUP_RESTORE)
Public Const REG_LINK = 6
Public Const REG_NONE = 0
Public Const REG_OPENED_EXISTING_KEY = &H2
Public Const REG_REFRESH_HIVE = &H2
Public Const REG_RESOURCE_LIST = 8
Public Const REG_RESOURCE_REQUIREMENTS_LIST = 10
Public Const REG_SZ = 1
Public Const REG_WHOLE_HIVE_VOLATILE = &H1
Public Const REGDB_E_CLASSNOTREG = &H80040154
Public Const REGDB_E_FIRST = &H80040150
Public Const REGDB_E_IIDNOTREG = &H80040155
Public Const REGDB_E_INVALIDVALUE = &H80040153
Public Const REGDB_E_KEYMISSING = &H80040152
Public Const REGDB_E_LAST = &H8004015F
Public Const REGDB_E_READREGDB = &H80040150
Public Const REGDB_E_WRITEREGDB = &H80040151
Public Const REGDB_S_FIRST = &H40150
Public Const REGDB_S_LAST = &H4015F

Public Const HKEY_CLASSES_ROOT = &H80000000
Public Const HKEY_CURRENT_CONFIG = &H80000005
Public Const HKEY_CURRENT_USER = &H80000001
Public Const HKEY_DYN_DATA = &H80000006
Public Const HKEY_LOCAL_MACHINE = &H80000002
Public Const HKEY_PERFORMANCE_DATA = &H80000004
Public Const HKEY_USERS = &H80000003

Public Const READ_CONTROL = &H20000
Public Const STANDARD_RIGHTS_EXECUTE = (READ_CONTROL)
Public Const STANDARD_RIGHTS_READ = (READ_CONTROL)
Public Const STANDARD_RIGHTS_REQUIRED = &HF0000
Public Const STANDARD_RIGHTS_WRITE = (READ_CONTROL)
```

```
Public Const KEY_NOTIFY = &H10
Public Const SYNCHRONIZE = &H100000
Public Const KEY_CREATE_LINK = &H20
Public Const KEY_CREATE_SUB_KEY = &H4
Public Const KEY_ENUMERATE_SUB_KEYS = &H8
Public Const KEY_EVENT = &H1
Public Const KEY_QUERY_VALUE = &H1
Public Const KEY_SET_VALUE = &H2
Public Const KEY_ALL_ACCESS = ((STANDARD_RIGHTS_ALL Or _
    KEY_QUERY_VALUE Or KEY_SET_VALUE Or KEY_CREATE_SUB_KEY Or _
    KEY_ENUMERATE_SUB_KEYS Or KEY_NOTIFY Or KEY_CREATE_LINK) And _
    (Not SYNCHRONIZE))
Public Const KEY_READ = ((STANDARD_RIGHTS_READ Or _
    KEY_QUERY_VALUE Or KEY_ENUMERATE_SUB_KEYS Or KEY_NOTIFY) And _
    (Not SYNCHRONIZE))
Public Const KEY_EXECUTE = (KEY_READ)
Public Const KEY_WRITE = ((STANDARD_RIGHTS_WRITE Or _
    KEY_SET_VALUE Or KEY_CREATE_SUB_KEY) And (Not SYNCHRONIZE))


Type SECURITY_ATTRIBUTES
        nLength As Long
        lpSecurityDescriptor As Long
        bInheritHandle As Boolean
End Type


Type ACL
        AclRevision As Byte
        Sbz1 As Byte
        AclSize As Integer
        AceCount As Integer
        Sbz2 As Integer
End Type



Type SECURITY_DESCRIPTOR
        Revision As Byte
        Sbz1 As Byte
        Control As Long
        Owner As Long
        Group As Long
        Sacl As ACL
        Dacl As ACL
End Type



Type FILETIME
        dwLowDateTime As Long
```

```
        dwHighDateTime As Long
End Type


Declare Function RegCloseKey Lib "advapi32.dll" _
  (ByVal hKey As Long) As Long
Declare Function RegConnectRegistry Lib "advapi32.dll" Alias _
  "RegConnectRegistryA" (ByVal lpMachineName As String, _
  ByVal hKey As Long, phkResult As Long) As Long
Declare Function RegCreateKey Lib "advapi32.dll" _
  Alias "RegCreateKeyA" (ByVal hKey As Long, ByVal _
  lpSubKey As String, phkResult As Long) As Long
Declare Function RegCreateKeyEx Lib "advapi32.dll" _
  Alias "RegCreateKeyExA" (ByVal hKey As Long, ByVal _
  lpSubKey As String, ByVal Reserved As Long, ByVal lpClass _
  As String, ByVal dwOptions As Long, ByVal samDesired As Long, _
  lpSecurityAttributes As SECURITY_ATTRIBUTES, phkResult As Long, _
  lpdwDisposition As Long) As Long
Declare Function RegDeleteKey Lib "advapi32.dll" Alias _
  "RegDeleteKeyA" (ByVal hKey As Long, ByVal lpSubKey _
  As String) As Long
Declare Function RegDeleteValue Lib "advapi32.dll" _
  Alias "RegDeleteValueA" (ByVal hKey As Long, ByVal _
  lpValueName As String) As Long
Declare Function RegEnumKey Lib "advapi32.dll" Alias _
  "RegEnumKeyA" (ByVal hKey As Long, ByVal dwIndex As Long, _
  ByVal lpName As String, ByVal cbName As Long) As Long
Declare Function RegEnumKeyEx Lib "advapi32.dll" Alias _
  "RegEnumKeyExA" (ByVal hKey As Long, ByVal dwIndex As Long, _
  ByVal lpName As String, lpcbName As Long, lpReserved As Long, _
  ByVal lpClass As String, lpcbClass As Long, lpftLastWriteTime _
  As FILETIME) As Long
' Modified so that data parameter is "any"
Declare Function RegEnumValue Lib "advapi32.dll" Alias _
  "RegEnumValueA" (ByVal hKey As Long, ByVal dwIndex As Long, _
  ByVal lpValueName As String, lpcbValueName As Long, lpReserved _
  As Long, lpType As Long, ByVal lpData As Any, lpcbData As Long) _
  As Long
Declare Function RegFlushKey Lib "advapi32.dll" _
  (ByVal hKey As Long) As Long
Declare Function RegGetKeySecurity Lib "advapi32.dll" _
  (ByVal hKey As Long, ByVal SecurityInformation As Long, _
  pSecurityDescriptor As SECURITY_DESCRIPTOR, _
  lpcbSecurityDescriptor As Long) As Long
Declare Function RegLoadKey Lib "advapi32.dll" Alias _
  "RegLoadKeyA" (ByVal hKey As Long, ByVal lpSubKey As String, _
ByVal lpFile _
```

```
   As String) As Long
Declare Function RegNotifyChangeKeyValue Lib "advapi32.dll" _
(ByVal hKey As _
   Long, ByVal bWatchSubtree As Long, ByVal dwNotifyFilter As Long, ByVal _
   hEvent As Long, ByVal fAsynchronus As Long) As Long
Declare Function RegOpenKey Lib "advapi32.dll" Alias "RegOpenKeyA" _
   (ByVal  hKey As Long, ByVal lpSubKey As String, phkResult _
   As Long) As Long
Declare Function RegOpenKeyEx Lib "advapi32.dll" Alias _
   "RegOpenKeyExA" (ByVal hKey As Long, ByVal lpSubKey As String, _
   ByVal ulOptions As Long, ByVal samDesired As Long, phkResult _
   As Long) As Long
Declare Function RegQueryInfoKey Lib "advapi32.dll" Alias _
   "RegQueryInfoKeyA" (ByVal hKey As Long, ByVal lpClass As _
   String, lpcbClass As Long, lpReserved As Long, lpcSubKeys _
   As Long, lpcbMaxSubKeyLen As Long, lpcbMaxClassLen As Long, _
   lpcValues As Long, lpcbMaxValueNameLen As Long, lpcbMaxValueLen _
   As Long, lpcbSecurityDescriptor As Long, lpftLastWriteTime _
   As FILETIME) As Long
Declare Function RegQueryValue Lib "advapi32.dll" Alias _
   "RegQueryValueA" (ByVal hKey As Long, ByVal lpSubKey _
   As String, ByVal lpValue As String, lpcbValue As Long) As Long
Declare Function RegQueryValueEx Lib "advapi32.dll" _
   Alias "RegQueryValueExA" (ByVal hKey As Long, ByVal lpValueName _
   As String, ByVal lpReserved As Long, lpType As Long, _
   ByVal lpData As Any, lpcbData As Long) As Long
' NOTE that if you declare the lpData parameter as String,
' then you must pass it By Value.
Declare Function RegReplaceKey Lib "advapi32.dll" Alias _
   "RegReplaceKeyA" (ByVal hKey As Long, ByVal lpSubKey _
   As String, ByVal lpNewFile As String, ByVal lpOldFile _
   As String) As Long
Declare Function RegRestoreKey Lib "advapi32.dll" _
   Alias "RegRestoreKeyA" (ByVal hKey As Long, ByVal _
   lpFile As String, ByVal dwFlags As Long) As Long
Declare Function RegSaveKey Lib "advapi32.dll" Alias _
   "RegSaveKeyA" (ByVal hKey As Long, ByVal lpFile As String, _
   lpSecurityAttributes As SECURITY_ATTRIBUTES) As Long
Declare Function RegSetKeySecurity Lib "advapi32.dll" _
   (ByVal hKey As Long, ByVal SecurityInformation As Long, _
   pSecurityDescriptor As SECURITY_DESCRIPTOR) As Long
Declare Function RegSetValue Lib "advapi32.dll" _
   Alias "RegSetValueA" (ByVal hKey As Long, ByVal lpSubKey _
   As String, ByVal dwType As Long, ByVal lpData As String, _
   ByVal cbData As Long) As Long
Declare Function RegSetValueEx Lib "advapi32.dll" _
```

```
    Alias "RegSetValueExA" (ByVal hKey As Long, ByVal lpValueName _
    As String, ByVal Reserved As Long, ByVal dwType As Long, lpData _
    As Any, ByVal cbData As Long) As Long
' NOTE that if you declare the lpData parameter as String,
' you must pass it By Value.
Declare Function RegUnLoadKey Lib "advapi32.dll" Alias _
    "RegUnLoadKeyA" (ByVal hKey As Long, ByVal lpSubKey _
    As String) As Long
```

You'll see actual examples that use this header in the chapter on the registry (Chapter 4). The good news is that the hard part is getting the correct declarations. Once you have those, the rest is easy.

Get the most complete and authoritative coverage of Visual Basic 5 object-oriented techniques from veteran programmer Gene Swartzfager. In this exciting book, you'll learn about:

USING A FORM IN AN ActiveX COMPONENT

4

Chapter 4 introduces you to the fundamental techniques for using visual GUI objects in ActiveX components. You will learn how to encapsulate a **Form** object in an ActiveX class library and how to display that form from an associated method. This is done by applying VB's **Show** method modally to the **Form** object from code within the method and, after the user is done with the form, applying VB's **Hide** method to return code execution back to the calling method. To master these techniques, you will create a **Delete** method and a Delete Files **Form** object and add them to the book's class library.

Chapter 4 also shows you how to internally test and debug a method in an ActiveX component. In Chapter 3, we stressed the importance of having someone other than the ActiveX component's developer externally test its public members. However, at design time, the developer also needs an easy way to debug and test a member's code. VB5 supports two different techniques for doing this and we examine both in depth.

We also discuss the pros and cons of the two different ways (the **CreateObject** function and **As New** statement) of instantiating a class in an ActiveX component. Finally, Chapter 4 takes a closer look at the private **CL** class of the book's class library and some of the **Form** object-related methods that it contains. The **CL** class contains many different general-purpose methods that you will find useful when you develop your own ActiveX components.

Encapsulating A Form Object

In Chapter 3, you learned how to write methods in a **ClassModule** object and call them externally by passing the required arguments. Many of the methods that you will write work in that way; that is, they take the arguments passed in to them, execute their algorithms, and return some value signifying success or failure. However, because Windows is a GUI operating system, there will be situations where you will want to write a method that displays some kind of **Form** object while the method is executing in order to accept input from the user.

Also, if you are a typical Visual Basic programmer, you have spent a lot of time creating and coding the same types of **Form** objects over and over again. Most of us have repeatedly designed and written code for such generic **Form** objects as:

- Splash screen
- File browser dialog box
- About dialog box
- Text editor
- Security password dialog box
- Search-and-select dialog box

Depending on the type of application programming you do, you can probably add several more types of **Form** objects to the preceding list. In the past, using VB3, you could create one of these **Form** objects in a generic fashion, but it was not easy to do or to maintain.

The obstacles to creating and using reusable **Form** objects with VB3 were many. The **Form** object's module had to be physically added to each new project to be able to be reused. And, if the code in the **Form** object's module was not completely encapsulated, a related standard module might have to be added to the project. Because most Visual Basic programmers like to keep all the files related to a project in the same directory, copies of the generic **Form** object and any related files proliferated. Because of the proliferation of copies, maintaining and enhancing the code was difficult to do on a systematic basis.

In a large-scale VB3 project, the logistics of trying to create and control the reuse of generic **Form** objects were a nightmare for any project manager. But that was then, and this is now. Project managers and Visual Basic programmers will be glad to know that VB5 makes it quite easy to encapsulate a reusable **Form** object inside a class library.

To show you how easy encapsulating a **Form** object is, I've provided the general steps to encapsulate a **Form** object in a class library and to enable it to be displayed from a client application:

1. Add a new **Form** object to the ActiveX component's project.

2. Add the control objects required by the **Form** object to perform its functionality.

3. Set the design-time properties of the **Form** object and its control objects.

4. Write the code for the **Form** object's and control objects' event procedures.

5. Write the required **Property Get**, **Property Let**, or **Property Set** procedures and general procedures.

6. Create and write a method that displays the encapsulated **Form** object using Visual Basic's **Show** method (*style* argument set to **vbModal**). It is at this point that code execution branches to the **Load** event procedure of the encapsulated **Form** object and temporarily pauses in the calling method.

7. When the user finishes with the **Form** object, an event is triggered (usually the **Click** event for a **CommandButton** object) and the **Hide** method is applied to the **Form** object. At this point, code execution reverts back to the calling method.

8. The calling method reads the **Tag** property or a custom property of the **Form** object, where any value(s) to be returned to the client application was stored, and then unloads the encapsulated **Form** object.

9. The calling method returns the value(s) to the client application that called it.

Encapsulating A Delete Files Form

Our first example of encapsulating a **Form** object in an ActiveX component will be to create a simple dialog box that enables a client application to select files located on a hard or floppy disk and delete them. Figure 1 shows how the **Form** object will look when it is displayed.

The **FileListBox** object will have its **MultiSelect** property set to 2 - Extended at design time. After the user selects some files to delete, the **Form** object will look like the one shown in Figure 2.

When the user clicks on Delete, the code in the **Click** event procedure of the **CommandButton** object deletes the selected files. Once this process takes place, the **Form** object will appear as shown in Figure 3.

When the user is done deleting files, clicking on OK or Close causes the **Hide** method to be applied to the encapsulated **Form** object. Then execution reverts back to the calling method, which will return **True** to the client application.

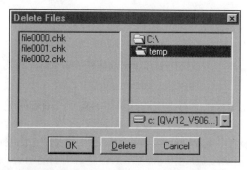

Figure 1   The Delete Files dialog box.

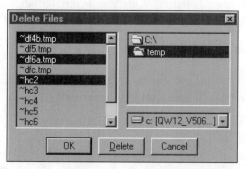

Figure 2   The Delete Files dialog box after the user selects files to delete.

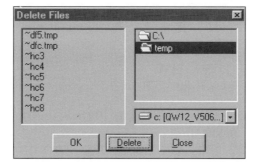

Figure 3 The Delete Files dialog box after files have been deleted.

ADDING THE FORM AND ITS CONTROLS TO AN ACTIVEX COMPONENT

Start VB5 and open the book's ActiveX EXE component project EFSE.VBP.

Select Project|Add Form and, from the Add Form dialog box, double click on the Form icon. Next add the following control objects from VB's toolbox to the form:

- **DriveListBox**, **DirListBox**, and **FileListBox**. Set their **Name** properties to drvDelete, dirDelete, and filDelete, respectively.

- Three **CommandButton** objects. Set their **Name** properties to cmdOK, cmdDelete, and cmdCancel, respectively.

You can set the various properties of the **Form** object and its control objects to mimic the size and organization of the dialog box pictured in Figure 1. A few properties, however, must be set to specific values in order to support the functionality of the dialog box as implemented by the code in the next section of this chapter. The properties and their settings are listed in Tables 1 and 2.

Only set the **Icon** property to (None) if you are running 32-bit Visual Basic. You can do this by selecting the (Icon) setting in the Properties window and pressing Delete.

WRITING THE CODE FOR THE FORM AND ITS CONTROLS

The code needed to enable a **Form** object and its controls to display and delete files is not extensive. In the process of writing it, you will learn some generic concepts about code for a class library that you will use repeatedly in this book. The first step is to make two declarations that enable the encapsulated **Form** object to call and use the services of members in **ClassModule** objects in the class library. When you instantiate an internal

Table 1   Settings for the **Form** object's properties.

Property	Setting
BorderStyle	3 - Fixed Dialog
Caption	Delete Files
Icon	(None)
Name	frmDelete

Table 2   Setting for the **FileListBox** object's properties.

Property	Setting
MultiSelect	2 - Extended

class that is part of your current Visual Basic project, you use a different syntax than when you are instantiating a class in a separate ActiveX component.

Write the code shown in Listing 1 in the General Declarations section of frmDelete.

Listing 1   Instantiating internal classes.

```
' Instantiate internal classes to reuse their members:
Private CL       As New CL
Private Dialog   As New Dialog
```

You should note these points about the code in Listing 1. First, the **Private** keyword is used to make the declarations. This ensures that encapsulation is not violated for these form-level object variables. Second, the **As New** statement is used to declare the object variable and to instantiate the class at the same time. Third, the type of object variable declared is the specific **ClassModule** object types **CL** and **Dialog** (that is, the **Name** properties of these two classes in the book's ActiveX component).

Using As New instead of CreateObject

*You can only use the **As New** statement, instead of the more commonly used **CreateObject** function, when you are instantiating an internal class or if you have previously set a reference in your Visual Basic project to the class library (Project|References). In ActiveX component terminology, this technique is called* early binding. *See* The As New Statement *section later in this chapter for more details.*

In the interest of writing readable, English-like Visual Basic code, the object variables in Listing 1 are given the same names (that is, **CL** and **Dialog**) as the names of the classes that will be instantiated and assigned to them. This is the only type of module-level declaration in the book's class library whose variable name is not preceded by a prefix indicating scope. Visual Basic has no problem keeping the same names straight when it executes calls to members of the classes.

Now we will continue with the rest of the code required for **frmDelete** and its controls. The code for the **CommandButton** objects is pretty straightforward. The **cmdOK** and **cmdCancel** Click event procedures are shown in Listing 2.

Listing 2 Code for the Click event of the command buttons.

```
Private Sub cmdCancel_Click()

    ' Reroute code execution back to calling method.
    Hide

End Sub

Private Sub cmdOK_Click()

    ' Reroute code execution back to calling method.
    Hide

End Sub

Private Sub cmdDelete_Click()

    ' Constants for literals:
    Const FIRST_FILE = 0

    ' Variables:
    Dim File        As Integer
    Dim LastFile    As Integer
    Dim Path        As String

    ' Enable error handler.
    On Error GoTo ET

    ' Delete selected files, repaint FileListBox
    ' object and change caption of Cancel button:
    Path = dirDelete & "\"

    If Right$(Path, 2) = "\\" Then Path = Left$(Path, Len(Path) - 1)

    LastFile = filDelete.ListCount - 1
```

```
    For File = LastFile To FIRST_FILE Step -1

        If filDelete.Selected(File) Then
            Kill Path & filDelete.List(File)
        End If

    Next File

    filDelete.Refresh
    cmdCancel.Caption = "&Close"
    Exit Sub

ET:

    Err = False

End Sub
```

You should note in Listing 2 that the **cmdDelete_Click** event procedure actually deletes files with Visual Basic's **Kill** statement. There are two points to note here. First, when you test this code, be careful to delete only files that you have made copies of or do not need (like those on the Windows temporary path). Second, this kind of code needs to be error trapped, and it is, but all the error handler does is set the **Number** property of the **Err** object to zero (**False**). We won't be dealing with implementing commercial-quality, error-handling routines in this chapter; that sort of code will come later in the book.

The code for the **DirListBox** and **DriveListBox** objects, in Listing 3, is minimal and goes in their **Change** event procedures.

Listing 3 Code for DirListBox and DriveListBox.

```
Private Sub drvDelete_Change()

    ' Update list of directories when drive changes.
    On Error GoTo ET
    dirDelete = drvDelete
    Exit Sub

ET:

    Err = False

End Sub

Private Sub dirDelete_Change()

    ' Update list of files when directory changes.
    filDelete = dirDelete

End Sub
```

Finally, there is the code for the **Form** object's event procedures. You need to write code for the **Form_Load**, **Form_QueryUnload**, and **Form_Unload** event procedures. Each one of these code blocks illustrates some generic techniques in coding class libraries.

The **Form_Load** event procedure has code that calls a method in the **Dialog** class called **ShowCL**. This method sets attributes of a **Form** object and its control objects to mimic the functionality of the dialog boxes in Microsoft's Office applications. The **ShowCL** method takes two required arguments: **Frm**, which is the **Name** property of the **Form** object to apply the method to, and **Properties()**, which is a boolean array. This boolean array may have from one to three elements, each of which is set to either **True** or **False**. The code for the **Form_Load** event procedure is in Listing 4.

Listing 4   Code for Form_Load procedure.

```
Private Sub Form_Load()

    ' Constants for literals:
    Const MS_BOLD = 0
    Const MS_DLG = 1
    Const MS_ONTOP = 2

    ' Variables:
    Dim Properties(2) As Boolean

    ' Subclass appearance/behavior of Form object:
    Properties(MS_BOLD) = True
    Properties(MS_DLG) = True
    Properties(MS_ONTOP) = True
    Dialog.ShowCL Me, Properties
    Dialog.Center Me

End Sub
```

You will learn more about the **ShowCL** method later in this book. Remember, however, that you can access the Help file topic for any member of the book's class library by viewing it from Visual Basic's Object Browser or by starting the class library's Help file EFS.HLP from the Explorer or File Manager.

The **Form_QueryUnload** event procedure has code that calls a method in the private, internal **CL** class. The **CL** class, which we'll cover in more detail later in the chapter, contains all of the methods that are called by more than one member of the public classes or their encapsulated **Form** objects. The **IsUnloadFromApp** method checks to see how the client application's user is trying to close and unload the **Form** object, and only proceeds to unload it if the user selected a **CommandButton** object or Control|Close. Finally, the code for the **Form_Unload** event procedure demonstrates how you should always explicitly free the system resources associated with any objects before unloading the **Form** object. The code for the **Form_QueryUnload** and **Form_Unload** event procedures is in Listing 5.

Listing 5 Code for procedures unloading form.

```
Private Sub Form_QueryUnload(Cancel As Integer, UnloadMode As Integer)

    ' Call object's member:
    If Not CL.IsUnloadFromApp(UnloadMode) Then
        Cancel = True
    Else

        If UnloadMode = vbFormControlMenu Then
            Cancel = True
            cmdCancel_Click
        End If

    End If

End Sub

Private Sub Form_Unload(Cancel As Integer)

    ' Free system resources associated with objects:
    Set CL = Nothing
    Set Dialog = Nothing
    Set frmDelete = Nothing

End Sub
```

The one tricky bit of code in Listing 5 is in the **Form_QueryUnload** event procedure. If the user tries to unload the form from the Control menu, the code cancels the request to unload and reroutes execution to the **cmdCancel_Click** event procedure. This must be done so that the **Hide** statement there can execute and reroute execution back to the calling method.

When you unload a Form object ...

*Visual Basic's Knowledge Base Help file recommends that when you unload a **Form** object, you set all its object references to **Nothing** (including itself) to avoid memory leaks and reinitialize any form-level variables.*

WRITING CODE FOR THE DELETE METHOD

Now that you have created the encapsulated **Form** object and written its code, you must declare and write a method that the client application can call and that displays the **Form** object modally. To begin this process, select the MISCEXS.CLS and, at the bottom of the General Declarations section, type

```
Function Delete() As Boolean
```

and press Enter. Visual Basic creates the opening and closing statements for the method. Write the code shown in Listing 6 for the **Delete** method.

Listing 6   Code for Delete method.

```
Function Delete() As Boolean

    ' Enable error handler.
    On Error GoTo ET

    ' Display frmDelete Form object modally so code execution pauses
    ' on this line until Hide method is applied to Form object.
    frmDelete.Show vbModal

    ' When Hide method is executed in delete files Form object—
    ' * Unload Form object.
    ' * Return True to indicate success.
    Unload frmDelete
    Delete = True
    Exit Function

ET:

    Err = False

End Function
```

Testing A Method Internally

In Chapter 3, we learned how to test a method externally by calling it from another Visual Basic project. It is now time to learn how to test and debug a method internally, from within the ActiveX component project that contains the method. There are two techniques that you can use to test an ActiveX component internally. The first technique works with both EXE and DLL ActiveX components under VB4, but it only works with an EXE component under VB5. The second technique works with both EXE and DLL components under either VB4 or VB5.

Technique #1—One VB Instance

With the first technique, you can test an ActiveX component internally without being required to start another instance of Visual Basic. To test the **Delete** method and its associated **Form** object with technique #1 internally, follow these steps:

1. Select Form1 and then select Project|Remove Form1.
2. Select Project|Add Form and, from the Add Form dialog box, double click on the Form icon.

Steps 1 and 2 are a quick way of cleaning out any previous test code and ensuring that you have a blank test form, which will simulate a client application's **Form** object.

3. Write the code in Listing 7 in the various event procedures of Form1.
4. Ensure that the **Form1.Show** statement in the **Sub Main** procedure in STARTUP.BAS is uncommented.
5. Select Project|EFSE Properties and, on the Component tab, ensure that Start Mode is set to Standalone.
6. Select Run|Start to display the simulated client application's **Form** object.

From here on, the process of testing a method internally is the same, whether you are using technique #1 or technique #2.

> **Note:** When you save, make and register an ActiveX EXE component's project, you can leave Start Mode on the Component tab of the Project Properties dialog box set to Standalone to facilitate internal testing. This is because an ActiveX EXE component's actual Start Mode setting is determined by how it is started at runtime, not by its nominal setting on the Component tab. For an ActiveX DLL component in VB5, however, the Start Mode setting is always disabled (a change from VB4).

Technique #2—Two VB Instances

With the second technique, you must start another instance of Visual Basic to test an ActiveX component internally. To test the **Delete** method and its associated **Form** object with technique #2, follow these steps:

1. Select Run|Start to run the ActiveX component's project.

2. Start a second instance of Visual Basic and open a standard EXE project that will function as a simulated client application.

3. Write the code in Listing 7 in the various event procedures of Form1 of the client application.

4. Select Run|Start to display the simulated client application's **Form** object.

From here on, the process of testing a method internally is the same, whether you are using technique #1 or technique #2.

Listing 7   Code for test form.

Code in General Declarations section:

```
' Form-level variable.
Dim MiscExs As Object

Private Sub Form_Load()

    ' Instantiate class. Programmatic ID has two parts delimited by dot:
    ' * Project name's entry on Options tab of Project dialog box.
    ' * Name property of ClassModule object.
    #If Win32 Then
        Set MiscExs = CreateObject("EFSE.MiscExs")
    #ElseIf Win16 Then
        Set MiscExs = CreateObject("EFS16.MiscExs")
    #End If

End Sub

Private Sub Form_DblClick()

    ' Call object's member.
    MiscExs.Delete

End Sub

Private Sub Form_Unload(Cancel As Integer)

    ' Free system resources associated with object variable.
    Set MiscExs = Nothing

    ' Force ClassModule object's project to unload completely.
    ' This is only done when testing a method internally.
    End

End Sub
```

At this point in the book, the code in Listing 7 should be clear. You are following the usual three steps: the declaration of the object variable in the General Declarations section, the assignment of the instantiated class to the object variable in the **Form_Load** event procedure, and the call to the object's method in the **Form_DblClick** event procedure.

After you select Run|Start to display the client application's **Form** object, double click it, and watch as the **Delete** method displays the Delete Files dialog box. Use the **DirListBox** object to find the Windows temporary directory (or some other directory) and select some files that you can safely delete. Once you have selected a file or files, click on the Delete button. The code in the **cmdDelete_Click** event procedure deletes the files and repaints the **FileListBox** object to confirm that they have been deleted.

When you test an ActiveX component internally, you can set a breakpoint on the calling statement by selecting Debug|Toggle Breakpoint, pressing F9 or clicking the toolbar button. You may then single-step through the method's code by pressing F8 or clicking the toolbar button. You can also set breakpoints in the method's code or do any other kind of debugging that you would do in a standard EXE project.

You can use the same code in Listing 7 to externally call and test the **Delete** method and its associated **Form** object, but you cannot debug the method's code when testing externally. For a review of external testing of procedures, see the section *Calling A Method Externally* in Chapter 3.

Now that you have internally tested the new **Delete** method and its associated **Form** object, you need to save the changes to the book's ActiveX component project. Be sure that the new form is saved to the same directory that contains the other project files (that is, C:\VBOOPEFS\VBCLSLIB).

Different Ways To Instantiate A Class

Our next step is to examine the ways to instantiate a class. In this section, we will discuss the **CreateObject** function and the **As New** statement.

The CreateObject Function

The **CreateObject** function is used to create a new instance of an externally creatable ActiveX component. **CreateObject** only creates a new instance of the object. You must first declare an object variable to which you then assign the instance of the object returned by **CreateObject**. In OLE Automation terminology, this way of creating an instance of an object is referred to as *late binding*. Using the **CreateObject** function to instantiate a class has several advantages:

- You do not need to set a reference to the ActiveX component in the References dialog box (Project|References).

- Version incompatibilities are not an issue.

- If you are instantiating an in-process, ActiveX DLL component, perceived performance is basically the same using the **CreateObject** function as when you use the **As New** statement.

Of course, we must also consider the other side of the coin—the disadvantages:

- Visual Basic does not provide syntax checking if a client application calls an invalid member or passes an invalid data type to an argument of a member. Instead, the ActiveX component must provide the exception-handling capabilities.

- The **CreateObject** function is slightly slower than when you use early binding and the **As New** statement on an out-of-process ActiveX EXE component.

Optimizing object performance

*You can optimize perceived performance by declaring the object variable with form-level scope and instantiating the class with **CreateObject** in the **Form_Load** event of the **Form** object that uses a member of the class. In this way, the instantiation (and the time required to do it) occurs only once.*

The As New Statement

The **As New** statement is used to indicate that a declared object variable is a new instance of an externally creatable object (for example, an ActiveX component). This statement can be used with these types of variable declarations:

- **Dim As New**. This declaration defaults to a public variable if declared in a standard module.

- **Private As New**. This declaration limits the scope to the module in which it is declared.

Used with a **ClassModule** object, **Dim As New** and **Private As New** both declare the **Object** variable and create a new instance of the object at the same time. In OLE Automation terminology, this way of instantiating a class is referred to as *early binding*. The early binding approach and the **As New** syntax are always faster than using the **CreateObject** function.

You can only use the **As New** syntax to instantiate a class externally if you first set a reference to the ActiveX component containing the class in the References dialog box (Project|References). If you do not set the reference first, Visual Basic displays the syntax error message *User-defined type not defined* when you try to run your project. When you instantiate a class internally, inside the class library itself, it is not necessary to set a reference because Visual Basic automatically sets a reference to the current project.

Regardless of whether you prefer to use early binding or late binding to instantiate an ActiveX component's class and reuse its members, the members should still provide their own syntax checking. There are two reasons for this approach. First, you cannot assume that everyone who uses the ActiveX component you write will use the early binding technique. If they use late binding, then Visual Basic cannot perform syntax checking. Second, some OLE Automation-compliant languages do not support the early binding technique (for example, Excel VBA).

Understanding The Private CL Class

Because you used the **IsUnloadFromApp** method of the **CL** class in the previous code related to the **Delete** method, I think this is a good time to discuss the difference between private and public **ClassModule** objects. The private **CL ClassModule** object can only be instantiated and used from inside the book's class library. A public **ClassModule** object can be instantiated externally and its public methods can be called from another Visual Basic project. If you select CL.CLS in the class library's project, you see that it is the only **ClassModule** object whose **Instancing** property is set to 1 - Private. All the other classes in the book's class library have their **Instancing** property set to 5 - MultiUse.

The private **CL** class (the *CL* stands for Class Library) contains all procedures that are called more than once by members of the public classes. Strictly speaking, this approach violates the OOP attribute of encapsulation, but in practice, most developers code this way in order to minimize the size of the ActiveX component. As long as all unencapsulated procedures are located in one private class, it is not difficult to understand what is happening or to re-encapsulate the common procedures within each individual class (if you so desire). You need to understand how some of the more broadly applicable methods of the **CL** class work because they use techniques that are essential to Visual Basic class library development. Some of these techniques are really workarounds that compensate for limitations in VB5.

Table 3 lists some of the most commonly used methods of the **CL** class.

HasHandle Method

The **HasHandle** method checks if an object reference has a handle. Three possible generic cases are dealt with. First, if the object reference does have a handle, the method returns a string set to "True". Second, if the object reference does not have a handle and it is one of the built-in Visual Basic objects, the method returns a string corresponding to the class or type name of the object (for example, "ListBox"). Third, if the object reference does have a handle and the handle evaluates to zero, then it must be Visual Basic's **OLE** container control object. In this case, the method returns the string "OLE". The code for the **HasHandle** method is in Listing 8.

Table 3 CL class methods.

Method	Description
HasHandle	Determines if an object reference passed as an argument to a member of a public class has an hWnd property (handle) and, therefore, whether certain Windows API functions can be applied to it.
IsForm	Determines if an object reference passed as an argument to a member of a public class is a Visual Basic Form object.
IsMDIForm	Determines if an object reference passed as an argument to a member of a public class is a Visual Basic MDIForm object.
IsDrv	Determines if a path-and-file specification passed as an argument to a member of a public class contains a valid drive.
IsDir	Determines if a path-and-file specification passed as an argument to a member of a public class contains a valid path.
IsUnloadFromApp	Determines how a client application is trying to unload a Form object from the class library.
IsWinNT	Determines if the client application is running under Windows NT.
IsWin95Shell	Determines if the client application is running under the new shell used by Windows 95 and Windows NT 4.

Listing 8   HasHandle method of CL class.

```
Function HasHandle(Obj) As String
' _____

' Purpose: Determines if an object/control has an hWnd
'          property (handle) and, so, whether certain Windows
'          API functions can be applied to it. Also serves as
'          indirect way to determine if object reference is to
'          ClassModule object.

' Called:  Internally from members of class library.

' Accepts: Obj: Variant that evaluates to VB object.

' Returns: String: "True" if object has hWnd property or else
'                   class name of Obj argument.
' _____


' Enable in-line error handling.
On Error Resume Next

' Try to get handle of object passed to Obj argument (causes
' error 438 if object does not have hWnd property):
If Obj.hWnd <> False Then

    ' If no error, then object has handle; so
    ' set function's return value to "True":
    If Err = False Then
      HasHandle = "True"

    ' Else if object does not have handle:
    Else

        ' Clear property settings of Err Object.
        Err = False

        ' Find its type name from groups below and
        ' set function's return value to that name:
        Select Case TypeName(Obj)

            ' Add-in objects:
            Case "Application", "Component", "Components", _
                "ControlTemplate", "ControlTemplates", _
                "FileControl", "FormTemplate", "MenuItems", _
                "MenuLine", "ProjectTemplate", "Properties", _
                "Property", "SelectedComponents", _
                "SelectedControlTemplates", "SubMenu"
                    HasHandle = TypeName(Obj)

            ' Custom control object:
            Case "CommonDialog"
                    HasHandle = TypeName(Obj)

            ' Data Access objects:
            Case "Column", "Columns", "Container", _
                "Containers", "Database", "Databases", _
```

```
                    "DBCombo", "DBEngine", "DBGrid", "DBList", _
                    "Document", "Documents", "Dynaset", "Error", _
                    "Errors", "Field", "Fields", "Group", _
                    "Groups", "Index", "Indexes", "Parameter", _
                    "Parameters", "Properties", "Property", _
                    "QueryDef", "QueryDefs", "Recordset", _
                    "Recordsets", "Relation", "Relations"
                        HasHandle = TypeName(Obj)
                Case "RowBuffer", "SelBookmarks", "Snapshot", _
                    "Table", "TableDef", "TableDefs", "User", _
                    "Users", "Workspace", "Workspaces"
                        HasHandle = TypeName(Obj)

                ' OLE Automation objects (Controls, Forms, Printers):
                Case "Object"
                        HasHandle = "Object"

                ' OLE Automation objects whose types are unknown:
                Case "Unknown"
                        HasHandle = "Unknown"

                ' Other objects:
                Case "App", "Clipboard", "Collection", "Data", _
                    "ErrObject", "Font", "Image", "Label", "Line", _
                    "Picture", "Printer", "Screen", "Shape", "Timer"
                        HasHandle = TypeName(Obj)

                ' Some other object (Form, MDIForm or ClassModule
                ' object), in which case VB's TypeName function
                ' either returns Name property of object (for Form
                ' or MDIForm) or results in run-time error (for
                ' ClassModule). Instead, HasHandle returns class
                ' name of object.
                Case Else
                    If IsForm(Obj) Then
                        HasHandle = "Form"
                    ElseIf IsMDIForm(Obj) Then
                        HasHandle = "MDIForm"
                    Else
                        HasHandle = "ClassModule"
                    End If
            End Select
        End If

    ' The OLE Container Control Properties topic in VB.HLP says
    ' the OLE Container object has an hWnd property; but, VB.HLP's
    ' hWnd Property topic says the hWnd property is no longer
    ' supported for the OLE container control. When you read it,
    ' it always returns zero and you cannot find its parent. This
    ' code returns its class name:
    ElseIf Obj.hWnd = False Then
        HasHandle = TypeName(Obj)
    End If

End Function
```

There are several things to note about how the **HasHandle** method is written. First, because it is a member of a private class and is not documented in the class library's Help file, a brief template at the top of the procedure documents the purpose of the member and its interface (that is, arguments accepted and values returned). Second, the three built-in Visual Basic collection objects (**Controls**, **Forms**, and **Printers**) are actually, at a lower lever of abstraction, OLE Automation objects. This type of object has the class name **Object**, which is how you must declare any argument in a member of an ActiveX component that accepts an object reference. Third, to determine if an object reference is to a **Form** or **MDIForm** object, **HasHandle** calls two other methods in the **CL** class: **IsForm** and **IsMDIForm**. We will discuss those methods in the next section. Fourth, there is no easy way to determine if an object reference is to a **ClassModule** object. The **HasHandle** method does it by brute force, so to speak, because it assumes that if an object reference is not to any of the other possible Visual Basic objects, then it must be to a **ClassModule** object.

Passing an object to OLE

*If you pass an object reference to Visual Basic's **OLE** container control object to **HasHandle**, it determines that the **OLE** container has an **hWnd** property, but that the handle is zero. This is a contradiction in terms because any handle Windows assigns must be a positive **Integer** or **Long**. In one topic, the Visual Basic Help file says the **hWnd** property applies to this object; in another topic, it says that it no longer applies. When you read the **OLE** container control with Visual Basic code, the control does have an **hWnd** property; however, it always returns zero and you cannot find its parent. This confusing situation probably reflects a bug in Visual Basic.*

IsForm And IsMDIForm Methods

The **IsForm** and **IsMDIForm** methods compensate for the fact that Visual Basic itself has no certain way of determining if an object reference passed as an argument to a member of an ActiveX component is a **Form** or **MDIForm** object. If you use Visual Basic's **TypeName** function on a reference to a **Form** or **MDIForm** object, it returns its **Name** property (for example, frmDelete) but not its generic class or type name. Visual Basic's **TypeOf** keyword will return the generic class name, but only if an inprocess ActiveX DLL component is running. For some reason, **TypeOf** does not work correctly on a **Form** or **MDIForm** object in an out-of-process ActiveX EXE component.

Both the **IsForm** and **IsMDIForm** methods use the same technique. The code tries to read a property of the object reference (**KeyPreview** for the **Form** object and **AutoShowChildren** for the **MDIForm** object). This property is unique to the object that is being checked. If the object reference has the property, no runtime error occurs and **IsForm** or **IsMDIForm** returns **True**. If the object reference does not have the property, runtime error 438 (Object doesn't support this property or method) occurs and **IsForm** or **IsMDIForm** returns the default value of **False**. The code for the two methods is shown in Listing 9.

Listing 9   IsForm and IsMDIForm methods of CL class.

```
Function IsForm(Frm) As Boolean
'  _____
'
' Purpose: Checks whether or not object is Form object.
'
' Called:  Internally from members of class library.
'
' Accepts: Frm: Variant that must evaluate to VB's
'               Form object.
'
' Returns: If it is Form object, True. If not, False
'          (uninitialized/default value of function).
'
' Notes:   a) VB's TypeName function returns Name property of
'             Form object, not generic class name.
'          b) VB's TypeOf function returns generic class name,
'             but it fails when used in out-of-process,
'             ActiveX component.
'  _____


' IsForm method follows these steps—
' * Tries to return value of property of Frm argument that is
'   unique to its VB class (that is, KeyPreview).
' * If property applies to Frm argument, no error occurs and
'   method returns True.
' * If property does not apply, error 438 occurs and method
'   returns False.
On Error Resume Next

If Frm.KeyPreview = True Or Frm.KeyPreview = False Then
    If Err = False Then IsForm = True
End If

Err = False
```

```
End Function

Function IsMDIForm(MDIFrm) As Boolean
'   _____
'   ' Purpose: Checks whether or not object is MDIForm object.
'   '
'   ' Called:  Internally from members of class library.
'   '
'   ' Accepts: MDIFrm: Variant that must evaluate to VB's
'   '                  MDIForm object.
'   '
'   ' Returns: If it is Form object, True. If not, False
'   '          (uninitialized/default value of function).
'   '
'   ' Notes:    a) VB's TypeName function returns Name property of
'   '              MDIForm object, not generic class name.
'   '           b) VB's TypeOf function returns generic class name, but
'   '              but it fails when used in out-of-process,
'   '              ActiveX component.
'   _____


'   IsMDIForm method follows these steps—
'   * Tries to return value of property of MDIFrm argument that
'     is unique to its VB class (that is, AutoShowChildren).
'   * If property applies to MDIFrm argument, no error occurs
'     and method returns True.
'   * If property does not apply, error 438 occurs and method
'     returns False.
On Error Resume Next

If MDIFrm.AutoShowChildren = True Or MDIFrm.AutoShowChildren = False Then
    If Err = False Then IsMDIForm = True
End If

Err = False

End Function
```

A trick with IsForm and IsMDIForm

Both **IsForm** and **IsMDIForm** use a generic coding trick that every Visual Basic programmer should know. Sometimes the easiest way to determine if an argument is passed a valid value or if an object has a certain member is to enable an inline error handler and then force a runtime error to occur if the argument's value or the member being tested is invalid.

IsDrv And IsDir Methods

The **IsDrv** and **IsDir** methods validate whether a string passed to an argument contains a valid drive or a valid path. The code for the two methods is shown in Listing 10.

Listing 10   IsDrv and IsDir methods of CL class.

```
Sub IsDrv(PathFiles As String, _
          Member As String, _
          Arg As String)
    ' _____
    '
    ' Purpose: Validates existence of drive.
    '
    ' Called:  Internally from members of class library.
    '
    ' Accepts: PathFiles: String expression specifying path or
    '                     path and file name(s) to check for
    '                     valid drive.
    '          Member:    String expression specifying name of
    '                     member from which this method is called.
    '          Arg:       String expression specifying name of
    '                     argument being checked.
    ' _____


    ' Constants for literals:
    Const NO_DRIVE = 1

    ' Variables:
    Dim Drive As String
    Drive = Left$(PathFiles, 1)

    #If Win32 Then

        If Drive = "A" Or Drive = "B" Then
           Drive = Drive & ":"
        Else
           Drive = Drive & ":\"
        End If

        If GetDriveType(Drive) = NO_DRIVE Then
           E.TrapSyntax 44, Member, Left$(PathFiles, 1), Arg
        End If

    #Else

        If GetDriveType(Asc(PathFiles) - vbKeyA) = False Then
           E.TrapSyntax 44, Member, Left$(PathFiles, 1), Arg
        End If

    #End If
End Sub
```

```
Sub IsDir(Path As String, _
          Member As String, _
          Arg As String)
    ' _____
    ' Purpose: Validates existence of directory.
    '
    ' Called:  Internally from members of class library.
    '
    ' Accepts: Path:   String expression specifying directory
    '                  to validate.
    '          Member: String expression specifying name of
    '                  member from which this method is called.
    '          Arg:    String expression specifying name of
    '                  argument being checked.
    ' _____

    ' Constants for literals:
    Const WILDCARD1 = "*.*"
    Const ATTRIBS = vbHidden + vbSystem + vbDirectory
    Const NO_DIR = vbNullString

    ' Variables:
    Dim DirName As String
    DirName = Path
    DirName = DirName & WILDCARD1

    If Dir$(DirName, ATTRIBS) = NO_DIR Then
        E.TrapSyntax 43, Member, "Path", Arg
    End If

End Sub
```

There are several things to note about how the **IsDrv** and **IsDir** methods are written. First, **IsDrv** uses the Windows API function **GetDriveType** to validate the existence of the drive. Unfortunately, like many Windows API functions, **GetDriveType** behaves differently under the 32-bit API than under the 16-bit API. The 32-bit version takes a **String** data type as its argument (for example, "G:\") and returns 1 if the drive does not exist. The 16-bit version takes an **Integer** data type as its argument (for example, 2 signifies drive C) and returns zero if the drive does not exist. Second, each of the methods is declared as a **Sub** procedure (unlike all the members of the public classes and the majority of the members of the **CL** class, which are declared as **Function** procedures). Three, no error handler is enabled in either of these procedures (or, for that matter, in any of the other procedures in the private **CL** class). The reasons behind the second and third points have to do with the error-handling scheme that the book's class library uses; you will learn more about that topic in Chapters 5 and 8.

> ### *Constants in the IsDir method*
>
> *Note the use of the Visual Basic intrinsic constants **vbNullString**, **vbHidden**, **vbSystem**, and **vbDirectory** in the **IsDir** method. Using these and other Visual Basic intrinsic constants makes your code more readable and reduces the amount of system resources used by an application or class library.*

IsUnloadFromApp Method

The **IsUnloadFromApp** method determines how a client application/user is trying to unload a **Form** object in the class library. Unless the **QueryUnload** event is triggered from the Control menu or from code in the **Form** object, the **Unload** event is canceled. There are five actions that can cause the **QueryUnload** event of a **Form** object to occur. These actions and their intrinsic constants are:

- **vbFormControlMenu** (0). The user selects Control|Close on the **Form** object.
- **vbFormCode** (1). The **Unload** statement is invoked from code.
- **vbAppWindows** (2). The current Windows operating environment session is ending.
- **vbAppTaskManager** (3). The Windows Task Manager is closing the application.
- **vbFormMDIForm** (4). A MDI child form is closing because its MDI parent form is closing.

The code for the method is shown in Listing 11.

Listing 11   IsUnloadFromApp method of CL class.

```
Function IsUnloadFromApp(UnloadMode As Integer) As Boolean
    ' ─────────────────────────────────────────────────
    ' Purpose: Checks how client application is trying to unload
    '          Form object in class library.
    '
    ' Called:  From Form_QueryUnload event of all Form objects
    '          encapsulated in class library.
    '
    ' Accepts: UnloadMode: Integer expression that is argument in
    '                      Form_QueryUnload event procedure.
    '
    ' Returns: If unloading form from Control menu or by code,
    '          True. If not, False (uninitialized/default value
    '          of function).
```

```
'  _____

   If UnloadMode = vbFormControlMenu Or _
      UnloadMode = vbFormCode Then
          IsUnloadFromApp = True
   End If

End Function
```

Call this kind of code from Query_Unload

*You should call this kind of code from the **Query_Unload** event proce-dure of every **Form** object. The best habit to get into is to not let a user close Windows itself without first being warned to close any Visual Basic application that is running.*

IsWinNT And IsWin95Shell Methods

The **IsWinNT** method checks if the client application is running under Windows NT. The **IsWin95Shell** method checks whether the client appli-cation is running under the new shell used by Windows 95 and Windows NT 4. The code for the two methods is shown in Listing 12.

Listing 12   IsWin95Shell method of CL class.

```
Function IsWinNT() As Boolean
   '  _____

   ' Purpose: Checks whether or not Windows NT is running.
   '
   ' Called:  Internally from members of class library.
   '
   ' Returns: If Windows NT is running, True. If not, False
   '          (uninitialized/default value of function)
   '  _____


   ' If 32-bit VB is running:
   ' * Size user-defined data type and fill it with data.
   ' * Get version and, if it is Windows NT, return True.
#If Win32 Then

      ' Constants for Windows API functions:
      Const VER_PLATFORM_WIN32_NT = 2

      ' Variables:
      Dim Win As OSVERSIONINFO
      Win.TypeSize = Len(Win)
```

```
    If GetVersionEx(Win) Then
        If Win.ID = VER_PLATFORM_WIN32_NT Then IsWinNT = True
    End If

  #End If

End Function

Function IsWin95Shell() As Boolean
    ' _____
    '
    ' Purpose: Checks whether or not new shell in Windows 95 or
    '          NT 4.0 is running.
    '
    ' Called:  From Form_Load event of all Form objects
    '          encapsulated in class library.
    '
    ' Returns: If Windows 95 or NT 4.0 is running, True. If not,
    '          False (uninitialized/default value of function)
    ' _____

    If FindWindow("Shell_TrayWnd", vbEmpty) <> False Then
        IsWin95Shell = True
    End If

End Function
```

The **IsWinNT** method uses the **GetVersionEx** Windows API function to determine if the client application is running under Windows NT. Because the Windows API function **GetVersionEx** only exists in the 32-bit API set, the code in the method must be conditionally compiled. **GetVersionEx** loads information about the version of the operating system that is currently running into the OSVERSIONINFO user-defined data type (represented by the variable **Win**). The **TypeSize** element must first be explicitly sized. You can then read the various elements of OSVERSIONINFO. In this method, the element being read is **ID**.

There are several reasons why the members of the class library that display a **Form** object need to know whether the client application is running under the old Windows 3.x shell or the new Windows 95 shell:

- The Control menu of the dialog boxes is slightly different in Visual Basic, depending on whether the new Windows 95 shell is being run or not.

- Certain features of the Windows operating system are only available when running under the Windows 95 shell.

- The dialog boxes in Windows and in the Microsoft Office 95 applications use a bold font for all controls when displayed under Windows 3.x or Windows NT 3.51. The same dialog box uses a normal font when it is

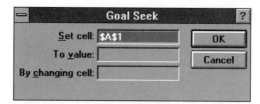

Figure 4 Goal Seek dialog box—Windows 3.x shell.

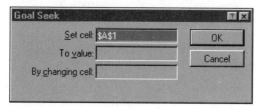

Figure 5 Goal Seek dialog box—Windows 95 shell.

displayed under Windows 95 or Windows NT 4. Figures 4 and 5 show the two different types of font displays (for the Excel 7.0 Goal Seek dialog box). To mimic this behavior, the **Form** objects in the class library call the **IsWin95Shell** method from their **Form_Load** event procedures to determine the version of Windows that is running. They then call the **MimicMS** method of the **Dialog** class to set the font to bold or normal.

The **IsWin95Shell** method uses the Windows API function **FindWindow** to determine under which shell the client application is running. In this usage, **FindWindow**'s first argument is a **String** specifying the class name (**Shell_TrayWnd**) of the taskbar window, which is unique to the new Windows 95-type shell. The second argument, if it is set to Null or the VB intrinsic constant **vbEmpty**, tells **FindWindow** to ignore the argument in its search. In another kind of usage, **FindWindow**'s second argument can be a **String** that specifies the window's title.

That's it for Chapter 4. By this point in the book, you should have a good grasp of the basic techniques of OOP development with Visual Basic and be able to try out some ideas of your own. In the next chapter, we are going to pull back a little from the level of detail in Chapters 2 through 4. Chapter 5 discusses the concept of the public interface of an ActiveX component and the principles that should govern the design of that public interface.

INDEX

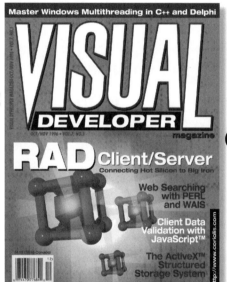

Solutions for Your World

It's easy to get lost in the online universe, but *INTERNET JAVA & ACTIVEX ADVISOR* will guide you in the right direction. Written by expert developers, every issue brings you vital information on the latest products and technologies necessary for staying ahead of the Internet Revolution. Take a look at what you'll get each month when you subscribe today:

New Product Reviews
What works and what doesn't

Developer News
What's happening and what's important

Behind the Scenes on the Web

Hands in Your Cookie Jar

Feature Articles
Developer insights on the products you use

Companion Resource Disk
Sample code, applets and programs in easy-to-use electronic format.

Companion
Resource

Disk

It's A Big Online World.